America Gives, and America Takes

America Gives, and America Takes

George C. Udeozor

authorHOUSE®

AuthorHouse™ LLC
1663 Liberty Drive
Bloomington, IN 47403
www.authorhouse.com
Phone: 1-800-839-8640

This book is non-fiction based on the life of the author and the actual events that took place to the best of the author's memory and perception as they happened. The author's accounts of the facts are based on his views, ideas, opinions, and understanding of these events and the people involved. Any reference to persons, agencies, governments, or any entity is the opinion of the author pertaining to the events which took place as they relate to him. The author makes no definitive statements or conclusions as to the character and intentions of each individual or entity mentioned in this book. The reader may make their own determination and opinion based on the information herein, as well as obtained additional information concerning the facts, from their own further investigation.

www.udeozor56@yahoocom

Published by AuthorHouse 12/09/2013

ISBN: 978-1-4817-4478-2 (sc)
ISBN: 978-1-4817-5828-4 (e)

Contents

Dedication ix
Introduction xi

Part One
Arrest by Abduction

One 3
Two 6
Three 10
Four 13
Five 22
Six 28
Seven 33
Eight 36
Nine 40
Ten 48
Eleven 53
Twelve 59
Thirteen 63
Fourteen 68
Fifteen 75
Sixteen 78
Seventeen 80
Eighteen 89
Nineteen 94
Twenty 99
Twenty One 104
Twenty Two 107
Twenty Three 110

Part Two
EXTRADITION U.S.A.

Twenty Four 117
Twenty Five 120
Twenty Six 126
Twenty Seven 136
Twenty Eight 143
Twenty Nine 150
Thirty 154
Thirty One 160
Thirty Two 165
Thirty Three 169
Thirty Four 175
Thirty Five 181
Thirty Six 185
Thirty Seven 189
Thirty Eight 194
Thirty Nine 201
Forty 208
Forty One 213
Forty Two 225
Forty Three 236
Forty Four 241

Part Three
Mother, Madam, and Maid

Forty Five 247
Forty Six 251
Forty Seven 256
Forty Eight 260
Forty Nine 264
Fifty 269
Fifty One 274
Fifty Two 278
Fifty Three 284
Fifty Four 289
Fifty Five 293

Part Four
United States Vs George Udeozor

Fifty Six 301
Fifty Seven 305
Fifty Eight 310
Fifty Nine 315
Sixty 319
Sixty One 325
Sixty Two 332
Sixty Three 336
Sixty Four 343

Part Five
Seeking Justice While Serving the Time

Sixty Five..361
Sixty Six..366
Sixty Seven......................................372
Sixty Eight.......................................378
Sixty Nine..384
Seventy..393

Epilogue..403
Acknowledgements..........................423
About The Author...........................425

This work is an extraordinary effort to explain how one man ran afoul of the Nigerian and American justice systems.

-Clarion Review

George C. Udeozor is a Nigerian-born U.S. citizen who spent nearly a decade in custody on charges he and his wife held a teenage Nigerian girl in involuntary servitude in the U.S. for five years . . . In *America Gives,* he details an ordeal that began when he was taken into custody in Nigeria in 2004 at the behest of U.S. officials. Readers follow him through foul and dangerous prison conditions and an equally perilous trip through the Nigerian and U.S. legal systems that ended with his guilty plea. Whether he is a victim, as he claims or a criminal as the U.S. government says—readers can judge for themselves—*America Gives* does offer a different view of the justice system . . . .

-Blueink Review

Dedication

I dedicate this book to the memory of my mother, Sussana Udeozor
and all others; deceased and living,
who have chosen to fight the disease of poverty.
Your fight is just and unlike most wars, it is winnable.
May God bless you and reward your effort.

Introduction

When in 1996 I took the oath of citizenship of the United States of America, a mixed feeling of euphoria and trepidation washed through my body—a curious response to a welcome and long anticipated event.

Euphoria because, considering the reduced circumstances of my birth and early life in Nigeria, clenching the evasive American Citizenship was for sure the crowning glory of a dream which had already come true for me—*The American* Dream!

Trepidation because, after living in America for upward of eighteen years to date, I had experienced the good, the bad and the ugly dimensions of my adopted nation… a nation whose delight in giving honor and glory is apparently only surpassed by her delight in taking them away.

My resolve to stay worthy of the generous gift of citizenship thus bequeathed on me was shortly put to test by a poorly reasoned deed of mine, which although imperfectly contrived, was nevertheless executed for a noble cause.

Having taken responsibility and paid society's price for my misdeed, I feel it my duty to many who out of genuine concern and curiosity or those who for their own sadistic pleasure rolled along as the wheels of our indifferent judiciary mauled me into wretchedness and penury, rendered my seven defenseless children fatherless at the most delicate developmental stages of their young lives by incriminating, convicting and sentencing me to ninety seven months in prison without a trial or any interest whatsoever as to my innocence or guilt.

By writing America Gives and America Takes: USA Vs. George Udeozor, my hope is to achieve a multiple purpose:

First, to reach out and explain to my family members and friends—my children in particular, the reasons they should not view my imprisonment with shame and despondency, but rather with understanding, courage, and gratitude to God.

Second, to respond to the perfidious lies of the young woman and her newfound benefactors whose greed and narcissism were, in their wisdom, compelling enough reasons to set my family up for ruin; as long as somewhere mixed up in the debris of my family's collapse, they found the "fortune" they sought.

Third, to contribute, even if in a very small way, to the often confusing discourse on the subject of servitude, with special and particular reference to the interplay between Foreign Cultural Values and American Jurisprudence.

Finally, to share some of my most fascinating thoughts and fantasies while living in confinement with nothing but time on my hands to spend as I well pleased.

It is the tremendous weight of these obligations, which I feel both in their psychological and physical dimensions, that has compelled me to write *America Gives and America Takes.*

This book contains a candid and unadorned account of my life. Although parts of this work may read as an attempt by me to shift blame which rests squarely on my shoulders, I hasten to point out that that is not the intent or motive behind those parts. In looking back over the span of my life covered in this account, I found that the things which hurt me cannot be divorced from the things which helped me. I imagine this paradox of life to be applicable in most other circumstances of life.

I can no more blame the United States for my woes than I can credit my childhood dreams of living in a land of utopia for my life's major successes. The simple truth is that pursuing the American dream straight out of Africa both hurt me and helped me just as I have helped and hurt myself in my effort to find balance in my life. I hope that both experiences would enable me to bequeath a fitting legacy on my children whom I love very dearly indeed.

It is my candid hope that the readers understand one thing, if nothing else, from reading this book: the truth has many faces; no individual, no nation, not even the United States, has seen the face of the unitary truth… nor does it exist.

PART ONE
Arrest by Abduction

Experience has shown,
that even under the best form of government,
those entrusted with power have, in time, and by
slow operation, perverted it into tyranny."
~Thomas Jefferson, 3rd" U.S. President

One

On the evening of Christmas in the year 2004, I was touched by doom. Three gruff and spindly looking souls led by a diminutive point man visited me, all of them armed with automatic guns and adorned in aprons marked in red with the letters EFCC.

Their blue aprons which turned out to be bullet proof vests appeared official, and had the wearers looked less menacing, my arrest would have struck my provincial town of Amawbia less like daylight abduction.

With a history of fierce rivalry within and outside its borders, Amawbia town is no stranger to upheavals. Within minutes, a motley crowd of young and able-bodied men had besieged my compound, barricading the armed strangers and other felicitating visitors within my high walled fence.

I was flattered, yet amazed at the speed with which the news of the looming melee in my compound travelled through the community.

My morale became immeasurably lifted seeing that these armed strangers, whoever they were, could not possibly have their way, their guns notwithstanding.

Buoyed by this show of strength and support, I approached the point man because he looked most like a leader and demanded to know who they were.

I could see from the troubled look in his eyes that the unexpected show of force took him by surprise and being a man of authority in law enforcement he must have felt uneasy at the chance of a very ugly turn if the situation was not properly managed.

Relieved at the opening offered by my query, he said, "I'm inspector Sani of the EFCC. Are you familiar with our agency?"

"No! What is EFCC," I responded.

"I will explain to you inside the house, but first tell your people to calm down. We are law officers. Not bandits!"

"You come into my compound waving guns like bandits and you want us to calm down?"

With that response from me the crowd bawled;

"We Amawbians fear no one.

You show us peace, we return the favor tenfold.

You show us war, we return the favor tenfold.

You leave us alone; we leave you ten paces away!

"Brethren, have I spoken the truth?"

A thunderous chorus of "Eeh!" or "Yes!" rent the dusty air. Meanwhile, the crowd continued to enlarge. Trouble was looming. The armed men were now tenser and highly agitated. They began assuming ready positions.

"Now, young man," the leader hissed in my ear, obviously panicked, "Open your eyes and see the truth. Can your people really fight armed men with their bare hands?"

He was right and I knew it. The sound of one of their AK-47s alone would trigger a mammoth pandemonium. Bloodshed was unthinkable to me. Knowing Nigerian law enforcement officers and their numerous "accidental discharge" fables, I could clearly see how close we had ridden to disaster.

Sweating profusely, I slowly tugged at Igwe's arm where he stood next to me and whispered a plea for calm in his ears.

He nodded and began inching his tall frame through the crowd, whispering my request to the principal crowd controllers known only to a few of us. Within thirty seconds calm was restored and Officer Sani and I were sitting at my dining table to try and make heads or tails of their unsettling visit.

"Who are you people?" I began.

"We are men of EFCC, Economics and Financial Crimes Commission," he replied seriously.

He slowly lowered his shoulders and bent forward staring intently into my frightened eyes.

"I am afraid I bear bad news for you. We are here to arrest you. Here, this picture should be familiar to you. Ehh?" he said as he removed a folded computer print of an enlarged passport image of me.

My eyes widened. My stomach heaved and I was suddenly feeling sick and claustrophobic. The air appeared to have vanished from the room.

The picture staring back at me was one I knew all too well, but it seemed to be from another life! It was a picture extracted from the MVA records of my last enhanced Maryland Driver's license taken nearly eight years earlier, some eight thousand miles away in Germantown, Maryland, USA.

When I separated from my wife and six children five years earlier, in 1999, I was as much a local dude as any other resident of Montgomery

County where Germantown is located. My attraction and attachment to this picturesque, serene county could not at all come as a surprise to those who knew that five of my seven children were born in North Potomac and Darnestown where six of them remain local youths to the present day.

My emotionally charged departure which I swiftly arranged as a very temporary measure while issues of my marital squabbles with my wife and in-laws were sorted and resolved took a turn for the worse upon my return to Lagos, Nigeria, where I owned a townhouse. The time of my return and reunification with my family thus became indefinite.

After twelve years of constant and pressured engagements in my business and family lives on two continents, in addition to the discomfort of the humidity and the incessant debilitating drizzles of Lagos and the harmattan fog of Abuja, not to mention the high traffic and crime rates in the large cities, it quickly became clear that neither Lagos nor Abuja was capable of providing me with a healthy living environment.

So, sick for the cool comfort of my home and children and realizing that our reunion was far from imminent, I chose to spend all my leisure time in my native land—the only place on planet earth I was sure to have uninterrupted and pressure-free time to meditate on my many issues of the heart.

I could not have been more off the mark with my choice for a quiet abode. Because now, as if to seal my doom, were these men from hell, my strife-ridden past life in their hands.

Two

As I stared unbelieving at my picture on that half-crumpled paper, the memories of my in-laws' acts of betrayal came as they always did, like a tempest to my senses… their endless nocturnal meetings with my wife, her younger brother Chuck's frontal attack on my family's quiet existence, and their joint instigation of police involvement in our daily lives. Those acts of betrayal had opened the gates on chaos, letting unstoppable havoc loose on my family. They literally turned my home into an unhealthy environment for children… a situation I judged unacceptable and which ultimately led to the total breakdown of understanding between me and my wife and to our eventual separation.

My mind made an instant sort of those who might list themselves as my enemies… those who might, for reasons certain only to themselves, find cause to send armed men my way and have the resources to sponsor the project. It was indeed a very short list. The list contained one name only; Chuck, my wife's younger brother.

Chuck is the mother lode of my in-law family.

My mind raced further down memory lane to my urgent decision to separate from my beloved family because I had come to the conclusion that to have to endure Chuck' recalcitrance everyday would try even the patience of a saint, not to mention his ever present alter ego and comrade-in-arms—his wife.

With my move to Nigeria, I reckoned that I had escaped Chuck's constant incursion into my family affairs. But I was wrong. His assaults and bug bites continued unabated. It did not matter that I had moved to Nigeria relinquishing the fruits of my lifetime labor to him by default. After all, his sister was in control. Nor would it suffice that learning to survive without my family was like learning to breathe air depleted of oxygen. No… this would not quench the hunger of this man's predatory lust for my flesh.

A memory icon constantly hovered over my senses, warning me that only my passage into spirit life would convince my in-laws to focus on other pursuits.

My mind was working at lightning speed—sorting, weighing, analyzing and evaluating. Could these strangers be connected with the bizarre plot that began just two months earlier in Abuja? Were they here to accomplish the will of my in-laws?

I had only seconds to process the mountain of data jammed up in my head. Luckily they were still fresh in my mind.

On a hot October afternoon barely two months ago today, a lean and hungry looking lackey of an accident claims attorney with whom my wife and I handled a fair amount of cases had somehow materialized in Nigeria at Abuja Central Police Station. His name at the time was Anuofia Adoga.

Without prior warning or even a hint of imminent danger I had been "invited" to the station by a team of three detectives.

When I demanded to know the purpose of this unusual invitation they simply retorted, "You will find out when we get there."

I was skeptical but not afraid of the police, perhaps because of my long history of association and friendship with members of the law enforcement institutions of Nigeria. Besides, my philosophy is that there never is a viable option to answering a call from law enforcement officers even under suspicious circumstances.

Before leaving with the dubious-looking detectives, I had taken one of the smartest cautionary actions in my life. I had called and informed my eldest brother whose office by lucky coincidence, was located adjacent to Abuja Central Police Station. On my instructions, he contacted two police commissioners at the Force Headquarters who were both my longtime friends. By the time we got to the Central Police Station, my brother was awaiting our arrival. He informed me that my friends at the Force Headquarters were neither aware of the invitation nor was there any record of it as was officially required. As a result, the H.Q. was dispatching a senior official to look into the irregular order and the official was already on his way.

As we wound our way up the flight of stairs toward the third floor, the female detective among them led the way while the other two, the echo of evil in each step they took, strode up behind me shielding my brother from my peripheral view. But I knew he was keeping pace with us.

Then it happened.

I knew it was impossible, but Satan himself was in my face as we entered the office behind an unpolished wooden door marked CID. It was as though a bowl of acid had just been dashed in my face. He had all the devices of wickedness radiating from around him. Hanging on his lean and hungry frame was an ill-fitting navy blue suit which I could have sworn was removed from the wardrobe closet in my Maryland USA home. My eyes burned fiery with hatred and damnation as I was overcome by an instant rage. The same kind of rage that nearly consumed me when I heard only a few months earlier how this snake of a man had so filthily wormed his way into my home and into my wife's affection upon my departure following our separation.

I had in the wake of that heart-rending news tried not to permit him or my wife such entertainments, for I regarded their acts as sinful… maledictions which call rather for pity and forgiveness than judgment and condemnation. It was not easy going, but with the passage of time and my reflections on the hallowed relationship that blessed my once enviable marriage to Stella, with six great children, I had relented.

Now, shaking with resurgent rage, hot with pristine anger, for hatred and anger are not among my character traits, I dashed toward this monster, yelling as I moved, also ready to die, "You slimy bastard…you evil dog… you lower than human…you…you…you…"

My voice boomed as I struggled to free myself from the restraining arms of my brother and the two evil detectives.

The commotion I caused took all, including the inspector who had invited me, by surprise, but none more than the slime bag standing in front of me who had stolen, and was now wearing my suit…as if to gloat and flaunt his prized trophy of my soul and inject salt on the open wounds of my life.

Whatever words he planned to utter upon my arrival were now frozen in his cold blooded, reptilian throat. He could not disguise the fright elicited in him by my entrance. He rose to his feet momentarily and stammered incoherently. Then he sat back down trying hard to gather himself and perhaps reorganize his thoughts.

My poor elder brother who had never seen me so utterly out of control continued his struggle to calm me, now that the detectives had loosened their grips on me and had moved over to report their "invitation" of one Mr. George Udeozor to their 'oga'(boss).

They concluded with their boss quickly, who then began his remarks by addressing my initial outburst. I ignored him and turned to face my brother.

My first words to my brother were, "That bastard sitting over there is Anuofia Adoga."

A sign of recognition flashed across my brother's face at the mention of that strange name with which he had become familiar. He nodded with a clear sign that he could now understand my outrageous and uncharacteristic anger.

Anuofia, on hearing my damning tirade turned to the CID inspector unable to fathom why the inspector's lieutenants had not seized me and cast me in the dungeon beneath the building which had earlier been prepared for me.

Anuofia stammered, But…But… I reported this man to you! Why is he here insulting everybody and nobody can stop him?"

Looking at this mid-level officer of the law, I understood his predicament, a situation clearly lost on Anufia Adoga, who relied solely and confidently on the legendary police corruption mantra of the old Nigeria Police Force- 'With the right amount of money, anybody can be made to disappear and nothing will happen."

The slime ball easily forgot three crucial new age realities. First, "a corrupt officer is the greatest coward in the police force." Second, certain people do not easily disappear. Third and above all, "There is a God," who sadly, many always overlook.

The events that followed; the hair raising drama of Anuofia Adoga's grand plan to dispatch me using the corrupt web of assassins operating at that time within the Nigeria Police Force to the netherworld became foiled as all evil plots and designs of the wicked eventually do.

As I sat in rigid shock ruminating on the eeriness of Anuofis's evil plot, my thoughts kept flowing like molten lava, unstoppable with such overwhelming force through my mind, that I remained for several moments oblivious of the present and more volatile drama unfolding right before my eyes.

Inspector Sani's voice was persistent as he called my name over and over and over asking, "Mr. George, are you with me? Mr. George, are you with me…?"

With a start, I returned to the present…worried that the timing and nature of the present assault on me bore an uncanny similarity to that recent attempt at Abuja.

Were these men of EFCC here to execute Anuofia's foiled evil plot on my life? Or, was there a more rational explanation for all this?"

Three

Thus, in my state of morbid fear and delirium, a state of mind antithetical to decision making of any kind, I was given only seconds in which to make decisions that had potentials for life or death outcome.

With only a crumpled digital photograph of me from halfway across the globe, no identity cards offered by my abductors, no warrants shown, and no entreaties entertained, I was offered two choices; either I submitted to the will of the armed men and allowed myself to be arrested and led away from my home to some undisclosed destination, or refuse to be taken by these strange men and risk whatever outcome… with a prayer of course, that their guns malfunction.

I had never been prone to thoughts of suicide, yet I knew that confrontation with these men was tantamount to mass suicide by all who would be within their line of fire. That was the unmistakable message of warning clearly etched in the faces of these men—Their eyes to be exact.

I decided that I would not be led away like a lamb to slaughter at any cost. Some form of explanation must justify my submission to the authority of these men.

I had not followed my dreams to America, pursued my education to post graduate level, pursued a career in business, married the woman of my dreams and fathered four wonderful sons and three angelic daughters only to duck from any hint that my life was in danger. Hell, danger had been my companion all along! One time I had ducked, not for dear life, but from the threat of a clash between action to protect my love for my family and the laws of the United States against such actions. This time I will insist on what was right—my right to be treated with honor and dignity.

"Yes, inspector Sani, I am with you, but I'm not leaving with you without evidence of your authority," I said, my voice regaining some of its strength.

Inspector Sani looked at me incredulous. He said, "Mr. George, you don't seem to understand. We will leave this place with you the easy way or the hard way. The choice is yours. But we will leave with you."

"Even if you deny me all my rights, you cannot deny me my honor and dignity. You do not have power over those," I replied.

"I have a job to do," he said, "please don't make it difficult, Dah Allah, Mr. George."

"I have rights, Inspector. Respect my rights!"

"Mr. George, this is not America! You seem to think you're still in America. In Nigeria, EFCC does not require a warrant or anything at all to effect an arrest. Maybe you should call some of your highly placed friends to verify my statement. But if you don't cooperate, I will call some backup and things might get ugly here."

I immediately seized that window of opportunity—*he had just offered me the chance of a phone call.*

I said, "Yes! Why don't I call the local state police commissioner to verify your authority?"

"Sure," he said. "We are not under his command and we do not need his approval to operate in Anambra State, but he is aware that we are here. In fact, I'll call him myself to make this quick." He was dialing some numbers as he concluded his speech. He continued, "Hello Sir, yes sir, yes, yes. The subject is resisting and there is a bit of commotion. We may need your help but it seems the subject knows you. He wants to speak to you." He handed his mobile phone over to me.

"Hello, hello, is it you, Felix?" I inquired.

"Yes George, how are you?" His voice was unmistakable.

I was instantly afflicted with an insidious case of panic fever…my thoughts whirled like a cyclone. The commissioner's voice on the other end of the phone was confirming my worst fears. These men were authentic officers of the executive branch of government. They were not impostors. Their claims and actions were fully backed by properly constituted authority. But why on earth were they arresting me?

Felix continued, "Well, I'm sorry George, I did not know they were after you when they checked in with me last night. You have to go with them. Maybe it's nothing serious. Maybe just a few questions. You do not have problems with anyone, do you?"

I knew I had to let Felix go. He was after all a policeman. His tone had taken on that professional edge that told me our friendship had to be placed on hold for the moment. I was a big enough boy to understand this.

"Thank you Felix", I said and hung up right away. It was decision time and I was on my own.

I turned to Inspector Sani and said, "Alright, I will go with you but I believe you owe me, at the very least, the honor of an explanation. Put yourself in my position and tell me if I'm being unreasonable." It was evident that I was trying to save face at this point—to achieve a small victory in a war which I had already lost.

He looked at me earnestly and said, "Mr. George, I will tell you truthfully, I do not know why you're wanted. All I can tell you is that it has something to do with the United States of America. But I know nothing of the details. Walahi talahi gaskiya (honestly)."

"OK, let's go," I said. I had lost my appetite and could not eat my first real meal of the day which had been served minutes before my abductors arrived.

Sani informed me that because it was already late—about 8PM, we could not risk the one hour road journey to Enugu where I was meant to catch a one hour flight to Lagos where the answers to all my questions waited at their headquarters. "Unfortunately," he said, "you have to spend the night at the police cell at the station here at Amawbia. Our oga (boss) will meet us early tomorrow morning to accompany you on the flight to Lagos."

Four

Upon being cast into the cell at Amawbia Police Station, my thoughts went to hell. My wish is that I am spared the misery and delirium of eternal torment, for if hell is even a little as diabolical as the dungeon which housed me on that fateful night, then hell is worse than my imagination previously held.

It is impossible to paint a clear picture of the experience of that night with words alone, but release you imagination and travel for a moment and experience the horror that I lived through, for only then will you get a glint of the interiors of this house of torment.

The cell was full to bursting, the stench of human bodies comingled with the already polluted air outside to overwhelm my usually powerful sense of smell.

It was baking hot as the cell was located near the waterline of Obibia River, a stream of muddy water which provided service water for the open abattoir nearby.

I looked around the cell in disbelief. It was hard to accept that a country like mine, Nigeria—the cradle of liberty for West Africa, fondly referred to as the giant of Africa, the land which gave so much to combat the evils of apartheid in South Africa, committed troops and sacrificed so many lives to free our brothers suffering under repressive regimes in neighboring countries and even as far away as Yugoslavia, could maintain such barbarously dehumanizing facilities for caging and dishonoring its own citizens who under the law were still innocent until they are proven guilty. The reality that in the twenty first century, Nigeria continues to shun decency in such basic human rights enforcement organs, as the police force, is beyond comprehension.

Imagine if you will, a filthy room which had remained unpainted, un-fumigated, un-sanitized, un-ventilated, and un . . .anything at all, for decades while playing host to a vast array of citizens; diseased, deranged, normal, elitist, eccentric, etc…

This cell's population rose to 169 (one hundred and sixty nine souls!) with the addition of my name. This dungeon which measures no greater than 30 feet by 35 feet inclusive of the pitch black enclosure that houses the "living dead" (as they were known to the other inmates), was playing host to the Okija Shrine priests and a fierce looking group of car-snatching armed robbers when I was delivered into its only entrance and exit door.

Admittedly, some of these creatures deserved harsh treatment for their heinous crimes, even the death penalty in some cases, but the sight of their gaunt and ghoulish bodies, the stench and noise of the sick, the twisting and interlocking of the limbs and other extremities and desperate search for resting position was deeply affecting. I could not help but feel sorry for them—It was as though I was having an out-of-body experience.

There was no furniture of any type, just the filthy concrete floor and a few straw mats tucked at the edges of the wall to the far left as you enter, perpendicular to the entrance/exit door. Those straw mats, I later discovered, served for the luxurious comfort of the cell "government executives" a few "wealthy" inmates into whose ranks I would shortly become enlisted.

As I picked my way through the mass of bodies, I was keenly aware of the over one hundred pairs of eyes that had settled on me and were following my movement. In that damp and oppressive room even the iron hearted is quickly tempered and rendered susceptible to the powers of unseen evil spirits which had to be in control of all goings on around the cell.

I said a quick prayer in my heart for God to restore my normally cheerful temperament which had been deleted by the experiences of that evening. I knew I would need a strong heart and a sense of humor to survive the next few hours and I silently promised that if God spared me overnight, I would commit many future days of my life to exposing and cleaning up the mess before my eyes. I did not know that the journey upon which I had just embarked would be so long, and that by the end of it, I would be jaded and cynical.

"Hey mister, where are you going?" The question came from somewhere over my head. The voice was icily soft and had a lisp which made the impression of the serpent behind me even stronger.

I froze on the spot. Unsure how to respond, I just stood there and waited for instructions from anybody anywhere. With their eyes, limbs, and bodies, the poor souls around me squiggled, squinted, and squirmed. It was obvious they were attempting to signal a message to me but I had not the slightest clue what.

When I finally heard laughter from more than a lone voice, I slowly began turning toward the source behind me. All eyes around me grew wider, then expectant, and finally surprised when nothing happened. I was later told that it was my calm demeanor and carriage that prevented the power players who ran the cell government known as "the state" from implementing the "welcome" ritual on me.

Ordinarily, upon the injection of an "alejo" (new inmate) into the cell, a spontaneous assault is launched on him during which he is stripped and dispossessed of all valuables. This act of rash intimidation was intended to and did serve to whip the newly admitted into voluntary and involuntary submission to the demands of the cell overlords.

As soon as our eyes aligned, the owner of the lispy, icy voice said, "Listen my friend, you've just entered my state, have you no respect?"

"Uh, I'm sorry… I didn't know… em… em … em, I stammered. "You are?"

"I am OBJ" he responded, and turning to his left with a wave of his hand at the fellow next to him, he continued, "and this is Atiku." That said, he paused for the effect of his claim to settle on me—OBJ and Atiku were then Nigeria's 'president' and 'vice president.'

It did not and I became even more fretful.

"OBJ? . . .Atiku?" … I repeated with a drawled and querying tone. "I am George…"

"Yeah, I'm OBJ you fool…the "president", and Atiku here is my "vice president". Now take those shoes off your feet, pick them up and give them to me!"

Beneath the comical appearance of the unfolding drama, there was no doubt about the seriousness of the danger I was facing.

There was no police guard in sight.

The only authority here belonged to the occupants of the cell. The officially designated police guards, who were conveniently absent, had long been in a conspiracy of silence with the cell overlords – a joint venture, the bountiful profits of which were unevenly shared in favor of the absentee official every day.

This harrowing reality put "OBJ" and "Atiku" in charge of my welfare for the night, and now they were about to show me who the real power here belonged to.

"Hey bro, let's talk now… I'm sure we can arrange something. We can make a deal here, you know… peacefully and like friends…" I could not recognize my own voice as I spoke these words.

"Shut da f…ff…fuck up! I'm not your fucking f… if… friend," thundered Lispy in reply.

Suddenly, I was surrounded by six haggard looking fellows who bore such foul and offensive body odors that I had to hold my breath to keep from throwing up.

As I stood there tense and growing pale outwardly, an inexplicable inner strength took over within me. I kept my eyeballs locked with Lispy and held him to the spot where he stood. He might be the devil himself but tonight I was determined to reach whatever little trace of goodness that I knew had to be somewhere within him.

Before I could blink, my sandals were off from under my feet. Six monsters worked with lightning speed. My gold chain and wristwatch had also been lifted from my neck and wrist before the now grinning President OBJ raised his right hand to signal his boys to stop.

Just as suddenly as they descended on me, the six monsters were gone in a blink of an eye. Thankfully, they also took the reek with them. Uhh… relief…some oxygen please!

"Th'o Mr. George, who is de oga here? (So Mr. George, who is the boss here?), Lispy asked.

"You are", I replied curtly.

"Who am I Mr. George?"

"OBJ".

"Who is OBJ?"

"The President!"

"Who?" he asked with his palm cupped behind his right ear.

"Mr. President!"

"Good, good, good, Mr. George." The fiendish grin on Lispy's face had turned into a happy one finally and for me a new way of life was dawning.

His authority was not in doubt. For the first time since I was delivered into his domain, "normalcy" was decreed by him. His happy grin was all it took. Every cell inmate knew better than me when to smile and be happy or when to freeze regardless of the emotions of the heart.

With OBJ's happy smile, warmth spread around the cell. Teeth began flashing around in assorted expressions of happiness and relief. Incredible, but even ghosts, such as they were, enjoy freedom and liberty.

Atiku, the vice president who had remained perfectly quiet during the president's discharge of executive orders to me finally had a role to play.

He waved at the six monsters who stumbled over from different corners of the cell to receive instructions. Their instruction was to clear a small space occupied by inmates and spread a mat for the president at the entrance into the cell—the only space in the room with access to air from outside.

The task was accomplished in less than thirty seconds to the chagrin of the squirming inmates who had just been squeezed into a much tighter space.

Atiku then invited me to join him and Mr. President to negotiate my fate for the night. His invitation was however an order: "Sit down here Mr. George." The remaining instructions, I deduced from his body language. In detention you have to fill in the blanks most of the time.

Mr. President's mood had surprisingly either calmed considerably or he was up to a new phase of his mind control game. I had no way of knowing. He invited me to sit with him and his vice on the mat for a chat and I did.

"Ah, Mr. George, you're too gentle for a big man, why?" he began.

"I'm not a big man," I protested.

"Oh, hmm, but you are! Look at you. Your skin shining… Mr. Spotless. Your clothes and your skin speak volumes about you Americans! You don't have to pretend. We can tell."

"If I was rich, maybe they wouldn't have been able to bring me here. Have you thought of that?"

"Oh sure, sure, sure, I've thought of that and I know the answer. They brought you here exactly for that same reason. Look. They brought you here at night because they know you will be out within a few hours if the court was still open. Your people will go to the judge and boom, you're out on bail. Not like any of us. I know that you'll be out of here before 9:00AM tomorrow. I know that already, so don't try to pretend or lie to me. I already know this."

"You are the boss OBJ, but you may be wrong. I do not even know who arrested me or why. I do not know their plan. So, I cannot be so sure that I would leave tomorrow. Frankly, I'm quite worried."

"Ha, ha, ha. Hmmm, Mr. George, don't worry. If there was foul play in your arrest, I would've been the first to know. I am the man to take care of such matters. Do you wish to see the last Americana they brought in here? He is in there and I tell you, he will not be leaving on his feet like he came. He will leave here in a lying position. If you know what I mean…"

OBJ was gesturing towards the dark enclosure out of which emanated scary guttural sounds as from impaled animals. He said, "Do you want to see him . . .? Go on, he is in there. Atiku, take him there and show him."

"No, no, no, I believe you. I don't want to see!" I pleaded. "But why is he there? What did he do?"

"He did not cooperate," he said evenly. "Ahh, but I know you will cooperate Mr. George, won't you?"

I now understood. The cloud was swiftly lifted from my senses. The entire rigmarole was designed to intimidate and frighten me. They were doing a great job of it. It was all part of the scheme— a well-rehearsed scam. Break him down; intimidate him into both voluntary and involuntary (if necessary) surrender to the will of the "president" (or simply, the big jail bully).

But upon reflection, I knew that neither the view before me nor the cries of anguish seeping into the cell was part of any scheme. These were real people in real human despair. I knew also that OBJ had the power to subject me to similar condition as these people, at least for the next several hours.

"Hey," I said in a voice thoroughly broken and as submissive as I could will it, "I don't play games. Here is my wallet. All the money I have on me is in there. You can have all of it. Just let me rest. I've had nothing to eat all day and I am exhausted. Please understand, I'm straight as an arrow. You may search me if you want to..."

His smile reminded me of the joker, played by jack Nicholson in Batman. My wallet was loaded with N1,000 bills that look and smelled right out of printing and minting.

OBJ quickly stowed the money underneath his beige caftan which must have been white at some point in its past life.

"I knew you were a big man Mr. George. You over there...you fucking mopol (mobile police)", he said, waving at the hood who had ferried away my shoes and jewelry, "give this man his shoes and wristwatch."

He turned to me with a devious grin and his gesture led my eyes to his chest where he was gently caressing my gold chain. He said, "Oga George, can I keep this one? . . .This little chain as a souvenir... something by which to remember this day?"

In my mind I was thinking, "Never, you bastard!" but I replied ever so carefully, "you know, it is really a gift from my wife. I'm not supposed to give it away...."

"But you just did, didn't you? Don't worry, your wife will understand, Women always do. They're better givers than us. Men always take, take, take...."

"Well, if you say so. I can't argue with Mr. President."

"Yee...yee...yearrh, this man is great," he said. "Mr. George, you will sleep here." He was pointing at a spot next to the mat where he sat, close to the entrance /exit passage which was currently occupied by no fewer than ten inmates squatting—their bodies linked into a human chain.

I ventured my first questions, "Where will all these men sleep? I am just curious. There is no space here."

Obj and Atiku laughed hard and long before OBJ replied, "You'll see in a few minutes… you'll see."

~

And indeed, I saw. Even unto this day it is hard to comprehend—a day which God had started with beauty and bliss—that it could end with a curse upon it, is a burden too heavy for my soul to bear.

The scene remains vivid in my mind over five years later—clear as the sky devoid of cloud, surreal from start to finish… At ten sharp, Christian prayers were announced and as if rehearsed, nearly all the gangly images of sorrow and grief were on their knees. All available spaces were taken. They were either kneeling or bowed; their hands clasped in prayer pose. Atiku led the session. They began with hymns of praise and worship. Hymns I had never heard, but the Christian rhythm of which was not in doubt.

From the corner of my eyes, I could see OBJ's lips in motion; invoking. His eyelids tightly shut, his whole body gyrating to the rhythm of the hymns…

"Let the spirit of the Lord come down…Amen."

"Let the spirit of the Lord come down…in Jesus' name…"

"Let the spirit of the Lord…from heaven come down."

"Let the spirit of the Lord come down."

I was instantly drafted—no invitation necessary.

There was no sign of coercion. These men were praying voluntarily. I had to pinch myself several times to be sure I was conscious. It never occurred to me in the past that murderers, armed robbers, extortionists, rapists, etc. had it in them to invoke the spirit of God in such manly voices, so pious you could mistake them for a school of cardinals in prayer.

In the midst of extreme anguish, sickness, and pain, these men were praying. Whether lip-syncing, cajoling, or truly supplicating, it did not matter to me. They were praising and worshipping God under conditions I knew I could not survive for one week!

I remember thinking that if this was possible, then God had to exist. It seemed pointless that they should be praying. They were already forgotten by their God and society. They were broken men brought to parity with zoo animals. For many months they had been tortured, caged, and starved. Their only defense and recourse was their maker and they seemed to know this.

After one hour of singing, praying, and invoking God, Atiku concluded by reminding "our Father" that we had obeyed His injunctions to;

"Seek and you will find."

"Ask, and it shall be given to you."

"Knock and the door shall be opened unto you."

"Now brothers, we've done our duty, we await God's fulfillment of His promises." He exhorted.

Moslem prayers were called at 11:15 PM. Two inmates from northern parts and one from the west began their last prayer of the day. There was no departure from the usual Moslem prayer that I could tell. No singing or testimony phase. They concluded prayers by midnight, paving way for the nightmares that haunt me even to this very day.

Before my God, I might not have believed this without the clarity of mind and heart which I had, even in my despair as I observed the events of that night unfold.

A clear sky and the full moon which seemed to be hanging outside the entrance/exit door provided enough illumination for the activities inside our god-awful cell.

Prayers were hardly over before I witnessed the brutal reality show which is the nightly lives of men in the dungeons known as police cells in my beloved Nigeria.

As if a prologue to the approaching omen, an evil bird, surely an owl, belched out several long hoots. Nobody spoke, only movements—crawling movements, as those privileged with authority took sleeping positions at the edge of the entrance wall to the right of it. At the wall across the room, the story was different. A line of about seven buckets stood with seven men astride them in half squatting positions while they dumped the wasted contents of their bowels in the buckets for all to see and inhale. The air went afoul as the steam from within their guts blended with the rot already smoldering me out of life bit by bit.

With a stone in my heart, I resolved to live through the unfolding nightmare however difficult.

OBJ and Atiku had graciously allotted a narrow space along the wall's edge to me. Atiku lay to my right next to the already slumbering President OBJ. But at our feet were piles of human forms in the same interlocking and squatting position that they had endured day after day and week after week. Now exhausted from heat, hunger and being bullied, they are made to sleep on their feet in the same position.

As I watched them and their expressions of melancholy, I was filled with loathing for the authority that allowed men to treat other men this way. Authority abused beyond comprehension.

One by one, they drifted into fitful sleep. I watched as bodies collapsed and piled on top of each other and as those crushed underneath awoke and angry protests and fights broke out. In silence, I watched as the fights were settled by no one at all—they merely fizzled when the combatants ran out of steam. Exhausted, they simply slumped on others too weak to protest.

The seven bucket business was an all-night affair. It was a mystery to me at about 5:00 AM when the buckets were removed that they were not filled up let alone over flowing. A simple explanation… there was little for the guts to dispense.

After the buckets were removed, two bodies also followed. Wrapped in their own clothes, they were too frail and with little flesh on them when they gave up their ghosts.

In my state of numbness and disbelief sleep was not at all on my mind. All I could think was, "when am I going to wake up from this crazy nightmare?"

Five

By dawn the next morning only a piece of me remained. As darkness slowly gave way to light, my thoughts began gathering its scattered pieces.

It was not a nightmare after all. Everything had been real. With sizeable effort I began repeated movements of my limbs and torso—an exercise to restart normal blood flow in my generally numbed body. Even though I was physically and emotionally drained, I knew the breaking day was pregnant with unknown puzzles. It was crucially important for me to be in the right frame of mind as we approached the hour to embark on the promised journey to Enugu and ultimately to Lagos where this ugly puzzle would be solved.

Slowly, the scattered pieces of me began returning into place and I was once again almost whole. My heart still kept a rate faster than normal and when I rose to my feet, I could barely stand. I was a physical wreck on my wobbly feet. But I did not fall.

At about 6:00 AM, I knew from the sounds of human traffic outside that commuters had begun their daily work-bound journeys. All I could hope for was a way out of the hell hole that engulfed me.

In daylight, the scene within the cell was even uglier than in the dark. Now, I could see the open sores all over the bodies of the human tragedies that languished under these repressive and inhumane conditions. The filth hanging everywhere you looked and the palpable odor of human illness and suffering were offensive beyond reason.

At about 6:30 in the morning, the image of my younger brother IK showed up at the entrance/exit bars like the apparition of an angel spirit—the best sight to assail my vision since the god-awful visit of the EFCC gang. I made a quick dash toward him at the bars. His expression was somber but reassuring.

He said, "Brother, don't worry. They're already here signing the papers. You'll be out very shortly. I have contacted brother Chiedu and he will meet us at Enugu. He has also contacted Barrister Mbonu. We will definitely find out what this is all about and hopefully put a stop to it."

I nodded and told him I appreciated his efforts. In his eyes I could see the pain and disbelief at what was happening. This was a most unlikely situation. None of us in the family could have anticipated even a remote possibility of it ever happening, and so, were unprepared and at a loss as to what to do.

Although our father had served in law enforcement as a police officer, moving high up through the ranks, he had discouraged us from having much to do with that institution.

He had warned us over the years that any invitation of the police for involvement or mediation in our affairs was like "opening the door permanently" for police intrusion—a license of sorts and a voluntary surrender of our privacy. He counseled us to have social relations with principal police officers and keep our acts clean. So far, I had found his advice meritorious and life preserving. At this juncture I was worried and was wondering how my harmonious and generally friendly relations with many in law enforcement would be impacted by the unfolding drama. This was however not the right time for such introspection. The issues of immediate concern to me were of hunger, hygiene, and spiritual strength. IK had come to try and provide me with as much of these as he could afford.

Among my 13 living siblings at this time, IK was the only one who ventured into the dreaded field of law enforcement. He was an operative of the State Security Services (SSS)… and he was a good agent.

I asked him, "What have you found out about these guys?"

"Not much, but when we get to Enugu, I will know more," he replied.

"You do think we can stop them from taking me to Lagos, even if I promised to report to their commission on my own?" I asked rhetorically.

"They appear determined, but we will try everything possible."

"I know."

From over IK's shoulder I could see Officer Sani approaching. He looked happy and well rested but much smaller than he looked the previous day, perhaps because he had removed his bullet proof vest and was now wearing casual western attire, just a pair of jeans and tee shirt. Behind Officer Sani was a local police officer with a key dangling from a rusted old key chain.

Instantaneously, OBJ, Atiku and a few other inmates began jostling around me, highly excited.

"I told you Mr. George, your kind never spend a full twenty four in our cell. Now you're leaving already. Please remember me when you're back to your house. All I need to get me out is N3,000.00 (about $25.00). That's all!! Please help me. God will reward you!" He pleaded.

I wish I shared his optimism, but I did not say so. I could not.

Others joined in.

Atiku said, "Oga George, me too, all they need to set me free is N4,000.00(about $35.00 dollars). Please help."

One by one, they began handing me bits of paper with their legal information scrawled on it. All imploring me to help free them, "in the name of God Almighty who has just rescued you from hell," they pleaded.

"I will do my best," I assured them, "but I cannot make any promises because I do not know what will happen next with me, but be assured that if and when my ordeal ends, I will not forget you."

"That's all we ask," they said, almost in unison.

"Good morning Mr. George, I hope you were able to rest," Officer Sani greeted.

When he got no reply from my sealed lips, he looked at me more closely and continued;

"Well, Mr. George, don't feel too sad, we also did not get much sleep. As a matter of fact we did not even sleep at all. We only got to the hotel this morning. No time to sleep before our trip to Enugu. Our oga is already on his way to Enugu to meet us."

As Sani was talking, the cell guard slid the barred door to the side and motioned for me to exit the cell. My thoughts were filled with unprintable curses for Sani and his gang but I kept a straight face. When I got outside, IK and I joined the other EFCC officers where their car was parked.

Officer Sani closed in and said, "Just a minute while I finish the paper work. We will be on our way right away."

When he returned, I turned to him, "Officer Sani, I have cooperated fully with your instructions, now I need the favor of your cooperation."

He looked up to my face and replied, "what do you need Mr. George?"

"I need a few minutes at my hotel, Georgian Villa, you remember, the venue of my arrest."

"Mr. George, that's a difficult request for me," he said, "do you remember the commotion yesterday? We almost had a riot on our hands..."

I cut him off, "Officer Sani, look at me. I am a mess. I need a shower, a shave and some food or else you may as well transport my corpse to Enugu."

"Hold on Mr. George, I don't enjoy this. I'm only following orders. Police work is not..."

"Sani, it was me who prevented the escalation of yesterday's imbroglio. Do you think I want to risk lives of my community members so recklessly? Hey, I have done nothing wrong to anybody. I deserve more respect and better treatment than I've so far received from you and whoever sent you. Da Allah, just respect my rights if not me!"

"OK, Mr. George, thirty minutes at your place. That is all the time I can afford.

"Thank you," I said and not another word was spoken as we drove the short one mile distance to my compound. I sat in back between Sani and one of his colleagues while the mobile policeman cradled his AK47 in the passenger front seat with the plain clothes agent who drove the car. I looked back to see IK following at a close distance behind us.

~

As our two-car convoy entered the gates of Georgian Villa, a state of nervous tension hung in the air. From all corners of the compound and from behind the tinted glass windows of the Villa, tens of pairs of troubled eyes peeped, unsure why this unwelcome vehicle had returned to torment them again so early this morning.

When I climbed out of the car however, the state of tension was quickly replaced by cries of confusion and despair. Some members of my staff hung their arms in limp surrender, obviously worried about how these events all play out for them, their jobs, and families. Others broke into instant song and dance jubilation in their mistaken assumption that the error of my arrest had been discovered and rectified. The scene was reminiscent of the tension that engulfed Okonkwo's compound following his strike at the eunuch in Chinua Achebe's epic novel, Things Fall Apart.

~

I was in torment and feeling like wood as we walked through the small foyer to mount the winding staircase that led to my permanent suite. IK's attention to all details, little and large came as a surprise to me. He took charge to see that my food was prepared quickly, that my clothes were laid on the bed and that bath water was warm and refreshing.

After one large cup of coffee, a hot meal and a warm shower, my whole body felt renewed, especially on the inside.

For one frightening moment I became assailed with thoughts of escape. The ordeal of the previous night had ignited a fear in me which I had never known. The thought that I could easily have lost my life without seeing or knowing who or what hit me, was greatly unsettling. Sani and his colleagues may have expressed regret about locking me in that god-awful cell but who was to say it would be the last experience? And how was I to foretell what was ahead, awaiting me in Lagos? There had so far been no warrant or explanation for my arrest.

My mind was making a compelling case for escape and mapping out an easy route to freedom.

I was alone in the bathroom. It was daylight. The only guard mounted by my adductors was out in the front of my compound. An easy slide down the side of the window and drop of no more than eight feet would put me on the ground in the back of my compound. Once down I could easily scale the low walled fence into my neighbor's compound and to total freedom.

All these thoughts came as a flash and went as they came because even as appealing as they played in my mind, I knew I was neither a criminal nor a coward. Escaping or even attempting to do so would make me both. That thought alone was all that stood between my freedom and an unknown unseen enemy.

My departure was as traumatic as it was emotional. Only a few hours earlier the mood at Georgian Villa was a festive one. Guests and residents of the Villa had streamed back and forth with their Christmas gifts and messages. A crew had arrived among these guest, from Anambra Broadcasting Services (ABS), requesting an interview with me to cover our community development and philanthropic activities. In focus was a Christmas party which we had jointly sponsored with the Mother Teresa Orphanage in Awka for three hundred orphans two days earlier.

All that, now seemed to have taken place a lifetime ago. At the moment my compound and Georgian Villa within its walls, was covered by a palpable cloud of cruel uncertainty. I could not provide my people with any words of comfort or assurance. My fate as well as theirs hung on a wavering balance.

I looked at them shrugged my shoulders and said, "Pray for my safe and early return. Everything will be alright. I will call you all soon."

They showed no sign that they believed these words of mine, but they nodded in agreement.

Our drive to Enugu took all of one and one half hours, instead of the usual 45 minutes. The badly degraded highway surfaces and the resulting go-slow traffic had gradually worsened over the last few years.

For me the journey was a torment. The heat and the bumps over large potholes were minor irritants. The real source of torment for me was what lay ahead at the point to which I was slowly making a final approach.

Enugu looked deserted when we arrived-far from the energy bubbling coal city normally was. Christmas celebrations seemed to have a way of sucking the life out of the acclaimed capital city of my people, the Igbo speaking people of Nigeria. As a result, once within the city limits, it took us just a few minutes to arrive at the Enugu Police Headquarters.

My brother Chinedu and Barrister Mbonu were the easiest two gentlemen to locate in the crowded parking lot facing the line of old bungalows that form the offices and cells of Enugu Police headquarters. They had apparently arrived very early and blended into a crowd of families whose loved ones were similarly afflicted with law enforcement issues.

Barrister Chuma Mbonu, a longtime family friend and school mate of Chinedu's had a reputation for practicality in law. He cuts to the chase—gets to the root of the matter without beating about the bush. The manner of his dialogue with Agent Sani was precise and impressive. Within minutes he returned to the EFCC vehicle where Chiedu, IK, and I were commiserating with one another to announce that our answer lay in Lagos. There was nothing anybody could do in Enugu because of lack of jurisdiction. EFCC was a federal agency with federal jurisdiction and reserves a right to choose its venues without legal challenge of its authority. Lagos had been chosen in my case and I had to be taken there whether I liked it or not.

As we set out for the ten minute drive to Enugu Airport, Chiedu assured me that he would arrange for me to be met on arrival at the Ikoyi headquarters of EFCC by a barrister before his arrival in Lagos on a later flight. We meanwhile rode in different cars to Enugu Airport.

Six

Enugu Airport is the scene of many memories for me—memories which span over many decades, some joyful and others sorrowful. No memories in between.

My earliest memory of this piece of historic property was in the early 1970's immediately following the end of the Biafra-Nigeria civil war. I was in my middle teenage years then, precocious and highly adventurous. Most of the children in Biafra had been forced into early maturity by a longsuffering civil war during which we were often forced into playing adult roles.

By this time in my development I was too young to be rationally seen as an adult but at the same time too mature to be considered a child. I was a man-child.

My older sister's fiancé had wowed everybody by announcing that he had secured a student visa to go, live and study in America. This news which made him an instant celebrity in our small community of Amawbia town had unlocked a catalogue of recorded dreams in my mind—dreams about this foreign land where I was sure that all the injustices of war, poverty, and discrimination did not exist. A land I was determined that I would make my own regardless of how unlikely it then appeared.

The memory of us—my sister and her fiancé, his siblings, nieces and nephews, myself and other relatives all lined up at the side of the colonial terminal building to be photographed as a final farewell documentary with our hero/celebrity before his departure to America became engrained permanently in my mind.

That occasion which tops my list of joyful memories of Enugu Airport was about to be matched by an occasion of equal impact in sorrow as we approached the now upgraded terminal building of the same airport.

My eyes picked out each landmark as we passed it in my idle countdown to an unknown, uncertain future.

As we pulled into the open terminal parking lot, I turned and peered through the rear windshield to confirm that my brothers were following. They were. The fact that they would shortly be unable to cast their shadow of protection over me made me feel as though I was seconds away from certain doom but hanging onto my last vestige of hope. Perhaps a miracle would happen. But I had my doubts.

Sani instructed everybody to wait in the car while he obtained flight information from inside the terminal building.

My brothers stepped out of the car and Chiedu began immediately to work the phone. After several brief conversations, they came around to the passenger window of the EFCC car to update me on their efforts thus far.

I was pleased to learn that Chiedu had managed to secure the services of a good barrister in Lagos who was glad to aggressively twist the arms of the commission (EFCC) until we unmasked my faceless tormentor. Although my brother had not met Barrister Dambo, he had it from reliable sources that he was equal to the task.

At this juncture it occurred to me that the moment had arrived to pull all possible strings, call in all intercessors, the weightier the better. Off the top of my head, I reeled out their names and phone numbers, the retired military generals who had until now remained my good friends, but only on a social level. The event which recently happened at Abuja had proved to me convincingly, that it is true what they said, "it is not always what you know, but who you know."

I repeatedly drummed it into my brothers head that he must call each of these gentlemen; "Tell them that I have been abducted by men of the EFCC for no apparent reason. Tell them they had no arrest warrant and that my life is in danger. Tell them about my night in the police station death camp. Spare no hyperbole in describing my plight."

My brother concurred and just then, Agent Sani returned to the car. He informed us that their boss had missed the earlier flight but was scheduled to arrive on a later flight in the afternoon. We had to find a quiet area of the departure lounge and await the boss's arrival. The boss was to clear from arrival and meet us at the departure hall to re-board the same airplane with me for the return leg of the flight back to Lagos. The whole arrangement seemed so surreal I was dazed. Me, of all people—after forty eight years of peaceful, largely uneventful livelihood outside the purview of law enforcement, was within twenty four hours, an ex-police cell inmate, and was now being moved across state borders in the manner of a fugitive. Yet my abductors, who were obviously law enforcement personnel, saw nothing wrong in keeping mum about my alleged offense. Knowing within my heart that I had not wronged anybody or group of people, this was a rather large pill to swallow. But my abductors were towering—the government and her unlimited chain of resources. A David and Goliath moment without the divine catapult… or, was it a sling shot that rescued David?

The departure hall interlude gave me pause to once again reflect on, and evaluate the tumultuous events of my recent past sequentially. I hoped somehow to narrow down the list of likely reasons someone would deem it worthwhile to amass the resources to hunt me down in my rural community of Amawbia.

EFCC, I had now been fully briefed, was set up with broad legal and territorial jurisdiction. Whereas the powers vested in this ubiquitous commission were arguably ad infinitum, it was generally understood that the focal purpose for setting it up was to combat financial crimes such as bank fraud. The name of the commission was after all EFCC which rolls out to Economic and Financial Crimes Commission and could not have spelled out its purpose any better. So then, why in the world would this commission's operatives be arresting me? I was not under investigation for any financial negotiations that had gone sour, and I had not sued or been sued by anybody for any reason.

With these facts crystal clear in my head, there could again be only two individuals who had made it their occupation to attach themselves to my private affairs.

A new thought immediately began to develop in my head. The visit of that sleazebag, Anuofia Adoga, could indeed have had a more ominous implication than I had earlier concluded. He could really have embarked on his evil mission on the behest of my brother-in-law who had vowed to make my life miserable from the day I served him with a notice to pack out of my property in North Potomac.

Were these EFCC officers carrying out orders which had been originated by these two fellows to fulfill their promises to do me some irreparable harm? Had my brother-in-law sponsored this inexplicable assault on me?

Sure, it was conceivable that he would and could plot to harm me. He had threatened and promised that much already. But, was he capable of engaging the services of Nigeria's much touted, incorruptible crime fighting commission, the EFCC? This was the question of which answer I had to uncover in Lagos. If he had achieved that, then I would never feel safe anywhere. Not even in the courts where verdicts have been known to be for sale. Never before in my life had I felt so powerless and unsafe. Little did

I know that the future held much more such puzzling questions for me to contend with.

~

My brothers and I had no choice but to sit with these officers and try to make light of my uncertain future. Sani inadvertently dropped a hint that he might have known more than he let on earlier. He said, "But George, you're an American, are you not? All you have to do is change some American dollars and whatever the problem you're having will disappear."

I was not at all amused by his remark. "First of all, how did you know I'm an American citizen?" I asked. "And even if I am, what has money got to do with my illegal arrest?"

"Come George," he smirked, "look how your skin is glowing. What do they feed you people in America? I can always tell the difference between an 'Andrew' and our sufferhead just by how smooth and fat the 'Andrews' are. You are definitely an Andrew, and you can't fool me, the dollars are there. Even Georgian Villa alone cost more than I will earn in my lifetime!"

"Look Sani," I said, "you might find humor in what is happening but I don't. I have been violated in a most humiliating way by you and your partners and although you claim to be following orders, it appears you're keeping something from me. For all I know, you may be working for some killers who are after my life. This is not funny to me."

Sani actually laughed out loud prompting his colleagues to join in our humorless dialogue. He said, "Mr. George, you take life too seriously. What is the worst that can happen, ehh? Nobody wants to kill you. I've seen bad things happen to people and you are certainly not looking like such people. Relax. It cannot be that bad."

We were getting nowhere with this line of discussion and I could not see that trend changing. I therefore decide to terminate the dialogue.

"O.K.", I said, "Sani, I will not press you for answers. You may or may not know what this is all about, but I can see that you will not share what you know or don't know. So please permit me to move to the other table and discuss important issues with my folks. I have to hand certain important documents over to them if you don't mind."

"Alright Mr. George, go ahead, but believe me, I'm not the bad guy here and I like you as a fellow Nigerian even if you have denounced our country."

I had to reply him on that last remark. I was hurt by it.

"Let me tell you something my friend," I said. "You arrested me at my property, in my village. If I had denounced my country, why would I build it and offer employment to the unemployed?" Don't you think that if all capable Nigerians living at home would do the same rather than stealing from Nigeria and laundering their loot overseas, our economic problems will be much less? I feel insulted by your joke and I believe you owe me an apology." He offered a lighthearted apology and my brothers and I moved to the table beside them to complete our parting arrangements.

Nearly five years has passed since that sorrowful departure and sadly, as I sit in America's Federal Correctional Institutions penning down these words, I long for the day when I will travel those roads of my youth again, under happier circumstances.

Seven

Out of nowhere the explosive sound of a lone jet aircraft split the silent sky over Enugu Airport. Air traffic is not part of the regular hustle and bustle of this region. On a busy day not even a combined twenty take offs and landings make Enugu Airport's single runway.

The crowd of waiting passengers erupted in their usual last minute scramble for flight tickets. Only foreign tourists and first time passengers are ever surprised by this peculiar unwritten air-travel culture in Nigeria. Since flight cancellations became a regular occurrence, passengers were forced to purchase tickets only for flights on the ground—no more anticipatory purchases based on promised or scheduled flights. They often disappoint and airline refund policies were often contentious.

Luckily, I did not have to join in that mad fray. My abductors had seen to all my flight details. All I had to do was turn when instructed, board the flight when instructed. Follow the leader.

The boss looked nothing like I anticipated. Given the gruff, ectomorphic appearance of my abductors, it was almost a relief to see a young-looking, polished gentleman, freshly shaved and with a mild trail of expensive men's musk hanging behind him as he walked by me to the table where his boys shot their out-stretched arms into the air in salute. He returned salute in like manner.

With a nod, he indicated his confirmation of my identity. Positive ID as they say. He smiled at his boys and said, "Good work."

Perhaps he felt his voice was too low for me to overhear him but I didn't think that my over hearing them bothered him. He waved for Sani to join him at the bar stools just across from where we sat. After they were seated, he looked at us as if to assure that we were outside earshot of them. He was not in luck, I could hear them, but he went on talking anyway.

Right in that airport departure lounge, the gentleman I now knew as the boss extracted a huge wad of 500 naira notes and handed them over to his presumed lead agent. Sani examined the money and after a brief light hearted exchange, the boss increased the wad of bills which Sani pocketed, a happy smile lighting up his face.

Agent Sani returned to the table where his colleagues were seated and drinking, though visibly excited and looking expectantly at the transactions taking place at the bar area.

One after the other they met with the boss and following the lead agent's example they each upped their bargain and got paid accordingly. Each returned smiling ear to ear.

As I listened in stone silence, each of these agents recounted to their boss how my arrest had been a tricky one. How their tactfulness had averted a bloodbath in the village of Amawbia. They all gesticulated as they dramatized the events of the previous 24 hours to demonstrate to their "oga" just how big a catch I had been. The deft negotiating skills of agent Sani and the intervention of the police commissioner who they were surprised to discover had been my friend. Each one of them concluded their sermon for high reward with the same pitch; "Oga na waoo." The entire scene filled me with pain as I sat there wondering what I had done to earn this horrible nightmare. I looked on in helplessness and resignation.

The boss having settled his boys walked over to my table and introduced himself. "I am Mr. Ade of the EFCC," he said. "Our flight will be leaving any minute now, are you ready?"

As he spoke, my eyes bore through his cold gaze. I could not have hoped for less than I got, he was after all a senior police officer which in Nigeria means that he had seen all that life has to offer. On my part, in twenty four hours, I had also learned not to expect things to be always as they seem. Some techniques I had learned theoretically many years before, now had a chance for practical application in my life. I had to accept, alter, adapt, or avoid these negative forces as they hit me if I hoped to come out of this situation whole. Right now I needed to accept that I was simply like fish in the net before these guys—nothing more.

"Sure, I'm ready when you are," I replied.

There was no time to waste, nothing more to say.

I hugged my brothers who tearfully tried to reassure me. I knew their hearts were hurting no less than mine. I nodded to their reassurances, feeling their love encircle me, making me stronger and more determined to live through whatever difficulties the future held for me.

The boss waved for me to move ahead of him as we strolled across the tarmac to board the Sosoliso Airlines plane for our Lagos journey.

Within minutes we were airborne. From my No 14A window seat, I followed the contrails with my eyes down to watch my brothers, Enugu, and my freedom disappear.

Eight

The boss and I sat beside each other, me on the window seat, he on the aisle seat, one empty seat between us. For a considerable length of time neither of us uttered a word. Then without moving his head he quietly offered, "I hope my boys were not too rough with you?"

I thought, "you must mean, I hope my boys gave you hell," but I answered, "I'm O.K.".

He nodded and the silence between us returned. For another 10 minutes not a word crossed the empty seat between us. There was however, a lot of chatter around us.

I knew we would commence descent pretty soon—the one hour flight usually felt like it took half that time.

The silence between us gave my body and soul time to coordinate in preparation for the unknown fate awaiting me in Lagos. Strangely, my mind had not dwelt on the last 24 hours during this flight—perhaps because the anxiety of what the future held was enough to freeze the feeling of despair already suffered, at least for the meantime.

Again, with his face fixed ahead, Mr. Ade said, "Are you ready to return to America now?"

I heard the question but the full impact of it did not immediately hit me.

I looked at him interrogatively, unsure his question was directed at me.

For the first time he met my eyes with his and asked me, "You are an American citizen aren't you? Don't you want to return to America?"

I had known all along that something was in the offing in my life; something major. But now I knew that I had underestimated whatever it was that loomed over me. Surely, it had to be of a cataclysmic scale. Mr. Ade's questions had finally confirmed everything!—from the assault staged by Anuofia Adoga to ice me at the Abuja Central Police Station, to the tango with EFCC abductors at Amawbia and now this hint that total strangers knew intimate details about me. They knew that I was an American citizen and even had the audacity to suggest that I should return there, as if my Nigerian citizenship was of no significance. None of these events happened in isolation. Of this fact, I was now sure. But what to make of it I did not know. All I could hope for now was clarity. Without knowing the source of my pain, I could never hope to alleviate it.

"How did you know I am an American citizen?" I asked. "I have not told you so, have I?"

He smiled mildly and underneath his smile I could see a satisfied expression that suggested to me that this guy had the entire picture down pat.

"Mr. George," he continued, "I do not know why the Americans want you, but your arrest has nothing to do with us at EFCC. We will be on the ground fairly soon and as soon as we get to our office, you will be brought to speed with everything. I merely want to prepare your mind for what to expect, so it does not come as a surprise to you."

"With all due respect, sir," I complained, "you have told me nothing that can prepare my mind for anything! What Americans want me for instance? For What? Why was there no warrant of arrest? This is really an abduction you know, Mister!"

His smile widened as he spoke, "You have really become Americanized fully. You Americans are funny, always quoting laws claiming rights. Well Mr. George, when we get to the office your people will be there. You can ask them all these questions and claim your rights. You might even sue them for damages," he joked. "That is the American way, isn't it?"

I was not satisfied and was not going to let him off the hook easy. He had opened the door to my questions. I was not about to let him shut it. Too much was hanging on the balance.

I said, "As a Nigerian and I am a full blooded Nigerian, you owe me an explanation, one Nigerian to another, one brother to another."

His reply was to make more Nigerians-in-the Diaspora jokes, "You mean that you're no longer Andrew?" But the Americans told us you are one of them, and from what I see, you look very much an American Andrew."

Of course, I had seen the satirical television splash which was politically contrived to deride the numerous Nigerians in the Diaspora returnees who cannot cope with their homeland's development pains but would proudly "check out" to enjoy the developed infrastructures of other countries after they had gone through their own growing pains. "Andrew" was the mock-heroic character of this popular TV satire.

There will be time in the distant future for me to join issues with Mr. Ade on his very expensive joke at my expense. Meanwhile, I knew that time was not my friend. I needed to have an idea what to truly expect down beneath us as we were now approaching Lagos in earnest.

"Mr. Ade, "I said," I am 48 years old, I'm the father of seven children. I do not have time to play "Andrew" games with my life. If you had asked your boys, they would have told you about their findings at Amawbia, my hometown. I bet you, "Andrews" do not take the pains to do the things I do for my people. I really need your help to understand what is going on in my life. This is a very serious matter for me you know."

I could not tell whether I had finally got through to him, but I could tell that he was listening.

"Mr. George, all I can tell you is this; somebody wants you back in the United States of America. As to whether it is the government of the United States or a private individual or both, I have no ideas or opinions to offer you. You are in a better position to know that information than I am. As I have promised you, somebody from the United States Embassy will come over to the EFCC to explain those details to you, if you don't already know. I cannot throw more light on the matter than that."

The thought of even the possibility that I was wanted by the United States government was so unnerving to me that I became momentarily dizzy. All I had known up to this point in my life about being declared wanted by the United States government were from scenes on that very subject in movies and television shows like The Fugitive, The Client, The Partner, America's Most Wanted, etc. These shows were always my favorites for visual entertainment because of my firm belief in social justice for all. But it had always troubled me when innocent people had been subjected in real life to the same overwhelming power possessed only by the United States government for bringing criminals to justice. In nearly all cases, even after innocence is proven, the lives of victims of a bully-styled justice system are never the same. In America it seems, honor once lost is lost forever. It is never fully regained. Some encryption in the cultural gene of America appears resistant to the acceptance of innocence in any persons on whom charges are brought. Leads me to wonder how innocent the remainder of our society on whom charges have not been brought really are!

I was still so overcome by Ade's words and the thoughts in my head that I failed to notice the descent of our aircraft and all the pre-landing announcements and preparations.

The hard landing and the screeching of the tires jolted me back to consciousness and to my prevailing issues.

~

We were met at the arrival hall by a gentleman who I presumed to be boss Ade's driver owing to the way he welcomed "Oga."

Because the only luggage we had was my carry-on leather bag containing two sets of change clothing and toiletries, we fast tracked arrival formalities and were soon at the parking lot.

I immediately gave up any hope that Barrister Dambo might be meeting me as I saw no sign among the waiting crowd that I was being expected.

Ade instructed the driver to head immediately to their Awolowo Road, Ikoyi office. Because I had paid very little attention to issues like time and weather, it was quite surprising when I noted that darkness was creeping in on us. I glanced at my wristwatch and was alarmed to discover that it was already 6:00 PM in the evening. Where had the day gone? What would become of me in the next few hours? I was, so far as I knew, still a captive of unknown, presumed officials of the Federal Government of Nigeria. My captors had flown me to Lagos, the scene of an untold number of bogus official arrests which turned out to be hoaxes orchestrated to cover up the actual act—kidnap. All I could do was look out the window and try to control my different erratic emotions.

Ade's double chamber pick-up truck finally came to a stop shortly after we exited from the third mainland bridge and I could hear the signal light clicking, tick-tock, tick-tock. I looked out and took note that it was about to turn into a driveway that led to a building I knew to be occupied by the SSS (State Security Service). I had been in this building numerous times in the past, albeit under happier circumstances. I was usually in the company of people who had something to say about how that service was run. Today however, I was on the other side of the fence.

One question was finally answered conclusively at this point. My abductors were not lone rangers. They were as officially real as any badge-wearing, flag flying Uncle Tom.

The obvious questions now were; how were EFCC services procured? And what will their next move be?

Nine

The road we were on has been the scene of innumerable historical and political events in Nigeria. I believe it is safe to say that no other street in Nigeria has witnessed more dramatic action or carried more controversial vehicular passengers than Awolowo Road, Ikoyi Lagos, from coup de tats to political campaigns, to armed robberies. These days, the newly dualized and beautified Awolowo Road plays host to a plethora of businesses including branches of Nigeria's new generation banks, digital filling stations, electronics stores, modern fast food stores all of which are advertised by bright and trendy neon signs. EFCC Lagos headquarters is nestled in a cul-de-sac off this poignant road and seems determined not to be outshone in the neon light competition. We were now signaling to drive up that short corridor.

As we turned into the driveway, a sense of un-wellness began developing in my gut. The kind surgery patients feel as they are wheeled into an operation theatre. The faces of the pedestrians milling around the check point up ahead held expressions of nervousness, fear, and gloom even under the poor street lighting. I did not need anyone to tell me that the only happy people here were operatives of EFCC and their business or social visitors. Others were doubtless in the mold of my brothers or other family members who were all in a state of melancholy.

As we drove through the check point, the guards saluted Ade even as they squinted and peeped to catch a glimpse of "Oga's latest captive"—me. Then, we were at the building entrance.

Throughout my current ordeal it has been my sorrowful observation that very few activities of man attract as much human interest as the suffering of others. It is also factual that rumor and innuendo grab our attention faster than truth and reality. As soon as I alighted from the pick-up truck I could see a number of faces peeping through windows, doors, and over counter tops. At first I could not tell what the commotion was about. It was not until much later—far into the night that I was informed that I was the star attraction of that evening and for reasons I found and still believe an aberration. The onlookers had been informed that a major international drug dealer had been arrested and was being escorted to EFCC that evening. Upon my arrival, word spread that the baron had just been hauled in for a transit period of a few hours until the late night special flight to the United States of America. The word was that I was a fugitive from American justice who had escaped a wide spread manhunt until my arrest the previous night. That, I was told, was the reason for the scramble to catch a glimpse of me before the FBI swooped on EFCC to haul me away.

Ade led me into his sparsely furnished office on the ground floor of the building. The furnishings which included a table, an executive chair and two arm chairs were so cluttered with manila folders and assorted paper correspondence you would think you had just walked into a civil service archive. Ade offered me one of the chairs and proceeded to catch up with goings-on while he was away.

It did not take me long to piece together the nature of EFCC's main assignment. Back to back reports were presented of one Italian and another, a Brazilian who were at EFCC on a funds recovery quest. They had been 419'ed by some of Nigeria's best practitioners of the illegal advanced fee fraud business. After doling out large sums of money as advance down payment fees they had both waited in vain for the promised millions of dollars to flow into their accounts. Subsequent investigations had revealed that they had been willing participants in a bogus arrangement to obtain payment from the Nigerian Government for purportedly already executed contracts. EFCC had been set up by the Federal Government of Nigeria to arrest and prosecute the proprietors of the illegal businesses, recover and return stolen monies and impound offender's properties among other activities.

I was able to glean that at the instance of the American Administration, sweeping powers were built into the Act which established EFCC. Because of the issues of overlapping jurisdictions, EFCC was usually at daggers-drawn with other law enforcement agencies of the country including the police. By placing a very strong mid-level police officer who was elaborately well connected at the helm of EFCC and placing the commission directly under the supervision of the presidency, it appeared that the commission had been handed a superior mandate over other competing law enforcement units. In addition to its superior mandate, the commission also seemed to enjoy the undiluted support and patronage of the United States Administration.

Before I could direct Ade's attention to the time which was already advancing towards eight o'clock at night, he said, "Mr. George, your matter is in progress. The Americans will soon be here, but meanwhile, as soon as our director is ready we will go to his office upstairs to discuss your matter."

"OK" I replied, "What does the man upstairs want to discuss with me? Can he tell me why I've been arrested? Does he have the authority to determine the matter? Is he the overall boss?"

"Mr. George, you ask too many questions. Anyway, he is the 2nd in command here at EFCC. Our Chairman is at Abuja. Have you heard about Mallam Nuhu Ribadu?"

The name struck a chord.

"Yeah, I've heard this name before," I said. "As a matter of fact, I am one of his growing list of fans even though I have not necessarily associated his name with EFCC. But I know he heads a new agency which fights money laundering by government officials. It is in that capacity that I've often heard his name."

"Yep, he is our boss and you're right. Most of our cases are financial crimes cases" I replied.

"Then why am I here?" I've had no monetary transactions of any kind that is contentious. I'm not a government official. I have no cases whatsoever with anybody!"

"Mr. George, you may be right that you have no case but as I already told you, we have no problem with you. Your problem is with America."

"Incredible!" I shouted. "Are you telling me that your agency works for Americans and that America sanctions your practice of abduction? You arrested me without a warrant, offered no explanation for my arrest and have detained me in a dungeon overnight. Are you telling me that this was all at the behest of the United States Government?"

"They are on their way right now and you'll get a chance to vent your anger at them." He said.

As new words were forming in my mouth, Ade was signaled to answer a call. He picked up the phone receiver, listened for an instant and said, "Yes Sir."

He turned to me and said, "We're getting somewhere already. Oga wants to see me regarding your matter. Be ready to come up shortly."

I said, "O.K., are the Americans here too?"

"No, but sit tight, I'll send for you in a minute." He said.

He left, and right outside his door I heard him say "Tunday, please go into my office and keep Mr. George company."

Tunday entered and sat on the chair next to mine. He had a pleasant air about him that made me at ease with him right away. I was the first to speak. Despite Ade's denials, I still believed that there was an off chance his statements were merely the sanctimonious rhetoric of a seasoned intelligence officer.

"Are you aware of my case?" I asked him.

"Nice meeting you too, my name is Tunday by the way," he replied jovially.

"I'm sorry," I said honestly, "My name is George. It was rather presumptuous of me to ask that question like I did. I've been overwhelmed with hysteria since my abduction yesterday by your men, I naturally assumed that all EFCC officers are out to get me. Maybe you can explain this whole madness to me?

"Honestly, you Americans are all actors. You sound like we are sadists here. We've heard about the hell you gave our colleagues at Amawbia where you were arrested. Is it true that inside your place is like America? They said you did not want to be inconvenienced at all. You were claiming your rights even inside a police cell. Mr. George, you have to calm down and realize that you are in Nigeria now."

"I'm not just visiting in Nigeria!" I protested. "I was born here and I grew up here! I am full blooded Nigerian and nobody has a right to treat me any different."

"But your driver's license and passport suggest otherwise," he said.

"Those are my United States documents! I am a dual citizen of both countries. There is no law against dual citizenship!" I insisted.

"I give up." Tunday submitted. "It is true then—my colleagues said you don't give up. But Mr. George, I want you to know I'm your friend. I can see already that I like your personality. Friends?"

"Friends." I said and we shook hands.

Tunday now opened the Pandora's Box.

He said, "You are a real fighter and you must be very well connected. Even before my colleagues took off to Amawbia for your arrest, the arrangements had been completed for your deportation to America. The official word was that you will be brought down to the Lagos office only for a few hours until your late night flight to New York. EFCC officials and FBI agents were to accompany you to New York where they would hand you over to American Authorities. But somewhere between your arrest and your arrival here we began to catch wind of a possible change of plan. We have received phone calls from very high up and it looks like there is a change of plan. Na waa for you ooh!

I could not disguise my shock. If what this guy was saying was true, then there were plans to bundle me to the United States! All my fears of the past 30 hours were resurrected at once. The welcome news that somebody or some people high up were already intervening offered me only a mild consolation. No assurances.

The kinship that was already developing between Tunday and I was good but offered no utopia for my heart's troubles. He had a job to do and given the choice between saving me and doing his job, there was no doubt what he would choose to do.

Moments after Tunday dropped the hint of EFCC's intentions to muscle me across the Atlantic to NYC, I was engrossed in hashing out in my mind how to respond to such an action when the time arose.

"Oya, Mr. George, let's go." Ade's voice came through the office door which was open a crack.

"Okay" I responded in a low tone. I followed him up the stairs and through a short hallway to an open office door.

The office was full of one man—a giant of a man. His face was meaty and his grotesque corpulence filled the space between his desk and the chair he was sitting on.

"Good evening sir," I offered instinctively.

There was no response. No acknowledgement whatsoever of our presence in his office.

Ade noticed my nervousness and waved at me to calm down. I do not believe that his plea of calm helped at all. I stood as close as was possible to the exit door not wanting to be trapped inside such an unfriendly surrounding. Ade stifled the laughter which was threatening to burst out from his stomach.

For what seemed an eternity, Mr. Director kept his face and interest buried in papers inside a bulky manila folder. Because Ade himself appeared tongue tied, I decided that this scene most likely occurred frequently and was accepted mode of practice at Lagos EFCC, Directors office.

When he finally lifted his face from the papers, he spoke without greetings or preamble.

"Why did you begin calling lawyers, threatening legal action and calling people all over the place? Do you think we do not know what we're doing here or that you can change anything by these erratic actions of yours?"

I was confused and unsure whether a response was compulsory, so I said nothing.

He continued to glare at me with eyes that seemed to bore right through my forehead. I continued to be non-responsive. Ade continued to look from me to the Director and back to me.

"General Shelleng is from my place. He is like a senior brother to me. If this matter was not an official matter, maybe I cannot refuse him. When he called me, I told him so. The United States is involved in your matter Mr. George. It is between our government and the U.S. government. Nobody in Nigeria can stop this action. Not even the president. So save your energy and stop drawing undue attention by making accusations against EFCC."

Still I did not respond.

He dismissed us with a wave of his large arm and returned to his earlier posture.

It was then I ventured a speech of my own.

"Sir" I replied with as much reverence as I could feign, "Mr. Ade assured me that the Americans who want me would be here to explain why they want me. It is now about 9:30 at night and they're not here. Can you explain what this is all about to me?"

The expression on his face was all Ade needed to decide his next line of action. He blinked at me as he turned from the Director's table. With a wave, he guided me away, his right index finger over his lips—a sign for me to say nothing more.

We returned to Mr. Ade's office.

"Do you have anybody here in Lagos you can stay with tonight?" He asked me as soon as we were seated.

I looked at Mr. Ade incredulous. He appeared opaque. I could not read his expression and after the dramatic episodes of the previous 36 hours, I no longer presumed myself a good interpreter of puzzling situations. Better to not get my hopes up too high.

"I have a lot of family members and friends here in Lagos. I will have no problem getting one of them to accommodate me," I replied.

"That's good but come with me to Tunday's office, he and Awe will be your case officers."

"My case officers?" I inquired, puzzled.

"That is how we operate. We have several units at EFCC such as 419 unit (or OBT Obtain By Trick), Money Laundering Unit, etcetera. I head the 419 unit. Tunday and Awe as well as Sani are all members of my unit. Your case is assigned to Tunday and Awo.

"You're confusing me again!" I complained with a very worried tone. "I have never obtained one dime from anyone in my entire life!"

"No, no, no, Mr. George, yours is not a typical EFCC case. Any unit could have been assigned your case. My unit just happened to get it. You worry too much Mr. George. Just relax with my men so that we may process you and hopefully get you to your people tonight."

His words did not comfort me one bit, but I knew I needed to cooperate with them to move things along—if only to discover the evil at the end of the tunnel. At least I would then be able to fashion a strategy to fight this onslaught.

I rose and followed Ade, but as soon as we turned to our right into the hallway, I looked straight to the end of the passage and froze in my track.

From behind rusted iron bars that form a makeshift gate I saw several men, some of them wearing nothing but wrappers or towels around their waists. Behind them were a couple of women. All of them were wearing these piteous smirks on their faces. It was obvious from their expressions and body language that they had long been expecting me to join them.

When Ade noticed that I was no longer following him, he stopped and turned. He had a knowing look on his face and was apparently ready with an explanation.

"Oh Mr. George, these are our con artists. You are not here for the same reasons as them. Do not worry or waste more time. We need to complete processing you so that we can all leave here before midnight."

I no longer believed Ade. I could feel it in my bones. It was déjà vu all over again. The memories of the night at Amawbia Police Station came flooding back. I was again, a fish in the EFCC net.

From the deepest recesses of my being, my storage of unspent will and power, my bank for divine assistance, I began to pool strength. No doubt was left in my mind that only God could protect and preserve me now. Not knowing how much credit I still had left in God's divine bookkeeping; if any at all, I began my supplication by promising Him that I would never take His love for granted as long as I lived, should He deliver me from the baffling trial I was going through. At this point, Ade's speeches to me were mere claptrap. I was buying none of them anymore. With my entire defenses entrusted in God's hands, I followed Ade into Tunday's office.

Tunday and Awe placed several forms on the desk that separated me and them.

Among them were;

(1) Nigeria's version of the Miranda rights.
(2) Bank Accounts Verification forms.
(3) Assets Declaration forms.
(4) Statement forms.
(5) Due Process Waiver forms.

The Miranda rights form was a joke of course, considering what the men of EFCC had done with my constitutional rights to due process. I merely ignored the form.

I told my inquisitors point blank that they had to murder me first before they would get a signed account verification form or an asset declaration form.

I completed the statement form in the standard question and answer police format. Tunday and Awo asked the question and I supplied the answers. All in all, I said in the form that I was abducted by men of the EFCC who claimed I had a case to answer in the United States of America. I challenged them to produce the American officials who they purported would come to explain to me why I was wanted.

The due process waiver form was the mother lode of treachery in high places. Had I signed that form that night, I would have been on the next flight from Lagos to New York, fugitive style—in handcuffs and leg chains. I also believe that without my brother Chinedu's efforts and prompt action in securing the services of a barrister and contacting my friends, the retired military generals, EFCC operatives would no doubt have forced a signature out of my hand and would have smuggled me out of Nigeria that night.

At approximately 10:45 PM on December 27, 2004, Tunday and Awe led me into the EFCC cell as inmate number 68. The cell was nothing but one open concrete hall with no living amenities fit for human habitation.

Ade was nowhere in sight but Tunday and Awe had thankfully become genuinely compassionate friends after listening to my story for one full hour.

Ten

I was once again in the midst of total strangers. This time, a group much less menacing it appeared on the surface, than my cellmates of the night before.

By now, I was feeling like I'd barely survived a bad train wreck. My head throbbed relentlessly atop my weakened and thoroughly fatigued body as I sidled toward an open spot on the cluttered concrete floor. The entire cell occupants diligently followed me with their eyes.

Before I could make it to the spot, a smiling middle aged fellow walked up to me with an outstretched arm. I took his hand and shook it.

He was the first to speak, "My name is Simeon, and we've been waiting long for you. Come, come and meet the Chairman." He was walking as he spoke, toward a frail looking gentleman who sat alone on a thick mattress that elevated him significantly above the crowd of inmates also waiting at his feet. "His name is Kingsley Ikpe," Simeon concluded.

I looked at Mr. Kingsley Ikpe and immediately knew that he was a wily fellow. He looked like a tired old leprechaun, withered and worn out, but determined to maintain a genial and courteous façade.

Ade had hinted to me that their regular detainees consisted of individuals facing OBT (Obtain by Trick or 419) and other fraud charges. From what I could so far observe, he was accurate.

Simeon indicated an open spot on the concrete floor with enough space to accommodate me in a sitting position and then officially introduced me to the crowd.

He said, "Mr. George, have a seat over there." And once I was seated, he continued, "Mr. Chairman, please meet the new man. He is George Udeozor. I've already explained to him that we have been set back because we were waiting for him. He is here now, so I now defer to you Mr. Chairman, for his welcome rituals."

"You're welcome to the state Mr. George", he began in a deep, clear baritone, "because it is so late, the night having been far spent, I will give you a quick rundown of the rules by which we live in this confined space, so we can all get some sleep."

He got my attention immediately. Since my unceremonious abduction from my home, I had not run into anybody with Kinsley's diction and eloquence. I had not expected to run into anybody with his composure in this god-awful dump. For the first time since arriving in Lagos, I began to feel that I could survive the new phase of doom in one piece. I reasoned that if a guy like this can adapt and survive, so could I.

He continued, "The issues we must address now are just two, the rest of our state rules will have to be addressed tomorrow when time is plentiful. First, you will need to pay a state fee of N4, 000.00 (four thousand naira; which converts to about $40.00). This money is expended on mosquito repellant, disinfectants and other hygiene supplies. Second, the sleeping space is allocated on the basis of first come first served and ability to contribute to the welfare of the state…."

At this point Simeon interjected, "Chairman, please Chairman, it is almost midnight. I will take things from there and get Mr. George caught up later. Let us get the Christian Worship started so that people can get some sleep," he pleaded.

"Sure Simeon, time sure flies when you're having fun. Doesn't it Mr. George? I sense we'll have a lot to talk about later."

He turned to his audience of inmates, "Prayer time, prayer time, its prayer time!"

Bibles filled up the whole place. Even I was given one. Again, I was in for a new awakening. The mood in this great hall of concrete and iron bars swung into evangelical mode.

Inmates who squatted motionless hither to the announcement of prayer time went in motion. Some swayed side to side, to and fro, some hobbled up and down, and others hummed and gyrated to their own musical renditions. This hall became electric.

Simeon pulled me to the side to ask when I could pay the state fee. "Business first," he said.

I promised to pay 50% of the fee after prayers and the balance upon my brother's arrival on the next day. It seemed my promise energized Simeon because he waltzed to the front of the gathered crowd shouting "Halleluiah, Halleluiah, God is good" to which he got a resounding "All the time!" He then gave a reversed chant of "All the time!" to which the response was also promptly reversed "God is good!"

Then, as if to quell the disorder in the house, Kingsley Ikpe raised the pitch of his singing with a new song;

"Children of God," he sang.

"Yearr!" Came a chorus response.

"Children of God, he repeated.

"Yearrr!" Another chorus response.

"Will you shout Halleluiah seven times?"

"Halleluiah, halleluiah, halleluiah, halleluiah, halleluiah, halleluiah, halleluiah!" Obliged the chorus.

As a life-long member of the Catholic faith, my religious life had been without the exuberant, almost noisy displays during prayers or other acts of religious worship as I was witnessing this day. As such, I was unsure what to make of the rapturous excitement all around me or what my role in it ought to be. One thing was certain; the sound being produced by these men in captivity was as captivating as whatever acts that got them there in the first place. No practice or rehearsals were necessary to join in their dance moves. Even the Moslem brothers who were there could not resist occasional nodding or swaying to the rousing tempo of the noise.

And so, I involuntarily joined in and experienced the miraculous healing of the ailments that had been tormenting me since I received the news from Ade and his boys that my abduction was merely a prelude to a much more ominous plot.

The throbbing in my head eased away. The fatigue that had been weighing me down gradually disappeared. With each dance step, I felt much lighter. Soon I was clapping and dancing like everybody else. The songs, although I was singing them for the first time in my life, gave the impression that I was a very well-practiced ventriloquist.

Changes were taking place within me of which only I was aware. The feeling of doom which had clung to my sense of wellbeing was taking a less severe toll on my faculties. The sense of loss which had been tormenting me from the very start of the ordeal was fading away.

After surviving the agony at Amawbia Police Station and also the twists and turns of emotion that followed until I ended up in the midst of my current companions, it began to dawn on me that at no time ever, had I truly and wholly been in control of my destiny. This realization which was clearly not new to me had never had the impact on my thought process that it should have—until now.

I needed a paradigm shift in my value system. I had to recalibrate my entire thought process. I now knew how needy for a time-out I was. But for now, I had to relish fully the miracle of freedom from pain which I was feeling. I chuckled to myself knowing that only a divine authority possessed the power to grant me the serenity I now felt in spite of my prevailing condition.

~

The praise and worship phase lasted about 30 minutes. A testimony phase was next and was followed by prayer requests and concluding prayers.

This experience which would be repeated every morning and night for my entire period of detention at EFCC helped me to reactivate my spirituality which had suffered a long period of stagnation, even decline, in the face of blinding worldly pursuits.

I do not presume to comment on religious issues better left to others who have earned either the credentials or the ordination or both to speak with authority on them. But I make bold to claim authoritatively that I received the mysterious healing and gift of a peaceful heart while at EFCC. I believe that this gift did not emanate from my personal piety or prayer intercessions. It was a love gift. I finally understood words I had hitherto spoken out of sheer frivolity, but not out of conviction. These simple words are... "God is Love!"

Thus, my earlier impression of God became permanently altered and firmly reshaped.

Today, I find God in spoken words, in beauty, in other people, in nature all around me.

Although there is no doubt He is in churches, mosques, and monasteries, being that He is everywhere, I no longer believe those to be His favorite sites. He might even prefer to be found in PRISONS—of all places!

After the prayers on that first night I gladly went to sleep on the concrete floor which was the standard welcome treatment for new inmates to the EFCC cell.

Thanks to a combination of exhaustion and my state of mind, I slept more soundly than I ever had in either the comfort of my bed or the luxurious suites of your five star hotels! I was not perturbed by the lack of a single item of convenience in this scorching, overcrowded dungeon infested by menacing, giant mosquitos. Despite these deliberate, egregious violations of our fundamental human rights, I felt no ill will toward anybody as I lay sprawled out in the presence of sixty seven other sweating and slumbering souls.

It was clearly as a result of the joy in my heart as I slept that I was able to rest so peacefully in the face of the daunting adversity which was confronting me.

By making the all-important decision to view this period of adversity as a well-earned time-out, I jump-started the most important resolutions of my life;

I would simply devote the time it would take to overcome this difficulty to worthy introspection. I would pretend that I was on sabbatical for an undetermined period of time. I would desist from paying attention to the shutting or opening of doors and gates on me and all forms of restrictions on my freedom, including the people whose duty it was to enforce the restrictions.

It was while I was lying there on the concrete floor, blocking out all pain except the serenity of these thoughts that I drifted into sleep.

Eleven

In the morning . . .
Early in the morning...
In the morning,
I will rise and praise the Lord...!
Rise up and praise the Lo...or...ord,
Rise up and praise the Lord,
The Lord is good!

These words floating rhythmically over me seemed to be filtering in from a distant place. As I skirted through the edges of consciousness, the pitch grew loud and then diminished; rising and falling evenly as if being manipulated for effect by a DJ.

Gradually, consciousness regained control of my senses and I could not continue enjoying the chorus of rough but melodious male voices which lost its great appeal once I was awake. Reality hit me then. My second night in EFCC captivity had been better than the first night, but it had exposed yet another dark realm in the precarious existence forced on Nigerian citizens who lack voice or means or both.

I sat up, leaned against the wall closest to me. Through the barred windows I could see the faint illumination of early dawn. I listened and observed as the morning devotion gradually wound to a close.

Just as at the conclusion of prayers the previous night, the inmates began shaking hands and hugging one another, wishing one another divine intervention in their cases. The scene had a striking air of sincerity and innocence; one could easily forget the character of some of these individuals. I certainly did and I certainly got burnt.

Simeon was all smiles when he walked over to where I leaned against the wall silently cataloguing my observations in my mind.

"Brother George," he said, "how are you this morning? I hope you were able to get a little sleep. When you are ready, just call on me so that I familiarize you with the way things work around here."

"Sure," I said, "kindly show me to the bathroom or a place where I can ease myself and freshen up some."

"Oh, sure, come with me," he said leading the way toward an open doorway which had obviously lost the part which opens and closes.

There were five men and one woman waiting to take their turn at the toilet.

"Men and women locked up in one open cell?" I thought, alarmed, but I could not voice those thoughts. I stood by the men hoping to observe a second door or anything that would indicate a different restroom for women. There was no new door and nothing to assuage my fear.

When it was her turn, the lady entered the room, took care of her business and walked past us by the queue which had grown longer by this time.

Once inside the restroom, I observed three doors with 8" openings at the bottom through which you could make out legs of any occupant standing within. The three toilets were separated by panel partitions high enough to prevent two occupants from eye-balling each other from separate toilets but low enough for occupants to scale over. In the days that followed, I witnessed activities that left me wondering who made decisions on the facilities and welfare of EFCC detainees and why it had not occurred to the commission executives that the arrangement within this facility provided inmates who were already guilty of some mischief the opportunity of increasing their debt to society right there in detention.

Simeon met me as I returned to the open cell. He offered me a seat on his mattress and said "Now, let's get acquainted."

"That's O.K. with me," I said, "You already know my name. So, tell me how things work around here."

"First, let me congratulate you for your first win against EFCC," he began. "The fact that you're here means that you must be a fighter. Before you arrived yesterday, Ade's boys told us that a kingpin had been arrested in the east. They said we may catch a glimpse of you but that you will be taken by late night flight to New York, USA from where you escaped and triggered a manhunt. Looking at you now, I can see that you're not what we expected. You do not look like a drug baron to me at all!"

I did not know how to start my response or even what to say, but I could see that Simeon wanted to hear something from me, so I said, "My brother, I do not even know the first thing about drugs. Quite sincerely, I do not know the difference between talcum powder and cocaine! As for EFCC, it might surprise you to hear that I do not even know why they arrested me. They have told me they did so at the instance of the American Embassy. They assured me that an embassy official would be here when we arrived from Enugu to explain to me the reason for my arrest. So far nobody has come forward from the embassy or from any other place with the promised explanation."

"That's outrageous!" Simeon yelled, "But it does not surprise me. Since the advent of Obasanjo's administration, Nigerians are constantly abducted from the streets and flown to the United States. You're not the first. As a matter of fact, I'm surprised they did not succeed with you. You better watch out. This thing is not over yet. If I know these guys, they will still try to smuggle you out. Be on your guard, Mr. George."

I was looking at Simeon, mouth agape as I recalled reading in the papers and news magazines a while back about one Tayo—a luxury car dealer who was seized from the streets of Lagos and smuggled out of Nigeria. I was incredulous at the thought that I could have faced a similar ordeal! I did not know then how close I had come to that fate in reality.

"Was one of those smuggled to the United States named Tayo," I asked.

"Thank you," Simeon said, "Tayo' s case is a celebrated one. There have been others done quietly which went unreported. Maybe with your case, if enough publicity is made on that subject, that abuse of process will stop. It is really a national scandal! Nigeria is really a banana republic!"

Simeon's vocabulary was impressive I must say. He was conversant with both the languages of the real and underworld for one who had never traveled outside Nigeria and apparently did not attend college.

"Well brother Simeon," I concluded, "trust me, I will see that whatever game they try to play with my life fails. One thing is certain, although I am not a saint, but in all my dealings and relationships with people, I go out of my way not go harm or wrong anyone. This case may be the one to expose the ineptitude of our government and their harshness on the common Nigerians. Now, please talk to me about the arrangements here. I will need a mattress and beddings. Things like that. I feel very tired and dirty as it is."

"Sure, sure," Simeon said, "Yeah, I can see that this is your first arrest..."

"Yes, it is, "I said.

"Okay now, just like in any police station, SSS, or other detention centers, when people are forced into a situation like this," he waved his hands to indicate the whole cell, "There is a need for order, or else life in here would be worse than hell. Here at EFCC, we have organized everything like you would in a city or state. That is why we call it a state. The Chairman, who was elected, is like the president. I assist him. We have a treasurer, a chief judge, inspector general (IG), provost, mobile police, etc. The duties of all officers are the same as in the real world. The laws of the state must be obeyed or else fitting punishment is meted out to the offender. The state is funded by the fee which each and every one of us pays when we are brought into the cell. The "state fee" is the equivalent of state tax. Those who are indigent and cannot afford the fee will be designated to the labor pool. They clean the cell and the toilets. Everybody must comply or they are made to comply. No exemptions. Our government works better than the Nigerian government," he joked at the end of his brief lecture.

"It probably does," I agreed. "It will surely take me a while to learn all the rules and remember them. Hopefully with time I will learn to cope.

"Sure," he said. "Nobody remembers every rule in the beginning. There are no signs or law books to refer to. We are the law here," he said, indicating Kingsley with a nod by which I concluded, he was talking about himself and the old leprechaun.

"I will certainly remember that," I agreed. "Now tell me, how can I acquire a mattress and other items I will need in the meantime?"

"Ooh yeah, as today is Saturday, you're lucky. Only a skeletal office staff works on Saturday— maybe the team officers only. So, as soon as it is 7:00 AM, you can get one of the guards a mobile policeman to dash to Obalande and purchase a mattress, pillow, bed sheets and other items you need. I caution you, they sometimes charge you up to double the price, since they expect you to cover the cost of transportation and a profit as an incentive for their trouble."

"Really," I exclaimed. "What about the indigent inmates? What happens to them?

"Oh, those unfortunate ones… well, as you know, God always takes care of the down and out. They usually live off the crumbs. When you purchase a mattress and beddings today, you're not likely to take it with you when you depart. It is the benevolence of the few like you "well –to-do" people who pass through the system that they depend on. Your leftovers are passed on to them, usually on a first come first served basis, unless you prefer to pass them to others of your choice."

"Alright," I said, "let me get started."

Simeon told me to queue up and get in the shower. He said by the time I was done, he would get the attention of one of the guards who would make the purchases for me.

⁓

It did not take days for me to uncover the depravity that is bound to result from the thoughtlessness or disdain for privacy rights that informed the cohabitation of male and female offenders within one open cell.

While I stood in the queue, I was able to observe that the only boundary between the male and female inmates was a mere doorway—with no door attached! From where I stood, I observed the women taking peeks at the bare chested men with only towels tied to their waists. There were many giggles and glances exchanged. Trysts were made with subtle body language. It was hard not to get aroused—not on account of the attractiveness of the women, but simply from the activities of hormones in healthy adult bodies. To say that the sexual batteries of inmates were always fully charged is to put it mildly when describing the goings-on in this place. How all out orgies were prevented is a credit to the moral few who frowned at these activities. But the truth is that while I was detained at this squalid cell, those of us who were incapable of risking our health and honor listened as the young adult males locked themselves in dog-style humping with mostly the older women inside the only three toilet/bath facilities provided for the convenience of all inmates.

The guilty parties in this perversion carried on with their illicit sex undisturbed every early morning or late night with full knowledge and protection of those charged in part to keep this from occurring. Their conspiracy of silence and collusion which came at a monetary cost of course, bound us all by one simple code which I later learned exists among inmates all over the world; you must not snitch! Snitching can cost you. Even your very life!

As promised by Simeon, my purchases were made for me by a mobile policeman who also as expected charged me double the price of the items purchased. How that formula was arrived at, I will never know.

⁓

At about 8:00 AM that morning, a local food vendor arrived with two large plastic food warmers. The containers which rested on the vendor's head and the head of her assistant who, from her looks, must have been her daughter, contained the breakfast for all sixty-eight inmate occupants of the cell. Certainly, if the food were half decent enough for all inmates to partake in the consumption of it, the portions would measure just as much as the communion bread in churches. Picture how filling that would be!

As it turned out, only the indigent inmates partook of the meal—to their fullness and satisfaction I hoped, although I had serious doubts.

For myself and other inmates who had relatives and could afford it, our meals were prepared at our relative's homes and brought daily to the cell for us. I still marvel at the devotion and dedication of family members. My cousin Uzo (DD) rose up to the task of preparing my meals. I owe her a debt of gratitude which I know I cannot repay it this lifetime. Family really is all we've got in times of trouble.

Twelve

Monday, December 30th, 2004 finally dawned and with it, significant events in my stand-off with EFCC.

The day started with an early morning visit from my brother. He had a restless weekend brooding over the inexplicable excesses of EFCC officials in their handling of my matter. Being employed as a senior civil servant himself, he was usually flummoxed by the recklessness of some of his contemporaries in office. He always lamented the irony that some people in government service often raised themselves above the law—the same law they impose and seek to enforce on those they are in office to serve!

I kept my brother company while his request for an audience with the director was being processed. He immediately assured me that my barrister was already at work. He explained that because the holiday period was likely to stretch into the second week of January, 2005, it was unlikely that my legal action against EFCC would be heard by a judge until after the holidays. In order to guarantee that EFCC did not spin a joker on us, my barrister would do whatever it took, including genuflecting before a vacation judge if necessary, to issue an interim order restraining EFCC from forcibly extraditing me to the United States without the due process of law. For the first time since receiving the infamous news of EFCC's plot to deport me to the United States, I felt like I could relax my mind completely.

My brother's visit with the EFCC Lagos Director was very brief. The moment I saw his face turn into Tunday's office doorway where we conducted our own visit, I knew the news of his short visit with the Director was not good.

Looking frazzled, my brother who usually spoke very little began talking before he got to his seat. "That is one difficult man!" He complained. "Can you imagine? He really has the God complex! He is all knowing and almighty! I could not even say a word to him once he found out I was your brother!"

"That does not surprise me," I said. "When I got here last week, I met him and I can tell you, it was not really a meeting. It was a crazed monologue, with him ranting about my audacious moves. He believes even I should have no say in my own matter!"

My brother agreed. "That was his exact attitude with me too! He believes everybody accused by government is guilty, and must submit meekly to any course of action the government decides to take. He is one big bully!" he said.

My brother went on to give us details of the exchange between them. In summary, the EFCC Director had said to my brother, "We will take George to the United States of America and there aint nothing you or he can do about it, period."

Tunday and Awe who both sat and pretended to be engrossed in their work finally chipped in their bits. They advised us that we should immediately seek a legal solution to the matter or else within a few days, the director would find a way to have me deported to the United States. They said they believed my case had become a quagmire for the Director because a lot of attention had been drawn to it. He had therefore recoiled to seek documented legal cover for his actions. They feared that soon, he would obtain the cover he required.

I was grateful for their advice but I made no mention of the actions we were already taking along the same lines.

At about 2:00PM, my brother left EFCC to get lunch for both of us. After we had lunch we continued our visitation until some friends began arriving to commiserate with us. With the visit of these friends, we began to learn all the gossips and innuendos making the rounds about my arrest. Different versions of my purported complicity with criminals were being circulated. Some were about my involvement in large scale fraud with government officials in Nigeria, money laundering or real estate scams. Others pointed their radar at the USA where I had purportedly escaped the authorities and was now declared wanted for offences which varied from civil to criminal depending on who was telling the tale.

The only troubling aspect of these rumors and gossips was about some of the people involved in spreading them. Without naming specific individuals, I think it is fair to say that these were people close to me, some of them even related to me, all of whom knew that the news they were peddling was total fabrication. Of interest also was the fact that the rumor mongers were people who pursued me relentlessly for financial assistance whether I was in Nigeria or the United States of America.

This was how I began learning my lessons about the price one sometimes gets to pay for offering himself as his brother's keeper. Somehow it had escaped my mind during my dealings with my in-laws and Anuofia Adoga that strangers can hardly do you any harm. That honor is reserved, almost exclusively, for friends and family.

During my visitation, a grand activity relating to my case was unfolding within the EFCC's legal department just one flight of stairs from where we were. It happened that my barrister, Mr. Dambo had secured the order restraining the commission from forcibly extraditing me.

This news was brought to us in person by Banister Dambo. The blow by blow account of how outraged the judge had been. How the judge had instructed that the bailiff treat the matter as priority by assuring that the notice is served on EFCC "this hour" before other notices in the bailiff's register.

Dambo went on to detail us on how he had accompanied the bailiff down to EFCC and how they had both spent the past two hours unbeknownst to us, <u>trying to serve the notice on EFCC!</u>

Apparently when he was consulted on whether to acknowledge the service by the legal department, an irate EFCC director, the know-it-all director, had threatened fire and brimstone on anybody who would dare to sign the bailiff's acknowledgement register. It took phone calls and the judge's ire to get the EFCC to accept the order and officially acknowledge that they had been served!

Dambo had earned more than his pay. We now had to wait for Nigerians to call off their nationwide Christmas/New Year jamboree and return once more to the serious business of building a nation, a job which only a few Nigerians appear truly committed to doing.

Barrister Dambo, my brother Paul, our childhood friend Dan, and myself put our heads together with my new EFCC acquaintances, Tunday and Awo, to try to come up with answers to the origin of this desperate attempt to turn me over to a faceless phantom prosecutor in the United States.

We decided that since EFCC was bent on shipping me off to the United States unceremoniously like a mere parcel, without due process, and without even the mere courtesy of a simple explanation of the reason I was wanted in the United States and by whom, we would take my inquires directly to the United States Embassy in Lagos. I enthusiastically agreed with this line of action and urged Barrister Dambo to write a letter to the embassy offering them my cooperation if there was any proof that this request for me to be returned to the United States was genuine and originated from proper channels of authority.

The good barrister offered to do more. He said he would write both the EFCC and the U.S. Embassy with my proposal. He would personally deliver the letters to the embassy as well as the EFCC.

I was totally pleased and convinced that at last I was about to uncover the demons feeding the fires of hell.

"Good night everybody and God bless you all," I said when the time came for me to return to my new abode. I hugged my brother Paul and bade him goodbye for he would be returning to his base in Port Harcourt early the next morning. I then waited for tomorrow to come.

Thirteen

Barrister Dambo undoubtedly worked through the night and early Tuesday morning because he returned shortly after dawn to see me with three documents that warmed my heart the way a fireplace warms a low basement room in winter.

I read and approved all three letters immediately. The first one was to EFCC stressing my willingness to return immediately to the United States where my six children had unfortunately had to endure the vagaries of youth without the love, protection, and stability of a father for five whole years—a situation which I was willing to give my life to remedy. The second was a letter to the United States Embassy forwarding the EFCC letter to them and further requesting their authentication of my arrest and detention and their involvement in the matter. The final document was the brief of my lawsuit against EFCC detailing their abuse of my civil and constitutional rights and the reliefs sought.

It is my privilege today, in hind sight to commend Barrister Dambo in the strongest terms for his calm demeanor, his intelligence and diligence. He is definitely a credit to the legal profession in Nigeria and I hope he climbs his career ladder to the highest bar possible in his field. He left EFCC and went to work right after I signed the documents.

With no work to do, no courses to study, no games to play, no room in which to exercise, my life behind EFCC bars was slowly turning me into a new creature.

I take my words back! I did have games to play while at EFCC bondage—mind games. Lots of mind games. That was how I won Tunday, Awe and their boss to my side.

Tunday and Awe both showed me real kindness. However although I was grateful for their assistance in ameliorating my discomfort at EFCC, a lifelong experience of disloyalty in the hands of many friends had taught me to exercise caution always in matters involving trust. Implicit trust robs you the room for quick recovery in cases of disappointment. There was an off chance that they truly believed EFCC higher ups had done me wrong by ordering my arrest and detention without showing probable cause. There was also a chance that their show of friendliness was part of their detective work; pretend to take sides with the accused, move in close, unveil the accused's weaknesses and then move in for the kill!

Whatever their own game was, it was comforting to know that I had no skeletons. If they were also playing games with me, then theirs, unlike mine, was a losing game. I had nothing to hide. So I kept digging for clues every day.

Tunday and Awe kindly made my cell phone available to me during daytimes. I was able now to stay in touch with the outside world from their dungeon. Thanks to these two angels, I was in touch several times a day with both my brother Paul and Barrister Dambo.

Minutes turned into hours, hours into days, and days into weeks. After the third week, Barrister Dambo visited me bearing with him the exhilarating news of the Lagos Court's ruling on my lawsuit against EFCC.

It was Monday morning. Sunday had come and gone like the three previous Sundays before it. I lay on my back on the hard mattress counting off the minutes until 8:00 AM when I usually queued up to take a shower. Suddenly, I felt a noiseless vibration underneath my pillow. Startled, I jumped up, only to see the flashing lights of my mobile phone as it splashed patterns on the pillow! I crouched low, pulled my wrapper over my head and whispered "Hello."

Tunday and Awe had allowed me the use of my phone over the weekends to enable me to stay in touch with my family and attorney. They however extracted a promise from me to be discrete with my use of the phone as other inmates were not allowed the same privilege.

"Are you sitting or standing, George?" It was the voice of Barrister Dambo. He sounded excited.

"None of the above, I'm lying down actually." I replied.

"Well then, good. Are you ready for some great news?" He asked, his voice filled with happiness.

"My head is about to pop man, give me the news!" I cried still struggling with the wrapper and knowing that others around me were listening closely.

"You guessed it. George, the verdict is out. The judge has ruled on your case. EFCC has been ordered to release you to my custody immediately."

"Omigod! Omigod! Omigod! I don't believe you! You're not serious, are you?" I yelled.

"Start packing your bag George. You're going home. I will arrive with the bailiff by about 2:00 PM this afternoon."

"Why up to 2:00 PM? Why not this morning?"

"Oh no. I'm still in my chambers. The court does not even open until nine. And then we'll have to wait for the judge to arrive and sign the order to EFCC for your discharge. All these take time. You know, other Nigerian factors like "Seeing" the court clerks and bailiff etc. I think 2:00 PM is a realistic time to expect us. Just be ready by that time."

I lifted my whole body in an attempt to get on my feet but realized that the wrapper was all that covered my nudity. I fell back on the mattress. With all my inner restraint, I kept myself from pulling down the ceiling. My happiness was immeasurable. Then my phone slipped from my grasp and fell. It banged against the wall next to me and dropped on the mat with a muted clang. The battery, sim card, and back cover scattered all over the floor. Everything was now in the open as all eyes focused on me.

I was on my knees and without a care in the world about who was looking. I gathered my broken phone. I whispered a prayer to God and began reassembling my phone. It was still working! Bravo Nokia, I yelled.

I pulled Simeon over to Kingsley Ikpe's corner and broke the news to them. That was when my joy was killed.

"I do not mean to spoil your celebration or dampen your spirit George, but EFCC has been known to disobey court orders," Simeon said.

In slow motion, I moved to the foot of Kingsley Ikpe's mattress and dropped on my butt.

"Don't get me wrong," Simeon quickly added, "that may not be the case in your matter since fraud is not involved. They may release you without a snag, but the EFCC record on disobedience of court order is legendary. Have you not been reading newspapers? Surely, you must have read about this before."

Indeed I had. But to my mind, that was what happened to other people—real criminals. Not people like me!

But even as these thoughts ventured to reassure me that everything was going to be alright, a silent worried voice hovered around at very close proximity, cautioning me to expect a good outcome while staying prepared for other possibilities, good or bad.

In low spirit, I stayed cautiously optimistic for the rest of the morning while I waited for Barrister Dambo. I prayed that EFCC would behave for once in my case, like a self-respecting commission and obey the court order.

There is however, something about truth one cannot deny. It always stands out. It is resilient. You may choose to ignore it. Pretend you did not hear it. But you cannot deny it. Period!

After Simeon drew my attention to EFCC's reputation for disobeying court orders, it rang true like gospel. I could neither deny nor ignore it. I could not pretend I did not hear it. My attempts to stay positive worked only 5% of the period I waited for Dambo.

At 3:30 PM, they arrived. They served the judge's order on EFCC before applying to have me brought to the visiting lounge at Tunday's office.

As if Barrister Dambo could read my mind, he opined that I did not look as happy as I had sounded on the phone.

I asked him, "Do you think EFCC will obey the judge's order?"

He replied, "That is what I was about to share with you. You are apparently already aware that EFCC tends to disobey court orders. I certainly hope they obey this order. If however, they don't I will file a motion at a higher court which will compel them to release you forthwith or show cause why they should continue to hold you. Believe me; the chairman of EFCC who is himself a lawyer, would have difficulty disobeying any order from this higher court because it is the same court that hands EFCC all the convictions that make them the popular commission which they are today."

I drew Tunday and Awe into the conversation. The exchange that followed could only be described as mere academic exercise. In the end, the consensus of opinion was; let us wait and see. I took that to mean that I should unpack and wait for a brighter day before I could hope to see my home again.

As the clock wound down to closing time for EFCC and all government offices, no sign of my imminent release was apparent. I had all but given up hope of that possibility but my "all glass-half-full" attitude to life's events kept a glimmer of hope alive. I could not totally shake that feeling of positivity off my mind.

When however, Awe who had been in conference with his boss Ade returned to his desk, he brought with him the sad confirmation that EFCC was not shifting from its tradition. The court order would be treated like others before it—mere bureaucratic mumbo jumbo.

I thanked my barrister, giving him my sincere assurances that I understood. He had no blame in what had just transpired.

As I walked back into the cell, sweat trickled down my forehead. A quiver ran through my entire body. My thoughts were trying to make sense of these sad events of the past few weeks. I remained unsure of who it was that was so audaciously ruling my life and by so doing, extending their influence to my family and friends.

I began recalling my brother Chinedu's failed attempt to get some answers from the EFCC Chairman himself.

Chinedu had taken time off and travelled to Kaduna along with my friend, Air Vice Marshal Chris Marizu. They were able to secure an appointment with the chairman who had been extremely elusive until that meeting in Kaduna.

The sorrow had remained with me for the past week that not only did the chairman offer them no explanations, my brother returned from that trip with an infection of meningitis. The sheer guilt and terror of the knowledge that my brother nearly lost his life to this god-awful disease on my account gripped me more on this particular night than when the event actually occurred.

I wrote two letters—one each to my sister and Dr. Georege Okafor whose timely intervention saved my brother's life. The letters were never delivered thanks to EFCC, but my heartfelt gratitude reached them both. My sleep that night was restless.

Fourteen

"Pick up your belongings right now and head outside!" Those words sounded so close, I felt they were coming from one of the cell inmates venting his frustrations by turning into a clown.

But instead a bulky scarecrow of a man barreled through the cell gate, his white flowing agbada trailing behind him like a wedding gown. He yelled as he strode in, "Are you all deaf and dumb? I said get your things! All of your things and move outside right now!"

Pandemonium broke loose in the cell. Simeon moved swiftly to where I was hungrily gulping my breakfast down. He whispered to me, "It is Sanda. He is the number two in command here. It looks like we are being moved to Okotiebo."

"Okotiebo?" I whispered back to him. "Where is that? What's going on? Has there been a coup?"

"No, no, no!" Replied Simeon looking scared now while he was busy gathering his belongings. George, you must pack your things or you'll be left behind and in serious trouble with Sanda. Okotiebo is EFCC main cell. It is located nearby at Okotiebo Street. It shares a fence with Ikoyi Club and is next to Dodan Barracks. We must leave now!"

"Go on without me. Do not worry about me," I replied. I had barely completed my statement when the barrel chested man in flowing agbada noticed me quietly consuming my meal.

He thundered, "Who is that fellow?" As he spoke he was making his way toward me. "Who do you think you are? Are you bigger than everybody else here? How dare you sit there while everybody else is doing as instructed."

I held on to my tray and the food midway toward my mouth and said nothing in reply. I just held on and kept gazing up at him.

Ade whispered something to him to which he retorted, "Is that why he thinks he can flout my order. O.K.Alright. The bus can go now. They can return and pick up the rest of them."

He turned toward me and yelled, "You better finish that food and be ready in 5 minutes!" Then he was gone.

I wiped the tears off my cheeks and resumed eating my breakfast. After about 5 minutes I finished my food, still feeling hurt and humiliated by Sanda's outburst.

It took me another 10 minutes to get ready and when we got outside the cell door, I noticed that all was ready and the bus was humming on idle, waiting for me. A second bus had been secured to convey us—the remaining inmates to Okotiebo.

One of the mobile policemen gave me a hand with my belongings and we were shortly out on Awolowo Road en route to Okotiebo Street.

Morning traffic on Awolowo Road is usually either a slow crawl or a virtual parking lot. On this particular morning, the road was a parking lot.

We did not mind this situation at all. I had been locked down for a little over one month by this time. The sights and sounds of street life had begun fading in my mind and this sudden thrust into one of Nigeria's busiest streets was a painful reminder that someone other than myself decided what my days would be like and where and how I would spend it. It was a hard pill to swallow, which was why I cherished this short drive as both a luxury and a reprieve.

After over one hour, we completed the journey which in normal traffic takes only five minutes. At Okotiebo we were deposited into a bunker. That was the way it felt inside that Hellhole.

The Okotiebo office of EFCC was different from the one on Awolowo Road where we had just come from. Although the staff appeared friendlier on the surface, the cells where inmates were accommodated was a completely different story altogether.

I describe this structure as a bunker for lack of a choicer synonym. The place was a box shaped concrete structure built with cruelty in mind. Its design and construction could not have been supervised by architects or engineers or else it would not have been erected. The structure has within its concrete outer walls, eight concrete cubicles. All cubicles were windowless save for tiny square openings that measure about 4 square inches up near the edge of the concrete roof. Each cubicle has only one of these openings. The openings which are not wide enough even to pass a premature baby through still have iron bars built into them. The builder's terms of reference must have been handed down from the slave dealers of the colonial era!

~

The occupants of these cell cubicles were drenched in sweat. They had no clothes on except the shorts or wrappers around their waists. It felt like an oven which needed no fuel or fire to cook its contents. We were literally cooking in there!

Many things baffled me about the condition in which these accused persons were kept but perhaps the two most poignant of them all were first, the question; "how could the government sanction such base treatment of its own citizens who had merely been accused and not had their day in court? Second, what type of conditioning could reduce citizens to this level of passivity?"

Mine became the lone voice of descent. Even though my protests received little or no response, I never quit voicing them. Other inmates thought I was merely shooting the breeze. EFCC officials felt I was merely thinking and talking like an American. Inmates and officials alike said I was a fish out of water. They felt time would bring me, like a chicken, back to the roost.

In my own private moments, I wondered how the United States could wrap herself in the words of a national anthem glowing with morality, touting the ethos of civility, respect for human rights and even the rights of animals, while at the same time encouraging other nations to abuse and debase their own citizens.

Some things surely did not add up. I was sure of it and with every new difficulty or hardship I experienced, my resolve grew stronger. I would come out of this ordeal much stronger.

~

Going by the information I was able to glean while in EFCC captivity, the commission was established at the instance of the United States Administration. The United States was feeling frustrated by the rising cases of Nigerians involved in the lucrative fraud business known commonly in Nigeria as 419. The perpetrators of these schemes merely promised a reward of millions of dollars to their victims for their assistance in laundering or stealing public funds from the coffers of the Nigerian Government. The only role required of the victim was to furnish an account number where the loot would be deposited. Up to this stage in the scheme, the victim risked nothing at all, except that their sense of greed had been triggered—they were now sucked in. The fraudster then demands for a good faith deposit to assist in any number of transactions toward consummating the "business."

The victim is promised a lion share of the "Windfall" upon the successful execution of the deal. These schemes became known as advance fee fraud.

In addition to the 419 schemes, there were also rising instances of Nigerians getting involved in schemes which successfully diverted funds belonging to customers of Western Union and sometimes public funds into accounts set up by fraudsters. These funds were usually lost and never recovered.

Yet another group of criminals conspired with insiders at banks, government offices, doctor's offices, etc. to steal the personal identities of unsuspecting individuals where after, they are stripped of their investments, savings, personal properties and in some instances, leaving their victims saddled with debts which they did not benefit from and are not even aware of.

As I listened to some of the inmates in EFCC net who were themselves involved in these crimes, my emotions ranged anywhere from pity to indignation. Even today, as I observe and listen to the criminals all around me, those feelings remain.

I had been victim of a number of these lousy creatures more times than any person deserves. Each scam had been different from the others but all of them had targeted a personal weakness, a situation which I was not in a position to detect at the time.

Before I became victimized by a group of these scam artists myself, I was outraged at the naivety of their victims. It was not until after my experience with the fraudsters who targeted me that I understood their level of sophistication.

Now that I was cast in their den, I was able to learn firsthand, from the horse's mouth what drives the advance fee fraud business and why it was unlikely to be successfully combated by EFCC.

Even though it is not the subject of this endeavor, it should interest all concerned with stopping 419, particularly the Americans exposed to the reaches of these fraudsters, that the only way to reduce or eliminate losses to the fraud schemes, is to work on the human weaknesses upon which the predators prey. One example of these weaknesses is greed.

Simeon put it this way, "EFCC is fighting a losing battle. 419 will go on as long as there are greedy people. If they close one channel, three new channels open up. The job of a fraudster is as easy as that of a preacher. In South Africa, to succeed, you preach miraculous cures for aids. In Nigeria, to succeed, you preach miraculous success through dreams! The key is, give people what they want. Not what they need! They will follow you to hell!"

It was a profound lesson to learn. Naturally, one would think this was a no brainer—they believe that only greedy or ignorant people fall prey for con artists. But no, I have seen more brainy victims of 419 than I can count.

My personal vulnerability was and remains even at present, my late mother. You see, love has always been my undoing. But not just love or loving for the sake of satisfying a personal urge. My mother's life from the time I was grown enough to view the world introspectively infected me with a brand of altruistic love that is so giving it has become almost an involuntary act for me.

I know it is easy to criticize my claim or dismiss it as excuses for inexcusable deeds but I'll have my critics know that for the greater part of my early youth, I criticized my mother similarly. That is until I began to ask myself what the author of humanity, the creator of our universe, whoever or whatever you may consider Him or It had in mind.

All I know is that at the point where I took leave from criticizing my mother and began the act of giving to others, the feeling of satisfaction that came with the act was more intoxicating than any aphrodisiac I had ever known.

Watching a grateful recipient of a gift beats winning an Oscar or Nobel Prize. I know because I have felt it. I know because I see it in the faces of many who were or are today, like my mother.

Bill Gates is one of them. Michael Jackson was like my mother. Oprah Winfrey is yet another one. They are everywhere. I am inspired by them all. But I am inspired more by my mother because she is unsung. I wish I had the resources to discover the few others who are like my mother. I would urge them to remain anonymous and unsung. But I would do for them the things that I still do for my mother's memory today, 8 years after her passing.

Here I was, in detention waiting to be charged with some alleged offenses amid a group of other detainees who were, judging from their self-admitted criminal profiles, guilty of fraud of some sort or another. In this kind of scenario, it appeared the sensible way to relate to these people was to build bulwarks between us. This was easy to see and yet impossible for me to achieve.

Against better judgment, I listened to the pleas of these individuals. What I saw was desperate individuals—unloved and abandoned individuals. They were all trying to fill in the gaps in their lives. To me, they were just doing it the wrong way. Their engines of common sense and compassion were not correctly tuned. And so, I began ministering to them individually as a pastime.

During my individual discussions with them I got to hear the sordid details of some of their heart breaking stories. Some of them had been in EFCC detention as merely accused people awaiting trial for much longer than their offenses, if proved, would earn them in prison time. Many of them needed as little as N4, 000.00 (about $40.00 USD) for bail or refund of their loot and for these reasons had been detained for over 12 months without formal charges in some cases! In one of the cases, the sick sister of the detainee, on account of whose illness he had committed a fraud, passed away. The inmate was not allowed to attend the funeral! The most disturbing of the stories was that of a guy arrested for being in the wrong place at the wrong time during the raid of the home of an accused person. He was in detention for no other reason but that he had no money or person willing to bail him out. There was also the outrageous case of a woman who was hauled into an EFCC cell with her 6 month old son because her husband, a fraudster, was eluding capture by EFCC agents! The tactic was used in order to coax her husband into turning himself in.

All in all, I assisted 6 of these individuals to regain their freedom. Five of them maintained contact with me while I was in detention out of gratitude. You can imagine what those visits did for my morale.

There was however, one of them who never returned to see me. One of the grateful ones, Emeka, later informed me that the fellow did not change his ways and had once again been hauled back into EFCC detention.

My lawyer Biriyai Dambo had given his all but neither EFCC nor the United States Embassy was responsive. EFCC maintained a disturbing tight lipped policy on my case, Dambo's numerous visits to the United States Embassy met with stonewall silence every time. They pretended they had not received any of our numerous letters to them—not even those which were hand delivered by Barrister Dambo.

We eventually discovered why the United States Embassy developed amnesia each time my case was brought to light. In a process which was a diplomatic anomaly, the FBI unit of the U.S. Consular Officer had written to EFCC urging them to arrest me for the purpose of having me returned to the United States to answer some charges pending there against me. By doing so, they were attempting to short circuit or bypass the agreed upon process which involved the red tape and bureaucracy of international diplomacy.

When I saw a copy of this letter, I was incredulous. On closer examination, I observed a few typographical errors. I also observed that the U.S. State Department seal on the letterhead bearing the request was not embossed on the original copy which was in the EFCC file. I concluded that this letter was a forgery. There simply wasn't any way I was going to be convinced that the United States would engage in this sort of practice. Events later proved me wrong!

There was no other plausible conclusion to draw at this time except that I was in danger. A faceless adversary was on my trail and had somehow engaged the support and assistance of forces against which I would ordinarily be completely powerless. But the USA is not an ordinary adversary, is it?

I made one important phone call. It was to a close friend who had extensive contacts and connection to many of Nigeria's legal luminaries. She was a legal practitioner and scholar herself, having graduated at the top of her LLB and LLM classes.

As it turned out, she knew just the lawyer I needed to contact quite intimately. His name is Festus Keyamo.

Fifteen

I knew what I needed. I did not know how to get it. What I needed was to embarrass the hell out of everybody. Then I would have received what I desperately needed… Attention!

That was it. Get the media to solve this problem for me free. No charge.

In the United States it is a right, not a privilege. There's no reason it should not be the same in Nigeria. But for sure, only the insanely naïve would believe this.

In the United States there would be media frenzy. There would be a public outcry; a U.S. citizen is locked up and dehumanized without warrant, without probable cause, at the behest of a foreign country—in direct violation of the sacred Constitution of the United States of America! For 3 months!

I could see the news headlines already…
SCANDAL!
IS OURS A PUPPET NATION?
TRAITORS IN OUR MIDST!!!
ABDUCTION!!!

I wanted desperately to figure out who my adversary was. Of course, I had a fair guess by now. But it was still a guess. If my guess was right, then the idea of the United States of America pursuing me with such vigor made no sense to me. If my guess was wrong, then I needed protection urgently.

I was willing and ready to board the plane and return to the U.S. at the drop of a hat at my own expense. Not at the expense of American tax payers. I had already made that known to the U.S. Embassy.

I had not so far been attacked in a way that threatened my life. But that possibility still existed. I was on guard all the time, making sure I did not isolate myself enough to offer a would-be attacker any opportunity to do harm to me.

As a matter of fact, when I shared my story with Simeon and the old Leprechaun, they both agreed with me that I should be on constant alert for my safety but they assured me that the cell, although grossly inconvenient, was the safest place for me at the moment.

These assurances and reassurances notwithstanding, it was clear to me that I needed the assistance of a legal eagle to achieve my aim. Enter Barrister Festus Keyamo.

Even speaking with him on the telephone, I knew I had made the correct decision by choosing Festus Keyamo for the legal/media battle I was about to launch against my faceless adversary.

Keyamo, at this point in his career, was not imbued with the legal appendage of Senior Advocate of Nigeria (SAN) – the favorite literary appendage with which Nigeria's Judiciary rewards experience, social status, and loyalty to the administration of the day, with emphasis on the loyalty tag.

He did however, possess a number of valuable personal attributes which some of Nigeria's SANS could never develop even after decades of toil, blood and sweat on the bench.

The aspect of these attributes which interested me the most at this time were;

- ✓ His media influence
- ✓ His knowledge of the law.
- ✓ His personality and presence.

It seemed to me that Festus Keyamo was the only lawyer in the country at this time with the courage, the vigor, and knowledge to go up against the establishment. He enjoyed the kind of distinguished presence and notoriety which the media could never get enough of.

In the late nineties and early tow thousands, Keyamo dealt the death blow on case after case of witch-hunting which was hastily put together by prosecutors eager to please the despotic power machinery of the Obasanjo/ Atiku PDP (People's Democratic Party).

My abduction by EFCC happened in this auspicious period during Nigeria's effort to construct a sustainable democratic republic, an effort which Obasanjo and Atiku had all but decimated.

Thanks to the Fawehinmis, Beko Kutis, Justice Oputas, Colonel Umar Kangiwas, and Keyamos of this world, Obasanjo's grand life presidency plot collapsed like a deck of cards.

~

As I waited eagerly for my scheduled upcoming meeting with Fetus Keyamo, I caught wind of EFCC's desperation to wean me off their list of inmates. The presence of my name in this list was apparently becoming embarrassing to the higher authorities, especially in view of the irregularity that attended my arrest and illegal detention.

Although it sounded like welcome news, I wanted my exit from the gaol into which I was so inauspiciously cast, to be on my own terms. I therefore kept praying and looking forward to ending my ordeal with a curtain raiser.

That was not to be.

Sixteen

On the weekend preceding my meeting with Keyamo, the head of EFCC's legal department visited me with a voluminous document.

While delivering the document he announced with visible relief. "You will now have your day in court. Here are your extradition papers. Get ready to be in court next week."

My jaw dropped. A shock ran through my nervous system from which I took a while to recover.

After three months of scorching cat and mouse game with EFCC, finally, a document to explain it all away!

Incredible!

"Their nerves!" I thought with hot anger in my throat. I could not articulate any words civil enough to prevent a riot, so I swallowed my thoughts.

~

To my mind, although I had not read its contents, this voluminous document had to be completely fabricated.

It was inconceivable, wasn't it? That a high profile government commission could flout the law the way EFCC had done with me when all the while an option was available to them that was not only lawful but also secured the rights and dignity of the citizen they sought to bring to justice.

Mind you, I had been arrested without a warrant or proof of probable cause. Even the arresting officers confessed their ignorance of my offense. I had been detained under deplorable conditions, in violation of both my human rights and court order for a period of nearly three months!

Now, out of the blue, this document shows up as if to clear the air, justify the injustice, and erase the gross illegality which the EFCC had done to me and the constitution it was set up to uphold and protect.

I was not buying it. Period!

Without uttering a word to the EFCC legal adviser, I took the document and returned to the cell to study it.

I willed myself to calm down. This took a little while but I calmed enough to concentrate.

First, I needed some privacy which is normally impossible in all Nigerian detention facilities due to overcrowding, EFCC cells included. But on this day, a welcome distraction was provided by a hotly contested championship game of draft (checkers) between the best two players, one each from among the inmates and the EFCC guard officers.

I stole my way into a deserted area of the cell and began reading the document titled "Extradition USA."

As I read, wide-eyed, my heartbeat rate increased by one beat with every next word or punctuation. The more I read, the more frightening the document's contrived implications got. My heart was hammering so hard I had to take a pause from further reading.

Unable to contain my emotions, I stood up and began pacing the length and breadth of the deserted cell. "It's not true! It's not true! It has to be a nightmare!" I remember thinking to myself as I paced back and forth.

After a few minutes of complete bewilderment, I stopped and whispered to myself. "Don't George." Then I took one step forward and stopped. "Don't George." Another step, "continue reading," another step. Finally, I returned to the document, sweat pouring down from my head into my long caftan. Many taps had involuntarily opened up in my head, apparently determined to drain life right of my body.

Just as the EFCC legal adviser had said, and also just as the title suggested, the document contained a compendium of official diplomatic jargon on papers which when all were put together, constituted an official request for my extradition from Nigeria to the United States of America.

But that was not the reason for my mental and emotional disquiet. Far from that, the rumble in my stomach, the panic in my sweat glands and the tightness in my chest were all triggered by an entirely different incident at which this document pointed directly and unequivocally.

Seventeen

I had seen these documents before! I was not hallucinating and most certainly was not having a nightmare!

I dropped to one knee and set the document on the concrete floor. I could read no further because the pages had become blurred.

Instead of the words, it was the apparition of a very evil man that flashed in and out of my view, blending into the pages of "Extradition USA" as if part of every page.

~

I was not wondering where I first saw this document. No. It was rather the place where I had seen it that was my consumption.

~

I saw these same documents, or copies of them, about three months before the previous Christmas, in the office of the Inspector General of Police of Nigeria at Force Headquarters; Louis EDET House, Abuja!

There it was.

The same old Satan haunted me still!

In order to understand the connection between the Extradition USA document and the Satan thirsting for my blood, it is crucial to lay out the events which gave birth to this entire saga of my life.

I lay great emphasis on the events that preceded the matter of my extradition because I feel it my duty to repudiate the accusation that I attempted to evade justice simply because I fought against a faceless adversary. I can imagine of nobody who would have done differently when confronted with the stark acts of evil and perfidy from people in whose hands I once entrusted my entire life.

~

First, when Stella and I got married, I was unpretentious with her about my conservative cultural ideology. I am first to admit that as far as marriages and families go, I am out of harmony with the times. Forgive me, but I am not in a hurry to replace this inclination.

Without excusing the inexcusable sin of the adulterous husband, I insist that the damage done by the adultery of a wife in a family blessed with children is by proportion far weightier on its long term impact in terms of the children's future functional stability.

Surely, I've often been credited with naivety on many of the world's complex social issues, but never with quickly accepting other people's views when dangerous risks are involved.

I am well aware that my brand of bold conservative cultural idealism begs for criticism from contemporary youth such as my lovely children, but I will remain steadfast with my beliefs, for it is impossible for the right handed to switch to the left at old age.

Having thus laid the foundation of my moral and cultural views on marriage and family, here is the position which this odious situation thrust me into.

I supported my medical doctor wife through her residency by working primarily as a defense consultant/contractor in Nigeria.

During that same period, we built a loving family together. We were financially blessed, especially from my end of the table, being that my services satisfied my employers immensely. My in-laws were happy to visit us from their various stations, both here in the United States and in Nigeria. I was happy to sponsor and assist them in any way I could. Life was great.

~

Six years into our marriage, in 1992, my wife successfully completed her residency program. This success constituted yet another of God's many blessings to us. However, by far the greatest blessing of all was our children whose number had grown to four by the time my wife completed her residency.

With four young children to cater to and provide for, it was difficult for my wife to hold down any job, even with assistance of full time live-in nannies.

As a conservative cultural ideologue, I deemed it my avowed duty as the natural provider for the family to accept, but not depend on any additional income coming from my wife. The idea was to build up the family on the strength of one income. This way, the second income will always be viewed and accepted as a bonus.

~

In hind sight I should have stuck to my ideals, but under extreme pressure from my wife who I loved beyond words, I succumbed and established a medical practice for her as a way of giving her independent management of her time and avoiding the necessity of seeking employment with others who disallowed the excessive tardiness which unavoidably comes with raising many children.

At first, the new medical practice did not disrupt our agreed upon principles of marriage and family, but as the practice took shape, my wife's lack of experience in the business side of medicine forced my deeper involvement in the day to day management of staff and finances. My wife heaped pressure upon pressure on me to involve myself even more. Her argument was that my involvement would keep me home here in the United States where she and our children needed me like never before.

If you truly love somebody, your position on issues can never be absolute, except on issues of moral principles. Even on such issues, one may consider shifting from their positions whenever the competing position is equally sound, especially in the interest of harmony and peace.

I loved my wife and children enough to shift my career plans in a major way for our family.

I shut down a significant portion of my consultancy and contracting operations in Nigeria. I did so because I saw no pursuit of wealth worth engaging at the expense of the people I loved the most.

~

With the reduction of my workload in Nigeria, I freed up a significant amount of time which made it possible for my family to enjoy some of our best years together.

The free time, as expected, came at a significant cost in terms of income, a gap which I quickly moved to bridge.

~

Shortly after scaling down my Nigeria based business operations, I changed the structure of the medical practice. This move which I made with the sole aim of compensating for the loss of income resulting from my reduced business activities in Nigeria produced many unexpected results, chief of which was the sad breakup of my marriage to my beloved Stella.

As in many events of life changing magnitude, the beginnings of marital problems come from one of many minute, harmless glitches in communication, visit of family or friend, choosing of a school for the children, enjoying meals together, etc. Just like cancer starts as a benign little mole and grows over the years into a festering sore.

Optimum Care Medical Center, LLC was the name Stella and I chose for the corporation. I was the CEO; my wife was the Medical Director. We delivered medical services to a paying public.

As the CEO, my duties included hiring and terminating employees, business development, overseeing billing and accounting, payroll, business client services and the like. At our peak, we owned three offices in Montgomery County, Maryland, employing four medical doctors in addition to my wife. There were over twenty support staff also employed. My wife's duties included practicing medicine and supervising all medical staff.

It is fair to say, in retrospect, that in the very short time which it took me to give the medical practice the facelift briefly described above, my wife never understood or appreciated what was happening. All she saw was God's blessings and prosperity of unexpected proportions. I too was immensely thankful to the almighty, for I knew He had willed good things to come into our lives. But from a business perspective, we were yet to begin experiencing the growing pains which all legitimate business owners have to plough through as they build up a client base, especially after finances from other income sources run dry. In our case, the $10,000.00 net monthly drawing with which I supported the family became eliminated with the scaling down of my business activities overseas. With that pivotal income which financed the purchase of our two homes and the establishment of the medical practice gone, we had little option but to pour in our every God-given acumen to ensure the success of our efforts. God rewarded our efforts with success, to the extent that we broke even within twelve months.

As the newly restructured medical practice began finding a foothold in the community, the income statement (profit and loss) reflected in its 2nd year of operations, a gross income (before expenses) of over $2 million. In sharing this success story with my wife, I did not believe it necessary to go into the detailed explanation of every single line of the income statement because I considered it self-explanatory. But I made sure to caution her to avoid getting carried away by the gross income figure without reflecting on the equally high expenses side. She also apparently did not care to know the details, as she showed no interest in them at all.

What I did not know was that she assumed, quite falsely, and naively, that most of the $2 million was ours to keep—a false assumption which she shared with her family members. That was the turning point in our relationship—the point at which the hammer met the brick.

My in-laws, operating on their misinformed assessment of our new found prosperity, swooped in on us, making demands, giving unsolicited advice and airing their views on how they felt my wife and I "just happened" onto such fortune all of a sudden and what their share ought to be.

Without a doubt, all members of my wife's immediate family shared these views but they had two actors on the ground—my mother-in-law herself, who was ably assisted by the family's mother lode Chuck, who was himself assisted by his loving wife!

It is not necessary to give a detailed account of the actions taken by the duo of mother and son, but suffice it to say that by the time they were done doing their deeds, my soul mate had become my soul nightmare.

At first, I treated my wife's tirades as a phase in our marriage which would pass as they often do in most normal families. Remember, I was not without my own faults or contributions to what ailed the marriage. My strong views on conservative family values which were not shared by my wife who preferred a much more liberal approach to raising our children had its own role. But I naively believed that our love which all evidence indicated as strong and exemplary would endure and outlast the current strife.

I was wrong. My wife's nocturnal meetings with her family increased. Every action I took at the office in the interest of the survival of the practice came under attack by my wife and her siblings under the chairmanship of their mother—my mother-in-law. These charades continued unabated, at the home of my brother-in-law, and sometimes at our office, or at any of the various other venues available to them.

Three incidents stand out among our many squabbles. The first was my firing of a physician assistant who had been repeatedly fingered as practicing medicine and had been identified as a doctor by unsuspecting patients. I fired him after he failed to heed repeated warnings to stop presenting himself as a "doctor" to these patients. He was not a licensed physician.

After I fired him, my wife chose to believe I had fired "this innocent man" because he often gave her a ride home from the office at about midnight. Although that had not been true, I chuckled and wondered aloud if that offense in and of itself was not even worse than the actual reason for his termination. Does a man who consorts with another man's wife deserve to keep a job with her and her husband? I began then to worry about my wife's perspective on many of life's complex moral issues.

The second troubling incident happened when I returned home after a busy day at the office to the thunderous sounds of heap dancing and yelling from our family room. Alarmed, I quickly parked the car, scanned the perimeter of my house for signs of trouble and then entered the room gingerly. What I found was my wife's lifelong friend who weighed toward the scale's highest calibration, pounding her supersized feet on the hardwood floor like a South African Ipitombi dancer invoking the spirits of her ancestors. I was gum smacked.

The sight of my wife cheering her on and my daughter wearing a confused grin but cheering along with her mother directed my thoughts toward a cheerful provocation for the loud outburst of happiness. I sank into the sofa beside my wife and gently asked, "What is the occasion? Did she win a lottery or better yet, did she find a husband?"

My wife giggled and gestured toward her friend, "ask her," she said. "She has the news of her life."

I did. I asked, "Ada Mazi, what is the news? Please let me in on the news and while at it, get my own champagne."

She widened her smile and increased the pounding of her feet. Then she began chanting hymns of praise to the "man" up in heaven.

"Look George, it is pink. Look at this sign. A plus sign! I'm pregnant! I'm pregnant George!" She finally said to me, out of breath.

I swung around to face my wife, then I shifted my gaze from her to Kimberly, our daughter, then back to the pregnant guest and finally to our other children, who were watching the entire show from the sidelines.

By this time, my countenance had gone through all kinds of changes and settled on gloom. I got up and went straight up to my bedroom.

I did not need to probe my wife further on this issue. It would have had the exact effect I sought to avoid. Any remarks would have raised the obvious question, "who is the father?" I could not raise the issue before my children! I already knew the sad answer to the unasked question!

When later I asked my wife in a bid to admonish her, the situation turned ugly.

My wife's friend was having an affair with a married man. The married man in question was not a stranger to us but a close family member—my wife's first cousin who had been very actively involved in our own lives in many positive ways.

I wondered out loud how young parents like us, raising our children to be morally grounded in all their affairs could explain to the same children that it was okay to have children outside the marriage. Even worse, to have babies with people who were already married with children! In other words, justify adultery!

I asked my wife, "would this have been okay then if I should return someday with a similar situation?"

To my dismay, my wife went wild with hysteria. She thundered; "Don't lecture me with your moral platitude. You do not know my cousin's wife the way I do. She has been going about acting as if she owns my cousin—like he is her private property! This suits her fine."

As I already stated earlier, I have never been a saint. There are sides to me which need constant work of improvement, but those sides of me have never been concealed. I dare suggest that it was the weaknesses I was born with, which I struggled with, as most mortals do, the demons within me, that my wife found attractive in me. The difference is that I do not defend those demons and I do not display them for my children to find. They have their entire future to deal with their own demons. I'll be damned if I was going to add to theirs or allow anyone else to offer them theirs.

This matter never got resolved the way I thought prudent. It simply hung suspended in the air of animosity hovering menacingly over our now troubled marriage.

Third and most devastating was the case of my failure to find a peaceful middle ground that would allow my brother-in-law Chuck to share in everything that had my name on it. His recalcitrance was so unnerving that I eventually moved back to Nigeria on his account.

Away from my family and my world—a world which I had shed my youth's sweat and blood to build. It was either I moved myself or I move him—he had no plans of allowing himself to be moved. I let him have it all—my home, the business, my wife. But our children, I left in God's hands.

Before I moved back to my roots, I promised my wife that her wishes to sacrifice what we had together, what we built together on the altar of sibling lunacy, would surely come true, but that the outcome would be far from her expectations.

As God, man, and woman are my witnesses, and those witnesses are alive today, I warned my wife that by the time her brother was through dealing with her, she would have no husband, no home, and no food of her own. I said to her, "You will go to Chuck, cap in hand, for school fees, housing, and food for the children."

In my tribal home, my remark is considered an "offor" which translates to "omen or portent."

It was not my wish or intent to bring this evil to fruition as I stood to be the single greatest loser should that ever materialize. I was struggling to turn my wife away from the war path into which she had thoughtlessly immersed herself, to my utter dismay.

Her response was, "You're not God. Go on, do your worst and quit acting like you know everything."

It is important to note that although a pacifist, I would not have felt any queasiness fighting fire with fire when my family came under attack. I take pride in recalling my father's logic when he refused to take flight from his home as enemy rockets rained into our compound during the Nigerian Civil War. He instead, dug himself into a bunker saying, "A man's house is his last line of defense, when the enemy chases you to your house, and your back is against the wall, you must then turn around and fight!" If analyzed vis-à-vis the American judicial system, my father's principle is much like The Castle Doctrine or the Stand-Your-Ground Rule.

But my father never had to contend with the logic and laws of the United States of America.

It was unthinkable to me. I know that I would most certainly have been dug out of my bunker had I followed my father's logic and confronted my in-law Chuck when he brought the fight to me at my home. I cannot begin to consider or speculate how law enforcement officers would have responded to that hypothetical confrontation, knowing as I did, that my own wife would invite the officers to help shape me up or ship me out.

Propelled by the weight of these events and my wish to spare my children the trauma of witnessing or disruptive showdown in the family between the same people who taught them daily, the virtues of love as against the evils of conflict, I decided that tough as it might prove, the only way to halt further deterioration of our marriage and the steady slide toward divorce and anarchy was for me to move to Nigeria. This way, I could explain to my children without guilt that I had returned to my Defense Consultancy business.

That was what I did.

On one fine Monday morning in 1999 following a pleasant Sunday evening with my children, I informed them of my urgent unplanned trip. With a heart the weight of lead and premonition of calamity, I braced myself, picked up my carry-on bag, said a prayer for divine guidance, and headed for Dulles Airport.

Even on my way to the airport I knew that a bad wind was blowing over my entire universe, but what was I to do?

A few weeks earlier, my wife had filed an ex-parte motion at the court in Rockville and obtained an order restraining me from coming within 2 miles of my home and especially my children. She cited rumors reaching her that I had plans to take our children to attend my brother's wedding in Los Angeles and onward from there to Nigeria without her consent and involvement. Both allegations, although false figments of her imagination seemed to me events she should not only support, but she ought to have been the one urging me to pursue.

In reality, I had purchased tickets for my entire family including my wife (especially my wife) to attend that wedding just as I had done without opposition from her for the weddings of three of her own siblings in Ohio, Boston, and New Jersey! I had purchased these tickets for my brother's wedding, ironically, from her close friend's travel agency with the full knowledge of my wife.

Events of the recent past had led me to conclude that my doting over my children and their warm reciprocal responses ran contrary to my wife's expectations. She, having selectively imbibed the American cultural values as they relate to marriage and relationship, wanted to provide the shoulder while I straggled behind her a backdrop to her vitality. I was to provide all the yam and garri, and the servants to do the pounding, the houses, and the cars— while keeping my distance from our children, except with her approval, as if they were her private toys!

My sympathy goes out to the many Nigerian men living in America and the other diaspora whose hearts have been squeezed into the shape of my wife's prescription for marital bliss. But I speak only of those still alive, for I have often found such names in the obituary section with the caption "Gone, too soon!—Survived by his HEALTHY, LOVING wife and "X" number of children."

Now, holding these extradition documents and realizing that they were the same as the ones I saw in the hands of my wife's pathetic lover at Abuja, in the Inspector General's office when that monster made his failed attempt at my life, I was convinced beyond any doubt that he was again behind my current ordeal.

Eighteen

My first meeting with Barrister Festus Keyamo took place as planned, over the weekend that followed the service of the extradition documents on me.

Before the meeting, I had called to inform him of the new developments—the receipt of the extradition papers and the court date set for March 23, 2005.

Festus Keyamo is a powerfully built young man. He is a physically imposing presence—taller than he usually appears on television. His strong facial features and square shoulders appear a match for any linebacker in American football, except that Festus is a better looker than most NFL linebackers.

These physical attributes which contrast significantly with his demure personality, I suspect are responsible in part for the love affair between him and those who know him up close, especially the media personalities.

When our conversation began, he sat impassively as I spoke, an air of the most complete tranquility upon him. At first, I thought something was amiss. The near garrulous television impressions of him had led me to expect a chatty conversation but instead he listened attentively, punctuating my remarks every now and again with a question or remark of his own.

It was not until I had taken up more than one whole hour telling him my story that the Festus Keyamo fire became ignited. I had hit the right nerve.

First he wanted to know whether I had decided to hire him to represent me.

"Sure, you're hired" I responded.

"O.K. then," he said, "here are my ground rules..."

He went on to lay out his list of rules and procedures at the end of which no doubt was left as to who was going to be in charge. He turned down my entreaties to work with another attorney even though I had assured him that the one my family had chosen was brilliant.

Least of Keyamo's rules detailed his fees which surprisingly, but thankfully, were not as high as I expected.

We arrived at full agreement on all aspects of the way forward. He requested and collected all documents in my possession to study before we broke up the meeting. By this time, word had spread that Festus Keyamo was in the house and not a few inmates and staff of EFCC positioned themselves to shake his hand or compliment him. Apparently, his numerous face-offs with government agents intent on perpetually disenfranchising a helpless populace, was winning many hearts and minds.

We adjourned with a tentative new date set for a final meeting during which Mr. Keyamo would layout his attack plan.

I now had a void to fill. With all legal documents relating to the issue on my hands gone, I had nothing else to do but begin reflecting on the most troubling aspects of my travail.

For several months now, I had been unable to face up to the sadness I felt about the eerie subject of Chinelo, the young lady who was probably at the heart of the entire unfolding family drama.

Never before, in my entire life, had I been so emotionally drained over an issue which was not life threatening in nature.

If the attached transcripts of my telephone conversations with Chinelo which form nearly a third by volume, of the extradition documents are to be believed, then Chinelo had assisted the FBI (Federal Bureau of Investigation) in attempting to entrap me into making damaging statements which no doubt portend far reaching consequences for myself and my entire family. Or was it the other way around? Could it have been the FBI assisting Chinelo to entrap me?

Wouldn't it be the most tragic event of my life knowing that I had perhaps done more to salvage this young lady from a life of destitution than I had for anyone else, only for her to deal me the hand of Judas?

I had numerous telephone conversations with Chinelo since my departure in 1999 during which I made spirited effort to calm her growing feeling of frustration about the state of her family's deepening mendicancy.

She was particularly upset that her family still resided in the same hovel which they shared with other relatives.

I had been to the place and understood why she would be so concerned.

I had also made promises to her that I would definitely go to the aid of her parents. I promised to build them a new home as soon as I was able to put the resources together.

As God is my witness, I meant to keep my promise to her. Meanwhile, I periodically sent assistance in the form of cash, food, and clothing to her family.

During this period, between 1999 and 2001, I was in the process of re-establishing my defense consultancy business after a long period of absence.

Absence is the greatest danger of all for a government contractor. Once out of the mind of his benefactor, it is difficult to fight back into esteem. Meanwhile, dependents have little patience with the sluggish flow of promised allowances. They are quick to interpret this period of drought as hesitation on your part and failure to deliver assistance promptly is regarded as a renege.

It was the case of Chinelo and her family that taught me a lesson about assuming things simply by appearances. The lesson is that poverty is not necessarily congruous with humility.

Growing up, I knew what poverty meant—the inability to access even the most basic necessities of life—clean water, food, shelter, and education. I struggled along with my parents and other siblings to change the circumstances that denied us this access.

I did all I had to do, including seeking the assistance of those who did not owe me anything. In other words, sometimes I sought to receive something for nothing.

The result was that when God turned our fortunes around, my mother made it mandatory for us, her children, to always go to the aid of those less fortunate than we were.

It was hence easy to assume that all such beneficiaries would always show humble appreciation. Wrong!

Chinelo was brought to live with me and my family in the spirit of my mother's philanthropy. Chinelo's parents were very poor, a situation they constantly blamed on her father's "evil" cousin who they insist even today, bewitched her parents, foreclosing any effort they made to become prosperous.

Having lived in the midst of superstitious elements in a few rural settings, suggestions such as these were rampant and rambunctious. We secretly laughed these suggestions off as envy which usually disappears once the fortunes of the sufferers improved.

We failed to detect the underlying malice that exists in some cases where even when their fortunes improve, those fortunes are deployed to settle scores and emasculate those previously held in spite.

I now understand that humility is not a virtue distributed by the author of life in any particular order. It is easy for even the smartest psychologists of our world to be beguiled by appearances.

Although it had not come as a surprise to me two years after separating from my family that Chinelo had engaged my wife in a war of words which then degenerated into a fisticuff, I was nevertheless saddened by that news.

If nothing else, I believed that Chinelo was narrow minded and mean, an observation which I had made just before leaving the United States of America and which I was in no position to forewarn my wife about. My wife, feeling like a woman scorned, had bonded with Chinelo as a mother and manipulated her into keeping a distance between her and my side of the family, although she was my mother's godchild.

Narrow minded and self-centered as she was, Chinelo played along and got generously rewarded with gifts of fashion items which matched or bettered those of our children.

Not willing to be drawn into petty games which I considered trifle, if not snide, I thought; "knock yourselves out!"

That was indeed what they did.

This was not the first time my wife had engaged in these treacherous little plots and this was not the first time it had back fired on her.

But this time however, it sank the precarious remnants of our family vessel.

~

My wife's bribes which purchased her loyalty were not enough to deter Chinelo from calling 911 the moment their relationship went sour. That single emergency call against my wife and many subsequent follow-up visits to the police, triggered investigation by the police, immigration, FBI, human rights advocates and child abuse shelters. Together, these agencies helped Chinelo achieve her agenda which was to remain in the United States; legitimize her illegal entry and give her long suffering family a new lease on life.

My humble self, my erstwhile soul mate and my children had apparently become expendable as far as Chinelo was concerned. The end justified the means in her well-considered opinion. Or else this story would never have been told.

It never ceases to amaze me. Indeed it surprises me, and even embarrasses me when very highly knowledgeable people act with little common sense.

When the news of the drama in my home in the United States broke, I was still smarting from the humiliation I felt from the knowledge of my wife's nefarious affair with the hooligan named Anuofia. But that hurt did not restrain me from reaching out through every possible channel available to get my wife to take pause and consider all the implications of Chinelo's allegations. My wife regrettably blocked all suggestions from me in the hope that all of Chinelo's allegations would bounce off of her and stick to me.

To people who know me and my family, it was a no brainer—the entirety of the allegations were spurious and extremely mean spirited.

But to uninvolved outside observers, the need to protect the displaced and down trodden has always been so great that there is a tendency toward overzealous prosecution of accused persons.

This is perhaps as it should be. The only problem is that when you are on the receiving end and you are innocent, you see so clearly that you wonder what has suddenly made the entire world around you go blind!

I was ready as I had repeatedly signaled to EFCC and the United States Embassy, to return immediately to Maryland in order to answer all the charges being made against me.

What I was not ready to do was to walk into a snare set by my wife's lover and whoever else involved in their conspiracy. The outcome of such a prospect surely would have been very ugly, very possibly tragic.

With these thoughts weighing constantly into my daily routines, I waited eagerly for my next meeting with Barrister Festus Keyamo.

Nineteen

The night before our scheduled final meeting I had only a fitful sleep. Although I had great confidence in the ability of Festus Keyamo to sift through the mountain of information which I had supplied him, I knew that without any personal involvement in the issues, it would be difficult for him or anybody else to fully connect all the different parts of this saga that I had lived in order to come up with the best line of attack.

Information which had reached me just hours before bedtime had it that the federal prosecutors for the 4th District of Maryland, USA, had begun the trial of my wife on allegations that she conspired with me to smuggle Chinelo into the United States for the purpose of harboring her involuntarily in our home and putting her to work as a nanny for our children and thereby obtaining financial gains through the savings resulting from her free services.

My wife's decision to proceed to trial without my input into her defense strategy was the single most troubling issue for me. It was perplexing indeed as I knew and possessed exculpatory evidence which was certainly not available to her and which would have helped her case. She rebuffed my family's effort to weigh in on her trial.

If God could be a witness in courts, my worries would have been much less, and although there is no shortage of Bibles and Korans in the courtrooms, God is not called to the witness stand and does not testify at trials.

I was in black humor at this point. I had given my wife every opportunity of saving herself and the family but it is said that "those whom the gods want to destroy, they first make crazy."

I had my work cut out for me. Festus Keyamo was now due to arrive and I had several of my own strategies cooking in my head but first the expert must speak.

Before retiring that night I prayed for guidance. Although no words of comfort came to me, I knew I had not been deserted by the Heavenly Father. My siblings and cousins from far and near kept in close contact, sending all I needed to keep my body and soul together.

Now I had a duty not to disappoint all these relatives who were as distraught if not more so than myself. I willed myself to be strong and sharp minded for my crucial meeting with Keyamo.

I had been ready and waiting for over two hours before I was invited for my meeting with Keyamo. As usual, we were given the courtesy of meeting in the shared private office of some EFCC field officers rather than the usually crowded visiting room. The gesture I was exceedingly thankful for.

When I arrived at the office, Festus got up from where he was seated to greet me, always the courteous gentleman in his well-tailored navy blue suit and a tieless open neck white shirt. We shook hands warmly and sat down to talk.

"Hope you slept well last night," he began.

"Not really."

"Oh? What happened?"

I shrugged, "Guess I'm a little anxious."

"About what?"

"It saddens me that this whole mess was actually avoidable."

"Indeed, but so is everything else, good or bad. They're always avoidable. Still they happen."

"Yeah, we are powerless against events in the past. Yes, I've heard it before."

"That is exactly right. We learn our lessons and avoid a repeat. Isn't that right George?" He asked with a penetrating look that bore through my forehead.

"That's right," I responded.

"Okay my friend, I've gone through the documents and also given much thought to the things you told me the other day. This is a very interesting case. In my opinion, it is winnable."

"Oh yeah?" I prodded. "Please give me your honest assessment of the documents. Do you think they could be fake?"

"Oh?" he said taken aback. "Are you still suggesting that these documents may not be authentic?"

"Hell Yes!" I shouted. "They're the same documents which my wife's hooligan lover brandished at Mr. Ehindero's office at the police headquarters in Abuja last October! If they were authentic, then tell me, how come the police did not arrest me? Huh? Tell me why the Inspector General himself would invite me, ask me questions about the documents and return them to the hooligan and send him away? Huh?"

"Are you serious Mr. Udeozor?" queried Mr. Keyamo, befuddled. "Did this actually happen?"

"Hell yeah", I screamed. "Even, think about it! How did this Anuofia guy obtain the documents in the first place? Can you tell me that?"

"Okay, okay, let us go first to what we know. We may then return and work our way back to the unknown, assuming it is necessary."

"Okay, I think I can handle that."

"As I was about to say, these documents are real. You can see them, touch them, and smell them. Regardless of who originated the documents, the Attorney General of Nigeria has acknowledged them as authentic. He has forwarded the document as required by law, to the courts to determine whether they meet the criteria for your extradition to the United States of America."

He took a pause which I interpreted as a gesture for me to weigh in.

"I am with you so far" I acknowledged, "go on."

"A judge has been assigned to hear arguments for extradition and also the arguments against it." Again, he paused.

"Yeah, proceed." I said.

"After listening to both sides of the arguments, the judge will make a determination whether there is merit to the request and he will give his ruling." Once again, he paused.

"Proceed."

"Thank you. Now, if either side is not satisfied with the ruling of the high court judge, then the dissatisfied party may decide to take their case to the appeals court and present their grounds for rejecting the lower court's ruling. In this case, the high court is the lower court."

Pause.

"Proceed."

"Now, even the Court of Appeals is not a dead end. There is a higher court still. Any side which is still unsatisfied with the ruling of the Court of Appeals can seek remedy at the Supreme Court."

Pause.

"Proceed."

"The Supreme Court is the final stop. I can almost guarantee that your matter will not go beyond the Federal High Court. But I wanted to lay out the legal procedures to you and explain the hurdles which the Constitution requires a matter like yours to complete before it is complied with."

Another Pause.

"Is that it?" I asked.

"No, there are more steps." He replied.

"There are more?" I asked curiously.

"Yes. The extradition of any Nigerian citizen is only carried out at the discretion of the Attorney General of the Federation. In other words, even after the court sanctions such a request, the Attorney General of the Federation has the power to stop the process from being carried out."

"What about the fact that I have maintained my offer to return to the United States of my own free will? Why is it necessary to go through all these processes when I can simply purchase my ticket and return to my home in the U.S. and report to the authorities voluntarily?"

"Perhaps I can raise that issue in court. But why would you make such an offer? I have read these documents carefully and I have found that the charges against you are simply not extraditable offenses. Moreover, the issue you raised about the origin of the request also needs to be addressed. I would suggest we proceed to the hearings. If we are successful, you may then follow through with the process of clearing your name."

"I agree on that score. But I am still not clear on the court procedures. Who will represent the United States at the court? What kind of hearing will it be? My accuser is not in Nigeria and cannot be examined to determine the veracity or otherwise of her allegations?"

"Yes I know, George, the court is not putting you on trial for any offenses. The Federal Government of Nigeria is not bringing any charges against you. You are a free citizen. The court is merely to determine whether or not the request of the United States of America should be granted. In order to determine this, the court must satisfy itself that all, I repeat all the criteria stipulated in the Constitution are met."

"Hold on Fetus," I interjected. "You could have fooled me! Did I hear you say that I am a free citizen? How would you like to visit that building back there?" Through the window, I pointed at the concrete cell block which was clearly visible from where we sat. Is that your idea of the home of a free citizen?"

"Mr. Udeozor," he replied, beaming with laughter. I have been guest of a far more brutal government agency than the EFCC. Do you know where I was housed? Underground! No electricity. No water. No mattress. Shit for food. People seem to have quickly forgotten the Abacha regime. Although the Obasanjo/Atiku regime is equally bad, it is still an improvement over what we experienced under Abacha."

"Halleluiah!" I replied.

Festus snickered, but continued, "Let me tell you one of my secrets George. I love Nigeria and I'll tell you why. The experimentation at building a nation combined with the madness that goes along with it is fascinating. Nigeria is like no other country in the world. It is unique. Tell me, is this not the only country in the world where a beggar or a mad man notices a traffic jam and jumps in to help direct traffic? And guess what? People appreciate this effort, applaud and reward them! We may appear crazy here but we are not stupid. I would never live in any other country. Trust me George, Nigeria will be great in its own unique way in the end and we would have built it all by ourselves."

"Amen," I said.

"Now, let me tell you what will happen in court on Tuesday."

Twenty

"You will be arraigned in court on Tuesday, George."

"Arraigned? I will be arraigned?"

"Yes, you will be arraigned. Do you understand what that means?"

"I think I do. I've read enough John Grisham novels in the course of my detention to not understand that word."

"Good. Then you know that you'll be sworn in as if a trial were being held."

"Stop there! That has been my fear all along. How can they put me on the stand and examine me when my accuser is not present in court? Am I now being accused by my own Nation? The whole world has seen the horrible internet junk accusing me of these unthinkable acts! The media both in the United States and here in Nigeria have been reporting these horrendous acts as if the whole thing has already been proven!"

Festus waived his hand, stopping me. "Mr. Udeozor" he said, "the judge realizes that these allegations are not proven facts. His job is not to judge your conduct while you were in the United States of America. His job is to ensure that the offenses which the United States wishes to put you on trial for are extraditable offenses and that, should you be extradited back to the United States, you will receive a fair trial and be treated humanely with all your rights protected."

I exploded. "Festus, I know what I want! It is sad, but I know that is not what the Nigerian Courts will do! How can they demand that I receive a fair trial and be treated humanely when right here in Nigeria they cannot even treat me better than a piece of wood? Tell me that! Huh? Look, the EFCC never cared to question such an odd request for my arrest. Even when a court ordered EFCC to release me, did they obey the court's order? Huh? Tell me Barrister Keyamo, who in Nigeria really cares what happens to me? I know it is only my family and my few friends who really care. I bet you, all this court wants to do is to ship me off to the United States and look good to the Americans. They would not give a rat's ass what happens to me afterwards...."

"Stop," Festus broke in. "But I care George! There are others who care. Why do you think I've been arrested so many times? Huh Mr. Udeozor? Why do you think GaniFawehinmi, my former boss was arrested and jailed at every heartbeat? Come on Mr. Udeozor, you're a man. Perhaps this is your own call to join in the effort to steer the system aright. Let's wage war against these clogs in our system. Come on Mr. Udeozor. Smile."

He had me floored... and I smiled. My heart was completely calmed. I had found my man! Whatever happened next, good or bad, I would take it like a man.

There is something liberating about true, honest effort. Anytime in my entire life I tried my best to achieve an objective, the outcome becomes a secondary consideration. Thankfully, I often achieved success this way. But whenever my efforts went unrewarded, I would not count it as a loss.

Today as I sit to pen down these words, I do not count my incarceration as the cataclysmic loss people everywhere project prison to be. But that is just me.

"Go on Festus. Educate me on extradition. How do we tackle this mess? I will no longer interrupt you."

"Thank you Mr. Udeozor," he said, a relaxed smile lighting up his face. "But I want you to feel free to ask any question at any point during my narrative."

"Sure"

"Try as much as possible to clear your mind of the anger and disappointment you feel about being falsely accused. You will not be brought to trial for those ridiculous charges. That is not what this Tuesday's preliminary hearing is about. I understand the urge to try and clear your name – that is what any decent person would want to do, and I also understand the frustration you feel as a result of your inability to immediately tackle it head-on. Be patient. There are a number of ways we can achieve that after we stop this extradition nonsense. Having said that, here is what we will do. Before Tuesday, my office will file a motion ex parte, asking the court to stop, reject, and discontinue the process of extradition in the case. We will cite several reasons to support this motion. These reasons will include, among others:

1. The three charges in the indictment filed against you are not extraditable offenses, which is in violation of the constitutional requirements that all offenses against a Nigerian facing extradition must meet.
2. Nigeria has no extradition treaty with the United States of America, which is why I believe they first tried to smuggle you to the U.S. using the EFCC.
3. The gravity of the offenses. By this I mean that even if the court accepts some offenses within our system as parallel to the ones in the superseding indictment, those offenses will not be serious enough to qualify as extraditable offenses. The only offenses in our system comparable to these charges are very minor ones. They are not extraditable. In order to be extraditable, the constitution requires that the offenses be punishable as a serious crime in both the requesting country and the surrendering country.
4. The court must be satisfied after considering all supporting documents that you will not be discriminated upon on the basis of race, religion, gender, national origin, or any other stereotype. From what we know, you cannot receive a fair trial based on prejudicial biases which the extensive publicity of your wife's arrest and trial has given the case. In other words, you've been convicted in the court of public opinion without a trial and may not receive a fair trial. To that, add the fact that racial discrimination is still a lingering unresolved issue in the American Judicial System. The courts here in Nigeria cannot guarantee fairness at a trial in the United States with regard to racial discrimination."

Barrister Keyamo paused for a while to sip from a bottle of Swan water which he brought with him. Then he concluded, "Mr. Udeozor, I'm going into these details to simplify the process for you. Tuesday's hearing will not address these issues. Once your case is called, we may not spend over ten minutes on it. The prosecutor will introduce himself or herself to the court. I will do likewise and the judge will ask you a few questions to ensure that you understand the process. He will then adjourn the court after fixing a date for the beginning of arguments."

"May I ask a question?" I inquired.

"Sure, go ahead, ask."

"Who will prosecute this case?"

"A lawyer from the office of the DPP will. DPP stands for Department of Public Prosecution. They work under the Attorney General of the Federation."

"Do you know the lawyer?"

"Not personally, but I've come across her a few times in court. It really doesn't matter if I know her or not. These kinds of issues are quite routine. My knowing her cannot add or remove the merits of our arguments.

"You're sounding so much like you trust the system of justice in Nigeria. That is rather a great surprise to me in view of the impression I have of you."

"No! No! No! you're mistaken. Quite the contrary, I distrust the system very much. That is exactly why my conduct as a lawyer has to be above board. Can you imagine what would happen if I should be found wanting in my ethics? It would be a bombshell. The government run media would go ballistic. This government sees me as a pain in their "you know where" and they would like nothing better than to catch me in a compromising position. Besides, I'm a Jehovah's Witness. That is something most people do not know about me. I kind of keep my religious beliefs private."

"I could never have guessed had you not told me. Barrister Keyamo, there really are many sides to you. I am impressed the way you're able to keep things in proper perspective. People out there actually believe you're an attention-seeking, celebrity-friendly lawyer while all the time you're really working on their behalf!"

"Things are not always what they appear George."

That is so true. And that also brings me to my next question…concern really."

"Ooh? Okay, shoot."

"Well, I understand your position about the process. I understand the fact that, although the allegations against me are out there in print and electronic media, they are not supposed to influence the judge's decision. But you and I know that both the prosecutor and the judge are human beings who have feelings and are bound to show sympathy for my accuser—especially in view of the nature of the allegations. Believe me, those allegations are spurious lies, but you have to admit that they are very convincing particularly in the absence of a rebuttal from me. There is not even a single evidence of exculpatory nature out there competing for the sympathies of the public. I have tons of witnesses from even among this young lady's family—people who know her motives and those in whom she or her family members have confided. I just feel this judge, whoever he is, is not as unimpeachable as you appear to believe."

"Look George…"

I interrupted him. "And barrister Keyamo, I have a confession to make. My decision to seek your counsel, I mean, to hire you was made in large part because of your relationship with the media. They love you. And although the government detests you for that, they pay close attention to everything you say, everything you stand for. I can believe that there is a love hate relationship operating right here. This is one cultural lesson the whole world seems to be importing from America and inculcating into theirs. When information is put out there in the media, a majority of the people who read or view it believe in the veracity. No further research is done. 'That's the way it is' was the way Walter Cronkite of the CBS evening news usually put it. As far as most who have heard, read, or viewed my story are concerned, 'that's the way it is'. Think about it. Who am I to challenge a story put out by the FBI, Washington Post, the large networks in America, WTOP in Maryland/Washington DC, etc.? Also here in Nigeria, This Day, Punch, Vanguard, Guardian Newspapers, even the major television channels. I don't know these people—the prosecutor and the judge, but my belief is that they're likely to be influenced one way or the other by a publicity of the magnitude which my case has received".

Festus did not say it, but the look in his face said it all. I knew he had heard an ear load from me. He sat there contemplative for a while before speaking.

"I've heard you Mr. George. You made a lot of sense and I tell you what, let us go to court on Tuesday. After that hearing, I will visit you here again. We will make a decision then on that issue. How does that sound to you?"

"Sounds good to me."

After Keyamo left I remember thinking, "Boy, this guy is definitely not the loud mouth people try to make him out to be. He is certainly a very knowledgeable guy."

The government-run media regularly portrayed him as loquacious and arrogant. Now I knew better.

Twenty One

I was in a very despondent mood when I called my Barrister, Festus Keyamo the next morning, Monday February 17. There was a simple explanation for this.

The previous night, after my meeting with him, I had returned to the cell and been approached by several friendly inmates, Simeon topping the list. They had monitored our meeting closely. How they did it remains a mystery to me. My only commentary today, after having experienced life behind a few bars is that there is a universal human relations skill among inmates the world over—an uncanny ability to tap into information no matter how secret it is classified.

These inmates had a consensus of opinion that I had chosen an attorney quite unwisely. They all acknowledged Festus as one of Nigeria's smartest attorneys if not the very smartest. They all however, believed his reputation as an activist who was in constant war of words with the government would surely hurt my case. They all insisted that his strict adherence to the provisions of the constitution with reference to the rules of legal procedure failed to consider the political realities of Nigeria. This, they suggested, cost Barrister Keyamo most of his cases which required political horse trading. Cases just like my own.

The more they railed out their views, the more I liked Barrister Keyamo. That is, until they shifted the focus to the judge and the prosecutor.

Listening as they described the presiding Judge as a government agent with a reputation for returning a nearly 100% conviction rate in favor of Federal Prosecutors and often in reckless disregard of constitutionally guaranteed rights of the opponents of the government, my confidence began nose diving. The inmates alluded to case upon case where this same judge, the one to whom my case had been irrevocably assigned, had thwarted all court rules including twisting the arms of the chief judge in order to have cases selected for hatchet work by the government, assigned to him. Once on the bench, this judge had been known to be fiercely defensive and protective of the position of the government on virtually all issues. They surprisingly credited him with high IQ, but accused him of applying that gift of intelligence toward cleverly circumventing laid down rules to deliver any ruling of government choosing.

As if this reputation of pathological judicial misconduct on the part of my assigned presiding judge was not enough to tame my thirst for justice, they brought in the story of the Federal Prosecutor to whom the DPP had assigned my case for prosecution. They described her as hateful and repugnant, always seeming at war with all men. They said she was probably the most unqualified lawyer employed by DPP. They said she tries to compensate for her scant knowledge of the law by her vicious castigation of the opponents of government. They concluded that the duo of this prosecutor and the presiding judge were the government's judicial patsies.

The transition from a free, contributing member of society to an idle, tagged property of government must rank extremely high among the most detested human transitions ever. This is the transition which, when incarcerated, I was forced to make.

The emotional highs and lows associated with this process are legion. My high level of confidence had just been dealt a blow and I needed it pumped back up. No one did so better than Keyamo. I telephoned him.

After listening carefully to my concerns about the presiding judge and the prosecuting attorney, Festus sad, "Look George, in the unlikely event that these guys are correct, there is a remedy. It is known as the Appeals Court. If you've been following the recent rulings of the Appeals Courts, especially their rulings on the election petition cases, you must have noticed how the rulings of the lower courts are being systematically overturned. Trust me Mr. George, your matter will receive the right kind of attention, hopefully at the lower court level. But in the event it does not, a higher court will deliver justice. It is really a new day in our judicial system. The era of corruption and ineptitude are being curbed, especially at the level of the Federal Appeals Court. Now, listen to me, get a lot of rest today, groom yourself properly and be ready for court on time tomorrow. I'll see you at the court before proceedings. Okay?"

His words worked like healing balm. The inmates who had rattled me with the disturbing information about the unethical practices of the high court judge in collusion with federal prosecutors looked expectantly at me as I got off the phone with my attorney. Not wanting it to seem as if their advice yielded no fruits, I told them that Keyamo had agreed to file a motion requesting a change of judge. I even went further to say that he had accepted that I should bring another attorney into my team who might have channels for a more political approach to resolving the matter.

They all applauded my smart handling of the issues they had raised about Keyamo who they again described as brilliant although in their view, better qualified for legal battles in a different judicial arena. Everybody was happy at bedtime when we said the Christian prayers. I received immeasurable good wishes for divine intervention at my arraignment.

Twenty Two

As dawn began signaling its arrival early Tuesday morning, I was already up, dressed and ready. I was finally going to have a day in court. Although Barrister Keyamo had explained that at arraignment the process was cut and dry, I fully intended to vent my anger and frustrations with the system that allowed such flagrant abuse of my fundamental human rights.

At about 7:30 AM, I and two other inmates who were also bound for Federal High Court, were led into a white nine-passenger bus for the one mile journey. The driver backed the bus down the short driveway and then onto Okotiebo Street which was already filling up with vehicular and pedestrian traffic. It took us a few minutes through the slow moving traffic to hit the busy intersection of Okotiebo and Awolowo Roads.

Over one month had elapsed since I last saw vehicular traffic. As a consequence, the sights and sounds of normal life, the hustle and bustle that characterize Nigeria's unique life-on-the-street, everything goes, high energy traffic jams had faded away from my immediate consciousness.

Now back on Awolowo Road, on the very short, one mile drive from EFCC Okotiebo to the Federal High Court Annex located a short distance from where we were caught up in the traffic jam, I watched the spectacle of Awolowo Road rush-hour chaos, aghast at what I saw.

It struck me with wonder how normal the scene appeared. Keyamo's paradoxical assertion that he would choose life in Nigeria over any other country because of the unapologetic spirit of tolerance and acceptance with which we Nigerians have embraced this chaotic way of living jumped into my mind.

I thought, "Son of a gun! Festus is right! Here's what makes the Nigerian unique; an enigma to an increasingly globalized human existence. Nigerians have the ability to make light what would have been considered a complex, impossible situation in virtually all other countries of the world. The unique ability to playfully untwine that impossible web of confusion and chaos, sometimes even without the involvement of law enforcement, and proceed as if nothing was amiss.

I realized then, watching this odd mix of people—my kit and kin, from costermongers to bank executives, all jostling for their individual and family livelihood, that none of us can escape from who we are. Not even spending a lifetime in America or long periods of incarceration can alter the essence of my life. This is who I am—one of these folks. It is indeed our way of living, our culture that prepares us for the seemingly inexplicable rate of success which we record in other countries, even in unfriendly environments. What the world often ignores and denies Nigerians credit for is that we are the world's most friendly people.

I resolved with determination that since I could still identify with this chaotic lifestyle after years and years living in America, then I would not allow life in confinement to change me either. Whatever the outcome of the unfolding drama, it would simply become part of the field trip which my life had unwittingly turned into.

~

We arrived at the court complex just as the time was coming up to 8:30 AM. Within the compound there were several buildings, some of them bungalows, but the main structures were one or two stories high. As I later found out, the smaller buildings housed mainly ancillary services to the courtrooms which were in the one or two story buildings. My matter was assigned to the Judge who presided over Court 10.

The escort led me into the door marked court 10 which was located within the main structure of the connected web of smaller buildings through a side door which was to the left of the building's main entrance.

~

Perhaps because courtrooms are usually quiet or maybe because of the unpredictability of the drama of any day in any courtroom, the entrance of a defendant is usually greeted with excited chatter from courtroom observers. It is of course easy to tell when a defendant enters a courtroom, for most often they are escorted by law enforcement officers of one type or another. In my case, my escorts were two; one plain clothes EFCC agent and one mobile police officer.

~

The courtroom was packed full of people, most of the lawyers draped in their black gowns, white button up collars and wigs. It did not matter what they had on underneath the gown. The lawyers took up about six of approximately nine rows of benches in the courtroom. The remaining three rows were the rows in the back of the room near the entrance through which we had just entered.

In this courtroom full of people, one man stood out like a bride at a wedding party. You could not help but notice him. He was the only white man in the entire courtroom.

Because of the oddity of his skin color, his casual American attire—slacks and tee shirt, his short hair and stern military posture, I had a good guess who he was.

Because I knew who he had to be, anger welled up from within me. I quickly suppressed this negative emotion to keep from making a foolish spectacle of myself.

He had to be the American, my fellow United States Citizen, perhaps an FBI agent but all the same, a fellow American, who having failed to have me smuggled forcibly to the United States, has now suddenly discovered the legal avenues for achieving the desired goal. It remained to be determined for whom he was working.

Twenty Three

As I was being led to the witness box, the room fell silent. It was then that I spotted my lawyer, Barrister Festus Keyamo seated at the front row bench with other lawyers who I could not identify. They sat to the right side of the aisle, close to the witness box into which I was ushered.

To Keyamo's left, on the left side of the aisle were two female barristers who I assumed immediately to be the prosecution team. It turned out later that I was correct.

It was after I was seated in the witness box that I first noticed my brother Paul along with other family members and friends all squeezing their bodies into the limited space on the benches which were packed with observers. I returned my gaze from the back to the front row and settled on Keyamo who gave me a reassuring grin and a confident nod of his head.

Suddenly, out of the far corner of the room from where I sat, behind the judge's platform, a door flew open. A police corporal emerged, carrying a briefcase with him. He walked briskly up the platform and laid the briefcase on the judge's desk. He then stepped down and turned to face the side of the platform. He cupped his right fist and banged it on the side of the desk producing three boom sounds; Boom, Boom, Boom. He shouted "Court!", and silence settled on the courtroom like cloud cover.

The eyes of all observers and lawyers shifted to the door out of which the corporal had just emerged. As that door swung inward, everybody struggled to their feet.

Out of the open door, a lean figure of average height, dark complexion and appearing of middle age emerged and strode up to the platform and behind the large desk. He swept the courtroom left to right with his eyes. Apparently satisfied, he sat down like a king claiming his throne, his eyes still sweeping the audience.

With a tone thirsty for respect he commanded, "Sit down." This judge clearly made no effort to mask his expression of smirking condescension for just about his entire courtroom audience.

He turned to me and asked, "Who asked you to sit?"

Puzzled, I replied, "You did sir, I just heard you say sit down to all of us."

As I made my reply to the judge, I noticed that one of the court clerks along with my barrister and a few other lawyers were all gesturing toward me to rise on my feet and disengage from my dialogue with the judge.

I complied, rising to my feet.

The judge, satisfied that he had put me in my place, proceeded to comment on various subjects in courtroom humor which all sounded dry to me but nevertheless drew lots of laughter from the audience of mostly his learned friends.

After making all the small talk and verbally berating a few lawyers about their poor dressing, he turned to his clerk who had remained on her feet all this while, holding a manila folder which she dug out earlier from the heap of worn folders on her desk.

He inquired from her, "Okay Madam, What is our next case?"

A few lawyers found humor in something which I had obviously missed and began a new round of laughter.

The clerk stood like a patient grandmother until all became quiet, then she announced: "The Federal Republic of Nigeria versus Mr. George Chidebe Udeozor, a case of request for the extradition of Mr. Udeozor to the United States of America."

With that announcement, the entire courtroom audience reacted, one way or another. Some gasped. Others who had hardly paid me any attention dropped what they were reading and began stretching to catch a glimpse of the bad guy—*me!*

Yet others began whispering in low tones. There was no way anyone in the audience could miss the judge's pleasure that his courtroom was the scene of such an important international diplomatic issue. His facial expression and body language were enough to betray his obvious enjoyment of this moment

He rubbed his hands together, turned to the bench by his right and asked;

"Who do you represent?"

Both ladies on the left aisle of the courtroom rose and spoke one after the other, each introducing herself as a prosecuting attorney appearing for the Honorable Attorney General of the Federation.

The judge then turned to Mr. Keyamo with the same inquiry.

"My Lord, I am Festus Keyamo of Festus Keyamo Chambers, appearing for the defendant George ChidebeUdeozor. With me is Barrister John, also of Festus Keyamo Chambers."

After that introduction, Festus sat, smiled again with a reassuring air of confidence in my direction, a gesture which he would repeat for the entire duration of the proceedings.

~

The judge, feeling in charge and in total control of even the oxygen in his courtroom now turned in my direction and said, "You may sit down.

I did so.

He signaled his court recorder, indicating that what he was about to say was off the record. The clerk replied that he understood.

The judge then began by asking both prosecuting attorneys; "How many of these extradition cases have we done in the last few years?"

The first prosecutor replied, "I can remember two my lord, but I believe it's been more like three or four."

"Poor memory… what do you remember?" the judge asked, turning in the direction of the second prosecutor.

"My lord, you know I'm still young in the office. It is only the case of Kayode Lawrence and this present one, I mean this defendant, George Udeozor that I've had the pleasure of handling."

The judge burst out laughing. "You mean the fake artist, the fellow that collapsed in the court?" he asked derisively.

"Yes my lord, the scared drug baron, I agree my lord. Even the doctor said there was no symptom of heart problem, and he was neither hypertensive nor epileptic."

"Where then did the foam from his mouth come from if he was faking?"

"It is still a mystery to me, my lord."

"He is seeking to have the case transferred to Abutu. I am sure he would do anything to accomplish that."

"It is so my lord."

"We shall see, we shall see."

~

"Now, Mr. Keyamo," the judge said.

At that same instant both the clerk and my lawyer began waving at me to get up.

I responded with a nod of my head and rose to my feet.

The judge continued, "Have you explained the process to your client?"

"Yes my lord."

They went on with a dialogue that lasted only a few moments. They discussed the attached affidavits, one from Seth Rosenthal of the United States Attorney's Office and another from the office of the Honorable Attorney General of Nigeria.

Barrister Keyamo proceeded to apprise the judge of the notice of preliminary objection which he had filed challenging the court's jurisdiction and the Attorney General's failure to comply with the due process of the law.

For another brief moment, the second prosecutor was brought into the exchange and a three way dialogue ensued during which the prosecutor referred to me as "fugitive criminal." This term, although in the context of this exchange may not have been inappropriate, nevertheless burned me worse than any smith's red hot brand could have. I was glad when the exchange which took place over my head as if I was not there ended.

The moment I saw the American official upon our arrival, I gave up my earlier plan to make a scene in court about the EFCC's abuse of my fundamental as well as my constitutional rights. Not knowing where he came from or who he represented, I had decided to approach the proceedings in a more civil manner than I had earlier intended.

However, just as the three way dialogue between the judge, the prosecutor and my barrister was being concluded, the American got up and walked straight up to the front row and bent over to whisper in the ears of the prosecutor. This struck me as irregular, so I paid close attention.

Everybody in the courtroom showed some surprise at the man's audacious attitude. He was not officially a party to anything going on in the court. He was not a witness. He was not named anywhere and apparently had no role whatsoever in the entire affair—at least not in this court. Moreover the judge had begun addressing the court and required silence at that moment.

The judge went off on this guy; "Who are you?" he queried harshly.

The man froze. He couldn't find the words to reply and so turned to the prosecutor for rescue. I'm sure his real problem was how to address the judge. He did not see him as "my Lord" being an American… perhaps "your honor" might have worked for the poor guy.

The prosecutor, obviously lacking totally, the gift of the garb, spewed out some garbage as explanation which drew a few snide laughter and some frowns.

The judge was forced to spew a lot of his own self-serving rhetoric; "That does not give you the right to come in here and behave any way you like. Do you realize that you are in a Temple of Justice? Nigeria's Temple of Justice? Can you behave so disrespectfully in a court in the United States of America? Huh? Do you think you can now walk into any court in Nigeria and act so arrogantly? So disrespectfully… ?"

The prosecutor jumped in; "My lord, my lord… eh… he is very sorry. He had a very important piece of information relevant to this case. That was why he felt the need to give it to me right away. As I said, my lord, he is sorry and this will not happen again."

"It had better not. You, madam prosecutor, should know better. This is not your first appearance before this temple. Now, have him return to his seat!"

"Yes, my lord. I am sorry," She said, an inexplicable little smirk on her face.

The judge pulled out a little notebook and began studying it. Again, like cloud cover, silence returned to the courtroom. The American who had returned awkwardly to his seat appeared the most quiet and also the most anxious to get some open air oxygen. He appeared to be suffering from acute claustrophobia.

The judge finally declared, "If it is okay with both of you, the court will adjourn until May 6th for the hearing of arguments. He waited for response, swinging his gaze back and forth between the prosecutor and my attorney.

They both, after consulting their schedule calendars and with the approval of the judge arrived at a new, more convenient date of May 8th, 2005.

"This matter is adjourned until 9.00AM on May 8th, 2005." The judge declared.

He then turned to face his clerk and uttered a word which I remember every single day with dread—"Remand."

PART TWO

EXTRADITION U.S.A.

"There is no one so enslaved
As the one who believes they're free"
~ Goethe

"A society that will trade a
little liberty for a little order
will deserve neither and lose both.
~ Thomas Jefferson, 3rd U. S. President

Twenty Four

With a dreaded one word directive from the judge, my fate for the next several years was effectively sealed. *Remand.*

The judge's clerk must have guessed what was coming, for she made herself invisible for a long while after that "Remand" order was issued. In panic, I dashed outside to get some air. Strangely, although I had never been in this situation in all of my forty-eight years of existence, I understood that the judge had decided to send me to prison!

Yes. I was to await trial. Yes. I was not guilty of any offense, unless and until proved guilty. But what was the difference? Huh? I will live like other prisoners, will I not?

That was the question I posed repeatedly to my cousin and her husband who was a lawyer and entirely familiar with the unfolding scenario. I knew that he meant well and was doing his best to console me, but what good did that do me? I was about to be sent to a real prison! I knew that despite his good-hearted effort, my life would never be the same.

I was soon the object of intense negotiations. The EFCC escorts wanted to be rid of me. The warders from Ikoyi Prison and those from Kirikiri Prison were pitching to have me remanded at their facilities. My folks and I thought I did not belong with any of these leeches and should be left alone. But we knew better.

Because we knew better, we laid out our preferences to my brother-in-law, Barrister Ilogu, who stepped up to help when he saw my diminishing state of wellness. First, he tried to reach the judge to see if he would not allow me to remain at EFCC and try to secure bail which would make it possible for me to attend court hearings from home. That effort failed.

Second, he confirmed that between Ikoyi and Kirikiri prisons, Ikoyi was much more conveniently located. Court attendance and access for family members considered. Kirikiri was out of the question. We settled for Ikoyi and my brother-in-law went to work. He succeeded.

At the end, I accepted my fate and we were on our way to retrieve my personal belongings from EFCC and into a new uncertain future.

It was a much shorter drive back to EFCC during which I sat in doldrums, isolated in the back seat. Then suddenly the bus jerked to a stop and began spinning in reverse. It was only then that I realized that we had just arrived at my much dreaded residence of the past one month.

Before I could organize my thoughts, the EFCC escort had thrown the side door open and was shouting orders at me; "Move it Mr. George, I did you a favor bringing you here to collect your properties. If it was someone else, I would have delivered him to the warders right there at the courthouse. Please let's go. Go! Go! Go!"

In bewilderment and confusion I ran into the cell, the mobile policeman on my tail, threw my collection of personal belongings together and as I stumbled out, unable to answer the barrage of questions being raised at me by my soon-to-be ex-cellmates, I heard someone say, "George, better take your mattress with you. There are no mattresses where you are going!"

I froze on the spot instantly. Experience is the best teacher. Memories of my first day in a cell, on that filthy concrete floor at Amawbia tumbled into my mind sending me back down memory lane. Not wanting a repeat of that ordeal, I ran back into the cell to retrieve my mattress against agitated calls from the escorts ordering me to re-enter the bus.

It was fast becoming a way of life for me. To be prepared at a moment's notice for any number of orders; stop, proceed, desist from any activity without question or choice. As I sidled through the crowded cell passageway which was cluttered with dirty, stinking mattresses, I tried to block off the voices coming at me, inquiring about the outcome of the court proceedings. I wondered why they could not put two and two together—the outcome was obvious from the expression on my face. It did not go well! Was that not clear enough for these guys? For crying out loud!

I picked up my already folded mattress and went off without a word. Now, I had become the picture of homelessness. That was the way I felt I looked—like the skid row dwellers that carried their entire worldly belongings with them everywhere they went.

In my mournful struggle to keep my composure I was slowly failing. The mobile policeman apparently observing my anguished look but not wanting to incur the wrath of my official escort spoke to me in a low tone; "Deeye, deeye (meaning: take it easy) Mr. George, here, let me help you." He picked up my overnight bag containing various food items, dishes, cutleries, and the like which had fallen away from my grasp.

I thought; "Only in Nigeria!" I knew in my heart that I made a very pitiful sight to all who watched and could see me then.

"Thank you very much," I managed between my sobs and my strides.

We got to the bus which hardly waited for our entire bodies and my baggage to get on board before speeding away.

As it turned out, Ikoyi Prison was a mere walking distance from where we were. Who in God's name would have known that? This was not your average Lagos tourists' destination. Not that I would have offered to walk instead. Or that they would have taken pity and given me all the time in the world to say my goodbyes. It would simply have been comforting to know that the current transition and torment would not last much longer.

Twenty Five

A green and white colonial portal embossed over the top with the seal of state authority announced boldly that we had arrived at Ikoyi Prison, Lagos.

From my seat in the back of the bus I could see a familiar small group of people that stood out in the crowd of animatedly worried strangers, the type of scene which in my erstwhile life, I simply avoided.

The familiar small group of people was a gathering of my family and friends who had traveled ahead of me to Ikoyi Prison to lend me their indispensable hands of support and encouragement. God, being all-knowing and merciful, seemed to realize that I could not have made it all alone and so, urged them along.

~

Until this day, I had the kind of dread for the vehicle Nigerians know as Black Maria that could only be described as haunting and loaded with ill omen.

For those old enough to remember the days when the Nigerian Judiciary carried out the death penalty by public executions under the recalcitrant military administrations of the nineteen seventies, this dread cannot come as a surprise.

There I was at Ikoyi Prison, and for the first time in my life, I was pulled up side by side with not one, but two of the dreaded Black Marias which for all intent and purposes, as far as I was concerned, were vehicles for the conveyance of only the mortally doomed. No one else knew the torment I secretly suffered at the prospect of being ushered into one of these vehicles at any time in the future. Having heard how some condemned prisoners asphyxiated in these vehicles before arriving the venue of their planned execution, who could blame me?

~

As I battled the many torturous afflictions of my soul, my EFCC escort battled with the paperwork that would relieve EFCC their burden of liability over me.

Finally, the time came upon us. The paperwork was done. It was time for prisoner transfer.

Thank God for family. The burden was shared just as if we all earned this scourge together. My brother-in-law, Chidi Ilogu, because he was familiar with the modus operandi at this prison, moved ahead of me and the others to see a man he described as the DCP (Deputy Comptroller of Prisons). He was supposedly at the helm of the Ikoyi prison management.

After Chidi disappeared into the DCP's office, the EFCC escort charged with my transfer emerged from the small gate which was to the side of the main portal, waving his hand in which he clutched the official transfer documents. The mobile policeman jumped off our bus and in military fashion, ordered me out.

I grabbed my mattress and in one instant, my brother and one other family member were at my side to give me a hand with my other properties. As we entered the gatehouse, I went rigid. I was frozen in disbelief at what I saw.

A crowd of about thirty gaunt and totally disheveled men of various ages squatted on the dusty concrete floor of the passage. At least three warders stood in their midst with batons and whips lashing out to keep them in line while two other warders stripped and searched two prisoners at a time right before all visitors; men, women, and even children!

My brother and others kept nudging me from behind to get moving as I stood paralyzed with my mouth in my throat.

It took the mobile policeman's harsh voice to return my limbs into motion, bringing me right in the midst of the group of squatting miserable souls.

From their looks, you could tell that these inmates were mostly men that had been badly battered by life and were now being vilified by the system.

It was interesting to observe that even the warders who were shamelessly rough handling these poor souls appeared in no better physical form than the prisoners themselves. They simply had the advantage of hiding there equally battered and gaunt frames inside their unkempt uniforms. These uniforms, their claim to authority, provided them the official mandate to intimidate, humiliate, and then disposes the prisoners of any valuables on their persons. I followed these events in horror wondering whether I was soon to receive the same baptism of fire as these poor souls.

It is amazing, the ability invested in the human mind to adapt to near impossible situations. When faced with few or no choices like I was, I have learned from my experience that a person may live or die based on what he believes. Everything depends on the individual's ability to internalize these beliefs and conjure them up at the relevant times, for it is true that our beliefs escape our minds in time of great hardship.

I found that in the past several weeks of incarceration, my life had narrowed right down to the thoughts in my head. Nothing else mattered but what my head told me—what I believed.

My beliefs in my current situation could lead me to either triumph or doom. I had chosen to be led to triumph through my beliefs so I had only to focus on conjuring them up and letting them guide me.

Right there in the prison gatehouse I began reciting in my head, the thoughts which I believed had guided me thus far and which I was convinced would guide me through the rest of my ordeal. I call it my God mantra:

- ✓ God is goodness and goodness is of God.
- ✓ Goodness is bonded to an undesired but inescapable companion known as evil.
- ✓ Only the invisible God is capable of breaking this bond of championship between good which is of Him and evil which is not of Him.
- ✓ Evil rules the world. Presently.

I did not know what lay ahead for me. Not even in the next heartbeat. But one thing I believed was that my war was against the forces of evil, regardless of where the physical enemy was coming from. Any adversary of worth must never be faceless. So, although a face had begun to emerge, it never should have been hidden in the first place, and even now that there is a sketch appearance, a silhouette of sorts, I ask… where is the beef? Will my real adversary please stand up!

It had taken me nineteen long years to earn the United States citizenship. All of my seven children were born in the United States of America; they all live in the United States and are hoping to contribute positively in the advancement of the American society. All these facts in addition to my own humble efforts which at last count had resulted in the employment of over twenty five American citizens in good paying jobs—I was not about to throw all that away!

It is doubtless that America made me who I am today. I make no pretenses about the privileges I enjoy. They extend even to my own native country, Nigeria. For without evidence of what America had given me, my own country of birth, Nigeria, would have given me nothing. Hurrah, the proverbial line, "a prophet is not recognized by his own kit and kin."

This is precisely why even with the appearance of Mr. FBI agent at the court proceedings, I remained disinclined to believe that the United States of America, the country to which I owed my sense of self-worth, was seeking to have me smuggled, forcibly extradited or railroaded back to the jurisdiction of Maryland. All I needed was a response to my letter and I would have happily shown up in Maryland at no expense to the tax payers.

Now, faced with my current situation—the humiliation of jail time in the deplorable conditions of Ikoyi Prison, one of the most notoriously overcrowded and most deficient prisons in the world, would it not have been more sensible for me to immediately waive my due process rights and return to the United States? Wouldn't it make more sense if only to escape the abuse which I had just witnessed and which I would surely own myself in due course?

Such had been the power of my conviction, or power of my faith, or power of my belief in America. Until my current ordeal, I believed the United States was incapable of injustice—that the system of justice in the United States was self-correcting. That even when a mean prosecutor, crooked judge, or biased jury, as a servant of the State imposed an unjust punishment or misused their authority in the name of America's institution of justice against any person, the invisible hands of justice upon which the foundation of the united states rests would clandestinely rise and reset the misdeed of the mean, the crooked, or the biased State servant… I was wrong.

My misplaced conviction was one of the many illusions which I had often mistaken for truth. Illusions which I am afraid many in the world share. Sadly, events of recent times have left us all wondering whether America is deliberately shedding the very ideals that made it the greatest, most loved nation in the world.

I refused to entertain the lucidity of the changing face of America and chose instead to believe that a different adversary was on my trail.

My thought was interrupted by my brother in law, Chidi, who emerged from the office of the DCP calling my name and motioning for me to join them. He could not have come at a better time it seemed, because he halted the evil designs of the warders who had shifted the focus of their attention to me after assaulting every last one of the inmates who earlier squatted at the passage of the gatehouse.

The head among them, a rotund, scabrous old warder with the ponderous bent of a vulture was still heaping abuses on me for failing to affix the "Sir" prefix when I responded to his order for me to squat down. The fact that we were to become good friends in the days that followed would have been enough to stupefy anybody who witnessed our brief exchange. (The Nigerian culture is uniquely structured to forgive and forget sins against each other).

He had turned toward me and called out, "you over there!" I looked in the direction of his call, not knowing that he was referring to me. I had heard his colleagues refer to him as "Baba Ade," so when he made it clear it was me he meant, I answered, "Sorry Baba Ade, I thought you were calling one of your men."

"Goodness me, prizonaar! Wetin you call me? Baba Kini?" He thundered.

"I thought your name was Baba Ade. Pardon me, am I wrong?" I asked with a shaky voice.

"Listen prizna, you don't think, you hear me? Next time you call me Baba Ade, you go tell weda na you be my wife wei born Ade! You hear me, prizonaar? You hear?"

I did not utter a word in reply. I gazed at him stunned as he made a word salad of broken English and his Native Yoruba.

He continued, "Let me tell you, as far as you are concerned, my name is Oga. You hear me? Prizonar, you hear me? Any time I call you, you answer yessir. You de hear me? Yessir, Oga Ade. Finish!"

Chidi walked right into the commotion, waiving and ushering me into the office of the DCP who was clearly visible behind him, waiting for me to enter. As I entered there was silence everywhere. Baba Ade became ice, his tirade prematurely terminated. Nobody else spoke.

"What is the commotion out there?" The DCP asked as I entered the office. My brother-in-law was shutting the door at the same time.

"Nothing Sir," I answered, not wishing to begin my journey through Ikoyi Prison as a target of ill will. "They were joking with words sir," I explained.

The DCP, apparently satisfied said, "Okay." He then went on to introduce himself to me directly. After he finished speaking, my brother-in-law Chidi and his wife, my cousin Helen, both explained to me in our native Ibo language, the cost of purchasing me a peaceful accommodation within the prison complex.

It turned out that a premium of N50, 000.00 (about $500.00 USD) was the going fee for residing in the "Whitehouse," the apex housing unit at Ikoyi Prison. For that amount, the inmate purchased a space in one of the six eight-man cells "Whitehouse." Supposedly, inmates in this housing unit would live there trouble-free in the course of their stay at the prison. I was soon to discover that the promise was as empty as a politician's campaign promise.

One step lower, was the housing unit known as the Sheraton. That accommodation would set prospective occupants back about N20, 000.00 (about 200.00 USD) with a commensurate promise of safety and comfort.

There were the other levels of accommodation between the Whitehouse at the apex, and the general housing units where criminals ruled supreme. At that base level were four dormitory- styled housing units known as A, B, C and D wards.

As I recall, "D" ward was the ward most noted for housing some of Nigeria's most notorious criminal elements. I was soon to discover things for myself.

Meanwhile, the DCP called the attention of his orderly and instructed him to see personally to my admission into the prison.

"Take this man to records. His name is Mr. George," he began. "Stay with him to make sure he is treated well. He is not to spend the night in the welcome cell. After records, take him to Aminu at the Whitehouse. Tell Aminu to situate him and then come back here with Aminu to see me."

"Yes Sir," the orderly replied, and turned toward me; "Oya Mister George, let's go."

I turned to my cousin and her husband and we said our goodbyes.

Out at the gatehouse, I said goodbye to my brother and other family members. It was a very emotional parting. Never to be forgotten.

Twenty Six

What can I say about my life behind bars except "thank you" to my maker, from the bottom of my heart? I recall, as if it were yesterday, that first night of my life in a real prison at Ikoyi, February 22, 2005.

Whoever God is; a whirl wind; a great man on a heavenly thrown; the forest of Congo and Katanga; a Buddha in Asia; a voice of divinity; a constellation in space; whatever He is, He was with me at Ikoyi, Lagos that night. He has indeed remained with me throughout my field trip through life.

It was all very surreal; stepping through that second gate and having it shut behind me. The jangling, clinking, clattering sound of the chain used to secure the gate. The ominous initial feeling of being swallowed and devoured by a mythical giant monster which lingered over my entire being as I struggled to get my belongings; mattress and all, through the gate, remains as vivid in my mind today as it was on that fateful night.

Only a skeletal number of office workers remained in the office as it was well past working hours, so there was an almost ghostly silence behind the gate. The DCP was apparently unaware how late it was when he instructed the orderly to get me processed. The orderly himself, in complete familiarity with what needed to be done, failed to point out how late it was to his boss.

The moment we entered, it is if a veil of darkness had been pulled over my eyes in my anxiety I hadn't noticed that the light in the DCP's office was supplied by a battery operated lamp. Darkness had descended on the compound while I was in the office of the DCP. Baba Ade and a couple of warders were all that remained with my folks when I said goodbye to them. Their only source of light had been just one kerosene lantern and two battery operated torch lights in the hands of two warders plus the little left of nature's light.

As my pupils readjusted to the small volume of light still being provided by nature, my thoughts went in one inexplicable flash to one of the games we played as children. In this game, we smoked rats out of their homes (holes in the ground), just for the sheer joy of chasing the poor, innocent, blinded creatures around until they became exhausted and could no longer run or hide.

It was interesting, I recalled, how sometimes some resilient rats fooled us. They remained in their hole as we pumped and blew thick, hot smoke into their dead end cul-de-sac hole-in-the-ground abode until the very last seconds of their lives before they scampered out, usually too tired to present us the opportunity of a good chase. Interestingly, those were the breed of rats that survived. They survived because in most cases, we gave up the labor of blowing smoke into the ground believing that no rat could possibly have survived all that smoke. The survivalist breed of rats would wait us out before crawling out to safety. Although some of them eventually died of asphyxiation or hypertension, most of them survived to taunt us in the future by outrunning us in a game of chase.

As I looked at the high 15 feet walls surrounding me in all directions, I was feeling exactly like one of the resilient rats at the beginning of one of our childhood games of chase. I could not identify who it was that hunted me. But although my eyes were being bombarded with smoke, I was determined to survive and taunt my tormentor at the end of the chase.

The DCP's orderly told me that it was too late to process me through the record office. He told me to leave my belongings on the dusty ground where we were and follow him. I did as instructed and followed him into a building across from the gatehouse. The two remaining office staffs in the building, tired from their long day's paperwork were expecting us. They quickly recorded my information and were about to open the door leading to what they described as the welcome cell when the orderly informed them that I was one of the "ajebotas" (pampered or privileged) on a one-way admission into the Whitehouse. There was going to be no welcome treatment for me, thank God.

"Oh, ooh, ooh, Mr. George, okay" one of the clerks exclaimed. "You have settled Oga already? Now it is our turn. Oya, settle us too. No be only Oga de chop. I hope you know."

I understood. He meant I that I should bribe them as I had done their boss, but I feigned ignorance and asked; "Settle you? I thought it was illegal to settle people for doing their job, right?"

"Kai Mr. George. Look at your skin. Na you be the real pay master. I have to thank Oga for leaving us for night duty. You have to settle us well. In Nija, settlement can never stop o. Your papers say you live in Abuja. You know say Abuja settlement better. Oya, oya, oya, settle us so that we can close."

"Mr. George, please find them something so we can go. It's getting late now. Oga will be closing any time now oooo (please)," the DCP's orderly interjected.

"Okay," I said, dipping my hand into my trouser pocket and pulling out two crisp N500.00 bank notes (about USD $10.00), "this is all I have left." I handed them each, one of the clean notes.

"Now you're talking," the first recipient quipped. Tonight will be bubbling at home!"

"Thank you Mr. George," the second warder said. Welcome to Ikoyi Prison. We will see more of you later. We know it's not a picnic, but since you're here already, don't let it wear you down too much, okay?"

That was a change from the usual assault and intimidation I had witnessed all evening. I tried to memorize this guy's face. Perhaps I had found my first friend at Ikoyi Prison.

With the day' official red tape now completed, we began the long walk to my new home, the famous Whitehouse at Ikoyi Prison.

I had earlier been briefed about what to expect but because the briefing came from one of my childhood friends, Dan Okafor, who had never been incarcerated, I took his advice with only a half grain of salt, although with much gratitude. He did however, supply me with valuable information about a prominent inmate residing presently at the Whitehouse who he believed might be of assistance in getting me adjusted to my new life. The prominent inmate was Emmanuel Nwude, alias Owelle Abagana.

Although I had not heard this gentleman's real name prior to arriving at Ikoyi Prison, I was completely familiar with his reputation and his alias by which he was known not only in Nigeria, but internationally, especially in Brazil and the United States of America.

It was Emmanuel Nwude, alias Owelle Abagana who allegedly masterminded the world's largest single bank fraud by deception (popularly known in Nigeria as 419 or obtaining by false pretenses). Through a web of deceptive meetings and promises of unrealistic windfall profits, Owelle and Co, was able to relieve a major Brazilian bank of the whopping sum of US $240 million!

As I noted earlier, and as is clearly demonstrated in every one of these "successful" fraud schemes, the fraudsters specialize in manipulating their victims and taking advantage of their greed. As I was to discover, Owelle Abagana and his co-conspirators would have been unable to perfect their deal had the Brazilian bankers who they defrauded not been inordinately greedy. But this is a complex subject of which I had no knowledge at all. I would talk to Nwude when I met him. For now, I had to concentrate on staying alive.

Down, midway into the concrete jungle of Ikoyi Prison, the orderly led me through yet another huge gate with rusted steel bars. There was no guard manning this gate but to the left of us as we entered, a smaller gate presented a view that shook the fear which was already festering within me out to the surface.

The orderly who was assisting me with conveying my belongings took immediate notice and began smiling. "I see you've never been inside a prison before," he remarked.

"No, never," I said, still panicked.

"Don't worry Mr. George, as you will soon see, the Whitehouse is very different. It is secure. Nothing will happen to you." He tried to reassure me.

We veered to the right into a long walkway between high walls that seemed higher than the 15 feet which I earlier estimated them to be.

The images of the half clothed crowd that stretched inward from the gate we had just passed and the plethora of odors oozing out of the barred gate trailed along with us down the walkway to the Whitehouse gate.

"Was that the sick inmates ward?" I asked the orderly.

"No, no, no," he replied. "That was the 'B' ward. It is just too crowded. Those inmates are waiting for the lock-up time. That's why they're outside. The warder is allowing them to get some air before lock-up. The prison is just too crowded. It was built to hold about 600 prisoners but we have 2,400 prisoners right now. It is very bad, but what can we do?"

"You're telling me that the prison is carrying about 400% its normal capacity?" I asked.

"Oh yes. Even that is far better than the police cells and the Federal Prisons at Onitsha and Port Harcourt. Nigerian prisons and police cells are badly overcrowded. Honestly. It's very sad indeed."

"They sure are," I said, wondering what my life in this place would be like.

Upon sighting us from behind the gate, a young man, built so powerfully you'd think he was Mike Tyson, flung the small gate open and brusquely sprinted up to us and with one swift movement grabbed the mattress away from my grasp and flung it on top of his head. At the same instant he snatched the two bags away from the orderly and began strolling ahead of us through a crowd of men sitting in disorderly fashion all over the "T" shaped compound created in the middle of three rows of dormitories.

"It's okay Mr. George," the orderly promptly assured me. "He is a Whitehouse helper. Helpers are young prisoners from the general wards who come over here daily to assist residents of Whitehouse and Sheraton with their chores and errands such as dry cleaning and cooking. In exchange, they get to eat well and stay out of the wahala (chaos) of the general cells. I tell you honestly Mr. George, life is not easy at the general cells. You will see that soon enough. It is survival of the fittest."

"Where is he going?" I asked. "He doesn't even know me or what we're here for!"

"You'll be surprised at how fast news travels here despite all odds. He knows more about you than you can ever imagine. Watch and see."

The powerfully built young man disappeared into the end unit of the longest row of the three dormitories—an imposing structure in comparison to the other two buildings which lay parallel to each other and directly in front of the block known as the Whitehouse.

The orderly led me into the same unit right behind the young man and my belongings. The young man had already laid my belongings down and was beckoning us to come right in with a wave of his right hand. His broad white teeth were gleaming as he happily announced, "the captain is waiting inside for you. Welcome… ha, ha, ha."

I knew I was not mistaken that the DCP had instructed his orderly to take me to one Alhaji Aminu, but this was no time to bring up such observations or any mix up. I was sure the orderly knew what he was doing. Moreover, the "Captain" was staring up at us from his lower bunk on a six spring double bunk bed that looked one century old.

The captain obviously earned his rank judging by his looks. Even though he was in a sitting position you could see from his tall frame, the rewards of nature and years of physical conditioning radiating from his lean and taught physique. He was all muscle as evidenced by his bare upper torso. A few scars held the tale of years of active duty in whatever field he previously cultivated. My first guess was a life in many fields of war, but I was wrong.

He was soft spoken but with a deep voice accented in harsh syllables.

"Tunday, I see you've brought us a good brother," he began. "Please have a seat," he said, waving at two makeshift stools placed behind a makeshift plank table. "My name is Captain Ayo, but around here everybody just calls me Captain. It is convenient because I am the only captain in the compound. Can I ask what your name is?"

The orderly answered him, "Captain, his name in Mr. George. Please explain the rules to him. Oga wants Aminu to come to the gate with me in reference to him. While you two gentlemen talk, I will go and inform Aminu so he'll be ready."

"Okay, brother Tunday, this won't take us too long," the captain responded.

The orderly got up to leave and I was in strange land again. It felt like each time I became relaxed with any person, then they'd have to leave or I had to be taken away!

The captain must have been reading my mind because he turned to me right then and with a gentle voice said, "Mr. George, relax. Nobody is going to harm you here at the Whitehouse. I remember my first day here. I felt as isolated as you're feeling. It is a dangerous place quite alright, but the Whitehouse is safe. It is good that you arrived late. The trouble makers have returned to their wards for lock-up. Tomorrow morning, I will show you their leaders, they will leave you alone. I hope you brought some money with you. Meanwhile, let us discuss the rules and regulations of the Whitehouse. Come with me."

I followed the captain to the passageway through which I had entered the cell. On the wall, just before the entry/exit steel paneled door, a wooden tablet hung suspended on a rope. It was simply titled "Laws of the Whitehouse."

On this tablet was scrolled laws and punishment for breaking them. The laws ranged from minor infractions such as poor hygiene through the more serious offences such as smoking marijuana and all the way to the horrible offence of sodomy. Punishments ranged from simple monetary fines to physical discipline. For the mother of all offences, sodomy, offenders are given the mob treatment.

Staring at the tablet, I could only think about the pictures I had seen of the Ten Commandments scrolled on a stone tablet. I stared in awe knowing that these laws and punishments were not the work of idle minds but rules which must be taken seriously, especially because no due process existed.

"Mr. George..."

The sound of my name coming from the captain returned my mind to the present.

"Yes Captain Ayo, I'm sorry, these laws... em, em, I was kind of lost reading them. Are they for real?"

"Oh yes", he replied. "You see, the State lives by rules or else this place will fall apart. Prison rules are stricter than the laws on the streets. Here, there is instant judgment. At the Whitehouse here, I am the I.G. which means the Inspector General. Aminu is the Provost and Tunday is the C.J. which stands for Chief Judge. Offenders are brought before us and judgment is rendered instantly. The fact is that here at the Whitehouse most people respect themselves, so we hardly have problems with anybody. It is a different story at the general cells. Each of the wards has its own officers and even more protocols than we have. At the general cells of A, B, C, and D wards, they have stricter laws and offenders are tried every day and punished accordingly. Instantly! No red tape." He paused.

"Now, let's talk about the State... I mean the Whitehouse. Here, we maintain this block by ourselves. Let me show you around. At full capacity the Whitehouse was designed to hold 48 inmates. There are three entrances into the Whitehouse. Each entrance leads into a passageway which splits the cell into two units. Each unit, left or right holds eight inmates."

He began walking me through the facilities. Along the passageway there were long benches with assorted cooking utensils—stoves, pots, and pans, strewn on them. On one of the stoves, a blackened pot sat with food stewing in it. Just past these improvised kitchens, two concrete step-ups led into a shower in the middle of two toilets which were obscured my two dwarf walls. The captain explained that the shower served all cell occupants while the right flanked toilet served the cell on the right side, leaving the left flanked toilet for the inmates in the cell on the left side of the passage. The point of the walk-through was to pre-empt any question or reservation I might have when he informed me that I had to pay a state fee of N50, 000.00 (about 500.00 USD) to him. He then took me behind the Whitehouse to show me two 2000 gallon cellophane water tanks which he explained were installed by the residents of the Whitehouse.

When we returned to his cell, the captain took time to explain to me that in Nigerian prisons, the operating law is survival of the fittest. Every prisoner's welfare is basically his own affair. By pooling the funds of the residents of the Whitehouse through the collection of N50, 000.00 State fees per inmate, an attempt is made to cater to their collective hygiene and security needs. But ultimately each inmate is on his own.

It seemed ironical to me that the three most important functions which any functioning government owed as a right, a *fundamental human right*, to prisoners or any detainee under its custody— hygiene/health care, feeding and security were the least concerns of the Nigerian government.

The question which repeatedly begged for answers in my mind since my ordeal began was, "if it was all up to the government to decide the fate of prisoners, shouldn't protection, feeding, and proper health care be part of the bargain?" As far as I had observed, what little effort by the system to provide these needs was as best, grossly inadequate.

As far as I could tell, all inmates, whether in prisons or police custody, who wished to retain any meaningful semblance of good physical and mental health had to provide it by themselves, ipso facto. Period! It appeared as if the government was suggesting that healthcare, nutritious food and decent shelter were somehow no longer necessities but luxuries!

Even more troubling, was the personal security of prisoners of lack thereof. The only aspect of security important to the system, it seemed, was the security against escape. From my observations, the authorities would rather account for a dead prisoner than an escaped inmate.

Captain Ayo pulled me out of my sullen introspection to inform me that we had to go and see the Provost, Alhaji Aminu.

The provost of the Whitehouse, Alhaji Aminu, turned out to be a very interesting young man.

In the history of Nigeria's intermittent love/hate relationship with military dictators, no personality has intrigued me personally as has General Ibrahim Abacha. Perhaps because by accident of chance in the early nineteen eighties, I drove into his home at Alexander Road, Ikoyi, which was adjacent to the home of my friend Air Marshall Ibrahim Alfa for whose gate I had mistaken Abacha's.

Abacha, who was the Chief of Army Staff and Minister of Defense at the time received me personally because his guards had let me through his gate unchecked because I arrived in Air Marshall Alfa's car with the window tinted black all around.

The exchange between the General and I left an unforgettable impression on me, but I never met him personally again all through his tenure as the President of Nigeria, which lasted seven years (1990-1997).

Aminu, the Whitehouse provost, was one of Abacha's BG's (body guards) up until his controversial death in 1997.

Aminu Mohammed, the Whitehouse provost had a body that fit the job of a body guard like a tailor-made suit. His solid 6'2" frame easily conceals a mass of muscular flesh that was sure to tip the scale over the 230lbs mark. His appearance alone was enough to persuade an uncooperative adversary that it was time for a change of heart.

He spoke very little, and when he did, it was in a low, almost shy voice that made you expect more clarification. You are left unsure when to begin your response.

"The DCP has spoken to me," he said. "I told him that they do their thing at the gate. We do our own thing here."

After a long pause, I had no idea whose turn it was to speak. Nothing he said so far made any sense to me. I kept my cool and Captain Ayo thankfully jumped in.

"Yeah," the captain said, "I took Mr. George around and showed him how we maintain the place. He understands and he has already paid N10,000.00. He said he will pay the balance next week."

"That's good," Aminu resumed speaking. "Otherwise we will cut them off as I explained to him. I cannot take nonsense from them. They cannot tell us how much to collect and expect us to maintain all the payments."

I now understood. The DCP had requested to speak with Aminu in order to weigh in on how much they should request from me as State fee.

Thus, within my first hour as an inmate awaiting trial at Ikoyi Prison, I had already begun to understand why the Nigerian prisons and detention centers became dysfunctional institutions. The inmates appeared to have more authority than their jailers. As the saying goes, "he who pays the piper dictates the tune."

I had to discount a great portion of the assurances of safety given by the prison authorities. They simply could not guarantee my safety. From what I could so far gather, my fellow inmates had much more to say about whether I lived or died while at Ikoyi.

Aminu and Captain Ayo both decided to assign a bed to me in the cell shared by Captain Ayo and Shola who was the Whitehouse C.J. (Chief Judge). It was a sobering discovery that it was they and not the authorities who decided where inmates were housed once the inmate was assigned to that dormitory.

I was glad to discover my bunk was the one directly across from Captain Ayo's. To my mind, that meant that any intending interlopers would be mindful not to incur the wrath of the iron fisted captain who I had finally discovered was the captain of an oil tanker being detained at sea on charges of bunkering.

~

On account of the very late hour, the duo of Captain Ayo and Aminu Adjourned addressing any further issues relating to me until the morning of the next day. It was, however, the beginning of a long night for me.

Twenty Seven

It was a hot and humid night, a perfect weather condition for insects and reptiles. I lay on my back looking up the wall beside me. Two wall geckos were making a play for food, I believe they were trying for the mosquitoes perched on the walls and windows bidding for the right time for their next meal of our blood. I watched the geckos run up the walls and then upside down over my bed, looking down at me. It was all so surreal. Me. In prison, and a meal for mosquitoes! A waft of breeze blew into the room carrying a stench so strong the captain woke up. He noticed that I was awake and advised me to try and catch some sleep. I thanked him and continued gazing at the geckos.

Meanwhile the captain rises from his bed, picks up a blanket, and walks to the window south of our beds. He throws the blanket over the window and secures it at the top with some weighted rocks. When he returns to his bed he explains that throwing the blanket over the window is the only way he can keep the stench from suffocating us. "Unfortunately," he explains, "the blanket cuts out the air from the cross ventilation, resulting in more heat and more sweating." He shows me a bucket of water which he swore was boiled and good to drink. "Just like bottled water," he jokes. "You need it to rehydrate after much sweating." Before the captain returns to sleep, he tells me that the stench was coming from an open sewer line which runs straight from the general cells right through the back of the Whitehouse. I put two and two together and figure out what manner of air we have to inhale all night long. I am certain that there would be no sleep for me through that first night.

I went to America because I believed it to be a land where opportunities exist for all willing to work for it, where merit is rewarded and mediocrity is discouraged, where the quest for human perfection retains only the humility and not the arrogance found in success and where justice and equality is the foundation of societal values.

I found all I ever dreamed of and even more in America, but I also found what now I consider my nightmares in America. I wish my dreams had warned me in advance about these nightmares, since in nature, good and bad always exist side by side.

It seems today, realizing my dreams about America had been unfair to me, for I only looked for the good in America and not the evil. But I found both. Sadly, I was unprepared for the evil I discovered.

Now, I am caught between two lands, worlds apart. One which I hate to love and another which I love to hate, both of which seem to love and hate me, all at the same time.

America, it appeared, judging from the extradition documents, was seeking for me to be returned to her bosom in order to punish me. I lay in my bed wishing it was out of love for me, just as a parent would punish his/her child. But deep down, I knew it was out of loathing for daring to carry my dreams as far as I had.

Nigeria, it appeared, judging from the same documents, was seeking to be rid of me out of fear of America. I lay in my bed wishing Nigeria would reconsider its actions and for once, stand up for her loved child and explain to America that her son had only erred in his attempt to be a good child by contributing toward reducing his parent's burden. I truly and sincerely believed that is what America would do for any of her children, even her adopted children.

As it is in nature, so it is within our spirits. As my disillusionment grew, my angst naturally turned more against my biological parent – Nigeria, than my adopted parent – the United States.

As the wall geckos, the mosquitoes and the mice were busy all around me occupying themselves in activities to keep their digestive systems from rumbling, I too needed some activity to keep me from falling over the edge of sanity in my new trap.

I crept out of my squeaky bed as quietly as I could, searched through my bag as quietly as I could and secured a ballpoint pen and my exercise notebook. I placed the notebook on a wooden stool and began instinctively writing about my observations in Nigeria that troubled me the most. Here are two of the several writings which I penned down that night:

1. THE CORRUPT POLICEMAN

Starched collars, belted trousers
Entrance backdoor, exit front door
Pretend Sheppard, public foe
Public's boogeyman, looter's guardian

Perverted justice, crippled truths
Filtered statements, blood-stained nails
Hammer protest, suppress dissent
Tyrant jubilant, masses forlorn

Highway mint, go-low twenties
Avid schemer, licensed killer
Masses bleeding, nation melting
Earlobe frozen, conscience atomized

My tribe, his tribe
Our tribe, their tribe
Help me, hate him
Spare us, roast them

Nations cancer, people's cross
Barbarous tumor, surgical knife
Willing surgeon, public theater
Diligent patriot, public welfare.

2. THE LAST DESPOT

Perfidious tyrant, infinite ambition
Portly character, ungracious presence
Known intransigent, socially intractable
Whimsical personality, Oedipus morality

Diagnosed malady, Mobutu Syndrome
Economic agenda, capitalize privatize
Kleptomaniac treasurer, tyrannical looter
National resources, farmhouse property

Political ideology, bombastic lies
Strong-arm tactics, proletarian disdain
Filched heroism, narcissistic despot
Dismal achievements, colossal ruins.

One learns every day. Writing my thoughts and feelings down was so relieving, so calming, I almost didn't feel the mosquito bites anymore. I lay there feeling satisfied with myself. I read and re-read THE LAST DESPOT with a wicked smile on my face. "Yeah," I thought, "that's what you get for abusing the people's mandate with impunity. For robbing and betraying a nation, while all the time spewing false sound bites that convince only your yes men Cabinet."

It must have been at least 4:00 in the morning by the time I sailed away. I slept so deeply that the mosquitoes must have felt very thankful for my cooperation with them during their mealtime.

In the morning, early in the morning,
In the morning I will rise and praise the Lord...
Rise up and praise the Lord,
Rise up and praise the Lord,
The Lord is good..."

The same lyrics as usual, the same time, as early dawn began filtering into the cell where I lay sleeping.

But this time, there was something different. I could not tell this new sound from what I was used to, but I knew there was a different flavor to it.

I turned over, trying not to wake up totally. I was not ready yet to face the future. But the mattress felt different. It no longer felt stiff and flat. Instead the squeaking sound of worn springs gave me a jerk from underneath. Nothing felt right except the pleasure of sound sleep.

But my instincts for wellness, the alarm bells of nature, shook away that enjoyable feeling without further delay.

It was then that I realized that EFCC cells had become part of my past. I now had a new, totally different life from the day before. Amazing that such transition could happen so fast.

The high pitched lyrics were accompanied in a soul-moving rhythm by musical instruments of various sounds. The beat was faster than the all-male vocals of the same songs which we sang at all our morning devotions at EFCC. The only problem here was that this morning, the sound of the music was coming from afar. I could not tell how far, but under the mistaken assumption that the gathering must be for all willing participants, I got up and began rummaging through my belongings to find my hygiene things so I could quickly clean up and join the group.

The captain returned to the cell just in time from the shower to direct me on their morning routines at the Whitehouse.

"You're up," he said. "I was trying not to wake you because I noticed you were up most of the night writing. Are you writing a history book or something?" he joked.

"No, no, no, "I replied. "Not a history book by any stretch. But what I'm writing is guaranteed to bring a smile on your face. As a matter of fact, I am writing down my fantasies."

"Uhmmm," he laughed, "that must be interesting can I read?"

"Sure," I said, "but I have not finished. I'll let you read it when I finish. Hey Captain, can I go to the morning prayers? I can hear people praying somewhere near us. Is there a central prayer assembly every morning?"

"Ha, ha, ha, Mr. George," I wish it was so. But to answer your question, the answer is; no. Every dormitory has its own prayer arrangements and schedule. The provost and his officers are in charge of that. If you listen carefully you will notice that the praise and worship songs you are hearing, they are all coming from different groups. The loudest is from "B" Ward which is closest to us. We used to have our own prayer band but after most of the Christians were released or sentenced, they were moved out. The band gradually disintegrated. But I will introduce you to our other cell mate. He is also from the United States. His case is just like yours. I'm sorry, maybe just similar to yours. He went through extradition hearings in the same court as you, with the same judge. His case is over now and he will be leaving for the United States any day now, possibly today. We just don't know. Come, let's talk to him. He and I say our prayers together every morning."

"Really?" I exclaimed. "Is he leaving voluntarily or is he being moved fugitive style? I mean, did he fight his extradition and lose?"

"Well, I believe he had no chance of winning and so did not really fight. I believe he simply went through the formalities. I really do not understand the process very well but I know that he had no chance of winning because he was tried for fraud in the United States and found guilty. He escaped jail time by jumping bail and running back to Nigeria. After two years he was arrested here in Lagos. That's why I think his case was not winnable."

"I see. You're right. His case is quite different. In my situation, I'm not even sure that the process is authentic. I had no case when I returned to Nigeria in 1999. Even as I speak to you now, I still cannot understand the charges against me because the allegations were made two years after I left the U.S. Even then, I'm willing to return to the United States and face trial voluntarily. I made a request for explanation of the charges against me, but the U.S. Embassy neither responded nor granted me permission to return voluntarily.

"That's okay. George. Here, I want you to meet Chris. We were too busy last night to discuss your case. I think we should say our morning prayers first."

"Sure, let me brush my teeth and clean up quickly, "I said.

At about 7:15 AM on February 23rd the four of us, Captain Ayo, Chris, Shola, and I were bowed down in prayer. Captain Ayo led us, imploring spirits of mercy, compassion, forgiveness and grace to dwell among us. I was again the odd man out. No matter how hard I tried, these prayer warriors beat me hands down when it came to interactive invocation. They spoke in tongues, quoted chapters and verses. Every last warrior outperformed the last warrior until it was my turn. I called for the Lord's Prayer and we zapped all the way through the "for thine is the Kingdom, the power and the glory, forever and ever, amen." I should have stopped right there but no. Reflexively, I went on; "hail Mary, full or grace…." Then I noticed I was alone and so, promptly stopped! I was later to learn that Catholics are rare in prisons. Catholic converts are however numerous; most of them converting as a ploy to seek charity or early release.

"Okay, alright." I stuttered embarrassed. The captain jumped in and concluded the prayer session.

The morning devotions concluded, the captain said he had to fix breakfast. He generously offered to make enough fried plantain and egg stew for everybody, myself included. I was thankful for his offer although food was not my primary concern that early in the morning. Since meeting Chris moments earlier, I had been dying to sit for a detailed conversation with him to find out as much as I could about the whole extradition process. I believed that his experience would help me review the wisdom of putting up a fight in the first place.

Whatever detailed conversation I expected to have with Chris was however not to be. Just as we were about to sit and begin talking, the DCP's orderly came in a hurry to our window and banged hard on it. When he got our attention he announced, "Hey Chris, the DCP wants to see you. I've called Adesanya to come open your cell. He will be here any minute. The DCP says you should get ready. The Americans are here to get you!"

Moments after I met him, just before we prayed, Chris had suggested casually that he was ready anytime the Americans came to get him. I envied his courageous mien then. But now that the messenger came with the dreaded message that the time had come, I could swear I saw the young man shudder and begin sweating more than normal, much more than any of the rest of us. I did not think any less of him, but I was surprised to see that his earlier cockiness was merely a show.

After observing this young, new acquaintance of mine handcuffed and shackled to a seat in an FBI van with nothing on him but a pair of unbelted jeans and sweatshirt, not even a single personal item of value to him, I decided that God willing, I would not be treated so dishonorably.

As Captain Ayo and I returned to the Whitehouse, bearing with us the disallowed, rejected personal belongings of Chris, my mind was in hell. “Some things are worth dying for, “I thought.

Was this one of such things?

Twenty Eight

"Man," I kept thinking as we walked along the walled walkway back to our housing unit, "if this is not slow death, I don't know what is!"

Darkness had concealed a lot from view the night before when I was admitted into Ikoyi Prison. Now, everything was in view and it did not look pretty. The smell of urine saturated the still, humid air around us. The entire yard looked like a demolition site. Broken down concrete and cement block structures were visible all around the yard. Just behind the record/intake/welcome cell block which I had visited the night before, a sewage gutter filled with human waste was being flushed by inmates with buckets full of water. Their bodies glistened with sweat even so early in the morning. I took notice silently wondering how long a person could survive intact in this environment.

The captain and I did not mention a word of what had just transpired with Chris until much later in the day. I guess we were in denial for a while.

We got back to our cell shorty before general opening at about 8:30 AM. The Whitehouse, it was explained to me, enjoyed many privileges over the general cells. The next block in line, the Sheraton block, enjoyed privileges too but not as much as the Whitehouse. The most significant of these privileges were, early opening and late lockdown of cells, cooking and self-feeding arrangements, conducting family visits in senior staff offices which comes with the added bonus of viewing cable T.V. programs while visits lasted, enjoyment of the only shower/flush toilet facilities in the entire compound, and easy access to officers and official visitors to the facility.

The list, which is quite significant, would make any person who concerns himself with social justice squirm. It made me squirm even before I could actually visit the cells where the general population lived. Out of a total population of approximately 2,400, only about twenty four of us in the

Whitehouse and about twelve others in the Sheraton block enjoyed what I considered fair accommodation in the entire prison.

When I eventually visited the general cell days later, my feeling of disillusionment at the system that would treat their fellow brothers with such ignominy rose to an unprecedented high.

I wished I could somehow bring myself to comfort some of these unfortunate souls; I knew exactly what I would do to the politicians, the bureaucrats, and the business men who feed fat and send their families on overseas vacations at the cost of the blood and even the lives of their poor souls. To this day, man's inhumanity to his fellow man remains a complete and baffling mystery to me.

Because I know that I do not have the heart to throw them into the same dungeons they created, I would simply get the inmates of Ikoyi Prison general cells to decide what to do with these heartless characters. It would be good for some of the criminals who sit in judgment of the others to sometimes taste their own medicine.

By the time I finished taking a shower and dressing up, it was nearly nine in the morning. The compound outside the Whitehouse was crowded with all manner of men, young and old, engaged in one form of activity or another. Some were hawking cooked meals of Akara, fried plantain and ogi, even lunch menus were available. Others were trying to fetch water or simply loitering. Yet another gathering at the far end of the Whitehouse was the source of so much animated chatter, I had to go see for myself. It was hard for me to believe that I was still in the same walled compound when I stepped outside our cell.

The scene was reminiscent of Oju Elegba junction but without the vehicular traffic. For those unfamiliar with Lagos scenes, Oju Elegba is perhaps the most notorious highway underpass in the city. Right underneath the busiest highway overpass all manner of human activities, ranging from street vending up to murder, happen in broad daylight and without as much as a shock effect on passersby. So, there's a dead body over there? So what? Mama Kemi still needs her tomatoes, Ambrose still has pool to play and the book seller has the new edition of Holderness and Lambert to sell to school pupils and their parent who must get their children educated even if there are no employers to hire the graduates.

That was the scene playing out right before my eyes in the compound of Ikoyi Prison's famous Whitehouse.

I stepped out cautiously, aware that many eyes were on me. I had been warned, albeit with some assurances of my safety both by the DCP and Captain Ayo.

Following the sound of chatter, I walked into the middle of the most impressive, crude gymnasium I had ever seen. Sit-up benches made out of rough wooden planks, weights fashioned out of concrete, crude dumbbells, improvised skip ropes, raised squat steps, etc. Everything you needed for a body builder's workshop, except that they were made of the crudest materials known to man.

Judging from the glistening tight muscular bodies of the inmates I could see in action, expensive gymnasium memberships are highly overrated and fraudulent. I had never seen a greater number of muscle men gathered in any single gym.

There are no inmate handbooks or "how to" books that instruct inmates on survival techniques at Ikoyi Prison. You either brought yourself up to speed or you lived to regret your naïveté if you survived… and that's with a big "IF".

The guys at the make-shift gym were the crème. Even the warders appeared in awe of them. The warders looked and acted like errand boys to these guys.

They simply called the warders attention and, you guessed it, the warder ran off either to shop for his inmate-boss or fetch a newspaper or any object of the inmates fancy. Mind you, newspapers were officially recognized as contraband in Nigerian prisons—among a long list of necessities which were also banned.

Captain Ayo had already noticed me in the audience of spectators. He waved me into the circle of the "big boys" before continuing his sit-ups. He alternated between sit-ups and pull-ups for a while and then came over to join me.

"Let me point out some important people to you so that you start getting yourself familiar with how Ikoyi Prison works," the captain began. "You've already met Aminu. Did I tell you that he is the overall General? He commands the highest respect in Ikoyi. Most inmates respect him more than even the DCP! As you can see, he is also very strong physically.

At the same time, Aminu was bench pressing weights that seemed to me like tons. At 33 years old, 6 ft. 2 inches tall and weighing about 240Ibs, Aminu was easily the most powerfully built man I had ever met. His physique was intimidating and being at his prime, it would be foolish to be on the wrong side of any argument in which he had interest. I could see plainly, the reason he was seen as one of the presidential body guards not to mess with.

"That one wearing black gloves," Captain Ayo continued. "Is Emmanuel Nwude, alias Owelle Abagana. He is a business mogul. He is the one accused of mega fraud of U.S. $240 million by a Brazilian bank. He owns some of Nigeria's best buildings in Lagos and Abuja. I think Obasanjo is just jealous of him. Otherwise, I see no reason he should be here. Anyway, the guy next to him is Azubuike. He is here for murdering his Lebanese boss and robbing him. Azubuike is Owelle's bodyguard here in prison. The one squatting with weights over there is Prince. You should have seen him when he first arrived here. He looked like a sick chicken. But now, two years later, look at him. He looks like a one man wrecking crew. Over there in the corner (he indicated two guys – a trainer and a young man wearing boxing gloves and pounding away), are Tunday and Ade. Tunday is the trainer...."

He must have pointed out over fifteen of the athletic young men busy working out when a warder arrived with a message for me to accompany him to the records office where my presence was required right away. I followed him and for the next one hour, the intake formalities were completed.

~

My late admission into Ikoyi Prison the night before had accorded me a relatively peaceful and uneventful walk through the most treacherous alley I had ever traveled. It had therefore been lost on me that this prison yard was at this time home to some of Nigeria's worst crooks. As I soon got reminded, there were armed robbers, trained assassins, narcotics smugglers, crude and distinguished forgers, clever thieves, even terrorists, housed within the walls of Ikoyi Prison. The presence of the well-established criminals alone was not what made the prison notoriously dangerous. It was more the presence of the young miscreants—thugs who took pleasure in unleashing terror as a prelude to extortion, on selected victims, particularly new comers like me who they christen "alejos." That was what earned this prison its vile reputation. These miscreants known in Lagos as "area boys" are like killing machines out on a cyclical calendar which corresponds with political campaigns for electoral offices. Politicians being the masters of disloyalty, routinely dump their usually well-financed "are boy" at the end of electioneering campaigns. The newly "elected" politicians, now with their stolen mandates, have no qualms using the state security apparatus to erect bulwarks between themselves and the area boys who handed them their mandates. The losers who used the miscreants as well, are now broke and without resources. They are deserted and abandoned by the area boys.

The area boys manage at the end of each cycle to retain their sophisticated supply of weapons, generously funded by the now, inaccessible political sponsors. Until the next cycle of elections, the area boys must eat. They must continue to sustain their elevated lifestyles—at whatever that lifestyle may cost—usually murder for hire and armed robbery of course.

The law enforcement system is also enthusiastic but clandestine partakers in the entire scheme... For good reason too.

The puzzling question is how a police rank and file member with an average family size of nine that includes about seven school age children, is expected to provide the financial needs of such a family on a meager salary which can scarcely sustain the bread winner alone?

With veils of denial pulled over their faces, the high and mighty sit in feigned incredulity, accusing, judging, and incarcerating these miscreants who were created by the high and mighty themselves in the first place. At the end of the day, all Nigerians live in confinement; the rich create their own prisons and the poor are thrown into prisons by the system. The nation ends up the loser.

As I strolled casually toward the alley which leads to the Whitehouse, I observed as one young man close by me broke into a run, signaling as he ran toward the alley gate. Without the slightest sense of danger, I strolled through the gate before an eerie feeling came upon me. The alley was too quiet for an overcrowded prison at about nine in the morning. Despite this feeling, I continued until I was midway down the alley way.

They operated with lightning speed. As I negotiated the turn into the alley of doom, I glanced straight down at the gate between the alley and the Whitehouse compound. The two figures approaching from that end bore no warning signs to signal that I was in any kind of danger until they drew close. Then, it was too late.

Despite the obvious futility of an attempt to escape, I was propelled by a surge of adrenaline to try anyway. But hell, it was a bloody waste of effort.

These guys had practiced and perfected their ploy. Surely, it had to be a repeat performance. I was already being shadowed from less than ten feet behind me by three hoods who were moving in fast. I was boxed in and cornered!

They were seven altogether—the five surrounding me where I stood on trembling legs, heart pumping violently, one each at both ends of the alley way keeping watch. Their leader raised his right hand and all four others stopped where they stood. In his raised hand an object gleamed, sending chills down my spine. The object was a dreadful weapon which left no doubt about the mess it would make of human flesh. Several razor blades were artfully welded or clipped at various angles to a wooden bar.

Holding the bar at its handle, his dead eyes somewhere at my neck, he drew close. He was the picture of Lucifer himself.

The terror in my eyes seemed to please him, so a grin cracked the sardonic expression he earlier wore on his face. Now the look of evil became complete.

Lucifer gestured to two of his lieutenants who moved in on me. They ignored my pleas and went straight for my wristwatch and the gold chain around my neck. They simultaneously lifted the wad of currency in my pocket. I had about N4, 000.00 (about $40.00 USD) loosely bundled in a money wrap. They handed everything to their leader who now moved close to me once more.

"Na me be Manager. They call me Manager. I will keep this money and your jewelry. My money is N10, 000.00. Look, na only N4, 000.00 I collect from you. When you bring the balance, N6, 000.00, you can collect your watch and your chain."

He raised his weapon, this time his boys also showed me their shanks. Then he continued, "If you open your mouth, we will take care of you." Then they were gone.

~

It had all happened in less than 60 seconds. All the while, I was expecting to feel the sharp pains or the stickiness of blood on my skin;

Nothing.

Only the face of this evil crossbreed and his gang hung suspended in my terrified consciousness. I stood there frozen and immobile when Captain Ayo came running. "Mr. George, what happened? Mr. George, what happened?"

Word had already reached him that manager had struck. He had been late, but the sight of Captain Ayo, the sight of a human being as against the crossbreeds of seconds earlier, worked like calming balm on my distressed, traumatized heart.

"They jumped me. I can't believe… you can't believe… what . . . they jumped me!

Captain Ayo led me back to the makeshift gym where Aminu and the rest of the guys were cooling off after the morning's workout.

Not a few of them found humor in the clear expression of terror still showing in my face.

Many spoke but the one speaker whose words I found genuinely comforting was Owelle. The reason was that he had experienced a similar ordeal on his arrival at the prison. We agreed to meet later to discuss that subject privately.

Sitting among Aminu, Captain Ayo, Owelle, and other Whitehouse residents were the provosts and Inspector Generals of the other cell wards. They all constituted the power brokers of Ikoyi Prison, the untouchables who ruled even over the authority of the prison warders within the high walls of the institution. These were the guys of whom the captain had earlier enlightened me. I had to settle them for my stay at Ikoyi Prison to be peaceful.

We made our pact right there and I promised to settle them in just a couple of days, little knowing that, that settlement was to become a mere opening bid for the purchase of peace of mind which these killing machines had now converted into a priceless commodity.

I placed a high value on my peace of mind; they treasured their daily fixes of marijuana and alcohol. "Pay for peace" they said, "value for value..." they get their value first then, I get mine.

Twenty Nine

It was indeed a very long day. By the time dusk signaled the day's exhaustion, I had heard and seen more evil than on any other day in all of my life.

In prison there is no time to learn the ropes. No time to equivocate. You hit the deck running. Very much like an infant attempting to crawl, stand, walk and run… all at once.

By the end of my first full day in Ikoyi Prison, I had learned these lessons:

- Virtues work in reverse in prison. Save your good virtues for the right time and place.
- Selfishness and self-preservation are the hallmarks of wisdom.
- Word economy is a must. Being miserly with words will serve you well anytime and place but it will serve you especially well in Prison. It could save your life.
- There is a need for compartmentalized thinking. In prison, you think like a prisoner regardless of guilt or innocence.
- Your peace of mind is a commodity. In prison it comes at a price.
- Righteousness has its time and place. That time and place is not in prison
- Get yourself in shape. Your life might depend on it.

The list goes on. Even today as I pen down the events that shaped my life in captivity, I have come to realize that these valuable, indispensable lessons are universally applicable to prison life regardless of where they're located.

However, at the time of my initial detention at Ikoyi Prison, an unusual anomaly was in place. Although it is not unusual for prisoners to sometimes grow both influential and audacious, for I had heard or read about such situations a lot, at Ikoyi Prison as at the time of my arrival in 2005, the prisoners were in complete control of all aspects of governance within the walls of the prison. Only the presence of armed guards stationed outside the gate served as deterrence to insurrection. Even then, there were widespread rumors among inmates that a riot was imminent.

The news of my assault, as with all news-worthy events in prison, had spread around the compound within one hour of the assault.

I found it interesting that the intervention of the Deputy Comptroller of Prison, the man who was supposedly at the helm of affairs in the prison, failed to convince Manager to return my properties or even to apologize to me for his actions.

I wondered; in what light was I now supposed to view the authorities in this institution when Manager himself returned my jewelry with a verbalized apology and a pledge of friendship with me, upon the intervention of the other inmates whose authority he dared not challenge?

If I owe a special debt of gratitude to any inmate at Ikoyi Prison at that early stage it is Captain Ayo. It was he who gave me the tips and physical protection from the great harm at the initial stage of my detention. Captain Ayo was a true marine captain. He had the fierce, rugged façade of a combatant. We were the same height 6' 1", but he was lean and mean-looking, with a matching baritone that reached both extremes of gentleness or roughness, as the situation demanded. He was feared, and for good reason. The last person who dared challenge him still cringes at the thought of his ordeal in Captain's hands. The scars remain permanent badges of remembrance and respect for his betters to this day.

But at Ikoyi Prison, you never say never—as in the case of hyenas and lions vying for control over a sumptuous meal. All the hyenas have to do is bide their time and wait for an opportune moment.

The area boys, Ikoyi Prison's hyena boys, operated like the hyenas of the jungle and a number of times, in Captain Ayo's absence I was rendered helpless by these predators. They usually looked so frail one wondered what they would do if they were cornered themselves without their blades and shanks. I bet only a few of them could survive a hot slap and remain on their feet.

But just like the hyenas, they always had the advantage in their numbers and weapons of choice. They also had each other's backs. Their eyes were sharper than the eyes of vultures. I now understood why the police were often helpless with these guys on the streets and highways of Nigeria.

For a great portion of my early incarceration at Ikoyi Prison, I lived in terror. I had seen a few young men from the general cells that had been worked over by the hyena boys with numerous razor blades, so I had no illusions about their willingness to use the same blades on me.

One morning I woke up to find myself all alone in the cell with Manager and two of his hoods. Both Captain Ayo and Shola had gone off to attend to their personal matters.

Manager was definitely a person to avoid. Standing over me, he was the pure image of evil. His lips, blackened by tobacco, were curled up in an evil grin revealing cakes of tarter on his few remaining teeth. His moistened lips and tongue moved menacingly as he began speaking. "I told you my balance is N6, 000.00. You think I'm a fool? Now, my balance is N20, 000.00 and I want it now!"

I thought "oh shit!" where do you begin in a situation such as this? These are not guys who reasoned with you. They do not understand any words outside yes or no. perhaps they will manage words with one or two syllables like 'o.k.' it is easy to connect with "yes." Any other response such as "give me a minute" or "hold on" simply means "no" to them.

Manager and his boys were also wily enough to understand the need to work at high speed. They knew that any waste of time could scuttle their mission and earn them the ire of superior forces. Therefore, while Manager was working to subdue me and make me cooperate, his brother hyenas were ripping through my belongings searching for "his" N20,000.00 (about $200.00)

They managed that evening to relieve me of the cash I had received from my cousin who had visited me the evening prior. Manager showed me his blades and promised to use them if I so much as hissed. Then they disappeared.

I had had it by this time. I had to act in my own defense. It was time to decide on a course of action, whatever the outcome.

Owelle and I had formed a bond of brotherhood by this time. We both hail for the provincial zone formally known as Njikoka Province. But that was not itself what brought about our closeness. We had become tight because the hoodlums who ruled within the walls of the prison had made both of us their prime targets. It was understandable that Owelle was targeted because it had been well publicized that through his 419 enterprise he was one of Nigeria's richest men. I, however, had the misfortune of being "that Nigerian American wee get plenty money." Explanations that I was not rich by any stretch of that magic word fell on deaf ears. They heard none of my denials. As they often said, "Look him body! That man I loaded! His skin just dey shine!" It did not help either, when my breakfast, lunch and dinner were prepared outside the prison and delivered to me every single day. That alone was enough evidence of my wealth as far as they were concerned. I quit explaining how bankruptcy was daily staring me in the face. Explanations were often interpreted as excuses and therefore made matters worse, stirring their anger even more.

Every evening, Owelle and I sat on the Whitehouse pavement sharing the stories of our activities that day. We played our routine game of ludo. Owelle's permanent bodyguard was a young man named Azubuike. He was the Hercules of Ikoyi Prison, bench pressing heavy weights of up to 300Ibs with unbelievable ease. Azubuike provided Owelle partial inoculation against incessant attacks by the hyena boys. But not even Azubuike's incredible hulk physique could provide complete protection. As I earlier observed, the hyena boys were imbued with the same coyness which the hyenas of the jungle apply to outwit their superiors in the contest for kingship in the fields. Although hyenas could never win that contest, to them, quitting is not an option.

Azubuike regularly attended court for his murder trial. Owelle himself frequented the courts for his trial. During these periodic interludes the boys found opportunities to get into Owelle's hair often with costly results.

Be that as it may, from speaking with Owelle, I knew I had to take actions one way or another to reduce my exposure to harm at the hands of the bandits of Ikoyi Prison.

Thirty

Five long days after my first arraignment before my presiding judge, my barrister, Festus Keyamo, paid me a visit at Ikoyi Prison. It was a visit I eagerly anticipated from the moment the court proceedings ending on February 22nd 2005. My mind was a cauldron of burning issues I wanted to discuss with him. Now, a more urgent matter even than my original concerns had taken center stage—what to do about the hyena boys?

Festus arrived with his shirt sleeves rolled up. He appeared battle ready to address all my worries and restore my peace of mind. He did not count on being asked how to battle a hyena.

Instead of the questions which he had prepared for, I asked him to get me the hell out of Ikoyi Prison right away.

When he heard the anguish in my voice, he imagined the very worst. He asked in what ways I had been assaulted.

I told him that if I had been assaulted in ways worse than what I had explained to him, I would be dead already. "These guys are psychopaths!" I exclaimed. "They will murder me if you do nothing!"

"Calm down Mr. George," Festus pleaded. "I will write to the judge to have you transferred to Kirikiri immediately. The only problem is that Kirikiri is a long distance away. Court attendance from there is quite a serious undertaking in Lagos traffic. Are you sure you want to deal with that problem?"

"I'm sure I want to live! That's what I'm sure of! I want some dignity man… my peace of mind!"

"That, I cannot guarantee you. Not even at Kirikiri. But I can guarantee that nobody will be attacking you at Kirikiri Prison. Inmates and staff are respectful to one another there. Don't worry, as soon as I get back to my office, I'll have John type up the request and by Monday, I will personally get it approved by the judge."

"You don't understand Festus," I protested. "I've been under attack daily since I got here! They come at you armed with razor blades and I have no doubt they're prepared to use them if they fail to get what they want! Every last one of them has scars all over from slashes they received. It is hell in here, Festus!"

"You've got to be kidding. What if I speak to the DCP? Do you think that would help?"

"That's a laugh. The warders are powerless against these guys. I worry that they're all in the pockets of the inmates. They've been either bought or overpowered by these guys. Trust me. When I reported to the DCP, he appeared incredulous. Reacting to the report of Manager's incessant attacks on me, he promptly summoned Manager who responded in a heartbeat. I thought my problems were about to be solved. But it was all a show. Manager swaggered into the DCP's office. In the typical Yoruba tradition, he prostrated and genuflected for several minutes. He appeared absolutely contrite when he apologized for his bad behavior. Responding to the DCP's instructions, Manager turned to me and offered what looked like a genuine apology. He then stretched out his deformed, treacherous arm in a conciliatory handshake. As we shook hands he said he was sorry once more, but he then winked at me from the corner of his eyes. Only I could see those sad deadly eyes and what I saw sent chills up my nape."

"I was relieved when the DCP let me out of his office ahead of Manager. There was no doubt in my mind that he would have laid in wait for me at the alley. In the end it was Captain Ayo who stood up for me by beating Manager into a pulp. I know it will take him weeks to recover and I fear that there will be reprisal attacks on me at any time. I am not safe here, believe me."

Festus stared at me stupefied. He was lost for words to express his shock at the state of things inside Ikoyi Prison. He admitted that I needed to be moved ASAP. But being a born fighter he advised me to pull courage from within me and find ways to contain the situation until he could work something out with the authorities at the court and also at Kirikiri Prison. Once again he reminded me that he had suffered many trials and tribulations out of which God saw him through. Similarly, he assured me, if I believed and exercised courage and patience, God would see me through.

~

Upon attaining adulthood, I realized that if I had to make any headway in life, I had to quit relying on God or blaming Him for man-made situations. To my mind, God had already done His own job by creating and arming me with the tools to accomplish my personal ambitions for myself in life. And although God's work in my life and in the lives of all His creations continues, it behooves on us to distinguish between our own responsibilities and His.

Therefore, when my attorney indicated that it was through prayer that I could survive until the Judge approved my transfer, I knew it was up to me to provide my own defenses, for I could not and did not know how to pray for Manager and his hyena boys to all die. Only death, they had vowed, could stop them from surviving the only way they knew how. As long as I was there, they asserted, they must eat from me. When I offered to provide assistance voluntarily to them, their spokesman and leader, Manager said they were not prepared to accept my crumbs. He said that was what "Big men" always did. He insisted that that was the reason he would always be an armed robber. According to him, "How me I got accept chicken change when I can blow you up and take everything? When I carry my AK, you are a small fry for me. You hear? Ahh Mr. Gerorge, you hear?"

Left with no other choice but to try and figure out a way to survive the attacks of the hyena boys on my own, I returned our conversation to the main subject for which we scheduled the meeting. I deferred deliberations on the matter of the hyena boys until another time.

"Okay Festus, I'll do my best to keep a distance between myself and the hoodlums. I'll find some creative ways to keep them from harming me. Now, let us discuss the matter of my extradition. You must have reviewed the entire case by now. What is your opinion on the way forward?"

"Yes Mr. Udeozor, I have indeed. First of all, I am convinced now that the request is authentic. You had voiced your apprehension about the authenticity of the extradition papers. You expressed fear that your wife's friend may be behind the request. What I think is that if your wife has a hand in this, then it must be at her instance that the authorities in America, i.e. the United States Attorney General, now got involved. But I am sure that the extradition request is not a forgery."

"Okay," I said. "If I accept your assessment, then how… explain to me how that man Anuofia, I mean the same person, my wife's boyfriend… how did he obtain copies of such sensitive documents before I became aware that they existed? With all due respect Festus, I know some hanky panky is in play here. But let us move on, under the assumption that the papers are not forged and that the request is genuine."

"Okay Mr. Udeozor. I may not be able to tell you how this fellow Anoufia obtained the documents, but that should not concern us very much. The answer to that question will eventually be revealed."

"Sure, I believe that," I agreed with Festus, "Now, tell me your... our plan of attack."

"Right," Keyamo began. "The first motion which I have filed, the Notice of Preliminary Objection, raises the issue of jurisdiction and requests the court to dismiss the entire proceedings against you," he paused and then continued; "This objection will most likely be denied and the judge will claim jurisdiction to hear arguments. All I can tell you is that although it seems pointless to object to the judge's jurisdiction knowing it will be dismissed, it is still important to do so as a first step."

"After the judge's ruling on the issue of jurisdiction, then based on the assumption that the court claims jurisdiction to hear the case, I will move for early trial. I am determined to have the entire matter resolved within three months."

"Hold it Festus," I protested. "You are not going to file for bail? I thought I could apply for bail. That would give me time to prepare for this trial and also get me out of this god-awful prison!"

"No, no, no, Mr. Udeozor, this is an extradition hearing not just a trial like any other case. There are issues of diplomatic nature to consider here. For instance, the United States of America insinuates in their request that you took flight from the United States simply to escape the risk of going to prison for these offences. They are sure to object to your being given bail. And you know the Obasanjo Administration will never challenge any request from Americans."

"That is preposterous! I had been living in Nigeria for well over two years before the incident that led to this matter occurred. Moreover, it was between my wife and this young woman, Chinelo that a fight broke out. My only involvement was that prior to leaving my wife, I did assist the young woman to enter the United States and also in bringing her to live with my family. But that is an entirely different issue altogether. I will address that when the time for that explanation arrives.

"That is just the matter, Mr. Udeozor. That is why I believe this matter could be resolved quickly instead of pursuing a futile motion to have you out on bail. If I apply for bail, it might take even longer to argue and obtain a ruling on your motion for bail than the actual extradition hearing. And then, if the bail is denied, as I think it will be, then we have to begin the trial from the start. Then you would have spent many months in prison—time which will simply go to waste. Trust me, Mr. Udeozor. Let's go straight to the trial and be over with the whole thing as soon as possible."

"Okay," I said, "I see the logic of your position. But how certain are you that we will prevail at the hearing? How are we going to challenge these ridiculous charges against me?"

"That is what I'm about to explain to you right now. If the judge, as expected, claims jurisdiction, then at the trial for extradition proper, I will use the same arguments; that the proceedings filed at the court by the Attorney General for you extradition fails to comply with the required due process of law. I will now go into details to marshal out deficiencies in the application of the Attorney General and show the judge that you cannot be extradited to the United States of America on the strength of the documents before him."

"Specifically, there are three broad objections that form our argument and I believe they are airtight. There is no way the judge can rule in favor of the extradition without violating the Federal Constitution. The three main arguments are:

1. The procedure adopted by the Attorney General in the case is a nullity as I've already explained; the court has no jurisdiction.
2. The offences of which you've been accused are not returnable offences and the law is specific about returnable offences. They must be reciprocal.
3. All the preconditions—about six or seven of them, necessary for the court to exercise its discretion have not been satisfied. As a matter of fact the Attorney General's submission satisfies only about 50% of these preconditions.

"Look, Mr. Udeozor, I am reasonably sure that unless the judge is under orders to rule against you or maybe if he is personally interested in having you extradited, there is no way he will rule against you. This is why I took your case. I am quite confident of victory here."

I was glad to have Festus Keyamo as my attorney. He continued every time we met, to help me repair my flailing confidence. Keyamo understands the law. But beyond that, he owns something which stands him out among the crowd in his crowded profession. He is able to decipher what his client seeks most, whatever it is; reassurance, confidence, publicity, privacy, etc… he approaches the issue of concern to his clients with wisdom and humility—traits which do not reflect in his celebrity persona. By the time he is through penetrating his clients' innermost thoughts and feelings, his clients are left little choice but to succumb to his approach. He is the most persuasive lawyer I had so far encountered.

And so, once again Festus calmed me down like a burning charcoal slowly doused with water. I agreed not to pursue bail and became determined to find a way to beguile or confront the hyena boys. One way or another, I would delist my name from their list of potential attack victims.

Despite the lucidity and rationality of Keyamo's recommendations for attacking the Attorney General's push for my extradition, one issue never stopped troubling me. The issue was the one-sidedness of the stories making the rounds about me. No media publication, radio, or television event had reported my side of the story—the side which would no doubt slow down or stop the speculative gossips making the rounds in the media about how Chinelo was a mistreated victim of the Udeozors. How I allegedly conspired with my wife to systematically abuse and enslave the "poor victim" without paying her or sending her to school.

Festus Keyamo's view on this total lack of rebuttal or publication of exculpatory evidence was that it would be beneficial and revealing after I have won the court battle to share my story of vindication then. I therefore kept silent about that eagerness bubbling within me. A silence I was soon to regret.

Thirty One

If any condition of living is capable of inducing a wish to self-destruct, it could be found at Ikoyi Prison. It did not come as a surprise to me when embassy officials came and negotiated bail or resolution of the legal problems of their citizens rather than accede to their detention in a Nigerian prison. Such negotiations happened frequently while I was in detention.

A young Chinese man Tsun, in his twenties was remanded not long after I arrived at Ikoyi. He was charged with smuggling textile materials into the country in order to avoid paying the duty imposed on such imports. He was guilty of the offence and tried to bribe the customs and immigration personnel who arrested him. He was unsuccessful and ended up in Ikoyi Prison.

Tsun obtained razor blades after his second day in Prison. Were it not for my personal intervention and dissuasion, he would have slit his wrist and bled to death.

Until today, I still find it troubling that some other inmates who tried to discourage my intervention were actually cheering Tsun on, urging him to prove to them the validity of the claim that when a "white" man died, he actually turned blue. In Nigeria, a person is either black or white. No shade of skin color is in-between. Spanish, Arabs, Indians, Chinese, Jews are all white men in Nigeria. As long as the skin and hair texture meet that perceived classification, they are grouped into that category.

Another incident which demonstrated the decadence and precariousness of life at Ikoyi Prison was the level of alcoholism among inmates at that time. One of the provosts had made a claim that he was the "last man standing" after an evening of wild boozing. The claim prompted another inmate to challenge him to consume thirty shots of kai kai—a local clear gin. He accepted the challenge and during the consumption session, he gulped down thirty five shots before staggering away. When he failed to show up the next morning to see Captain Ayo, we went looking for him.

The warders led us to the gatehouse where his corpse was lying next to the corpses of two other inmates who had passed away from other causes.

In the course of discussing these incidents I got to uncover some vital information which I believe eventually saved my life.

I was shooting the breeze with one warder with whom I shared a love for reading. He purchased a number of novels for me which kept me occupied any time I had privacy, especially at night. During one of our conversations, I complained that the stress of day to day living at the prison was wearing away at both my physical and psychological wellbeing. He agreed, saying that my distress was showing in the way I was gradually deteriorating. I was losing weight and my mood was melancholy. He confided that he could assist me in securing an appointment to be taken outside the prison for medical reasons. All that was required was the cooperation of the medical personnel within the prison. He specifically suggested that the in-house doctor at the prison could make it possible. He explained that once approved, he would be assigned as my guard to the hospital visit. I will then be able to visit my folks within Lagos and experience some normalcy once again.

The information was what I needed to give me hope that Ikoyi Prison would not end up sending me 6 feet under. I took up the task of setting up the initial visit at the prison clinic. As it turned out, my blood pressure had indeed shot above the safety mark. This was the first time in my life that I had suffered the condition.

After that doctor's visit within the prison, things moved so fast, they had to be divine-propelled. Within just a few days I had been scheduled for a hospital visit at the Lagos General Hospital, Marina-Lagos.

There is no doubt in my mind that when, in our lives, we consciously and deliberately awaken the spiritual dimensions of our being, subtle messages are revealed to us, perhaps in the form of premonitions. If we let the sprit guide us, I believe we're able to achieve our goals or avert the path of harm. As they say, to be forewarned, is to be forearmed.

By following the guidance of a trusted unseen hand, I relentlessly pursued the paperwork and was cleared for the hospital visit and assigned my friend as the escort warder. I had two lucky strikes on the very day of that hospital visit.

First, during that very first visit I met a young physician who not only gave me the best medical attention I had ever received anywhere, but also became a friend—a friendship that endured throughout my time in prison and until today. He scheduled me for admission at the hospital. I had however, to return to the prison while the hospital administration department made a secure room available for me.

Unbeknown to me, my second lucky strike of the day; a lifesaving strike had taken place at Ikoyi Prison just minutes after I exited the prison compound on my way to the hospital. I had narrowly escaped a well-planned attack organized by the combined efforts of a group of outlaw inmates and some warders. The outlaws and the warders conspired to open out all notoriously violent hyena boys very early in the morning of that fateful day.

Their mission was straightforward and their targets defenseless—my humble self and Owelle. They were to swoop in on us, and pound and batter us straight out of bed, strip us of all money and valuables even before the official opening of the Whitehouse.

That was indeed what they did except that Owelle had to endure my share of the punishment as well as his own.

The story was that minutes after I left the prison at about 6:00 AM, en route to the hospital with my escort—unknown to the general staff, the perverted warders crept into action. They opened the Whitehouse unusually early but without raising any suspicion. They then opened out all the senior outlaws and finally the hyena boys. The warders then withdrew to the gatehouse turning a blind eye on activities within the compound as the sounds were easily drowned by the usually loud praise and worship sessions.

The unsuspecting Whitehouse occupants, my cell mates, had thanked their good fortunes for the early opening and proceeded to start their morning workout session earlier than usual.

The first batch of outlaw inmates to gather around my cell mates did not stir any fear or uneasiness, since they usually participated in the morning workout. However, when they failed to join in as usual this morning, Owelle turned on a pleasant smile and asked their leader what was keeping them from the action.

What he got in reply was a wham so hard; Owelle hit the ground with his rear. Then all hell broke loose. The hyena boys were led in by a band of outlaws. The leaders momentarily left the trashing of the Whitehouse inmates to their boys while they themselves moved into the two targeted cubicles— Owelle's and mine.

It was said that from the time of their arrival, they fumed with rage that I was nowhere to be seen. The evidence of their rage was visible everywhere from the rummaging they had given to my belongings. It was like the scene of a plane crash.

After beating Owelle to near death and carting away both our belongings—money, electronics, jewelry, clothing, shoes, even hygiene items, and then giving our cubicles each a deliberate run over, they left the Whitehouse in a shambles and laid in wait for me at the alley.

My life had been spared. I had also been spared major bodily injury. I had even been spared the loss of vital personal items which I had carried on my person. But upon our return from the hospital, and totally oblivious of what lay in wait for me, I carried a huge shopping bag of sporting goods, colognes, body lotions, health care needs, packaged food items and entered ahead of my security escort into the main portal entrance.

Baba Ade sat on the edge of his chair at the intake desk looking infernal as he checked me back into the prison compound. Although I shared N1, 000.00 (about USD $10.00) among Baba Ade and the two guards manning the gates, none of them warned me about the looming danger. Even today, I still cannot say for sure which warders were among the co-conspirators in the assault on the Whitehouse that day.

As I made my way into the compound, I found it a bit odd that the usual crowd of young convicts who hung by the gate in hopes of earning some small cash handout for their assistance with chores such as conveying food or other effects from the gate to the housing units, seemed to ignore me this time around. A couple of them who usually ran to my aid in the past appeared eager to talk to me but for some reason could not approach me, they signaled from the edges of the dilapidated buildings or the prison walls but I failed to decode their frantic signals. They watched me crestfallen as I strolled into the alley of death.

It was reminiscent of the first attack of the hyena boys on me. Once again, I was trapped midway down the alley of death. It was also the alley of choice for the hoodlums of Ikoyi Prison for their nefarious activities. Within seconds, my bag of goodies was gone, my wristwatch and Nokia phone had been snatched and I had been socked front, side, and rear. Were it not for the intervention of Owelle's boy, Azubuike, who happened to be passing by, I would have received the beating of my life. Azubuike kicked and chased my attackers away from me where I had dropped to my knees in shock and disbelief. He led me back to the Whitehouse where I got the sobering tale of the out of control assault which had sent Owelle into admission at the clinic earlier that morning.

I sat in stone silence as Captain Ayo, Shola, Aminu, Papa and my other Whitehouse mates recounted the blow by blow account of the day's horrific assault on Owelle. I listened to the story of the frantic search for me and the anger expressed by the bandits upon learning that I was outside the compound and out of their reach. As if in answer to the question in my thoughts, Captain Ayo said that the mob which was surprisingly led by guys who were generally friendly toward the Whitehouse residents showed no mercy. Aminu had to stay neutral or face the ugly consequences of the confrontation with a mob of out of control hoodlums who had nothing to lose.

In the end, not even Aminu himself, Captain Ayo, Shola, or even Papa, all of whom every inmate deemed untouchable were spared a painful brush with the hyena boys when they attempted to rescue Owelle. For some inexplicable reason, Owelle's protector-in-chief, Azubuike was not seen during the no-holds-barred assault.

Everybody in the hallowed Whitehouse was nursing some kind of wound or cut—a sight which despite the seriousness of it, I found irresistibly comical. I fought hard from underneath my breath to stifle the laughter which kept surging from my stomach.

We all knew there would be bitter fallout from the events of that fateful day but we had no idea what form that fallout would take. Time would surely tell and eventually did.

Thirty Two

All in all, it took a total of nine court sittings from February 22, 2005 to arrive at the judge's ruling in my extradition case on June 16th 2005.

With the following concluding statements, the judge sanctioned the Attorney General's request for my extradition to the United States;

"In the light of the foregoing and considering the order under the hand of the Attorney General requesting this court to deal with the case in accordance with the provisions of the Act, it is my humble view that the applicant have placed before this court all the necessary materials for the extradition of the defendant. Consequently; the defendant GEORGE CHIDEBE UDEOZOR is hereby committed to prison custody to await the order of the Honorable Attorney General of the Federation for his surrender to the United States of America after the expiration of fifteen days hereof."

Signed: The Honorable Judge
16/6/05

As the judge read these final words of his very lengthy ruling, I was thinking in my mind; why, your lordship, you belligerent patsy of the despot, you. You have your instructions. Your mind is made up. Why wait fifteen days? Have me shackled and shipped to America tonight!

The entire court process had been a charade—a formality. As learned people usually say… "mere academic exercise." Nevertheless, it was a process already in motion. It had to be followed to its logical conclusion.

From the opening salvo, it was pretty obvious that the Judge and the Prosecutor were in bed together on my case. But with the open and shut nature of my defense, I felt it a worthwhile occupation to remain at the ringside as an observer in my own case.

Everybody in my own neck of the woods knew that at the end of the process, win or lose, I would return to the United States. That much I had already made clear to my attorney. My entire family knew this. Only the judge and prosecutor seemed to be in the dark about this.

My hope in going all the way with the process was partly to begin a process which I hoped would ultimately vindicate me. Lingering suspicion remained in my mind as to the authenticity of this extradition process. But most poignant now was the need through the process, to go on record with my assertion that the entire process was unnecessary. I departed the United States a few years earlier of my own volition. I had done no crime and I was not wanted for any offences whatsoever. I wished to return to the United States where I still had a family, including seven children that I missed dearly. I wished to return a free man. I was willing to answer any allegations against me. But first, I wanted to be treated with dignity. I wanted my constitutional rights respected.

But it appeared clear to me from the proceedings that both the judge and the prosecutor, although in the business of justice delivery, in actuality did not know what justice truly looks like. To them, the destruction of all people accused by the government is synonymous with delivery of justice.

From the days of my childhood I admired the men and women of the legal profession. In the University I played with the idea of reading law but my interest in business carried me in another direction. My admiration of the showmanship of the legal profession however, never died. Instead, I was driven in my romantic life to date a few female lawyers. I was intrigued and captivated by their wit. But upon my arraignment in court, with the junior prosecutor sitting a mere three yards from the dock where I sat, not even my love for her profession could shield her undesirable, dry persona.

It did not appear that make-up did anything for this prosecutor. She always arrived in court wearing a sour expression, lips in a thin straight line. Her face and other visible skin were usually sparsely oiled as if she did not have enough for an even spread.

The prosecutor's longsuffering façade gave the impression that she might have been a house girl earlier in life. If that was the case, then it would easily explain the aggressiveness with which she prosecuted my case. It is doubtless that one who had been abused could never make a good and impartial arbiter in child abuse cases. I was willing to bet that the prosecutor fit my assessment of her, perfectly.

As for the judge, what can be said about a man in his position? No honorable judge would accept a job as hatchet man for any government, let alone a government known to be so overtly oppressive that even the masses acknowledge that they have no government. Between 1999 and 2007, Nigeria was ruled—not governed. This judge thrived in office during this period. I had to admit that any chance of his objective evaluation of the request for my extradition was void *ab initio.* He boasted in open court that his pedigree in law was under the Attorney General's tutelage as a prosecutor—the same Attorney General that submitted the request for my extradition. He openly declared that my barrister, Festus Keyamo, was misguided in suggesting that the Honorable Attorney General of the Federation failed to place before the court, all necessary materials which were constitutionally required for my extradition. He practically suggested that the Honorable Attorney General was infallible.

Yet, the Attorney General's regular abuse of the Constitution in those days, particularly in the resolution of election dispute was so glaring that every proletarian in the country took easy notice. But then, such was the tradition of the ruler of our nation at the time. The constitution was, after all, drawn up at his instance and quid pro quo—by himself. He had the right to violate it.

~

It was a no brainer. The judge had to have known even while crafting his ruling in my case. I would be appealing his ruling. So, hand in hand with the delivery of his ruling, he instructed his clerk to immediately reproduce the copies of the process for Keyamo. He joked. "I know you're heading for the Court of Appeals right away."

Indeed, my barrister had with him, our prepared Notice of Appeal. He had discussed with me the possibility that the judge might find a clever way of shifting the burden of giving a negative response to the Americans to someone else.

It all came down to courage or the lack thereof. Even in spite of the judge's display of fake hubris, we knew he did not have what it took to say no to the Americans. Bullies rarely venture outside their sphere of influence. They detest being humbled, and America will humble you. The world is full of Noriega types.

My barrister was disappointed at the court's ruling for one major reason – he believed the judge was clever and had knowingly and cowardly subverted the course of justice. Career advancement was perhaps his motive, but to Keyamo, that was inexcusable. His main premise for feeling let down was that after the fall of military dictatorship against which Keyamo risked his life on the streets to protest, he had hoped that the gains made in Nigeria's judicial system would endure. The Judge's ruling dealt a great blow on his hopes and aspirations for a country he loves.

Festus stood outside the courtroom with me and my family members and vowed to put up a hard fight against the court's ruling at the Appeals Court. He took time to explain the process to me and pleaded with me for patience and courage.

One part of me wanted badly to throw in the towel right there, sacrifice my right to be treated with dignity and ignore my sense of decorum, get shackled and transported fugitive-style to go face my accusers. The other part of me, the one which insists on holding out, trying my best always, with all of my God-given abilities until I had no more fight in me, won the contest. I said, "Let's fight."

I turned to Festus and went on, "Please do this. Let the judge know that he lied in his concluding statement when he ordered that I be remanded in prison custody to await the order of the Attorney General for my extradition. I have been in custody for nearly one year already. I am willing to remain there as long as it would take for justice to be served."

Thirty Three

I lay in my narrow, sagging, six spring bed, restless. The air is still, thick, clammy with the breath of my sleeping cell mates. It stifles me. I open the make-shift cover with which we keep out the stink from the sewage pipe. Looking out, I can scarcely see through the damp smog hanging like smoke from a burning bush outside the window bars. My pupils begin to adapt. Finally I begin picking out profiles of the adjoining building and the 18 ft. walls.

God is great, I thought finally, dawn approaches! I sit up on my squeaky bed and creep slowly up to reduce the disturbance which might awake my cell mates. Quietly I retrieve my soap and towel and sidle blindly across the room, out the door and into the tiny shower. Ahhh, the feel of clean, cold water on the skin with pores sucking the air for oxygen!

In no time, I am dressed. The morning is still young. The time is 5:50 AM.

My bags are already packed. I saw to that duty the night before. Nothing of my own doing was going to delay my departure or scuttle it. In exactly 40 minutes, at 6:30 AM, the warder, the one that God has assigned to me, would arrive and I would walk out of Ikoyi Prison. We would catch a taxi right outside the prison gate and we would be on our way to Lagos General Hospital in Marina where I would be admitted for the management of my failing heart.

My failing heart? I smiled. No, I thought. My heart never felt stronger, it was my spirit which was wounded. I knew that the moment I walked through those gates and onto the streets, my blood pressure would compete favorably with those of infants once again.

At Lagos General Hospital I was admitted into a private hospital room which had a private entrance. The room was surprisingly spacious, even for the two patients which it was designed to accommodate. A call button, beside lamps, a cabinet—with built-in refrigerator, and a full bath shower were all part of the facilities that gave my hospital room the ambience of a double room in a three star hotel.

From the outside it would be hard to guess that any attention would have been given to the comfort of patients in a hospital that catered largely to the indigent population of one of the world's most populous cities—Lagos. But to my amazement and pleasure, I found both the facilities and services of the hospital professionals to be excellent. My room had recently been painted and still retained the smell and freshness of new construction. The air conditioner worked flawlessly although I scarcely needed it— my windows were usually open to admit the cool sea breeze of Lagos Lagoon through the Marina corridor. In short, I felt like one rescued from hell's inferno and delivered into the heart of Eden.

For three months I was free in captivity—paradoxically speaking. But to anybody who witnessed my hospitalization at Lagos General Hospital there was nothing paradoxical about my claim.

The fact is that the warders assigned to guard me at the hospital knew me. They knew that I would not attempt an escape even if I was paid to do so. Such was my reputation at Ikoyi Prison. How did they know this? Well, for one, after one of my trial hearings, the Awolowo Road traffic had, as usual, ground to a complete halt. The entire stretch of Awolowo Road from Kingsway Road junction to the Race Course was one long parking lot. My warder escort suggested we beat the traffic by hiring two motorcycles. He rode behind me to keep an eye on me. However, a short distance from the courthouse, the guard and his carrier hit the road curb and fell behind. They sustained injuries and their motorcycle broke down. All this happened unknown to us. When we got to the prison gate and discovered that my guard had fallen behind, I instructed my carrier to trace our steps backward. We rode all the way back to our embarkation point but failed to run into my escort. At this point, I returned to the prison gate alone and waited out of the view of prison staff until my escort showed up hours later looking a ghost of himself. He was battling in his mind how to prepare an incident report.

When I trotted up to his side, winking to alert him that nobody had noticed our separate arrivals, he almost toppled over in his tracks. Wide-eyed, he walked up and gave me a hug. He let his friends at work know what had occurred.

It got to be known from this and other incidents at court and elsewhere that I was an unusual prisoner. When prison guards had a reason to worry about inmate flight from custody, my name never came up at all.

The hospital authorities were initially concerned about my free movement around town. They were concerned about possible exposure to liability in case I escaped. After a few days of anxiety they realized that I was not a flight risk and promptly gave up their worrying. That was how I became a free man in captivity.

With my reputation for reliability assured beyond all doubts, I began to press my escorts for more freedom and liberty. I knew quite well they had issues they would prefer to attend to rather than spend their hard-earned money on public transport only to come and spend eight hour shifts sleeping at my door entrance. I took advantage of their needs to make a pitch for my own need for liberty.

First, I came clean with the friendliest among the guards assigned to duty at my door. I told them I needed an occasional walk or visits to the shopping malls of Lagos. Without hesitation, they obliged. We easily convinced the hospital authorities that occasional strolls would help restore my health and strengthen me. They joked in response that I might consider trading places with them since I was now healthy enough to lecture them on the values of exercise.

They cooperated and my first few outings went without incident. But on about my third outing, the Assistant Comptroller of Prisons (ACP) visited the hospital for an unscheduled inspection. The nurses on duty, although they were in on my scheme were caught off guard. They were unsure how to respond, and so contacted my Attending Physician. My quick thinking physician backed me up with the report that I had gone for a laboratory test which he purportedly sent me to the mainland to do. The ACP would've returned to his office satisfied with the doctor's explanation had he not run square into me and the guard who was meant to keep watch over me as we charged up the stairs, clutching several shopping bags full of purchases in our hands. Our attempts to explain the inexplicable fell on the ACP's deaf ears. He insisted that I was clearly well enough to return to the prison yard.

In life, every situation, every problem, every question, has a solution or an answer. The trick is in finding that solution or answer. The ACP's sudden appearance at the hospital immediately created a Maalox moment for me. Returning to Ikoyi Prison so early after my liberation was not an option to even consider. I needed to remedy this situation fast. Now!

"Sir, there's an explanation," my voice quivered as I began speaking. Let us go up to my room. We are blocking the stairs for patients. The hospital authorities do not take kindly to people holding conversation on the stairs and hallways, Sir."

"Sure," he said. And as we began ascending the stairs he continued speaking; "The nurses and your doctor have already explained about your laboratory test on the mainland. But their explanation said nothing about you bubbling with strength and going on shopping sprees. Well, I have news for you. You are still in prison custody. Right now you are looking and acting like an emperor."

"Sir, please give me a chance to explain," I said. But I was thinking, "Phew! He has already spoken to the nurses! And the doctor too! My God! They even covered for me? Oh, what angels they are!"

"Sure Mr. George, you'll have your chance to explain. But I'm not sure it will do any good."

I could hear my own heart as it over worked itself banging on my rib cage as my mind tried to come up with a story convincing enough to explain away my unholy adventure. Unbeknownst to me, my salvation lay in the hands of my accomplice—the warder, standing with his back to the closed door smiling.

Before I could speak, he held his first finger to his lips, "Shhh." He whispered. "Come with me."

He led me to the far end of the room and spoke in a hushed tone…

It's only going to cost you money, Mr. George. Now, you can actually work out a plan so that you can make regular visits to town. As long as Oga knows, you're safe. Everybody knows you have no plans to escape. We all know you and nobody is worried about you, Moreover, it is a shame that you're being held in prison for assisting a fellow human being. It is like this, even though I am lying to help you now, I cannot think of any reason why you would turn me in tomorrow for helping to save your life. It just doesn't make sense."

I said, "Thank you very much for this godly analogy. That is exactly the same situation. Meanwhile, what do we do about your boss outside?"

He said, "Oh that is simple. Find him something big enough to convince him to look the other way. He never saw us returning, if you know what I mean… he never saw us return from town because we never left the room at all, get it?. He visited and found you in your hospital bed, receiving treatment. As a matter of fact, if you make it good every time he comes for inspection, you may remain here until your matter is over."

Now, this was music to my ears. I would have a fuller discussion with this young warder later. Now, I had business to attend to.

As they say… "Money talks and shit happens." Indeed money talked but it was no shit that happened—instead, my life was saved.

That was how my cat and mouse game with the warder men of Ikoyi Prison began.

It began with those initial visits into town accompanied by a warder on each visit. A number of times we ran into the warder's co-workers on the street. It was easy to explain that we were out on a hospital related appointment. I generously rewarded the warders for their cooperation and offered them the option to skip coming altogether if they should choose to stay home. They took the bait and for most of the evening and night watch, I was by myself. Unguarded.

When I began sneaking out by myself to visit friends, go shopping, or to the cinema at Citi Mall, I waited until dark to ensure that I was not recognized by any prison staff that might happen by chance to be in the area. But finally I began to risk daytime outings especially to attend church services on Sundays.

I have to admit that there is an indescribable feeling of accomplishment associated with breaking an unfair law and getting away with it—a certain kind of high. Almost like the high of scoring your first goal.

I understood clearly that if caught by the wrong person on the street by myself, the matter would be treated like an escape from prison. That fear was however not enough to dissuade me from walking like every other free citizen through the narrow streets and alley ways of Obalende, Mandilas and Race Course. This was becoming for me, a new kind of adventure. I was not an outlaw, but I felt like one. Any call from behind me gave me the shivers. Sometimes I would freeze right on the spot, thinking I had finally been caught. I would turn around to discover the caller busy attending to someone else altogether.

At age 49, I had led all my life free entirely from entanglements with the law. If I may indulge in a measure of immodesty, I was good for most of my life. As a result, I made a poor escape artist now that I put myself in a position where I could be legitimately accused as an escapee from prison custody. At the same time I did not give a rat's ass what it cost me. I was going to keep living on the edge as long as I could. The high I got from it was exhilarating. Freedom is priceless!

One time on Broad Street, I had gone to a branch of my bank to withdraw some money. I completed my transaction and the moment I approached the exit door, a senior warder stood frozen on his way into the same bank. We both paused and stared at each other for one moment, speechless. I bowed toward him and exited the bank. When I turned to check on him, he was still standing there motionless. I waved at him and he shook his head. He turned and went into the bank.

I expected a delegation of armed men at the hospital for two days before I realized that this gentleman was a real saint. He had not sold me out! The incident went unreported and nothing was said of it until months later when I returned to Ikoyi Prison once more.

~

I gave the warders reason to trust me and it amazed me that rather than betray me, they would fall with me. I spent my entire period of hospitalization acquiring friends among prison and hospital staff. I hope that someday in the future, I would be able to sit across the table from these people to whom I owe my life to share with them the story of their gifts to me.

Thirty Four

One of the greatest systemic failures of successive Nigerian Administrations on its citizenry is the inordinately long periods which accused people are forced to endure under inhumane conditions awaiting trial. This failure of a system designed to protect the innocent is often waved aside by bureaucrats who refuse to acknowledge their actions as the abusive acts that they really are—criminal abuse of discretion.

Most of the inmates who populate Nigerian prisons remain in custody on awaiting trial status for several years. In many cases, they remain in custody for periods far exceeding the prison tern prescribed for the offence for which they were remanded in the first place. What usually happens is that the criminal elements who are arrested and injected into these populations find the prison a fertile ground for recruitment and training of new bandits. The hyena boys typify these ready-made prospects. They are usually youths brought in from the streets. Their only offences were usually "wandering," which is one word for "being at the wrong place at the wrong time." The common denominator for these unfortunates is poverty.

The Whitehouse was part of their induction into their new career in crime. Their recruiters who also serve as their training officers usually spent a little time in custody before easily purchasing their freedom through one brand of the many brands of "bail" available to moneyed criminals.

During most of my daily visits, I witnessed a retinue of these "bailed" criminals who now drab themselves in "godfather" togas, to pay celebrated visits to their trained recruits who remained behind bars awaiting trial. Dramatically, these recruits—the ones who had successfully graduated in banditry, soon regained their freedom following these visits. They are granted the same bail which had eluded them all these years, i.e. until they met their mentors in crime.

After the assault on the Whitehouse, the internal controls which had kept news of the attack strictly within Ikoyi Prison walls, failed. Inquiries began spreading through the prison community—investigators persistently solicited information from both inmates and staff. We soon began catching wind of possible personnel reshuffle.

From my hospital room, I monitored the events as they unfolded. The more I learned of the rapid decline of order, the more thankful I was to be away from that god-awful environment. I knew, and everybody else also knew that it was no longer a question of *if*, but rather *when* a complete collapse of warder authority would trigger intervention from law enforcement—police or even military. The inmate outlaws had become totally out of control. Marijuana and other drugs of all kinds were easily smuggled into the prison and hawked openly. Attacks on detainees believed to possess interesting valuables, not to mention cash, had become open and brazen. Alcohol consumption, sodomy and rape had become preferred entertainment for the powerful outlaw inmates. Although these practices remained unlawful and were considered grievous sins, only the lesser thugs were punished for engaging in them, unless of course their exposure implicated one or more of the powerful outlaw inmates. It was a period of learning, observation, and growth for my timid mind. I realized how little I really knew about what goes on in the world while my family business and social lives kept my mind focused on their demands.

It happened without warning. At least not the kind of warning I expected. I had expected a more gradual progression toward an assault on Ikoyi Prison by law enforcement. A stand-off while negotiations went on with the inmates the kind I had seen during prison breaks or riots in the movies. But no, not at Ikoyi Prison—I believe, not in any prison in Nigeria either was that even thinkable. Our system seems decided on a familiar approach; spontaneous anarchy.

Lying in my hospital bed with my hand under the bed covers, I groped for the TV remote control as I routinely did every morning. My face cracked into a grin when I recovered it from between my thighs where I had hidden it from the nurse earlier. She had needed an excuse to spend more time in my room and I wouldn't give her one, so she had to leave. I cut the TV on for a moment. The picture on the screen seemed a blur—perhaps because I was not prepared to accept the images flashing before my eyes.

I shut my eyes, rubbed them and reopened them. The images became more real and more incredible. A police armored tank, policemen in battle gear, more battle ready uniformed men from other military formations, vehicles of all descriptions and news reporters were all mingling and milling around the unmistakable background of Ikoyi Prison!

Gunshots rang out as if on a battle ground. Smoke from a burning building mingled with smoke from teargas canisters to give my unbelieving eyes a picture of complete and uncontrolled chaos. Nobody seemed in charge of the combined team of law enforcement officers deployed for the assault. They fired as they ran and took cover. Guards fired their guns from their position atop the 18ft walls around the compound. Reporters, in their confusion, kept dishing out estimates of the dead and wounded. Stories of people trapped in the burning administration and records building. Horrific inferno! Incredible destruction! Armed inmates on the rampage! How in the world did inmates secure machetes and guns? Such explanation and questions filled the air waves. I gazed at the television screen every few hours overnight, incredulous. It was all too surreal!

⁓

At about 4:00 PM, following a few breaks in the transmission of news, finally, the Minister of Internal Affairs and the Comptroller General of Prisons stood in the middle of reporters at a joint press conference, stating how the indiscipline, corruption and decay going on at Ikoyi Prison had been obliterated. They made unconvincing remarks at the low cost in human lives, especially considering the extent of indiscipline among the inmate population. Beads of sweat covered their foreheads as they tried to explain how order which had broken down completely had been restored. They explained that the most troublesome of the inmates had been disarmed and moved to another prison where discipline was not a problem. All in all, they painted a government picture of the assault which was now on its second day of unfolding. Reporters were now able to capture pictures of truckloads of inmates as they were being shipped away to new locations. I lay on my sick bed, sick in my stomach with worry about my friends at the prison. I knew that there was damage control reporting built into the government account of what was in actuality still an unfolding event. I knew that accurate numbers would not be made available anytime soon. But even the government's conservative estimates of thirty dead and dozens wounded was troubling enough for me. I was beside myself with worry.

That night, I received visits from my friend who was also my attending physician, my dietician, and the nurses assigned to me. Each one of them had mixed feelings about the news of the law enforcement assault on Ikoyi Prison. On the one hand they were sad about the high loss of life, but on the other hand, they were thrilled for me, especially because the event validated my assessment of the threat posed by the unruly inmates; an assessment which triggered the fear that ultimately saved my life.

The next morning I woke up early. The television stations had changed their focus to other issues for their morning news. I sat like a statue, feeling both horror and excitement as I watched other new events with no interest. My thoughts were still hovering around the vicinity of Ikoyi Prison. I felt a surge of energy erupt from inside me. Without thinking, I got up and quickly threw on a tee shirt and sweat shorts. I slipped my sneakers on and began working out. It was grueling—as I had abandoned my routine since I became admitted into the hospital. Something told me that I would soon need some energy. After 45 minutes of push-ups, squatting and skipping rope, the sweat was rolling down in streams. I threw the door open and went for a walk around the hospital compound.

When I returned, my guard was at the door, pacing side to side, somewhat nervous. He was my friend and so his presence did not trigger any alarm bells. But I was pleased that he had showed up. I was sure his version of the events that occurred at Ikoyi Prison would be more accurate than the television accounts which had filled the air waves. I practically pulled him into the room with me. I poured us both some juice and sat on the bed facing him on a chair positioned for my guests.

"The situation is very bad, Mr. George," he began. "Honestly, I've seen prison riots before, but this one was horrible! Worse than any other I have witnessed." He paused and began mentioning and describing the dead and wounded. Some names I recognized, some I did not. But the shock was no less terrifying. "George man!" he exclaimed. "One of my egbon (close friend) confided that bodies were everywhere. The armed guards were firing live rounds man! No more friendship… oooh. All my colleagues who usually decried the empowerment of the inmates moved in for the kill! You know Felix and Obaika, the two ACPs. They were like field generals in battle. Those warders you thought were wimps. Woo, they're fired up now. They marched into the yard with batons, machetes and rocks and they were mowing down inmates as if they were swatting flies. No friendships. No sacred cows. The smart inmates sustained only injuries from whips and batons. This was because they wisely stayed in their cells. But they were still not spared horrific beatings. Every single inmate was beaten. George, you're the only one spared. People are marveling at how you managed to escape these incidents. You are the talk on everybody's lips at Ikoyi now. Some warders are joking about how they would've reduced you to a mouse with their batons and whips. Even me myself, I've been wondering about you. God really loves you very much. Somehow you always manage to escape harm. You know what my people say, the first escape is just luck, and the second may be spiritual intervention, but the third time? That one na juju ooo (magic charm)!"

We both laughed very heartily. But my friend was serious. He said although he was aware that I did not believe in voodoo or the occult, he and many at Ikoyi Prison believed very much in supernatural powers. He asked me to come clean with him. Did I possess some Igbo talisman?

"My only talisman is my love of God, my self-love and my love of humanity. I hate to see people suffer. It follows that I do not enjoy suffering myself. Now, that is different from enduring the process of suffering. You see, as long as I satisfy myself that I have done everything to avoid suffering, whatever degree of suffering persists in spite of my best efforts to avoid it, I embrace. In other words, I am quite capable of dealing with unavoidable pain. It will surprise you, the pain I can endure."

The warder paid attention as I spoke. He nodded and said seriously, "Mr. George, nobody was killed at your housing unit. Thank God for that. But they have been reduced to the status of caged animals. They have not seen the sun for the past three days. They are forced to eat the same food as other inmates when it is available, and as you know, that food is just like dog food. They've not taken showers. Even sachet water for drinking is scarce. All phones have been seized or destroyed. Not even the Whitehouse has one single working fan. They are all in their underwear. It is hot as hell. Honestly. I do not wish to see you put through the torment these guys are going through. They have all seriously emaciated. Some of them look so gaunt that you will hardly recognize them. It is really, really sad indeed."

"But they're all alive! Thank you Lord!" I shouted. For the first time I felt relieved that I did not have to mourn the loss of a personal friend. The sadness in my heart was not replaced by this feeling of relief however; it merely felt good knowing that that sadness would not become a personal one. The feeling of guilt which I would surely have felt had been graciously spared me.

"Yes, they're alive, but barely. It has only been three days, mind you. If the rumors going around are true, then the situation might go on for months. And that will spell disaster for everybody, the warders included. You see, there is an irony in the whole affair. Some of the warders have been short sighted as they celebrate what they deem the restoration of their authority. They believe naively that their new found power to discipline the inmates has no negative side to it. Unfortunately something is disconnected in their minds. They seem to be pretending that they can somehow make up the large payoffs they receive daily from the inmates. That is foolish. I bet that within one month the trend toward forceful control of inmates will begin to slacken. It has to. The government does not pay enough for any warder to give up the extra income which comes from no other source than the inmates. In some cases, the government payroll serves as the supplemental income to the income generated out of soft warder-inmate relations. No doubt about it. My problem is simply… what happens between now and when the authorities begin to relax their hard grip?"

His words were logically and realistically grounded. I was almost moved to tears. This guy who on the surface appeared carefree and just average, you easily overlooked him when it came to analyzing even a mildly complex issue, was indeed very thoughtful. "What do you think I should do? Is there anything I can do about this situation?" I asked him.

"Fight for yourself Mr. George! Talk to your doctor and the hospital authorities. They are Nigerians like you. They saw on television what happened at Ikoyi Prison. They will not send you back there in good conscience if they can help it. You've been a model inmate and a model patient here. If you wished, you would've long since gone. Escaped! End of story! In the end the sky would not have fallen. After all, what crime did you commit? Talk to them. They can, and will stop the authorities from bringing you back to the prison until your appeal is concluded and you go home."

Unable to hold the tears back, I ended our conversation with two simple words; "Thank you."

Thirty Five

My appeal of the High Court ruling in my case was not going well. It was not going at all, actually. While my entire life hung in the balance—dodging death in detention, coping with seismic loses at all fronts in my family life, the ruling cabal was busy making changes—playing a game of chess with government postings.

With every move in the country's judicial chess board, new Court of Appeals Judges were appointed who in turn forced a postponement of sittings in my case. Then, by the time the new set of judges became familiar enough with the subject matter of my appeal, the entire nation's judiciary waltzed home for a year end recess for Christmas-Sallah-New Year celebrations, a jamboree which lasts over three months!

Faced with the perplexing indifference of this system that appears desensitized to the plight of a good number of Nigeran citizens seeking justice, I began wondering how long I could carry on with my silent crusade and of what value it would be if it did not benefit anybody.

Unknown to anybody but just a handful of my relatives and my friends at the prison, I was not fighting my extradition back to the United States to avoid returning to face justice. Had that been the case, the fight would've been long over. I would've been free by now. I was in the fight to draw attention, albeit in a very subtle manner, to two issues which affect the lives of a great number of people whose voices had never been and would probably never be heard. At least not until someone had enough courage to speak up.

Festus Keyamo was sympathetic to my cause although his life-long battle against Nigeria's successive administrations had been only on national issues not issues with international ramifications. He nevertheless saw my fight as a just one.

First, for whatever it was worth, I was determined to draw attention to those of us naturalized American Citizens who followed our dreams to achieve the greater dream in a land which rewards merit regardless of race, religion, or gender. On the surface, this dream—the American dream, is offered to all equally, but to my dismay, it seemed that once the dream becomes reality for a certain category of us, we are made targets of intense and unwarranted scrutiny by some who believe us to be undeserving of our achievements.

Where others are examined with cursory glances by the police, we are body searched and cavity searched regularly . . .

Where reporters of rowdy parties are calmed with a mere telephone call or the visit of one patrol car, squads of hostile, aggressive officers are dispatched to our homes for the job....

Where a grand jury would normally find no probable cause for indictments to be issued, a series of indictments and superseding indictments are handed down to us....

Where prosecutors would normally consider house detention or mild sentences, they aggressively request the maximum punishment under the law....

Where cultural values cause us to transgress, sometimes in violation of the law, we are treated as criminals for actions that amount to mere misunderstandings to us....

Yet, it must be stressed that being more or less first generation Americans, we are the most ignorant of the laws of this vast and sophisticated land—the most diverse in the history of humanity.

My list of grievances applies to so many who suffer in silence and obscurity. We have no defenders and our rights appear to exist only in writing. We are made pawns of vicious stereotypes. Even by judges!

Second, on the home front, here in Nigeria, the corruption and ineptitude of our judiciary reflects the attitudes of a broken people. Nigerians appear to have resigned to their unwholesome fate. The fate that in Nigeria ordinary citizens cannot aspire to any condition higher than that which they met on the ground, and until benevolence of divinity stirs the wind of change—usually by way of a coup d'état or the strong arms of dictatorship, then status quo must remain.

~

My loss at the High Court made me angry and strengthened my resolve to fight against extradition. This way, I would throw some light on the plight of many of us who had unwittingly become victims of the cultural system that made us who we are—a system that sadly sits as imperator, basking in our glory when we triumph but shamelessly recoils away from us like scared amoeba when our cultural values come under assault.

The truth is that most Nigerians are industrious. Even the criminally minded Nigerians are a lot easier to rehabilitate than most people I have come across around the globe. But my case is not being made for the criminally minded. Those may be left to fend for themselves and face the consequences of their deeds. My crusade is for those whose circumstances are so dire in Nigeria that they are forced to seek secure livelihood elsewhere. And who, upon achieving a measure of their dreams, generally returns the rewards to their "beloved" nation which selfishly welcomes the rewards but rejects the earner of the rewards.

Glued to my issues as outlined above, I waited and suffered rejection and abuse. I spent my lifetime earnings during this stressful period, trusting as I still do today, that in the end good will prevail over evil… as it always does.

While I waited in prison, the nation's political overlords and their ruler-in-chief were embroiled in a game of Machiavellian chess in which the ruler-in-chief sought to perpetuate himself in office for a lifetime, a crazed ambition which inspired me to write Nigeria's Last Depot. The despot, being a master of his games, knew better than to trust any of his overlords implicitly. He therefore resorted to using agencies like the EFCC and the nation's judiciary for all messy jobs such as forcible extradition.

And so it was that every time a group of three judges at the Appeals Court were assigned my case, I waited, hoped, and prayed for quick deliberations and decision. This hope however, would soon be dashed by either the dismissal or reshuffling of the judges. When judges were not being changed, the nation's entire judiciary seemed to proceed on an exodus of one form or another, judiciary conferences, inaugurations of one form or another, or vacations that seemed endless.

This cycle went on for month after month while my life within the high walls of Ikoyi Prison, or one hospital after another, presented me with experiences that were gradually transforming me from who I had been all along, into a new person who even my imagination was as yet unable to construct.

Finally, after 20 long months of judicial rigmarole, a hand-picked panel of judges of the Federal Court of Appeals was ready to render a decision in my case.

Meanwhile, after months of on-again-off-again news of sittings by the three assigned judges which produced no ruling on my case, I had given up hope of any meaningful outcome from that Court. On my instruction, my sister In Maryland, USA enlisted the services of an attorney to look into my case, research it and begin putting a defense together. My cause was to me, a worthy one, but upon reflection and deeper introspection, I began developing the idea of writing a book. At that stage a tell all book had begun looking to me like a more practical way of exposing the cause which was already becoming for me, the cause of my life—my raison d'etre.

While my barrister, Festus Keyamo, was preparing for D-day, I was daily on the telephone with my new attorney in Virginia, USA digging to unearth the genesis of my extradition request. Who was behind the request? What was the United States Attorney planning to use as evidence? As I could think of nothing I had done to anybody, I wanted my attorney to investigate the origins and veracity of whatever materials the Prosecuting Attorney planned to table as evidence against me. My mood had begun to adjust to, and even anticipate a dramatic court battle once I returned to the United States.

My attorney In Nigeria, Festus Keyamo, meanwhile had begun weighing in on the likely outcome of my appeal. There was obviously only one of two possible outcomes—one in favor of my extradition or one against it. Following the inexplicable last minute changes in the final make-up of the three man panel of judges who sat on the matter, both Festus and I were no longer iron-clad certain of a positive outcome. We knew that it was highly irregular for a judge who was newly appointed to the panel and by the way, the most junior of the final three judges to preside over the ruling in a high profile matter such as the extradition of a citizen. But of course, in Nigeria it cannot be irregular to break the law or abuse official discretion as long as it is government sanctioned.

My mind was already keyed into the American justice system as I waited for the ruling from the Nigerian Court of Appeals.

Thirty Six

My sleep had been restless throughout the night. Now I knew why. As the footsteps rose and fell with military precision somewhere in the interminably long hard concrete hallways of Lagos State Hospital in-patient wards, I knew they were headed for my room. Nobody said they were. I just knew.

Just before the guard posted at my door departed to be with his sick daughter the previous night, he had asked me to cover for him anyway I could in case one of the supervisors decided on a middle of the night inspection. Of course, as usual, that did not happen. But we also had not counted on a dawn visit by the most militant senior warder at the prison.

My muscles tensed, sending the wrong message to my private nurse who was curled up next to me still sound asleep. She stirred and slowly turned to attend to my needs but I placed my first finger over her lips and signaled her to listen. Confused, she sat up and we both listened for a moment as the approaching footsteps grew louder and louder.

Finally, the footsteps slowed and stopped abruptly right outside my door. What sounded like about a dozen feet began shuffling to and fro' all over the place and then, a mixed salad of male and female voices began filtering in through the cracks between the door and door frames.

My eyes became the size of the new silver naira. I whispered under my breath, "Obaika, ohh noo!"

My private nurse went berserk. She let out a stifled cry, "What" Who? Who is Obaika?

"I can't tell you now." I replied in panic.

"Please tell me. What do we do? What can we do now?"

"Come with me," I said as I sprinted on my tip toes toward the bathroom. She followed and when I looked back at her, my arms went limp. She was not dressed!

"Please, please, grab your clothes!" I pleaded with a desperate voice.

As she dressed up, I tried to evaluate the situation in a few milliseconds. That voice was unmistakable. It had to be ACP Obaika. No one else sounds like him. At the prison, we usually referred to him as Amin Body-double on account of his uncanny resemblance of the famed Ugandan despot, Idi Amin.

"Where is my guard?" he bellowed.

"I said you should calm down Mr…ehh Kini… calm down. The patient is in his bed and that is the only agreement we have with Ikoyi Prison. We are not here to guard your warder!" I heard the matron's authoritative voice reminding Obaika that she knew her onions. But I wondered in terror how she would explain why the hospital allowed me the company of my own private nurse who also shared my bed!

I knew what Obaika's mission was. He could not have come for inspection—he was too senior for such duties. Moreover, from the footsteps I heard earlier, there were at the very least, three officers outside that door.

I sidled noiselessly toward that door and made sure it was locked and bolted from the inside. I would not let anyone into my room until I absolutely had to. If they chose to, they could go ahead and break the door down.

"Okay, where is my prisoner?" Obaika demanded. "We are here to return him to the prison right now!"

"Hold on, hold on, officer. Your prisoner is a patient of this hospital. As far as I can tell, his doctor has not discharged him yet. Unless I see the doctor's discharge order, nobody can remove him from here. "

I could have hugged this matron right then and there.

"Do you know who you're talking to madam? I am Assistant Comptroller of Prisons Obaika—A level 13 Officer in the Federal Civil Service. I will make a report on this hospital and the hospital will be disciplined for your unprofessional behavior!" Obaika thundered.

That was what it took for the matron to lose her cool. Like a ticking time bomb, she went off on Obaika; "Heh, heh, heh, Mr. Obaika or whatever you call yourself. I don't care what level officer you are at Ikoyi Prison and I don't care what uniform you are wearing. This is Lagos State property and you have no authority here. For your information, I am a level 15 officer and Deputy Director of this ward. That means I am two levels your superior. Do not think you can walk in here like Idi Amin and everyone will fall on their faces before you." The matron's voice was on fire as she spoke to Obaika, moving closer and closer to him. "You had better leave this place right now! Do not return until you have necessary paperwork to remove the patient or I will have you removed! And please tell this man to put down that stupid gun. Patients are upset by you and your guns! Am I clear enough for you, Mr. Oboaka?"

I knew I was in the dog house but I could not help thoroughly enjoying this dialogue. Obaika had been cut down to size. I damn near choked as I struggled to hold back the laughter. Obaika of all people was being disrobed with words by a diminutive nurse. A woman for that matter! I knew how he always felt about women in authority. During the daily visits at Ikoyi Prison, he and his buddies would sit and make disparaging remarks about inmates who appeared under the spell of their "controlling" spouses. They felt those were the runts of society. Here he was now, all decked out in his "powerful" uniform being reduced to his true size. I would have given anything to see his face right then and there, but no such luck. Instead, I heard him stomping away. Just like when they arrived, their footsteps, with the clack of military precision began rising and falling again. Only this time the sound progressively faded until… nothing at all.

The matron and an entourage of nurses and other staff of the ward showed up at my door shortly after Obaika stomped out. I stood my ground, refusing to unlock my door until the matron spoke to me with a knowing snicker in her tone. She said that Oboaka had left and I was not in immediate danger of being bundled away.

I threw the door open and gave the matron my best smile. I also threw in a peck when she responded with a conspiratorial smile of her own. She told me that the situation was dire and that she had doubts that that animal warder would give up. She said he had commented that he would be back. It had been fifteen days since the September 20th riot at Ikoyi Prison and I had somewhat relaxed my worries and anxiety that the authorities might decide to interfere with my healthcare rendezvous at the hospital. Now my good fortune had all but eclipsed.

"Hey, Mr. George, you rascal, you better get your visitor packed out before that Satan comes back," the matron began cautioning me. "We allowed you a family visit and as far as we are concerned, this young lady is your cousin. Sorry ooh my sister," she gestured toward my private nurse. "But you have to leave. Oya, Mr. George, get back into bed. Let us get you back on drip. The doctor ordered another one for you." She concluded with a wink.

I immediately understood. They were going to try to keep me at the hospital for further treatment. Perhaps, that way a case could be made for the extension of my admission.

"Yes ma." I replied. At the blink of an eye, I was tucked in with a drip line running at the back of my hand. I winked at the nurses and put on my best sick face. It was the sweetest conspiracy I'd ever known. I fell in love with the matron and all the nurses around me at that moment.

The matron was first to leave, and the group of nurses followed shortly afterwards. My private nurse then began packing her overnight bag. It was as if a tap had opened up somewhere inside her head. The tears streamed down her lovely face in torrents as she shuttled between the bathroom and my bedside. Hard as I tried, I could not shut my own tap, but I managed to only let the tears out in trickles. We held hands and looked at each other through wet, cloudy eyeballs. We both knew freedom was only hours or even minutes from being taken from me once again, but neither of us had the courage to say goodbye.

Because we were so absorbed in each other's bittersweet pain, neither of us heard the military foot-falls. By the time we figured out that Obaika and his men were back, they were already at my door. The guard on duty entered first. As we separated and simultaneously shifted our gaze to the door, it was too late. The armed guard closely followed by Obaika was already within the view and inside my room.

All eyes were on the young, curvy lady standing by my bedside. Obaika's jaw dropped as he gawked from me to her and back.

Thirty Seven

As Obaika and his men drove me to Ikoyi Prison, I nearly blacked out from hyperventilation. My chest felt like a ton of lead had been dropped on it. Outwardly, I tried to keep a straight courageous face but in my mind, I was terrified of what would happen once we got back to Ikoyi Prison. I did not have to wait a long time.

Obaika marched through the prison gate like a lucky prize fighter displaying the prize of his latest conquest. There was no prisoner in sight, not even the few inmates normally designated to maintenance duties around the compound.

The warders at the gate were jubilant. They appeared to be celebrating an important occasion but when I looked around, I did not notice food, beverages, or any signs of fanfare—just a gay mood in faces which were usually made ugly by misery. It never occurred to me that the occasion being celebrated had anything to do with seeing me marched defenseless back into the prison compound and into a new era—one in which the warder man had reclaimed his lost glory.

As we walked solemnly through the compound, Ikoyi Prison, which only fifteen days earlier was the scene of a very ugly bloodbath, stood violently still as we strode across the naked yard. The air was thick and ponderous with humidity. The clay soil around the yard had not seen human traffic for over two weeks and had broken into an endless blanket of small clay patches with shrubs sprouting at their edges as if nature had made tiles of its caked uneven grounds.

The smell and feel of death hung purposefully over the prison even as life in various forms and sounds surrounded the compound outside its 18 foot walls.

I clutched tightly to about six plastic bags of bottled water, groceries and my personal effects, thankful that my weeks of physical training combined with the adrenaline of the situation to give me the strength to carry my possessions which weighed tons.

My heart rate doubled as we approached and turned into the alley of death. In my minds eyes I could see the ghosts of Orji; Manager, and the hyena boys lurking at every corner. The two warders accompanying me were not feeling talkative but their boots sounded like little explosives with every step as we turned the corner toward the Whitehouse. There was no soul in sight, not even Chinese and White, the two cats that gave us hours and hours of playful interludes in-between the stress filled joblessness that was our daily lives at Ikoyi Prison.

The sound of silence was suddenly broken by the shrill applause of flaccid voices coming through the security bars at the cell windows. I stopped, looked around, saw nobody. I turned around and squinted but still saw nobody. The warders then urged me forward. The voices grew louder and more strained.

Finally, through the darkened windows, their gaunt, disheveled forms began to appear. Big white teeth formed into smiles of misery and helplessness—they were wounded and defiled and bitter. Most of them were.

"Welcome back George! Mr. Hospital, is that you? Your head is the noose now! Why did you let them bring you back? You should've run! Man! You're sooo stupid coming back here!" the questions and comments rained through the windows as we quietly made our way to the entrance of my cell.

As a welcome gift, the warders allowed me several minutes to walk up to Aminu's window, and Papa's window too. I saw my few friends and passed some of my bottled water, bread and other goodies to them. Celebration broke out spontaneously. They had not seen bottled water in over two weeks. Even the sachet water known in Nigeria as pure water had become a rare commodity. My cell mate Captain Ayo was the only person who looked his former self, perhaps a testament to the ruggedness of his training and career as a sea man. The loss of a few pounds merely exposed more of his muscular build. The story was different for Aminu, Papa, Shola and Bola. They exhibited the same response to starvation—they looked thin and wasted. I found it interesting that weight loss does not affect both the teeth and the eyes. They don't lose weight. My friend's teeth and eyes stood out prominently.

For the next two weeks I did not—could not, see the sun. When the tap ran, it was a major event. We were able to fetch enough water for drinking, bathing and re-cooking the daily ration of Ikoyi Prison beans. We ate beans for breakfast, lunch and dinner. We found that having the free tap water from the public reservoir stand overnight or until the sediments collected at the bottom, gave us water which, boiled or not, tasted better than pure water which came at a price. Also, our daily ration of beans when refried or re-cooked with red palm oil had a palatable taste to it—especially after the taste buds are restrained to see no evil and smell no evil. One day at a time, we were making it out of hell's precipice.

With my return, morale was significantly lifted at the Whitehouse. Every new day, changes that might appear insignificant were added. For instance, one table fan which Captain Ayo had hidden in the ceiling through a concealed opening was retrieved and warders were convinced to overlook our unauthorized use of it. Within another day we were allowed to purchase a boiling ring for a premium. Then we made a giant leap when the first mobile phone was smuggled in. Now, we were able to reach out to family and friends and when a few more phones made it into the Whitehouse, we could call each other and share our latest triumphs or frustrations. The cumulative effect of these small strides was a gradual return to normalcy in our lives. But if there was anything guaranteed never to return, it was the status quo ante bellum.

Then, after two clear months of total lockdown, the Whitehouse residents were once again allowed to have meals prepared and brought in by family members. Limited family visits were restored and a number of privileges were either officially restored or allowed at the discretion of the warder on duty. The one contraband which remained strictly prohibited was the use of cell phones. Authorities insisted that cell phones in the hands of prison inmates were as dangerous as explosives strapped to the body of terrorists. I disagreed with them but I was only an inmate. My position on the issue and my protests that inmates should be provided with telephones or else be allowed to procure the use of one merely caused the prison authorities to watch me more closely than other inmates.

It was not long after the relaxation of the strict clampdown and lockdown policies that warders began to show their true colors. My friend's prediction on the effects of the new policies on inmate/warder relations was prophetic. The warders had in their celebration of their restored power over inmates underestimated the impact which the loss of the daily payoff from inmates would have on their economic and financial fortunes. Two months without the payoffs was enough to clear their heads and teach them better appreciation of reality.

Each one of us shut down the flow of out sustenance money into the prison from our families. The monies we managed to smuggle into the prison, we stowed away into the many crevices which we expertly fashioned out of window and door hinges, wall partitions, and even the floor. We had gotten used to the warder man's raids and now knew how to outsmart them when it came to our routine hide and seek games. That was what their shakedowns amounted to.

The warders were hurting and we knew this. We let them stew. When they tried to strong arm us, we found humor in their empty threats. We knew how empty their threats were. Without evidence they could not hurt us. Even when they had evidence such as a lucky chance upon an inmate using a cell phone, we knew that all it amounted to was an opportunity for one warder to make a few bucks.

We had a ball playing Popeye and Blutto game with the warders. When we noticed a warder lay siege at the smelly gutter that runs the entire length of the Whitehouse backyard, we let him strain himself running up and down with his ears tracking the source of our make-believe telephone conversations. We pretended we were oblivious of his presence and ran the conversation from one cell to another with raised voices; "Hello Sir," I would say, "When you get to the prison, call me. I will meet you at the gate." We would then monitor the warder's footsteps as he scurried toward my cell. At that point, my friend Papa would take up the make-believe conversation at another cell, causing the warder to change course. When finally exhausted, the warder would burst into a cell and into a staged arrangement believing he had made a bust. His frantic search however, would yield no fruit forcing him to reluctantly and grudgingly give up. Occasionally, they got lucky and made a good bust and the culprit got punished if a deal was not worked out.

Among the Whitehouse residents, I was the one most affected by the poor condition of living at Ikoyi Prison. Although I had learned how to read a book many times and still enjoy it, even that pleasure in addition to all my other devices, were not enough to inoculate me against occasional attacks of anxiety and depression. As usual, the cumulative outcome of these swings in my mental state began driving my blood pressure up and breaking me into little disjointed bits of myself. After about three months since Obaika snatched me from the hospital and returned me to the life of misery at the prison, I was back at work plotting my way to return to my life of quasi freedom and the excitement of dodging wardermen on the streets and alleyways of Lagos.

The unseen hand once again took control of my providence. From the day I returned to Ikoyi Prison from admission at Lagos State Hospital, I told myself that it would be my end if I resigned my fate to whatever the system had to offer. I was already in the process of setting goals for my life after my current burdens—the burdens of prison life and my war against the legal systems of Nigeria and the United States. Clearly, my life would never be the same again after it is all over. I had major plans to layout and Ikoyi Prison was not the right environment for that mission.

Just at the right time, the most auspicious for me to change my dwelling condition or else face extermination, the unseen hand sent the sadistic resident physician of the prison on vacation. The young doctor who was sent as his relief was such an amiable young man; we became an item immediately he reported for duty. It was as if we had been friends for ever. He was sympathetic to my plight and decided to help alleviate my suffering.

Based on his referral, I was admitted at the Military Hospital on Awolowo Road, Ikoyi early in 2006. As a tribute to the hard life of the warderman, I composed the following poem on my first night of admission at the Military Hospital:

WARDER MAN

He is a soldier without a gun
He is a teacher without a classroom
He is on duty; his master's tool
He is angry; he needs to vent
He is hungry; but his tray is empty
He looks to heaven with tear-soaked eyes

He then asks the Lord if He had on hand
Anything left that his master forgot.
Yes, the Lord replies, I had plenty on hand,
But I left it all at Aso Rock.
The fact is warder man, the stuff's so hot
You can't use it in the hell you're at.

So the warder man looks around his duty post;
If this is hell he wonders, then who's in charge?
Whereupon he asks aloud; who the hell's the man in charge?
Screaming, the devil appears fork in hand;
Look around you stupid, or I'll poke your eyes out!
If they protest, don't call me, Abuja will help.

Hell yeah, hell yeah, the warder man yells,
I can see clearly now, the scales are gone!
Turning to his prisoners, the warder man scowls;
I want this, I want that… or ya ass is mine!
Sure, the prisoner agrees; you can have it all, if you'll be my boy….
When he accepts, the prisoner smiles; now stupid, ya ass is mine!

Thirty Eight

"Naw… naw… naw… not again!" I yelled as I scaled the low fence and into the lagoon. I felt myself sinking with great thrust, as though weighted with concrete glued to both of my hands. Fearing that I would slam my face into the untold monstrosities that inhabit the ocean floor I began kicking with all my might. Noohh… no… no… no. I thought I had just seen the ocean floor as I sailed downward head first. Then, my kicking seemed to start paying off. Gradually I began slowing, until finally, I was able to maneuver my body by wriggling it as I kicked.

What do you know? I thought with a smile as I suddenly began floating like an Olympic swimmer. My God! I could move! What was I? A man fish? Who the hell cares I thought. Yippee Obaika…! Must not be your lucky day… ha, ha, ha!

"George, George; Are you alright? Mr. George, wake up! Are you okay?"

The two military nurses stood with their blood pressure kit and a thermometer by my bed with puzzled looks on their faces. I jumped up, blinded by the bright fluorescent light overhead. Through my squinting eyes, I could not recognize the two soldiers looking down at me. I threw down my notebook and the pen with which I was trying to paint a word picture of Obaika and his fellow warders.

"Is he here? Where is he? Please… please… don't let him take me! Please…!"

"Don't let who take you Mr. George? Who wants to take you?" The female corporal spoke first.

Then the sergeant added, "Calm down Mr. George, you're at the military hospital. Nobody can take you away from here. Please calm down.

"Okay," I said, gradually collecting my thoughts. As my thoughts returned, the obvious slowly began to dawn on me. It had all been a horrible nightmare. "My God," I whispered, feeling relieved and ashamed at the same time.

"Please forgive me," I pleaded with them. Was I really screaming? Was I loud?"

"Hmmm, oh yes Mr. George. You were loud but because you're in a private room, I do not think many people heard you. Anyway, it really doesn't matter much. We're used to hearing screams here. It is a hospital. But we must attend to everybody who screams even if we know why they're screaming. Now, relax, it is 6:30 AM. We have to take your vital signs now."

No offence to the many excellent male nurses who do great work in the profession, but this particular female corporal was my idea of what a nurse ought to be. Her words were so unbelievably soothing; I longed to have her attend to me in the days that followed... every single day. To appreciate my biased favor for this soldier, one needs to be her patient. That way, they'll feel what I felt—they would've been touched by an angel.

Shortly after the nurses left my room, my warder guard stumbled in still giddy from his body's need for more rest. He lied that he saw my door open from the end of the hallway where he kept watch at my room and so rushed to ensure that all was fine.

I assured him that all was fine and that he needn't worry about me. I gave him the names of his colleagues who had guarded me in the past and would be prepared to vouch for me as character references. He confirmed that he already knew that I was not a flight risk at all. He was only concerned about his bosses who might drop in for inspection at any time and without warning. We both agreed that as time went on, their bosses would relax and the warder guards attached to me could better use their time attending to issues of more value to them. As we spoke, the door swung in and his relief entered. It was my best friend from the prison yard. I smiled. Things had already begun looking up for me.

We winked at each other as the two warders performed their exchange duty procedures. Thirty minutes after his colleague left my friend said, "Have a nice day Mr. George. I have family matters to attend to. Please do not get caught wandering around Lagos by these hungry warders. You know that this is warder territory. "Bye." And he was gone.

My freedom came much quicker than I had anticipated. And it could not have felt more liberating. No more walls. No more bars. No more angry guards!

I never knew that the joy of freedom could also be so incredibly therapeutic. I felt as though my mind had just been drugged. I quickly went through my overnight bag and fished out my hygiene pack and my towel.

Confused, I lay them beside me on the bed and put my head on the pillow. As by a thief, consciousness was immediately snatched away from me. The combination of joy and exhaustion is truly a virtual drug—potent beyond belief. Fast acting too!

One hour later, I got up. I walked into the bathroom where I stood, full of vigor under the shower feeling electric. Instinctively, I turned the louvers of the window next to me. Light rushed in ahead of the fresh morning breeze from over the Lagos Lagoon. I squinted at the view from my third floor window. It was breathtaking. But as I swept the scenic view of the street along the south side of the lagoon with my eyes, my heart sank. My chest began to tighten. I broke down and began sobbing.

Standing imperiously within the familiar low and elegant fence which itself is barricaded for security with concrete barricades, was the American Embassy building. A building perceived by many a Nigerian youngster as their only hope—their only avenue to succeed in life. They come, their hopes bundled inside large envelopes—some of them forged or stolen passports, bank statements, invitation letters, wedding cards, photographs of arranged overnight marriages and borrowed babies, wives or husbands. They come with their rehearsed stories. They come with disguises which they hope would give them the acceptable appearance—older or younger, elderly or youthful, as necessary. They come with their life savings, ready for the steep visa fees, and bribery if necessary. They come because their spirits tell them to. Because they believe in the dream of America—the same dreams I once had. The very same dreams that I had followed to heights I never believed possible and from which the hand which lifted me up seemed now bent on pulling me down. Down below my point of entry!

I yelled, "It's only a misunderstanding!" But no reply came back. Nobody heard me. Nobody was listening. Nobody cared.

By this time, I had been working the telephone for a while with the lawyer who my sister had hired out of Alexandria, Virginia to defend me. I had briefly summed up my story to her, telling her how I had departed my home in 1999 after persistent disagreements with my wife threatened to escalate even more when I insisted on resolving our differences by ourselves. How my wife went on to involve the police and the courts in our family matter prompting me to separate myself from her rather than engage in a drawn-out ugly battle which I had feared would damage our children psychologically. An outcome which I judged unthinkable, especially considering how focused they had become on the promises which lay in the future for them. I felt that they were inspired to do great things and that it was my wife and I who by our examples had set them up with such high aspirations. I considered it immoral and self-serving to allow my own selfishness to derail them.

Whether my judgment was right or wrong was immaterial at this point, I explained to the attorney. What was relevant was that I left my home. It was my departure that caused everything in my home to spiral downward into chaos. It was indeed my departure that resulted ultimately in the breakdown of communication between my wife and the young woman in the middle of my extraordinary case that was now known as United States versus George Chidebe Udeozor. A Superpower versus whom... Me?

As I kept my gaze focused on that great building, the Embassy of the United States sitting on its tree lined Walter Carrington Street address—a scenic half crescent street formally known as Eleke Crescent, I wondered in my long suffering mind why nobody in there cared enough to reply to my various letters seeking clarification on the genesis of this unnecessary diplomatic battle. I was offering to return to the United States voluntarily for God's sake! If the object of this elaborate, painful and expensive process was just to return me to the jurisdiction of the United States, then how in the hell could it be more desirable to engage in this process than me bringing myself to the courthouse where I was needed? The taxpayers would be spared the huge expenses and justice would be better served!

My attorney had explained to me that once I was arrested, the Embassy would be unwilling to allow me to return of my own volition at that point, the reason being that I might be a flight risk. On hearing that explanation, I thought with a devious smirk; "if only they knew!" the truth is that I personally could never accept the type of freedom that would have me live a life on the run. Never. To my mind, only the criminally minded could live such a life.

Here I was, free like a bird. Free to return even to the United States undetected or to go to any country of my choice. Or better yet, melt away to any location of my choosing in Nigeria. But I would rather be subjected to a deadly scourge than be named a wanted man. That choice—the choice to take flight from any situation that would cast doubt on my honor, never even received a second thought in my mind. But how could I get bureaucrats to know this?

Feeling helpless, I withdrew back into the bed where I wrapped my body in a blanket in order to keep from freezing. My teeth clattered from a combination of the effect of the morning chill and my emotional exhaustion.

With my mind made up to return to the United States, it became for me, just a matter of when; at what cost to my integrity; and at what stage of the ongoing extradition proceedings?

Should I insist on winning my extradition battle first and then board a plane and return? Or should I terminate the process by accepting the judgment of the lower court regardless of its implication for my principled opinion—being denied my right to due process?

I suspended the decision to await the outcome of my appeal. Meanwhile I began adjusting to a life of quasi freedom once again. During this period, I availed myself the opportunity of studying in more depth, the character of my Nigerian people at the grassroots like I never would have been able to do had this tragedy not befallen me.

While it is frustrating to belong to a breed of people who appear hell bent on saluting Jesus and Prophet Mohammed but embracing and enthroning the currencies of the world, a people who covet the order and egalitarian principles and policies of civilized societies but act as though those principles and policies are too good for their own society, I also came to see from first hand observation that Nigerians are among the most resilient, most patiently aspirational breed of people on the planet.

The trouble with Nigeria is the lack of honest and committed leadership—period. As I spent my days and nights visiting every establishment that I possibly could, it was easy to observe that wherever there was a good leader; Nigerians were willing and eager to follow. I would sometimes walk up the entire length of Awolowo Road and find not a single soul controlling a gridlocked traffic. Then as I made my way back, the seemingly impossible gridlock would have disappeared and normal traffic flow restored. This usually resulted from the effort of a volunteer—the kind of selfless individuals fit for leadership. But most often, these sorts do not get to become leaders because Nigerians are yet to discover that leaders are meant to serve. To my chagrin, I found this tendency in all levels of Nigerian society; sadly, even among those who should know better—especially among such groups!

The world seems to believe that Nigeria is doomed and I could see why. The trouble with this world view of Nigeria however, is that Nigeria is graded by the report cards of the Nation's leaders. As I strolled through the streets, store fronts, backyards and alleyways of Lagos, I had the privilege of meeting and interacting with Nigerians who inspired me and gave me hope. There really are warm, resilient Nigerians who give their all every day waiting patiently for the day when true leaders, the leaders who would serve the people rather than themselves, finally take up their mantles. Perhaps the glory days of which I speak are near. I would not know. But my gut feelings are that those days are nearer than the world presently believes. I only hope I get to see those days or even better, help make it possible before I am gone.

When the ruling of the Appeals Court was finally delivered, there were no surprises. It had appeared for a while that the Ministry of Justice was having difficulty finding judges at the Appeals Court level who would follow the tradition of ruling at the pleasure of government. But after over two years in detention, on Monday the 26th day of February, 2007 before their Lordships:

Monica B. Dongban-Mensem, Justice, Court of Appeals;
Paul Adamu Galinje, Justice Court of Appeals; and
Hussein Mukhtar, Justice, Court of Appeals;

A ruling prepared and delivered by Monica Bolna'An Dongban-mensem, JCA JPT, read and affirmed by both Paul Adamu Galinje and Hussein Mukhtar, upheld the ruling of the Federal High Court.

I immediately understood why the judgment had to be delivered by someone with a name like Dongban-Mensem. Because it was a don-gone-mission of government to deliver me to the United States regardless of reason… or the Nigerian Constitution at that. As far as the government was concerned; "who cares what the Constitution says?"

On page 17 of her ruling she wrote: "…the nations of the world have, out of the need to make the world a safe place for its people, agreed to cooperate in curbing the excesses of suspected miscreants. The courts and law officers MUST NOT ALLOW TECHNICALITIES TO FRUSTRATE THIS EXERCISE. Accordingly, I uphold the submission of the learned counsel for the respondent, that Section1(3) of the Extradition Act applies to the United States of America subject to the provisions of the Legal Notice No 33 of 1967."

I burst out laughing as I read out loud "… out of the need to make the world a safe place for its people…."

"What a comical travesty of the law of the land!" I thought. A cooked up Act now trumps the Constitution of the land so that a Nigerian justice could make the United States safe from miscreants like George Udeozor? Give me a break! By the way, at the time of this ruling the home State of this presiding judge, Plateau State was mired in mindless violence due to poverty and involuntary servitude. But instead of saving the world from that scourge, the learned justices assigned themselves the hallowed duty of saving the world from ME! It surely made me cringe that at the time of my arrest, I had in my employment three indigenes of Plateau State in good paying jobs. God only knows how they've been faring since. God help us all.

What a laughable lampoon of a judgment!

Thirty Nine

During the entire period of my incarceration to this point, fate had been brutally unkind to my family. My personal travails began to pale in comparison to the collective losses which providence visited on my siblings; my mother's passing in 2000 having rendered us orphans. It was only my frequent escapades into many nooks and crannies of the fascinating streets of Lagos that usually chiseled me out of my morbid introspection whenever I was alone in my hospital room where I was usually in a state of melancholy.

The first blow came early during my life in detention. My immediate elder brother, Paul who remains my best friend in addition to our biological ties, was cut down by meningitis after a visit to Kaduna, in Northern Nigeria. Aside from the pain of having a brother who I loved immensely come close to losing his life to this dreadful disease, my torment over his misfortune ran marrow deep because his visit to Kaduna was on my behalf. He went up to Kaduna with my friend, Air Vice Marshal Chris Marizu, after they failed to nail the EFCC chairman down at his office in the days following my inexplicable abduction by men of his commission. They travelled to Kaduna based on a reliable tip that the slippery chairman of EFCC could be cornered therewith his guards down and would as a result be forced to explain the questionable circumstances of my abduction. My guilt over my brother's contraction of meningitis was exacerbated by the fact that I urged him to travel to Kaduna despite what I'd heard about the EFCC Chairman's reputation to stonewall those who tried to hold him responsible for the excesses of the organization which he proudly headed and defended stoutly against all complaints.

I had seen the EFCC Chairman the week before my brother's visit to his home in Kaduna. Even knowing his reputation, he did not look at all like any evil tyrant. He had watery eyes that blinked as if unaccustomed to light, and the meek expression of one who wished desperately to be accepted as humble and kind. If pushed, I would have placed him as a gentle Imam eking out a quiet existence in an affluent Katsina neighborhood where government has no business. Yet he was hard, immutable and insouciant as my brother and Air Vice Marshall Chris Marizu found out in Kaduna. He was every bit a government man. In the usual duplicitous manner of government men, he told my brother and AVM Marizu that my matter was beyond his pay grade. He said it was an issue between the governments of the United States and Nigeria, and that he couldn't comment beyond that. Little wonder the United States preferred working with this man—sidelining the properly constituted chain for diplomatic cooperation. In my case, rather than depend on the police force to secure a warrant of arrest and pursue due diligence, the FBI branch of the United States Embassy wrote directly to the Chairman of EFCC and his men to have me arrested for extradition back to the jurisdiction of Maryland, U.S.A. where I was wanted to face charges for some alleged offenses. I suspect that the FBI knew full well what method the EFCC would apply in my arrest and extradition. That method—abduction and forcible extradition had thankfully now been scuttled midway because of my quick thinking relatives and friends who acted with dispatch to counter the process which was already in motion.

Thankfully, through all his hurtling around the country in a bid to stop the great injustice targeted at me, my brother's life was spared. I know that had he died from meningitis, I would have held the EFCC Chairman personally responsible along with his Commission, the FBI, and the State Department. As it turned out, he survived even if fate did not retract its brutal onslaught on my other loved ones.

In the fullness of time, all people, even those with bionic body parts must die. This much I know is true. This fact however accords a father or any parent little consolation when his baby dies. On December 20, 2005 shortly after Obaika callously plucked me out of my hospital bed to return me to the drudgery of prison, the unthinkable happened. Richard Udeozor fell, and his fall was an eternal fall.

Richard Udeozor was the first child of Mr. & Mrs. Paul Udeozor, which made him my nephew. As you may recall, Paul is my immediate elder brother as well as my best friend. When I moved to Abuja in 2002, Richard had been accepted and was a student at one of Nigeria's premier Secondary Schools—Loyola Jesuit College, Kado, Abuja. He was among the school's top academic performers with a near 4.0 grade point average. Loyola Jesuit College was also the institution of first choice for my children's High School education but the logistics of relocation to Nigeria scuttled the idea.

I find the guilt of losing Richard especially haunting because he died in an airplane crash. Richard usually spent time with me at my Abuja home before proceeding back to his parent's home in Port Harcourt, usually by being picked up by his father. This routine had been maintained over all of

Richard's holidays until I was arrested by the men of EFCC. On December 20, 2005, because I was not in Abuja, but incarcerated at the request of the United States and the order of a judge of the Federal Republic of Nigeria, he boarded an ill-fated charter flight along with about seventy of his school mates. None of them survived the crash of the Sosolisso Airlines flight of December 20, 2005. Neither my abductors who remanded me in prison nor my accusers who requested for me to be so treated was responsible for Richard's death, but they denied my solemn petition to be taken to his funeral even if I had to go in hand cuffs and leg chains while also covering the entire cost of the journey. I am however thankful to the unseen hand which always looked out for me. I was able with the aid of a smuggled cell phone to send my eulogy by text message for my beloved nephew Richard in my own words to his father. Although these words which were read at his graveside do not erase the guilt which I still feel for his loss, they have somehow continued to provide me the sustained solace that Richard received my farewell message to him:

"Beloved Richard,
Yes, your body is now still,
But, your silent footsteps walk on,
Yes, your body is not moving,
But your tender voice speaks on.
Though today we commit your body to mother earth,
Out of our sights,
But we know that you now enjoy God's eternal life.
I will forever see you
On the quiet macadam of Loyola Jesuit College.
I will forever hear your footsteps
In the walk of us all whom you left behind.
The sublime nature of your
Love-filled, sin free life
Is indelible.
We pray to remain spiritually connected with you
Until we come to live with you forever
In God's celestial light
Amen.

~Uncle George

The chances of being switched at birth according to hospital statistics was about 1 out of 5,000,000 in 1975. At the same time, the chance of being born just minutes apart from one's first cousin at the same hospital and being switched with her was about 1 out of 50 million. Yet that was what happened in 1975 at the University Teaching Hospital, Enugu, Nigeria where my niece Bene Nworah and her cousin were mistakenly switched at birth.

This sad error by the grossly incompetent nurses who took delivery and care of these two babies didn't become obvious immediately although they exhibited strange responses to normal natural activities like breast feeding. By the time they were two years old, even skeptics who doubted the possibility of such unwarranted and inexcusable error knew that the children had been switched at birth. Because each set of parents and their extended relatives on both sides had bonded with the "wrong" baby, neither side had the courage to address the issue let alone suggest a reversed switch of these beautiful, adorable infants. But as they grew and the error became too pronounced even in their physical appearances—especially their faces and heights, people began to speak up and even allude to possible medical reasons which could present future nightmares if the error was not acknowledged and corrected. After several heart breaking family deliberations, the reverse switch was made.

Bene, who had suffered severe psychological damage before the reverse switch had to struggle and suffer greatly to readjust to a liberated life, a life she had never known. But when her mother, my biological sister Ethel Nworah, nee Ethel Udeozor suddenly died in 1989, all the developmental gains made by Bene were shattered. An emotionally decimated young woman, Bene continued her brave struggle until I became incarcerated. Bene grew up a devout Catholic. During my last contact with her, as she had done previously all of her life, she shone with love while she prayed with me for peace and protection in our riotous and strife torn world.

I was inconsolable when I got the news of Bene's passing after a brief illness. Again, I was helpless and mourned my niece morning, day and night on my tear soaked pillow, unsure what news tomorrow held for me.

My phone seldom rang while I was at Ikoyi Prison. That was because it could not ring when it was switched off, which was most of the time. To keep from being betrayed by a ringing cell phone in prison, you simply switched the electronic nuisance off. Then you turn it on only when you make phone calls. Common sense tells you that, Right? Well, not always.

Like clockwork, I automatically hit the off button after each call. But being human, mistakes happen to us from time to time, as it did with me shortly after I received the news of Bene's death. I took the chance of getting busted and answered the call. Another bad idea, I felt at first. Well, not this time. At the other end was my half-brother Obiora who sounded like he had just returned from outer space, transfigured. I did not recognize his voice at first. But when he identified himself I asked him why he sounded like an alien from outer space. I jokingly called him ET and we both laughed. I knew he did not know who ET was but he seemed to find my comment funny. Having been raised entirely in the provincial town of Amawbia, our ancestral home, he was richly bequeathed with native intelligence by the many elders who seemed to hang onto life just long enough to pass their wisdom from the soil to him. With the little grasp of western concepts and terms he had been exposed to, he chuckled when I explained ET to him. Then he grew quiet and in a distant philosophical tone he asked me to listen carefully. I did.

He said he called to wish me well. He said to me: "Dende (my family pet name), I bet you're surprised I called you. Well, I got your number from Gilbert (my oldest biological brother). Please listen carefully. Hold onto your ways and never depart from them. Your path in life has been invaded in order that you may be tested, but if you stay strong, you'll prevail in the end. I am…we are all praying for you, even people who you do not know. Your good deeds cannot destroy you." When he paused, I was close to tears. It seemed he sensed my demeanor and so, quickly continued, "Please forgive me for any times in the past I offended you. You know I was sometimes mischievous. Please forgive me. You're a good man."

That did it. I began sobbing—my eyes and nose dripped like cracked sewage pipes. For a while neither of us spoke. Then, I noticed that he had joined in with broken sewage pipes of his own. After we were both satisfied, with neither of us consoling the other, I thanked him and we said our goodbyes.

I still ask myself today why I failed to detect the underlying message in Obiora's phone call to me.

One week after I spoke to Obiora, during one of my regular daily phone conversations with my brother Paul, he said he had bad news. He knew I could ill handle suspense so he gave me the news straight up. "Obiora died last night," he said in a tone soaked with emotion. "We couldn't save him. Last month he surprised me with a phone call. When I answered he requested assistance. I rushed the money to him but his illness had advanced beyond cure. We lost him."

Obiora was not a paragon of good health but he had a firm, rounded exterior which some of us mistook for *healthy and well fed.* He also hardly ever complained of ill health. I therefore failed to capture the essence of his valedictory phone call to me. My belated adieu to Obiora is thus one of my messages to my loved ones who passed on during my sad period of indisposition.

Sometimes I die. Then I inexplicably find myself alive in my bed. Quite distinct from reveries, day dreams or nightmares, in these deaths which I have only experienced less than ten times in my life, I return to the same scene and meet the same people, but they are usually not present when I turn up in my bed. Sounds like clairvoyance, Right? Perhaps so, but to me they have always felt like death.

During the entire period of my incarceration, I have died only twice before finding myself alive again in my bed. I died the night after I had a telephone conversation with my younger sister Susan earlier on the same day. When this event happened I was already petitioning the courts to withdraw my legal appeal against my extradition so that I may be brought back to the United States to confront my accuser.

My immediate younger sister, the only one out of nine of us born to our parents who possessed the tenacity to go on digging in the elite club of academics, who still found room for erudition after post graduate studies, was diagnosed with colon cancer early in 2007. She was married and blessed with five living children. Although marriage mandated her to change her name to Mrs. Susan Dikas, to me she was always "Uche"—short for Uchenna, my little sister. Whenever I was able to confirm that our telephone conversations were not being monitored by her husband, I teased her about her about her foreign sounding marital last name; "Dr. Uche Udeozor sounds better than Dr. Dikas. You'll always be Uche Udeozor to me, and anybody who disapproves can jolly well go and perish. I could never be more proud of anyone!"

My sister never challenged me when I played my vicious game of "discover" with her—my little game to try and uncover her secrets which dates back to our childhood. She knew I only wished to reassure myself that she was happy in her marriage. She also never gave much away about her relationship with her husband, for she was welded to her Christian beliefs as if with a blow torch. Christianity ruled her life. She taught me in our few last conversations that in these debased and corrupted times we live in, there are still people who still know the meaning and value of honor. With the purity of a child, she thought and acted in such noble and simple manner that I found myself mending the things which were wrong in my own life after every conversation with her.

As excruciating as the disease of cancer can be on its sufferers and their loved ones, I can say, although with great bitterness at the disease, that metaphorically speaking, good always can result from the experience of contending with its destructive power.

It multiplies my grief that it was after my little sister Uche came down with the disease that many of us to whom her treasured gifts of compassion and wisdom were available realized the need to harvest those gifts. Nevertheless, I thank God for the time, however small it was, that I had with heron the telephone in those last days, for I am a lot wiser for it. My siblings all over the United States and Nigeria thankfully experienced along with their families, the spiritual and physical rewards of Uche's sage words and love impulses.

I suppose by now, I have made it clear that Uche, my little sister, has already been claimed by cancer. The trouble for me is that I believe she still lives. "Why?" you may ask, do I believe she still lives. The answer is quite simple; my little sister promised me that we will be together again. In all of her lifetime she never uttered a word of promise which she failed to keep. When I died in my jail cell after that conversation with her in early 2007, I met her for the first time at that eternal address where I have been a guest after my every death. It was there that she made me the promise.

Unlike the case of losing Richard, I would have declined any offer to be brought to Uche's graveside. Perhaps then she would have truly died—a situation which would have stolen my immortality from me. That way, the unkind brutality of fate would have gladly consumed me.

Forty

It would amount to a boring exercise to go through the detailed account of all the wrangling that preceded my eventual departure from Nigeria to return and face trial in Maryland, USA. But to fail to at least shake my fingers in the faces of those who made the process hell for me is to condone their many acts of subterfuge. And lest those, whose acts of perfidy brought these painful memories to fruition now wish to repudiate my record of the events, let them be warned that I have in my possession, hard copies of the evidence of their perfidious acts.

Festus Keyamo, my barrister and friend, went into law practice ahead of his time in the development of Nigeria's judicial system. I believe this to be so because his handling of my case stands as an undeniable testament of that fact. After the Federal High Court ruling which ordered my extradition to the United States, I did not hesitate in marching up to the Court of Appeals with my barrister. I could tell then that he was no longer involved in my fight for monetary profit. Although I paid the fee which he charged, I could tell that he barely covered his expenses which were quite steep. Then, although by the time the bombshell ruling of the Appeals Court was so savagely and insouciantly delivered my mind was already made up to return to the United States, an incensed Festus Keyamo went into war mode. He was so angered by a ruling at the Appeals Court level which unequivocally unmasked the incompetence of government appointees to offices even as high as the nation's Appeals Court. The justice who wrote the judgment did not understand our argument. Pure and simple. Festus implored me to dig in the deepest recesses of my mind to find the forbearance to go through a Supreme Court appeal of the two lower courts' error drenched rulings. To demonstrate his confidence that we would prevail, he waved all fees. He would win the case at the Supreme Court, and he would correct the errors which stank to high heavens for now and for posterity.

I wished so very much to indulge my friend. After all there were already two signs that he would deliver on his promise. First, a precedent had already been set while I was still in detention which set the record straight on the matter of extradition between Nigeria and the United States of America. While I was still living at the Military Hospital, on admission and awaiting the outcome of my appeal, a highly moneyed young man was remanded at Ikoyi Prison, also at the request of the United States. The request for this young man's extradition was stopped dead on its tracks at the High Court, with the request being tossed out the window by a different judge from the one that presided over my case. Curiously, the attorney for this young man used the same argument which Festus Keyamo had so artfully articulated in my case. Second, through a dear friend of mine, I got a retired Supreme Court Justice to look my entire case over and afterwards, he was incredulous at the judgment delivered at the High Court and particularly the one delivered by the Court of Appeals. In very few words, he urged me to take the matter to the Supreme Court.

The ruling that set the young man free had made nonsense of the rulings rendered by the judges in my own case. Of particular significance was how this judgment debunked the assertions of the two courts which placed the Attorney General of the Federation above the constitution of the Federal Republic of Nigeria.

What Festus could not see was that I had become content with myself seeing the outcome of this young man's effort. By the judgment which set him free, the brave judge who stood up for the rule of law with courage regardless of possible political backlash or career setbacks had ostensibly proved my point. There was no longer any need for me to win or prove a point. His win was a judicial triumph for the whole nation. Had I been the winner in my case, I would have taken the first available flight and would have long been in Maryland and the United States District Court at Greenbelt. So, the question had become; "why not do just that?"

Because I knew what winning this case at the Supreme Court would do for the brilliant career of Festus Keyamo, the man I considered to be among the best lawyers in the country at that time, I began diddling on how to break the news to him that I had decided to accede to my extradition to the United States on the strength of the order of the Federal High Court Judge. Festus had made a powerful case for the need that we finish our quest for justice and help rewrite an inequitable treaty—a treaty that would not truly exist if the Nigerian Constitution were to be treated with the respect that it deserved. In response to my acceptance of the judgment which quashed the extradition of the young man as a vindication of the principled position that informed my own fight, Festus made another deeply compelling argument. He observed that because the freed young man was being sought for criminal offences which violate all known moral and ethical values, his would be the wrong victory with which to make our case for equity in the treaties entered into. My case on the other hand he contended, would be invaluable to address cultural and systemic failures that go far beyond treaties with nations that think so little of our values.

The truth sometimes cut deeper than a razor sharp knife. Festus was cutting me with his words but could neither see my wounds nor my bleeding. I was in Nigeria only in flesh. My soul was in America. Although born and raised in Nigeria, I grew up into a man in the United States and have not known any other country. In short, I love both countries just as a child would love his biological parents for giving him life and his foster parents for giving him a sense of meaning and direction in his life. Every child who is fortunate enough to be provided with such balance would rather hang than acknowledge any act of subterfuge by either of these parents. Regrettably, callow as it is for me to admit, families are only as good as the parents who head them, just as ***nations are only as good as their leaders!***

The culture of any group of people shapes the people in that group, including its leaders. In Nigeria, a majority of adults grow up in homes outside the home where they were born. Through one form of customary arrangement; apprenticeship, guardianship or philanthropy, a child born into poverty will seek to better his or her lot in life. For generations which predate the dark era of slave trade, this practice became a trite cultural norm. Some of Africa's greatest people like Nelson Mandela have been products of this cultural practice. The world admires and applauds the success stories which emerge at the end but feigns amnesia or selective memory to the cultural engineering that made the final product even possible because we find the process offensive. Joe Jackson, without whose efforts, the world would never have known of Michael Jackson, is today vilified by many as evil. Those who have the courage to eulogize him for his sacrifices are accused of condoning his excesses. One never gets it right with human beings!

People cannot influence the location of their birth, and they also cannot contribute to the fortunes of their parents prior to the time of their birth. But once born unto this earth, regardless of the circumstances of their birth, they must seize the opportunities that the environment provides them to both benefit themselves and contribute to society. The provision of those opportunities is a major reason why governments are created. To my mind, it is only a government which has done its due diligence toward its people that has the moral authority to make and enforce laws on them. Although no nation is without injustice, there is no question that in terms of due diligence toward its people, Nigeria cannot stand on the same platform with the United States. Comparing Nigeria to the United States because they are both sovereign nations is literally like comparing a mouse to an elephant because they are both four legged animals. Once this fact dawned on me and I realized that my cry for justice would never be heard if I sat there in a Nigerian Prison, I knew I had to make a move.

Against the background of my status as a dual citizen of two countries that promote dissimilar cultural values while attempting to apply the same laws in governance, I knew I had been snagged in between a rock and a hard place.

My mind had however already been made up that I would accede to the order for my extradition and I was not about to change it. So, after much humiliation in the hands of those empowered by the system to decide right from wrong and crime from innocence, I was ready to embark on the journey of my life. Whatever good intentions there were behind the covert formulation of a treaty of extradition between Nigeria and the United States, are to me, lost on the altar of inequity. I believe so because the President of Nigeria, his Attorney General, and on down to the last Nigerian is potentially guilty ab initio, of any offences covered by the said treaty if they violate the Nigerian Constitution and their accepted way of life.

I understood the reason the United States frowned sternly at what the system perceived as the subjection of another to involuntary servitude and would seek to bring offenders to justice. What I could not understand was why Nigeria could not decide based on accepted Nigerian cultural, economic and moral platitudes what would constitute involuntary servitude in Nigeria and then take a stand on it. Especially considering that the Nigerian President, his Attorney General, State Governors, Judges and Prosecutors would themselves be found guilty of Involuntary Servitude as defined by the United States. Perhaps the United States could become persuaded to be more accommodating of the cultural practices of other responsible nations even when they are in conflict with those of the United States.

In view of the ramifications of these clearly complex socio-cultural issues, and hoping to convince the United States Justice System to temper justice with mercy in the interest of cultural accommodation and tolerance, I began putting in motion the preparations for the long flight to the United States. I had decided that I, my attorney Festus Keyamo and our cause will be better served if I terminated all legal actions in Nigeria and returned to the United States immediately.

Forty One

I sat in stone silence as the North American Airline's wide body jetliner curved on ascent directed by GPS to face northwest on our one way, nonstop journey from Lagos, Nigeria to New York, New York, USA. Through the window my eyes followed the curved contrails trailing behind us against the background of a dark night over the coastline of West Africa—my birth place. As we progressed high into the sky, and Lagos disappeared behind us, my mind flickered randomly on different scenes of the dramas that played out on the days and hours that preceded our New York bound flight. I also remained conscious of the two pairs of law enforcement eyes boring into the back of my head.

When I signaled my intentions to accept the order of extradition handed down by the High Court in my case, by filing a motion to withdraw my appeal, I believed the process to be a simple matter which merely required confirmation that it was a voluntary choice on my part. However, upon packing and unpacking my travel bag several times in readiness for my extradition and still there was not a hint that the withdrawal process had been completed, I began wondering what could be slowing the process down. Three months appeared much too long of a period for the simple task I imagined the process would be.

My pressure on the Attorney who had filed the withdrawal motion on my behalf opened up a can of worms such as I could never have imagined. The process required a sitting of the Appeals Court Panel which had deliberated on my earlier appeal against the High Court ruling. I could never in my wildest dreams guess that I was going to relive the up and down hassles of sitting in jailhouse limbo while court dates were assigned and cancelled, while prosecutors requested adjournments for unprintable reasons and junior court staff demand bribes before they would do their assigned paperwork. But like it or not, those were the painful agitations I had to endure. Sounds ironical, doesn't it? That I had to pay for a process that ran at major cross purposes with my own wellbeing? If that is not the way it sounds to you, then well come to Nigeria, where life is a game for the rubber-hearted.

Now, the tables were turned. I had gone from fighting to stop the system from extraditing me to fighting to make the system extradite me! Incredible! Right? Do not take my word for it, check the records. It was as though I had been forgotten or abandoned—left to rot in the prison. And it even got worse!

After four exhausting months of bureaucratic dallying which left holes in my pocket, I was relieved when on Monday the 4th of June 2007, the withdrawal was effected. I was again thrown into travel mode. My expectation was that within two weeks, the combined team of FBI and Interpol agents whose duty it was to carry out the physical transfer of my person to the United States would show up. That did not happen, and to my chagrin, two weeks slowly and torturously turned into two months. That was when I began wondering whether ours was indeed a member nation of the much touted new world order, the purported new global community. Forgive me, but I will not subscribe to the notion that to compare the justice system of Nigeria with those of advanced nations is somehow unfair to Nigeria. To accept that ludicrous notion would place a higher value to the human rights of some human beings over those of others; depending on nationality or place of their birth.

It is doubtful that most Nigerian government employees are even aware that they're involved in nation building of any sort. If they were, then they wouldn't be quick to retort: "This is not America" whenever one complains about workplace laxity or corruption—a response that suggests that in America, a secretary has a higher calling than his or her counterpart in Nigeria. If indeed truth be told, then the Nigerian secretary has a higher duty call as the challenges of a developing nation tower above those of developed nations. Yet, the people wallow in misery and apathy as though without options in the hands of pockets of their fellow citizens, who having sacrificed principles, impose themselves on the population that they are meant to serve.

As I waited for action from the government, it began to gradually dawn on me that I had a choice to make. I either kept mute, stayed in prison, abandoned like the other helplessly weary souls or I kicked up some dust. I chose the latter.

~

On August 8th, I wrote to the Nigerian Attorney General basically reminding him that I was awaiting the execution of his order. I took no pleasure in having to write the letter but because there was a great deal less pleasure in sitting abandoned in prison, I chose the more sensible option.

When no reply came as I half expected, I contacted my friend Barrister Ivienagbor who filed a motion on my behalf on September 4th, 2007 at the Federal High Court, Lagos requesting the court to issue an order compelling the Attorney General to surrender me to the United States within seven days or else release me from prison custody.

As the motion was being filed, I was worried about its bad timing. I feared that September was too close to the end of the year. I did not share my worries with anybody else but I tried as much as I could to lock in an early hearing date. My feeling of disquiet was because of the dreaded upcoming year-end jamboree which saw most Nigerian workers anywhere but at their offices working. Most government establishments are guilty of participating in this annual jamboree but the justice system appears the one with the most guilt. The court staffers simply vanished for a period of 3 months!

Needless to say that my efforts failed and I simply cannot recount the horrific emotions exacted on me by the fear of the ensuing delay. It remains a mystery to me how I survived the interminable minutes and hours which were so painfully boring, but if I had not lived through them, then I wouldn't be here now, would i?

~

With that motion filed at the High Court, I got the attention of the Department of Public Prosecution (DPP)—the Lagos office of the Attorney General of the Federation. DPP which is clearly peopled by bean counters as most government bureaucracies are appeared to smell blood. They quickly sat up and in a matter of days, they filed a counter affidavit challenging my assertions that I had been left to rot away, abandoned at the prison. Their challenge was however nothing more than their typical reaction whenever they were fingered in a threatening way for their habitual abuse of public trust. In fact, at the time, as I am quite sure it remains today, there were hundreds of inmates who remained similarly abandoned at Ikoyi Prison who would spend years, and perhaps their entire lives without a chance of ever being tried.

I was unable to persuade the Chief Judge of the Federal High Court to assign my case to a judge before the mass judiciary exodus of the year 2007 began in October. Despite my spirited efforts and the tireless but failed scampering of many of my dear friends to secure a hearing date, I had to brace myself for the long and painful period of subjugation in prison squalor that was to follow.

My period of waiting in prison yard oblivion was on November 13th, 2007 abruptly interrupted by an unscheduled and unexpected visit by a representative of the Office of the Commissioner of Police, Interpol Section, Force C.I.D. Alagbon Close, Ikoyi, Lagos. It was then that I realized how much heat I had ignited on the staffers of the Department of Public Prosecution. I knew that the visitor had to be a representative of a panic-stricken prosecutor somewhere scampering to have me extradited before a rogue judge heard my case and set me free. Before going to respond to the visitor, I had a quick bite to eat, unsure whether or not I would be taken away to the United States that evening.

As I entered the office of the Deputy Comptroller of Prisons, I was nervous. I held my breath for a fleeting second, and then stepped into the office. The DCP indicated a seat and said, "Give me a moment." He was on the telephone rounding up a conversation.

The visitor, a Chief Superintendent of Police (CSP) is an Ibo man, meaning that he hails from my tribal area of Eastern Nigeria. Still, I did not feel comforted by his kinship as I took a sidelong look at his powerfully built frame. I could feel his police mind's radar drill through me, assessing me, sizing me up. I felt myself squirm as fear crept up my back. The courage with which I had been anticipating the journey to the United States as a fugitive had all but totally evaporated. All I really knew about extraditions apart from the dictionary meaning of the word were from the various movie scenes where wanted bandits are shackled with chains, padlocks and handcuffs in their prison jumpers, escorted by mean looking FBI agents or United States Marshals. The bandits usually looked their part, like Tony Montana in Scarface—not wimpy and paralyzed with fear as I was gradually becoming.

When my knees began knocking and my stomach began to tighten, a voice in my head came alive. "Pull yourself together George!" the voice ordered. "You've waited like a trained dog for a chance to reunite with your children! Now, that chance is here and all you're worried about is the inconvenience that will not last a full 24 hours? Snap out of it!"

That was what it took to pacify me. I felt a rush of excitement as the DCP ended his conversation and began introducing the Interpol Superintendent to me. I greeted my visitor, half expecting him to inform me that the time had come for me to go face justice in the United States. Instead, the man dropped a bomb on both the DCP and me.

My jaw dropped, my eyes narrowed and I began quivering as the impact of the words just spoken by my visitor began to weigh on me.

The DCP snapped his fingers, incredulous at the same information. The CSP had just told us that he came over to the prison to meet me and clarify my identity. He informed us that upon receipt of the order of the Attorney General of Nigeria commanding Inter pol to collect one George Udeozor from Ikoyi Prison for the purpose of surrendering him to the United States authorities in New York, he had been directed in accordance with diplomatic procedure, to go and arrange with the US Embassy for the logistical implementation of the surrender. He informed us that the embassy officials who he spoke with did a thorough check of their list subjects scheduled for transfer to the United States but failed to find my name on that list. He said that as a cautionary measure, to be fully certain, he had requested the embassy officials to double check their information and after they did, they returned with the same result, whereupon he decided to visit Ikoyi Prison to confirm that the name George Udeozor was indeed flesh and blood.

"Voila!" I yelled. "Voila, Mr. George Udeozor himself! I am Mr. George Udeozor. I am not only flesh and blood; I am also a U. S. citizen. For the past three years, somebody has been making my life a living hell! Now I know that this whole sordid affair is the work of a monster. I will find that monster and I will unmask that monster! Somebody will pay for this travesty. I will find the monster and I will make him pay!

Both the CSP and the DSP looked on puzzled. I went on to give them a brief rundown of my life's sojourn in the United States. My family saga and the incident that triggered the problems which I believed were at the root of my ordeal. When I finished I asked the CSP how and when the Interpol would brief the Attorney General about his findings. I told him that I did not wish to remain in prison indefinitely. I also informed him that I was actually anxious to return to the United States and could use his assistance in getting that information to the Attorney General to perhaps expedite my release from prison so that I could leave for the United States right away. He told me unequivocally that it was not the duty of the Interpol to get involved with making recommendations to the Attorney General of the Federation. He said the Interpol was finished with my case until they received further instructions from the Attorney General. "The ball is in your court now Mr. Udeozor," he concluded before we said our goodbyes.

The ball was in my court alright—and I wasn't going to miss that striking opportunity. Overnight, I managed to track my friend and barrister down on the telephone. I informed him that I was calling a meeting of my war council. I had a war to wedge. In a few words I gave him an account of the CSP's visit the previous night. Even over the phone, I could feel how incredulous he was.

On the next day, after meeting for several hours strategizing on the best approach to tackle the DPP and the order for my extradition, the war council agreed to carry out our own independent investigation into the CSP's revealing visit before we took any action. Remarkably, when my attorney visited the Interpol and the U.S. embassy two days later, both agencies corroborated the information I obtained during the CSP's visit.

One week later, on November 21st, 2007, we fired our first missile in the form of a motion to the Federal High Court demanding that the court issue an order revoking the orders for my remand in prison and for my extradition to the United States which the court made on June 16th, 2005. We decided that other motions would follow as the court's response warrants.

It took the DPP nearly three weeks to react to my application for the revocation of the court's order in my case. The affidavit in support of my application provoked just the right amount of indignation in the prosecutor for her to lose a lot of sleep. I was tickled when I learned this very pleasing news because I sensed that she took personal pleasure in my demise—not the uninvolved just-doing-my-job approach which I expected from a prosecutor under the unfortunate circumstances of my matter.

By her reaction, it was clear that she was thirsting for red blood like a Tasmanian vampire. And she indeed found vulnerable source for blood to suck. Not mine, but the blood of the CSP! When I saw the CSP's affidavit filed on November 21, 2007 denying just about every single one of his statements to both me and the DCP of Ikoyi Prison, my hands dropped limply by my sides in disbelief and resignation.

I was not angry with the CSP. I understood right away why he had to bow to superior authority. After spending a lifetime building a career, it would have amounted to extreme recklessness to risk losing the benefits of his life's work at a late age and at such a difficult period of economic downturn in the country. He obviously had no choice but to disclaim his own story. That was why even though our own independent investigation at the U.S. Embassy confirmed his story and also, although the prison DCP would have corroborated my account of the CSP's conversation with us, I chose to not pursue my latest motion any further. I chose instead to focus once again on my prior motion to compel the Attorney General of the Federation to either enforce the pending order for my extradition to the United States or else release me immediately from prison custody.

~

Looking back now at those last few days, I find it remarkable how we, the mere mortals that we are, sometimes work ourselves into a frenzy chasing shadows when all we really need to do is exercise patience and wait on God. After the whole imbroglio over the CSP's visit to Ikoyi Prison, without a single effort from me personally or my legal war council, my motion to compel the Attorney General to enforce the order of court for my extradition was assigned to a judge who was entirely God-sent.

The court was already in session when I was brought in. it was a full court, with law interns occupying about six rows of benches as observers. My family and friends were also present. When we walked into his courtroom, this judge whose name I was still learning to pronounce, flashed a dazzling smile in my direction. First thing I noticed was how he seemed to fill the entire courtroom even though he was just a man of average size. He wore his good-fitting robe well, covering a slightly portly torso. I was immediately at home in his courtroom.

He resumed interviewing the prosecutor on the matter at hand after I was securely caged in the docket. It was then I understood the reason this courtroom was so cheerful and warm. This was a people-friendly judge whose mastery of his art co-mingles easily with his self-confidence to create a sedate, yet pleasant atmosphere where people are not afraid to speak their minds.

The judge apparently did not require my physical production in court to decide my matter but now that we were already there, he appeared pleased to put a face to the "fugitive Criminal" which the prosecutor enjoyed tagging me with. The judge took exception to that term, preferring to address me as Mr. George Udeozor whenever he needed to. This sign of respect earned him my eternal gratitude as it made me feel like all hope was not lost for Nigeria—with judges like him still on the bench.

"Returning to your name counsel," the judge resumed, "did I pronounce it correctly?"

"You did okay my Lord." The Prosecutor replied.

"What a name! I believe that name has a Plateau ring to it. Are you from Plateau State?"

"No, my Lord. Benue State, my Lord, it is a Tiv name my Lord."

"Is that so? I have great friends from Benue State. They cook very well, I must say. I had the best egusi soup ever at my friend's home. By the way, is it true, story about Benue hospitality…?

"Yes indeed my Lord… I… eh…"

"I'm still speaking. Let me land…"

"Sorry my Lord."

"As I was saying… or getting ready to ask; is there any truth to the story about Tiv hospitality—the story that a Tiv man would offer a visiting close friend the affection of one of his wives as part of his expression of good will or appreciation of their friendship?"

"Oh no no no, my Lord. That is ancient history. That no longer happens. You will see when next you visit Tiv land. Ask any enlightened Tiv person. I must say my Lord, we still cook well and we are still friendly and hospitable. When next you visit Tiv land, come visit us. I will cook for you, my Lord."

"Oh no, no. But I do plan to visit Tiv land again sometime, but you will not get a visit from me. I don't trust you."

"My Lord! But I'm a good cook. Egusi and dried fish is my best dish. I will make you the very best." The Prosecutor protested.

"I have already said no to you. I'd rather have a tall pretty Tiv girl cook for me. I cannot trust you at all at all… Errhh, now, let us go on record. By the way, I hope all these have been off the record?" the judge concluded, now facing the court clerk.

"Yes my Lord," the clerk replied amid tumultuous laughter from the enthralled courtroom audience.

I was particularly captivated by the exchange and I laughed so exuberantly that it would have been impossible to believe I was the same aggrieved detainee who had been made cynical by the dreadful condition of Ikoyi prison life.

~

The judge now focused on the matter of my motion and opened a tripartite dialogue between himself and the prosecutor on the one hand and then with my barrister, Lucky Ivienagbor on the other hand.

For the first time in three years during which the Nigerian justice system had so callously abused my honor and my birthright to be treated with dignity, an angel in a black robe-de-chambre spoke up for me. After hearing my humble submission through my barrister and the equivocations of the government's respondent which was nothing but a lot of babbled legalese, this god-sent judge gave me the opportunity to address the court—it was an unexpected platform. One which I had been denied by the EFCC, the United States Embassy, the Presiding Judge for my Extradition hearing and the Appeals Court Justices.

My brief emotional speech which I deliberately punctuated sporadically with piercing tirades against the system and those who operate it was well received by the judge and the audience which listened with rapt attention.

In ruling, the judge appeared to have studied my mind because he addressed issues which were not even mentioned in the course of the court session—the issue of Chinelo, the young woman who made the allegations which ultimately put the United States Justice System on my trail. The judge obviously studied and understood the issues at play. He berated the prosecutor for her insensitivity to the plight of people awaiting trial in detention, abandoned in prison for long periods unnecessarily. Addressing me by my first name, he said, "George, you are being punished for your humanitarian deed, I know, but go back to the United States and to your family. Even if you should be made to serve prison time, do it with your chin up. You will come out better in the end. The perfidious young lady who did this to you will reap her reward in her own currency."

He then gave the prosecutor a period of three weeks and ordered that we return to his court on February 12th, 2008 when he would release me in the event that the government failed to implement the order of the court for my extradition to the United States.

On hearing the judge's ruling, my hand flew up like the hand of a 3rd grade student vying to supply a great answer to the teacher's tough question.

"Yes George," the judge indulged.

"My Lord, three weeks is much too long! Can't you make it the one week I prayed the Court in my motion?" I pleaded.

The judge laughed fitfully for one minute before replying. He said, "George, you sound like the middle aged man who remained childless for twenty years after he got married. When finally the doctor informed him that his wife was two months pregnant and would be delivered of the baby in seven months, he began complaining hysterically. He felt that seven months was much too long and said to the doctor; "Doctor why does the baby have to take seven whole months? Why can't we have the baby in seven weeks?"

It took a while for the judge's anecdotal message to process through my clogged mind and when I finally joined the court audience in their hysterical laughter the judge saw that I finally got it. Only then did his gavel come down. "Court dismissed. Adjourned until 9:00AM February 12, 2008"

I was walking on air as we returned to Ikoyi Prison. The judge had lifted my spirit beyond the clouds of heaven!

On February 10, 2008 I got a visit. My visitors were two, a male and a female, from the Embassy of the United States. The gentleman was an FBI Agent and the lady was a representative of the State Department. She took a photograph of me and explained that it was to be used in preparing a passport for my journey back to the United States. When I queried her about their reason for failing to visit me in the past three years, she swore that she never knew that a U.S. Citizen was being detained at Ikoyi Prison. I exchanged glances with the DCP and we shared a knowing smile. Only both of us had the knowledge we shared—the secret knowledge about the Interpol representative's visit.

It was thus no longer necessary to engage the unseemly prosecutor or even set my eyes on any other apologists of our oppressive judicial system. But I made myself the promise that whenever my ordeal ended I would return to seek out this judge in order to pay him my respect. I know that unless I do that, he may never know what role he played in restoring my self-confidence and reassuring me that charity remains one of God's indispensable fruits. He might not have been aware that his words got through to me, so much so that I resolved that despite being vilified for helping to rescue Chinelo, I would go on doing the work I believe all of humanity are called to.

Deciding what attire to wear was no easy task. I spent the entire day brooding over the subject. Three years earlier I witnessed the humiliating experience of Chris, on the night of his extradition, within 24 hours of my arrival at Ikoyi Prison. He had also agonized over what apparel would be most suitable, and had decided on casual combination— blue jeans, tee shirt and a blazer. I still had a clear memory of how his belt was stripped off his waist and the blazer peeled off, leaving him with nothing but a pair of jeans which were so loose at the waist they threatened to fall off his rear, and a tee shirt which was ill-fitting. Not wishing myself the same awful experience, I decided finally to be clad in a caftan—the closest attire to a track suit which I had in various color combinations. The caftan is also the trendiest statement of contemporary Nigerian fashion. But to me it was the most practical way of avoiding the harsh treatment which I feared was now inevitable. As it turned out, I ought not to have worried about a thing. Not at this stage. Not yet!

To start with, the FBI agent designated to accompany me to New York was the same one who had visited me on the 10th of February with the representative of the State Department. He presented me with my new travel documents and gave me his marching orders: I had two choices—either we did things the easy way, in which case, I cooperated with him, giving him no problems or we proceeded the hard way if I chose instead to be an asshole and spin some spider's web. Either way, I will be brought to New York leisurely as if we were pals, or on the other hand in hand cuffs and leg chains. With his penetrating turquoise eyes searching my own pair of brown eyes from barely one inch away like laser beams, he waited for my response. I could not hold back a chuckle as I responded; "Are you kidding?" he found something very funny because he smiled. Perhaps despite my attempt at bravado, he saw in my eyes whatever it was he was searching for. I suspect his probing eyes were searching for sincerity and I was eager to project through my eyes the picture of a meek lamb ready to be sacrificed. I must have succeeded, for a hint of satisfaction was mixed up in his smile. In a cracked voice, I assured him that he will not have any problem with me.

Time seemed to stand still for me as the FBI agent and his Nigerian Interpol colleague quickly processed me. The FBI agent graciously allowed me to bring along my overnight bag which I had packed, fully expecting that I might not be allowed the privilege of travelling with it. As I was being patted down, my throat felt as though a fishbone was stuck in it. I was unsure what to expect. My memory of the indignity suffered three years earlier by Chris as he was going through similar processing for extradition occupied my thoughts. Although I had so far been treated quite decently, the paralysis of fear elicited by the unknown would not let me relax. Yet, a feeling of optimism kept building up in the back of my mind as we neared the completion of the process of prisoner transfer between the DCP and my two escorts. Then, the announcement by the FBI agent; "I guess we should be on our way," finally eased the fishbone out of my throat.

I squared my shoulders, released my held breath, picked up my overnight bag and said goodbye to the Deputy Comptroller of Ikoyi Prison. In a surprising display of humanity, the FBI agent allowed me to hug my friends Aminu and Papa, the two inmates with whom I had grown quite close while we shared the humbling experiences of awaiting trial in a Nigerian Prison. And then it was time to head for the airport en route to Greenbelt Maryland, USA.

Outside the prison gate, two official vehicles waited with their engines humming on idle. As we approached them I caught sight of my brother's black Toyota Tundra, also humming on idle along with the official vehicles. I stopped myself from my first impulse to dash across and say goodbye. The eagle eyed agents quickly noticed my move, forcing me to explain that the man behind those wheels was my immediate senior brother, Paul. Again, I was allowed to say a quick goodbye even though my brother joined our convoy to the airport.

I sat between my two escorts staring blankly at the familiar Lagos scenery as we crawled through the streets and highways of one of the world's most populous cities to the equally historic and famous Murtala Airport, Lagos.

After a check-in process that felt like going through an obstacle course in the Amazon Jungle, we got to the boarding gate. It was only then that the fast moving time seemed to suddenly stop. My mind resumed functioning properly again. And as we waited to board the flight, it slowly dawned on me that new detention facilities, US Marshals and Courtroom dramas were all only hours away in my future.

We were soon airborne and there I was at last, shivering from two kinds of cold. One, very real—spewing from the air conditioning vents overhead. The other, imagined, from the dread of the unknown arsenal of manufactured evidence thrust in the hands of an unsuspecting prosecutor who was eagerly waiting to do damage to my life.

Forty Two

I could not summon the calm necessary for sleep, so while it was quiet all around me, save for a number of passengers snoring, and others who moved about answering the call of nature, I sat in my seat, now projecting my thoughts forward to the events destined to come in a matter of just a few hours. Every time I stole a glance behind me, the two pairs of eyes shone back at me like laser beams. My two escorts apparently did not factor any sleep as part of their agenda for this journey. I could feel their radars drill through me.

Finally, after eleven grueling hours of nonstop flying, sitting tongue-tied and miserable, anguished at the thought of what was to come, I felt the airplane jerk and begin pointing its nose downward. We had started our gradual descent into New York City.

Like a programmed computer I began a silent prayer as I often do during times of grief. I recited the sorrowful mysteries while I prayed the rosary in my heart.

Why do I pray the rosary during times of grief? Simple; I pray the rosary for the solace which I derive from praying it. Forgive me, but I find my reflection on the sorrows of other people as the quickest route to peace of mind. And whose sorrows better to reflect on than those of one who knowingly embraced it? I do not pray for my sufferings to be lifted—I know better now. After being married to my misery and torment for so many years, I had come to terms with the real value of prayers in my life. I respect all opinions on the value of prayers, including those of people who pray for miracles. But since I have yet to experience divine miracle in my life, even the lifting of my smallest burdens, through prayer, I find it redundant to pray for them knowing that they would go unheeded. Since my prayers for companionship through difficult times are always answered, I value with extraordinary relish, the strength and courage released in me during those times. I have come to the sobering conclusion that God would rather stand with me, suffering along with me while he provides me with the strength and courage to overcome adversity than to grant me miraculous solutions or the painless lifting of my burdens. That is the reason I pray—to call up to the surface, the God within me whose companionship I can count on, one hundred percent of the time, particularly during the most difficult of times.

Things had so far gone so well for me that I had foolishly assumed my escorts would simply walk me up to some U.S. Marshals upon our arrival at the JFK Airport for onward transfer to Maryland. That was the extent of my ignorance and naiveté on the workings of the United States law enforcement even after over two decades of living in the United States. I had simply followed my father's sage advice during my youth to avoid having any entanglements whatsoever with law enforcement officers. He had warned us, his children, that, "Once you invite the probing eyes of the law into your affairs, they are there to stay, with or without invitation." It turned out that my father was right, as he should, being a British trained police officer himself.

It was not yet dawn when we arrived at JFK, but with the airport so brightly lit up by over 10 million points of light, nothing, no transactions, could be conducted with secrecy. That, I believe, was the reason the FBI agent stopped me when I picked up my carry-on overnight bag and moved to join other passengers to disembark from the aircraft. "Hold it George. Sit back down. We will be the last to disembark." He said. I knew right away that my new reality was about to kick in.

In a matter of minutes, all passengers had disembarked, leaving only me, my escorts and a few flight crew members. My time was up. I waited; surprisingly calm judging from my callowness vis-à-vis the long arms of the law.

The sound of handcuffs is distinct when it is about to be put to use. The familiar "click click" sound coming from behind me sent me up on my feet. As a defense contractor, I had put many a handcuff to test before ordering them for my clients. Now, I was about to experience the difference when the cold metal is snapped on one's own wrist for real and not for sampling.

"Turn around George." That order hit my ears like a slap. I turned around and nearly bumped into the FBI agent where he stood inches away from me, the silver handcuffs glistening in his hands. "I'm sorry George, but we are now on United States soil. We will now proceed with U.S procedures. I have to handcuff you." He concluded.

"I understand. But can't you wait till after we've disembarked?" I pleaded.

"I'm afraid no. This is not personal. I wish I did not have to do this. You're quite a nice guy. But if I lead you out without handcuffs, I might not have a job by the end of the day." He said.

"Okay, you have to do what you have to do."

"Thanks George."

"Sure."

I dropped my overnight bag on the seat and shot my two hands out to surrender. But the agent shook his head.

"No George, behind you. I have to cuff your hands behind."

"Oh my God! Really?"

"Yes, really it won't hurt. You'll see. C'mon, be a man George...."

"I sure don't feel like one now. Believe me, I don't."

"You'll do alright."

Click...click...cra...cra...cra... k!

As we walked solemnly through the arrival hall past other passengers who had just arrived on our flight and were queued up for customs and immigration processing, I noticed as many of them who had seen me on board the aircraft gawked at me, wide-eyed and incredulous. I was marched past them by my escorts, leaving them to make their conclusions about what they had just witnessed.

Most of the activities that followed right after we disembarked remain, even today, quite surreal—like an out-of-body experience to me. I remember being led into a room full of uniformed law officers. I remember being moved from one desk to another to face many different officials before finally being handed over to two people, one woman and one man, who were not in uniforms. At this point, the FBI agent told me these two were U.S. Marshals and that his duty ended right after he handed me over to them. That was when the unthinkable happened.

The handcuffs would not come off! No key in the whole of J.F.K. could unlock the handcuffs! Every police officer in sight tried their own keys. No luck! The FBI agent gazed in disbelief.

He said the handcuffs were from the newly issued batches specially shipped to the embassies around the world by the State Department.

After many failed efforts to unlock the handcuffs, it was decided that since the law enforcement officers attached to the airport were not equipped to unlock or shear it off my wrist, I would have to be transported with the handcuffs to the courthouse where they had all kinds of gadgets which could easily do the job. On that note, the FBI agent and his tag-along Interpol colleague said their goodbyes to me for the first and last time since we left the Nigerian shores.

I followed the U.S. Marshals; dazed like a lamb being led to slaughter toward the airport terminal exit door. The female Marshal grabbed me by my left elbow—a firm grip which surprised me considering her diminutive stature.

~

Nine straight years in the tropical climate of Nigeria had dimmed my memory of what cold winter weather felt like, so when the exit doors were parted by electricity, an explosion caused me to take a backward skip. The two U.S. Marshals were beside themselves with laughter which I found odd in the circumstance. "George", the male Marshal said with a grin, "it's a really nasty day to come to New York from Africa. It sure is cold out there although I see you're fairly well prepared for it. But I bet you did not know it was going to be this cold. It is the coldest it's been this winter… 15 degrees below."

That was when I silently thanked my sister Chinwe in my heart. It was she who alerted me over the telephone to dress as warmly as I could to prepare myself for what was indeed a brutal winter season. I was glad I brought a thick sweater along which the FBI agent allowed me to put on in-flight.

The explosion I had heard was from the mingling of air pressure between the warm air-tight interior of the terminal and the freezing cold outside air. I was now better prepared for the weather assault when we burst out and sprinted to their truck which was a little distance away, thankfully, illegally parked on the roadside and not in a clogged parking lot one mile away.

Although it was yet to strike six in the morning, traffic had begun building up heavily on the freeway to Manhattan. We were lucky finally to make it to the courthouse in Lower Manhattan in just less than two hours. It was a tortuous journey which I can never forget, much as I would prefer to do so. The scars left on my wrists by those States Department issued handcuffs took over six months to heal.

Both of my hands, especially at my knuckles, turned pale from shortage of blood. Blood flow was badly restricted at my wrists by the pressure from the handcuffs when I was forced to sit on my hands. I still have the taste of pain in my mouth from the rough and sharp tips of the heavy pliers, clamps and scissors that impaled my wrists over and over while the U.S.

Marshals and a police officer at that courthouse basement struggled to free me. Each prick from those tips and jagged edges sent piercing pains which felt like electric current through my entire body. By the time it was over, I was exhausted and my wrists were covered with abrasive wounds, but I was glad to finally be free of the clamping restrictions of those handcuffs. I was then led into a lonely, cold but brightly lit holding cell and informed that U.S. Marshals were already en route to New York from Greenbelt, Maryland to collect me.

Looking back now, many years after the fear-inspiring events of that day, I marvel at the efficacy of faith—the kind of faith in God that frees the soul of expectations and selfishness, and as a consequence, free of fear. True faith does render the heart fearless. The sad story here is that I am unable to sustain that level of faith for always. Perhaps God made it so, lest I would naively deem myself invincible.

On this day, I was invincible through faith, or else I would not be here today. Before you dismiss my claim as frivolous, consider the ordeal which I endured before the end of my first day back in the United States after a nine year field trip abroad:

Following the painfully scary experience with the jinxed handcuff—the State Department-issued handcuff which affixed itself to my wrists like a leech, I was dumped in a totally bare holding cell with the air conditioning blasting at full throttle despite the numbing winter cold that seeped steadily into the cell. Exhausted, hungry and convalescing from my wounds, I waited for over four hours, coursing in and out of consciousness. I remind you, at the time of our departure from Nigeria less than 24 hours earlier, the average daily atmospheric temperature was about 90 degrees F.

At about 12:30 PM, when it appeared that my soul wished to separate from my increasingly frail body—the soul remaining stronger than ever before, sounds of human activity returned to the below the ground establishment which surrounded the holding cell in which I was confined. Male voices, sharp as blades cut into my space sending chills over my already frigid form. The chills did not however come from further decline in room temperature; it came instead from my body's reaction to the subject matter of the conversation coming from the sharp voices.

Three voices in all were involved in the exchange, leading me to conclude that we were only four in the whole establishment; me and the three of them. For easy reference I identify them as Voice A, Voice B, and Voice C:

Voice A: "About time you got here. It's been lunch time forever. I was wondering if something happened to you guys."

Voices B & C (together): "The drive was nasty for a while, leaving Maryland—up around Baltimore. But it got better. Oh hell. What are you complaining about? We're here, aren't we?"

Voice A: "Yeah…yeah…come to claim you cargo?"

Voice C: "Uh huh . . . Where is he?"

Voice A: "Back there in the holding."

Voice B: "What's he look like? Trouble?"

Voice A: "Some African Tribal Chief or something. Don't know what to make of him. Ain't heard a peep from him."

Voices A,B & C: General laughter, then, incoherent chatter.

Voice A: "Who knows? He's probably iced out. They brought him in on handcuffs that won't come off. He got pretty battered up when we tried to yank the things off. Guy's pretty strong. But he was poked here and there and his wrists are sore from the poking."

Voices B & C: "Ouch! Then general laughter,"

Voices A: "Let's hope he's still breathing. I know it's like the Arctic back there. By the way, what are things like on the streets in your neck of the woods?"

Voice C: "You don't wanna know. They're mostly killing each other now. It's like a war zone now. Especially in P.G., you won't believe what these guys do these days!"

Voice A: "How do you cope? Are they being put away?"

Voice B: "Hell no! That's the problem. It's frustrating! They're back on the streets in a blink. Some of these judges are idiots. Especially the n--ers ones. They're assholes."

Voice C: "You remember… (says an inaudible name)? You know… the cop. One of these bastards… a doped up dealer… it was not a full month after he was released. He traced down… (Inaudible name) and shot him. These judges just don't get it. These n--ers are animals."

Voice A: "Why don't you guys do what the boys do up here. Just silence them. No body. No case. No paperwork. Nothing… period."

Silence. Not one more word.

Finally, after minutes of eerie stillness, human activity returned—this time eerily close to my confinement cell. I heard footsteps, voices and puzzling sounds—the sound of chains clattering on the concrete floor ceaselessly. The voices, still engaged in conversation were now drowned by the metallic sound of clattering chains. I was exhausted, worried, even terrified, but I was determined that I would comport myself in a dignified manner, whatever evil intended by the men behind the voices, my companion was with me, within me, supplying me with strength and courage while we waited together to overcome the terror advancing toward me. My body was weak but my spirit was unyielding.

Without warning, the cell door swung inward and a plain clothed man entered with a document out of which he tried to read out my name. I was by myself and it was therefore not difficult to figure out that I was the object of his search. "Yes". I replied to his enquiry. "I am George Udeozor."

"Thank you Mr… whatever. Get yourself sorted out. Use the bathroom now if you need to. The Marshals are here to get you." He shut the door before I could ask any questions.

Thankfully, I had no need to use the bathroom for I would have had to do so in the presence of the two young Marshals. They marched into the holding cell within just seconds on the heels of my last visitor, dragging behind them several long chains with handcuffs of various sizes and padlocks attached to them.

They walked into the cell, looking through me as if I was not there. They then walked around me to a spacious part of the cell and finally dumped their chains in a large heap. One of them poked around the empty cell like a sniff dog before joining his colleague where they both began sorting the chains, handcuffs and padlocks.

If their deliberate handling of those fettering gadgets was meant to intimidate or terrify me, they succeeded. Both men were young and powerfully built. They appeared fiendish, especially following their earlier conversation with their New York colleague which continues to send cold chills through me, years after that god-awful day. My only thought was; "Whatever your intentions, please make it snappy." While I waited, I betrayed no emotions. Had they known how terrified of them I was, I believe they would have approached me gingerly, if only to reassure me that beneath the Lucifer perceived by my sensibilities, they were actually humans, with flesh and blood and feeling too. Instead, one of them ordered me:

"Take your garments off."

I was caught off guard. Nothing could have prepared me for this moment. Nobody said, "Hey George, your dignity has been purchased. You are now an item—tagged like any furniture in any department store." The only difference is that unlike furniture, I have feelings which can be bruised, but furniture does not. On that score, furniture would fare better than I was doing, subdued as I was before these two young men. Even in my situation of helplessness, I still felt entitled to some respect and dignity. This would be the first time in all of my lifetime when men would order me to disrobe before their eyes. I could not help but ask them why I had to disrobe before them.

Both men answered spontaneously. But their answers were not harmonious. The younger Marshal seemed angered by my question and retorted, "Because we say so." The older man who appeared a lot more mature had more authority behind his reply, "Because that is the rule."

Still nursing hunger pangs and feeling as if drugged from exhaustion, I began slowly peeling off my garments—first the caftan, then the sweater, my inner shirt and finally my shoes. I was shivering now from the cold which began to freeze the tears that were gradually dripping down my cheeks. The two U.S. Marshals who were comfortably dressed in layers of clothing underneath their overcoats began methodically unfurling, searching and examining every inch of my articles of clothing with their gloved hands. After they were done, the older Marshal asked me to remove even the last bits of garments left on my body—my boxer, singlet and a pair of socks. I looked at both men convinced that the last order was a joke. Their expressions left no doubt that they were serious. At that point, as at every low point in my life, I found strength. I also found courage. In a swift move, I stripped all articles of clothing off my body and threw them into the waiting hands of the Marshals. I asked them. "What next?" The younger man was visibly angry but seemed restrained from acting out. He said viciously, "Squat down and cough." I squatted down and coughed. "What next?" I continued. The older Marshal stepped in, apparently noticing some testiness in our brief exchange. "That's enough, George, get dressed up," he said gesturing toward my clothing.

They waited while I put my clothes back on. My hands were steadier now than when I undressed. Must be spleen, I thought. Anger does do some good after all. I had forgotten about food for a moment, perhaps because I saw none and smelled none. My mind was so consumed with rage at the humiliation I had just suffered that I paid little attention to the physical trauma that followed. To me nothing, no amount of shackling with handcuffs, chains and padlocks could rival the humiliation of being disrobed and violated the way these Marshals had just done to me. Well… Maybe not.

In just minutes, I had been shackled with chains at my ankles and torso. My wrists were cuffed and linked to my torso with a padlock. Just like they do in the movies!

I could not disguise my contempt for these men as they led me through the narrow hallways and out to the indoor parking garage where their car was parked. They equally had no qualms about treating me with disdain as they shoved me into the back of their car which was made tight and cage-like by the Plexiglas paneling that separates the passengers from the Marshals in the front seat.

During the drive from New York to Greenbelt, Maryland I was barely conscious. I faintly recall being thrown about in the cage as the car speeded recklessly south-bound. I recall with bile the pain at my wrists from the wounds inflicted on them by the handcuffs earlier in the day which were re-opened once more. Mostly, I remember my attitude of defiance. Not that the Marshals cared. No. No. No. It was also not because of my pent-up anger or even rebelliousness. It was rather my only way of coping with overwhelming sadness and grief. It may sound unsavory for me to say it, but quiet defiance of oppressive authority has an appealing eloquence about it. I felt good knowing that if I should lose my life in that cage, I would've gone at the hands of another—not due to a fate which I brought on myself.

At about 4:30 PM when I felt the car begin to make a number of slow maneuvers, I bounced out of my delirium in time to see the car pull into the rear entrance of an underground car garage. Two gentlemen who I later saw regularly approached the car and let me out. I could barely stand on my own but because no assistance was forthcoming, I drew strength from within, the very last my spirit could muster, and began the zigzag walk at the limited pace possible with leg chains in place. The four Marshals walked behind me even as they showed me the way up the staircase until we got to the first floor landing right in front of a walkthrough metal detector door.

The two new Marshals leaned me against the wall at this point and began unlocking the padlock, handcuff and leg iron. After they freed me from their shackles and chains, they ordered me to walk through the metal detector door while all of them began again to unfurl and search my articles of clothing. I frankly found it very perplexing that although I had not met with anybody from who I could have received the smallest item whatsoever, I had actually been mute and semi-conscious and entirely in the custody and full view of law enforcement officers, yet they found it justifiable to give me the most invasive body search at every turn! Open your mouth, wiggle your tongue, turn around, squat down and cough, drop your underwear, open your cheeks with both hands—no not those cheeks these ones… yes those! Lift your… yes those! The most humiliating treatment possible for someone who had merely been accused of alleged offenses and who had never had problems with the law.

I groaned. Surely these men could not know any better, I thought. I felt a need to rationalize on their behalf, their obvious insouciant attitudes toward me. No self-respecting person who has travelled the world and experienced jetlag and the associated harsh environmental changes would add starvation to those drastic disruptions of body functions unless they did not know better. That would, and did amount to torture. And so, as the Marshals went about discharging their duties, nonchalant to my misery, I felt myself slowly perishing….

Finally, a glimmer of hope—they were done processing me. For the first time since we landed on U.S. soil, someone remembered that I was human. I was ushered into a cage-like holding cell with two others who had just been before a judge. I was handed a filet of chicken sandwich and a Styrofoam cup of cola. I gulped it all down in an instant and settled to allow my digestive system acknowledge receipt and end my hunger-induced delirium.

Minutes into my slumber I was suddenly awakened by one of the U.S. Marshals named Charlie. He announced that I had a visitor and walked me across the hallway and then through a door. Sitting on one side of the small room across from a thick glass partition was a fragile looking woman. I sat down at the only seat on my side of the room and picked up the telephone which she indicated with her free hand.

"It is perhaps not the best way to meet," she began, "but you're welcome back to the United States. I am your attorney."

Still smarting from my many wounds and gradually now recovering from hypoglycemia, I was still sufficiently disoriented that I couldn't hold a coherent conversation. But time was running out on us. I had earlier been informed that I would be brought before a magistrate for a brief pre-trial hearing. The purpose of the hearing which was to me, a mere formality, was to determine whether there was sufficient evidence to prosecute me. Also, to be determined was whether I was eligible for house detention pending trial. Finally, the magistrate was to explain to me, the court procedures applicable in my case and set a date for further pre-trial hearings. With the information I just received, I knew that the process must go on regardless of how I was doing.

"It's good to finally meet you in person. How are you?" I inquired.

"As good as can be expected, considering how busy I've been lately. My new office is starting to take shape; maybe I can finally slow things down a bit"

"That's good. Now, please tell me, have you seen my sister Chi?"

"Oh yes. She's somewhere in the building. You'll get to see her in the courtroom shortly. But a word of caution; you will not get to converse with her. I know that that seems unfair, but that's just how the rules are designed.

Our visit was a very brief one indeed. My attorney explained that all she needed was for us to get acquainted as we had never physically met each other before. She explained that I was not to make any oral contribution to the process. The trio of the magistrate, the prosecutor, and herself the defense attorney, would do all the talking which should last under thirty minute's altogether.

As it turned out, we spent nearly one whole hour at that preliminary court sitting. During that process I was beside myself with shock and disbelief. Even in my state of delirium, when I thought my condition could not be made any worse, I found myself sinking further into oblivion. It was difficult from the very start—to sit silent while my character was viciously maligned by the prosecution. I cringed as I felt the impact of the prosecutor's every word, as if impaled with a long syringe. She had painted the perfect picture of a depraved lowlife by the time she was done. The courtroom fell silent.

Even with my attorney sitting just inches next to me, I felt all alone. My faith in her ability to defend me had been dashed during the prosecutor's verbal assault on my character. Side by side with the prosecutor, my attorney emanated zero confidence. She sat beside me like a beautiful partridge in a deadly gun sight. When the magistrate indicated that it was her turn to speak, she reluctantly and delicately got on her fragile feet. She ignored the note which I slipped to her expressing my outrage at the prosecutor's false and malicious invectives and offered such a feeble response that left me tongue-tied and miserable for the remainder of the process.

Given the dismal performance of my attorney, nothing in the order of the judge came as a surprise to me. There was to be no freedom or house detention for me pending arraignment for bail hearing. The judge then ordered my detention at MCDC (Montgomery County Detention Center) at Seven Locks, Rockville Maryland—a short distance away from the home I relinquished to my wife nearly ten years earlier.

Forty Three

"One endless day!" I thought, as I sat upright, mute like a statue, avoiding body contact with the seat-back of the cold steel bench in the holding cell beneath the court building. I had never felt colder inside any room. But then, it was not in a normal room that I now awaited the infamous United States Marshals. Instead of a heater, the air conditioner wheezed, full blast, from vents overhead! Inside any normal room, the heater would at this time be blowing full-blast considering that February 12th 2008, the date of my arrival back to the United States after nine years in simmering Africa, was that winter's coldest day.

I strained to remember everything that had occurred in the last 24 hours before and after the North America Airways plane landed at JFK, Airport early that morning. Before depositing me and my thoughts into the frigid, solitary cell, the U.S. Marshals had hinted that it would be a long while before they were ready to transport me to my new home at Rockville Maryland. The new home, Montgomery County Detention Center (MCDC) located about thirty miles from where we were and just 15 minutes' drive from my home in Darnestown, is also known as Seven Locks. It felt surreal that this institution which I whisked past uncountable times in the past, without even a glance, as if it were a leper colony was soon to become home for me.

As the incredible scenes of the last twenty four hours started tumbling into my heavy heart, I clenched my fists and began gritting my teeth. A tremendous pressure quickly built up, swelling my heart. My chest rose and fell rhythmically until the thumps it produced became the only audible sound in the room. The scenes in my head were like nightmares from a fitful slumber. As though my thoughts were being pumped into my head from a source outside of it…

With one swift overnight flight, I had been transplanted from one world to another. The world before me now was neither the one that welcomed me in 1977, and which I departed nine years earlier, nor the familiar and much loved chaotic existence in the land of my ancestry which had just been so abruptly terminated. This was an alien world to me, a world marked by cruelty, metal and monologues. The entire events still seemed like an out-of-body experience—a nightmare from which I was to awaken shortly....

My morning had begun at Ikoyi Prison like all other mornings; first, a large cup of coffee, then ten minutes of aerobics and a two mile run. I had lost appetite for real food. I was aware that another undesired new phase of my life was shortly to begin. My hormones were already responding to the many unknowns and unpredictable of my future life by creating new responses within me. My attempt to stay calm was merely a ruse—my friends easily saw through it. But they were compassionate and understanding. They assisted me through the long exhausting day. They force-fed me and reminded me to take a shower. Finally, by 6:00 PM, I was dressed, ready and waiting. Shortly afterward, above the silence which had enveloped the entire "Whitehouse" wing of the prison, the crisp sound of footsteps on the rough macadam coming from a lone prison warder signaled that the waiting was over. It was the orderly of the Deputy Comptroller of Prisons.

"Mr. George," he called out, "they are here."

That was all he needed to say.

"Let's go," I replied.

My friends, Aminu, Papa, and a few others could not be stopped. They took that long walk through the alley of death to the gate with me.

Looking back as I sat, brooding, in the freezing courthouse holding cell, it became clear to me that it was the free flow of the current of charity from these men that saved me from certain emotional rupture even before I could embark on this fateful journey. It felt to me as though it was that surging current of love that overflowed through me unto my two escorts, the FBI and Interpol agents who instead of "conveying me," chose to "accompany me" to the point of my delivery to the United States Marshals in New York. They treated me with unexpected civility. No handcuffs. No leg chains. Plus we shared our meals and drinks as though we were old buddies.

Sadly, it was not up to these gentlemen to decide how I was handled in the hours following our arrival in the United States. I shuddered as I reflected on the rapid decline of my self-worth from the moment I was handed over to the United States Marshals to my present state in this god-awful holding cell. I was astonished at my limited understanding of the operations of America's law enforcement. I remembered feeling like a piece of defective furniture in the hands of wreckage disposal workers. The expression, "America's long arm of the law," it turned out, is hardly just a cliché. Within the first few hours of our arrival, those arms had touched me in ways I would never forget. The more I thought about the details of that experience, the more I recoiled at the inference forming in my head.

Was it possible to infer otherwise? I wondered seriously. Was this not a case of abuse or bullying? Surely, if the unfounded charges against me qualified as abuse of a minor in the eyes of the law, then the entire judicial system was guilty of abusing and bullying me, in my opinion—only on a much grander scale! My lack of understanding of the American judicial system notwithstanding, it is widely known that it sometimes grossly exaggerates the facts on crime related issues. It was painful enough that I had been wrongly and maliciously accused, but more painful was the fact that the system had swallowed up all of my accuser's deception and was now seeking to punish me severely for them. Without any knowledge of it, I was sobbing. Where was America's sense of proportion? I lamented in silence. The fearsome events of the last twenty four hours had greatly heightened my uncertainty.

The tears were now flowing as from an open tap. What manner of crime could warrant such base treatment as I had endured even before a trial? Was not trial required any longer before one was chained and shackled like Hannibal Lecter? And was not that level of cruelty meted only if it was determined that the accused was guilty as charged? What is society's gain but sadistic pleasure, in having a man, accused he may be, but not yet declared guilty; stripped naked, violated and humiliated over and over while in continuous, uninterrupted custody of law enforcement officers?

I could not help reflecting on the ideals which sparked a global American Cultural monomania among the youth of the world—a mania which remains alive in the hearts of many across the world. Is America selling the world a hoax? Or is the world simply intent on viewing America with scales in their eyes?

Forgive me, for I may be out of harmony with the current branding of America in world view, but the slogans, declarations, and proclamations which captured my youthful adulation appear to exist today among Americans only as sources of intense regret and grudge rather than the sources of pride and promise originally intended, and which endeared America to an adoring world audience. Americans now seem to be wondering whether their investments in those ideals are still worthwhile.

In my despair inside my frigid confinement cell, I began recalling some of those unique one line slogans with teary eyes:

- ✓ In God We Trust
- ✓ Land of The Free

- ✓ Land of The Brave
- ✓ Innocent Until Proven Guilty.
- ✓ Home of The Free
- ✓ Land of immigrants
- ✓ All Are Equal Under The Law

Above all I recalled mentally, the declaration of independence preamble which to me is the Holy Grail of the promises of America: *We hold these truths to be self-evident that all men were created equal, that they are endowed by their Creator with certain inalienable rights, which among these are; life, liberty, and the pursuit of happiness...*

I speak only for myself, but I am convinced that I speak the minds of many who are similarly bound, oppressed and afflicted by an intractable system of justice when I ask, "America, whence the lofty promises?"

Images of my agonies were still rattling around in my head when the unmistakable sounds of clicking handcuffs and rattling chains returned my consciousness to my more immediate situation. It was then that I noticed the Marshals leading two women, obviously Spanish judging by their appearance, past the front of the cell where I waited. Within seconds, two Marshals, one of them Black and the other Caucasian were at the door to lead me away.

Again, leg chains, handcuffs, more chains around the waist and torso and finally anchored with a large padlock, were all fastened and locked around my body and limbs. Before this, the strip, squat and cough routine had of course been repeated for the fourth time in under six hours of continuous uninterrupted custody in their hands,

My tendency to dwell on and emphasize the cruelty of this unnecessarily repeated, highly invasive routine most likely portrays me as a weeper. But I know myself well enough to ignore this false notion and proceed to expand on the impact which the routine had on the final outcome of my case.

Like millions of immigrants who arrived in the United States and went on to become naturalized citizens after attaining adulthood under another cultural banner, I have many issues of honor and conscience which may be irreconcilable with my new cultural reality as a first generation American. Where we foreign-born and bred Americans run into problem is the point at which the cultural practices, into which we were born, overlap with our adopted American culture. At this juncture, I'm afraid to say, the laws of the United States grows snobbish or deaf, or even both snobbish and deaf to our plight. This does not need to be so, and can be made to not be so, for if patience and wisdom are allowed to prevail, it would be discovered that in every clash between two cultures, the best resolution must take into account, the best elements of both cultures while also equally discounting the negative elements of both. This way, punishment for misdeed will be fair where it is called for.

The truth is that I believe most thinking naturalized citizens of the United States would continuously live in conflict between their consciences on the one hand and the law on the other until the judicial system grows sensitive enough to their plight to begin to apply appropriate mitigating measures. Thankfully the age-old legal doctrines MENS REA and ACTUS REUS read as though ordained for that purpose. MENS REA requires the prosecution to prove that a defendant had when committing a crime; criminal or recklessness. ACTUS REUS also termed mental element; criminal intent; guilty mind; is the wrongful deed that comprises the physical components of a crime and must be coupled with MENS REA to establish criminal intent.

I suspect that a large number of alleged offenders who share similar backgrounds and experiences as me are languishing, imprisoned in their minds or like me, in one of America's numerous lock-ups trapped in this avoidable spin with the American Justice System.

I am a telling example that if nothing else, this sad situation creates more victims than it renders justice. In my case alone, although my side of the story had not even been heard, let alone tried in court, there were already scores of victims who lost their livelihood in addition to my family and the taxpaying public. All these casualties as a result of the perfidious lies of one young woman whose motives of monetary extortion and a ploy to secure a green card have become commonplace. Like Judas she claimed her bounty but as what cost? It is not my place to pass judgment but my heart bleeds today even as I proceed into a future pregnant with uncertainties and hostilities brought on me in part by my own recklessness but mostly by people for whom I had once risked everything.

My mind was still locked in deep thought when the prisoner transport van hit the uneven levels of the open parking lots leading up to the MCDC, Seven Locks entrance. From there the US Marshals led us into our new home which I entered feeling as though I was approaching the twilight of my life.

Forty Four

The world can change in an instant. Or it can change over time. But change it will. Nothing stays the same forever. In the beginning, the "harmless bickering" between my wife and me seemed a safe enough indulgence for our blissful marriage. Our marriage was indeed one that was destined to last forever. Or so we deluded ourselves into believing. And so, we indulged in more and more harmless bickering.

Not so harmless on that cold winter night. Our bickering was all along, perfecting the most unforeseen outgrowth which at the time, neither of us could have foreseen—prison.

Any illusions suspended in my subconscious mind that the treatment I was to receive would improve at MCDC because I was innocent until proven guilty were totally shattered the moment the United States Marshals escorted me into the facility. Interestingly, the first correctional officer I made contact with was himself a Nigerian national—also a naturalized U.S. citizen. Now, here is what I call a strange situational oddity.

Without even a hint of difference between his attitude and those of the U.S. Marshals themselves, he ordered me to strip down to the sole of my feet. I gazed at him in bewilderment. The place was a beehive of activity and I was not about to flaunt the entire over fifty years relic of my manhood before total strangers. It was then he realized that I did not know what he was talking about. Simultaneously, we both noted for the first time, our common ancestry.

"Oh My God." He exclaimed under his breath, "You be Nija!" Nigerian Lingua for, "Oh my God, you're Nigerian!" Ordinarily we would have hugged each other and loudly exchanged banters and perhaps kicked off a friendship, but I weakly acknowledged his equally softly expressed camaraderie.

"Yes my brother, it's been an extremely long day for me. Are you serious about me stripping off all my clothes?" I asked him.

"Oh yes," he replied. "My brother, I cannot ask you yet how you ended up here. You see those dark globes? They are all cameras. Uncle Sam is watching my every move." He gestured toward a small screen and said; "Over there. I know that for a Nigerian family man, this is like going naked in public, but most of the inmates here are old customers. They've been through our system many many times. It's like second nature to them. In a flash they're done. Please, just change into the uniform in that container and place your clothes and properties in the container." He gestured at a plastic basket.

With no choice but to comply, I hauled as much of my stature as the screen could cover behind it and did as ordered—stripped, squatted down and coughed.

I could now sense my world changing completely, for although I had not seen a mirror since departing Lagos the previous night, it was clear that I no longer looked myself. And the change was only beginning!

With my new uniform—a large orange jumpsuit in place, the easy part of my transition from family man and provider to prisoner and government property had been kicked off in earnest.

My first order of business was to have a mug shot taken of me.

Then, in descending order; finger printing, height and weight measurement; identification wrist band strapped, and bio-data questionnaire completed.

Sensing my exhaustion and disgust with the experience, the correctional officer gave me a brief reprieve. "Mr. Chi Udeozor," he offered waiving at a bench, "have a seat over there; I'm not done with you yet."

He signaled for the next in line, a woman who was obviously inebriated, to approach. It was a white woman, but by the way she wobbled and danced toward the officer, I was momentarily befuddled.

She conducted herself with the decorum of an untamed pit bull—charging, cursing and demanding her freedom. Although in return she was treated with civility, and the scene she started quickly diffused, I could not help wondering why the issues of race, gender and culture are beyond human resolution.

Here was an awkward moment—a trick played by the evil known as social injustice in the minds of the oppressed. It had always seemed normal to encounter a black person, or a person from an oppressed minority group in the position of this feisty, bedraggled white woman, but unusual among whites, even when their economic conditions are identical. Why was it that this woman had the audacity to demand respect and freedom although merely seeing and listening to her, one knew she was guilty? And why did her ranting attract immediate response whereas the ranting of a black person in a similar situation would obviously not? Could it be that before the law all people are not equal after all?

~

While in detention in Nigeria, I learned one universal lesson about prison. That lesson is that prison is a world apart. Life behind prison walls or fences bears very little resemblance to the world outside them. But they do function under similarly structured codes of conduct being that both worlds are inhabited by human beings. Prisoners attempt to create their own code of conduct among inmates along the lines of the exact same issues which defines the society outside the walls and fences.

Only twenty four hours earlier in Nigeria, the issues had centered on the gross inadequacy or total lack of provisions for the legal resources, healthcare and welfare needs of inmates. Now the issues had been completely flipped. Whereas the central issues of concern to Nigerian prison inmates do not even rise to any level of worry here in the United States, the issues of concern here are to me, more troubling. First, I was stripped of my ***dignity*** as a man by the numerous orders to strip, squat, cough, wiggle, etc., in addition to being chained and shackled up like Hannibal Lector. Second, I was stripped of my ***identity*** and assigned a number in replacement. Finally I had been served a visual recipe of the pervasive issue of ***racism*** which features prominently in U.S. prisons.

How was I now to adjust to my grave new world? Surely, if prodded to choose between enduring racism in heaven or enjoying freedom and dignity in hell, I'd hurry to hell. I knew that I would never adjust well in any environment where these toxic issues are simply a matter of course. I therefore made up my mind that while my ordeal lasted, I would create an entirely new world of my own, in which I would live for that entire period. The world I created was the one I promptly moved into—it was all within me—body, mind and soul.

~

Once securely moved into my new world, I turned to the topic at the root of my incarceration—the allegations against me. While I lived in

Nigeria, my mother's godchild, Chinelo had had a fall out with my estranged wife which snowballed into various allegations culminating in the allegation of Involuntary Servitude against both of us. Although I vehemently deny her allegations and am now here to present a different version of the events, in the eyes of the U.S. Justice System, slavery had been committed and since someone was required to pay a price for that crime, whoever the "victim" named or linked to that act, was guilty as charged.

The long arm of the law had already snagged my wife as a co-conspirator in the enslavement of the alleged victim. Sitting now in cell C-12 gnashing my teeth, determined to live through the night, my thoughts migrated to the three women in my life who feature proximately in my dilemma. I refer to them as "Mother", "Madam, and "Maid."

PART THREE

Mother, Madam, and Maid

"To marry is to halve your rights and double your duties."
~Arthur Shopenhauer

"The person who seeks to change another person in a relationship
basically sets the stage for a great deal of conflict."
~Wesley Snipes

"She said I was mean to her children . . .
Now I will show her Jezebel."
~Chinelo Anyadeigwu

Forty Five

I lay on my back on that narrow bunk bed, awake and covered head to toe, in two blankets. Thanking the father above for the gift of solitude at last. But more for the extra blanket meant for another soul on the empty bunk inches across from me.

Staring blankly at the wall, I could make out the grooves of a narrow window obscured by frost. As I sat there in my misery and thoughts, I could hear little other sound than my slowly beating heart. I suppressed the ferocious and overwhelming hunger which mingled with my despair to focus my energies on the thoughts in my head . . .

Even in my lethargic state of mind, I could not restrain my mind's musing as I recalled a conversation I once had with a friend years before. This was no whimsical friend and so I usually held his views in high esteem. Our chat this time was centered on the women in our lives. He made many observations but the one poignant point that sparked debate was his assertion that we men were the inferior of the two genders. He shooed away my argument that both genders were equally endowed. He asserted that all our lives, until we die, we work and toil all for none other than the women in our lives. I refused to concede to his views in whole without a little sparing although we both knew he had won the debate. The one area though, where he admitted defeat was when I told him that he was wrong about the number of genders in existence among humanity. In answer to his genuine surprise at my light-hearted challenge to him to name the six genders of humanity I said they are male, female, gay, lesbian, hermaphrodites and the blank or unidentifiable genders. After a fitful laughter, he looked up into my face and said, "Only in America… only in your country."

In a world where the guilty blames the damaged, the damaged becomes the guilty and the system designed for justice, sees beyond its duty, a chance to make a fortune. Guilty or damaged, what's the difference? And what do we really have after all?

Lying there, I turned these thoughts around and around in my head as I tried to answer for myself where things began going wrong. I came to the conclusion as I always did in the past that beside God, all we really have is ourselves and our family—if we have one.

If all we have is ourselves in the family, why then did all the problems in my life have their origins from within the family?

That was when my friend's theory about the women in our lives began having its most powerful impact in my thought process. His robust common sense had always impressed me. But I had seldom delved into their real life implications, until now. His light-hearted remarks, it turned out, were not simply harmless words of wisdom; they're sage words that apply in the life I had so far lived. Without the involvement of the three women in my life; my mother, my madam (of holy matrimony) and my self-proclaimed maid in my affairs, my life might have turned out different.

While I was living my entire married life under the delusion that I was the "man" of my home, these three were really the ones who wore the pants. It was impossible for me to know this at the time, as I am sure it is at the moment for many a man's man.

From the moment I took my first breath, love was my doing and undoing. At that time the world was my mother. I loved her so much; a whip in her hand was as destructive as candy cane in the mouth. She used the whip alright, which leaves me wondering even today why I only felt the swelter when the flogging was done by my father or a teacher.

That was the power of my love for my mother. It was impossible to not love her that way for that was the way she loved too—with commitment and devotion. Her commitment and devotion to us, her children, was only surpassed by that which she showed to God and His affairs at St. Matthew's Catholic Church, Amawbia.

We had to attend mass every Sunday and morning mass every morning when we were opportune to do so. We had to live our lives always mindful of the Satan and his evil influences. We had to love our neighbors as ourselves and in our interactions and relationships with others we had to be polite and avoid those who would put our mortal souls in danger. We had little option but to copy our mother's examples. After all, what child did not gloat in the face of steady and unyielding compliments?

"Oh, him? He is one of Susanna's children. That's why he is so well mannered."

"She is so intelligent, whose child is she?"

"Let's have one of Susanna Udeozor's children come to the front of the line."

"The winner is... Udeozor."

That was how I became the young man George Udeozor. It is fair to say that by the time I got married I had not learned that the word "love" had two force fields; The bitter/sweet force fields.

With my mother, I only experienced one of love's force fields; the sweet one. My marriage to Stella in 1986 began with the same field, and then opened up the second field—love's bitter force field. We survived and overcame the onslaught of trials and tribulations which all successful marriages must pass through. That was until our ninth year of blissful relationship. Some members of my wife's side of our extended family decided that we must allow them free and unfettered use of every possession of our union. The line between my nuclear family and my in-law family which was already blurred was a threat to their designs and they sought to do away with it altogether. I felt it was time to stand up... and I did. My wife however, remained sitting.

At first I believed that my wife's reticence was a sincere and deliberate strategy to diffuse tension by staying neutral. That appeared both justifiable and logical. And so, believing that we were on the same page on the issue of balancing out both sides of our extended families, I surged with my in-laws, determined to draw the same protective line between us which I had earlier already drawn between my nuclear family and my own side of the extended one.

Betrayal packs enough power behind its punches to knock out any bonding known to man. From the moment Stella and I met, our hearts bonded. Our heads were full of sin and excitement. The first chance we had alone together was the day after we met. We were driving in my car after I picked her up that evening. We stopped by a Spanish costermonger (fruit vendor) where she picked up some deep red malformed strawberries. They looked vulgar, and we both looked at each other knowingly. She smiled and opened the strawberry slits (or splits) even wider. While feeding them to me, she asked what they looked most like. When I told her, we came near falling into a ditch on account of our excitement. It was on that night that our first daughter, Kimberly was conceived. It was also on that night that we formed a bonding which I believed to be unbreakable. Little did I know that bonding is powerless against a traitor, for the traitor fights from within, approaching you unexpectedly from your blind spot.

Because I am now more mature and wiser, having learned about the bittersweet nature of love, I now appreciate my mother's brand of love even more. She loved all people and kept the door to her heart open to them. It was through this door into her heart which my mother kept open until her death that the young woman who dealt the game-changing blow to my world found her way into my life. Her name is Chinelo, a teenage daughter born into one of the many peasant families of our local community in Amawbia. She plays such a large role in the saga of my life because it was she who set in train, the events which gained me the most formidable adversary on planet earth—the government of the United States. That role has earned her a place among the group of three women who ran my life for a period covering over one quarter century.

To truly understand my story it is necessary to set out clearly my account of events, starting from the very beginning—my marriage to Stella and the linkage with my mother and the maid.

Forty Six

Under two months after Stella fed me the vulgar red strawberries, she came to me, her entire body in flames. She brought more strawberries which tempted us into a repeat performance of our first night together. Then she began sobbing.

"What's wrong Pumpkin?" I asked her. "Did I hurt you?"

"No, no, no, Darling, it's just that… that…" she stammered.

"That what, baby?" I was all fired up again and….

After it was all over, her whole body trembled and the flames seemed refueled even more from within her. But instead of an ice pack, she requested that I cover her with more bedding. She was with fever.

I lay beside her for a long while when from underneath the layers of beddings, I heard her voice again; "I missed my period."

"You missed your what?" Her words formed no meaning in my head.

"Darling, I think I'm pregnant." She purred.

Three months later, because we could not bear to bring forth our bundle of joy before we were married, we wrapped ourselves in each other's affection and presented before God at the altar of Holy Matrimony at Holy Ghost Cathedral, Enugu.

It was a memorable wedding—well attended and well received. Some of our family members felt it was the best they had ever attended. Stella's friends and family were magnificent, loving and proud. My friends and family were very supportive and very loving. In our native State of Anambra, Nigeria, ours was one of the weddings of the Christmas period of 1986.

When the wedding pictures came out, Stella was ecstatic. Her wedding gown looked regal and shielded the holy sin of our first night together. She took my hand and guided it to the side of her stomach where I felt

Kimberly's heart beating. It felt like rapid string of soft taps from under her skin.

On the night following our wedding, it felt as though it was the best day of a five month honeymoon. We agreed that we did not require a special hotel suite for our honeymoon. Nothing in any hotel suite could top the laser borne ecstasy between and around us. Being with well-wishers was our preferred way of sealing our bond of affection.

Before departing Nigeria to return to the United States as a married couple, we visited both our families in their remote villages. For any African who bears my level of cultural grounding, departure from custom is not just like pulling one tooth; it is like pulling out the entire jawbone. Unthinkable.

Images of that visit has followed me ever since. They were the best scenes yet in my adult life, suspended in time. I review them each time I think about my daughter Kimberly. The rest of my children too: the scenes of our arrival at Amawbia; the chauffeur-driven convoy of cars; the hooting; the gathering crowd of villagers; the drumming; and finally, the appearance of my mother herself, hooting and ululating with happiness. Money cannot buy that.

We all know that the getting of children is easy—a simple function of biology in the natural act of playing being all that is required. Any couple can do this. Except, of course, those not yet of age or well burnt out already or yet the few who due to some unfortunate circumstances, known or unknown, are therefore precluded. It is the raising of children to become contributing members of society while at the same time achieving for themselves the fulfillment of their life's purpose that sets parents apart from those who simply engage in the enjoyment of that vulgar act of nature at much cost to society.

The arrival of my daughter Kimberly became my epiphany. I had decided that we would be real parents to our children. Not just two adults caught in the heat of passion, and having babies only as a consequence of that act. It was time to sit and talk with my new bride about our future as man and wife—as family.

Had I been properly schooled on the intricacies of love and marriage, I might have noticed this early into our marriage that we failed to begin our planning from the beginning rather than in the middle. In hindsight it is clear that our skittish rush to the alter robbed us of the time and task of first addressing issues of fundamentally greater importance than a wedding. For what value is a grand wedding if the couple should shortly thereafter entertain the same audience with a grander spectacle of their uncouth lives? We unfortunately placed total reliance on our professed unconditional love for each other as the only key for the success of our marriage. Well and good, but I tell only the truth. I am satisfied that the facts will speak for themselves.

The birth of our first child turned my wife into a warlike mother hen. She was young, as I was too. Catholic, as I was. Driven to build a strong family on solid foundation—so I believed. But events later proved me wrong. Our values were not in sync. Only at the eleventh hour did this crucial reality dawn on me. That was when my life in limbo inevitably began. I have learned now, perhaps a bit late, yet, better than never learning at all, that one of the greatest paradoxes of youth is that youth assumes that all will be well. And so, the young often jump into marriage thinking little at all about the possibility of disappointment and failure. I am convinced that the author of life made this so—with His own trusting assumption that parents will play their own role; of guiding their youth through the tough obstacle course of transiting from youth to mature adulthood with all the attendant wisdoms through that experience. It was clear that neither of us entered into our marriage fully equipped.

I return now to where all the trouble began. We jumped into marriage without planning. When we started planning, we began from the middle rather than starting with first things first.

Following a string of successful stints in Banking, Accounting and a job as a Research Assistant at the University, I deferred my preferred career path of becoming an Attorney; I started a business career in Nigeria as a Government Contractor and Consultant targeted mainly at the Ministry of Defense. Providence permitted me modest but promising success as I advanced.

That was when I met my future wife. She had, at the time just arrived in Los Angeles, California where I resided, with two desires; to secure a resident study/work Permit required in order to be admitted in a teaching hospital for a four year residency program in medicine. A brilliant student, she had obtained her medical degree, MBBS in Nigeria before arriving in the United States. Her second desire was to meet and marry her soul mate. She later confided in me that she had arrived in Los Angeles shortly after pouring out her desires in a prayer to God and receiving His assurances that He had secured such a man for her.

Upon meeting her, I wasted no time filling in the blanks left by those two desires. I was swept by the roaring tide of affection into a life working for the love of my life.

During our heart to heart discussion I was disarmed by her teary eyed revelation that she was driven by the memory of her late father's demise to become a doctor. Her father, who was himself a doctor, was reputed as a kind and unassuming young physician who touched numerous lives, saving them from the scorches of Nigeria's diseased and degrading civil war of the mid 1960's—a war which claimed his kind soul. She stated that some elements of her extended network of family relatives who later came into money, some of it ill gotten, were eternally jealous of her father's noble accomplishments and felt unshackled by the disappearance of his towering image and so, celebrated his death believing that his offspring will come to naught.

So compelling and moving was her account that I vowed to make it my life's duty to stand by her, come rain or hail storm, until she achieved the kind of success that sends doubters and detractors scampering for refuge.

That was when I took the decisions that sealed my doom. First, I decided to extend the moratorium which I placed on my career plan. After all, I was already quite successful working as a government contractor. I had also drawn up an impressive resume of accomplishments while I was still in the University. Most importantly, while Stella was busy working on her residency program, someone had to shoulder the staggering cost of maintaining our immodest lifestyle. I felt ordained for that lofty role. Without much ado, I got on with it.

A certain deceptive aura of affluence surrounds some people in the eyes of many who rely on appearances alone to make their judgments. I have had the odious fortune of being frequently placed on a much higher pedestal than the one upon which I truly stand. When so elevated through no fault of your own it is sometimes difficult to climb down. Not necessarily due to getting acclimatized to the false and bloated image of yourself, but due to a willingness or eagerness to resolve the genuine needs of people you care deeply about. That was the case in my relationship with my wife.

Upon the birth of Kimberly, my wife Stella expressed extreme nervousness about ever leaving our bundle of joy in the care of nannies. Remember please, that those were the latch-key-baby days when the airwaves were filled with breaking news of the atrocious acts of many a nanny against defenseless babies left in their care.

Stella believed, with a measure of support from me that nannies from our local communities in Nigeria were unlikely to get abusive with babies in the manner we were witnessing around us. My wife was a pack or nerves anytime we were forced to deliver our baby in the home of a sitter or whenever we had one do the sitting in our home.

My wife's hysteria over this issue increased exponentially with the expansion in our family after the birth of our son George Adam. Also, because I was usually overseas on work assignment, I succumbed to my wife's pressures. I labored hard until I engaged the services of a nanny from Nigeria. My mother, bless her soul, suffered tirelessly in search of an energetic young woman fit for the duty. After she found one, I went through the uphill battle of securing a visa for her and the atrocious expense of funding her travel and salaries.

Sadly, the arrival of Comfort, the nanny, only marked the beginning of my multiple years' run-in with the job of hunting for nannies to cross the Atlantic for the job of providing the services demanded by my wife—services they all found daunting and often complained went unappreciated.

It will serve no useful purpose to dwell on the details of my humanity expended on every single nanny who crossed the Atlantic to cater to my wife's demanding duty roster. It suffices however to say that it was the fifth such traveler (in under eight years) who, although was not even contracted as a nanny or maid, brought my entire family to its knees. Her name is Chinelo—The maid.

Forty Seven

It would serve me ill if I began my narrative of the ugly outcome of Chinelo's sojourn in my home by suggesting that she was a curse through and through while in my family's guardianship. As a matter of honesty, quite the opposite of that suggestion, she was mostly a positive addition to the family upon her arrival and during a great portion of the time during which she resided with us.

As I have hinted earlier, her perfidious and treacherous lies when faced with a real possibility that she might be deported to Nigeria as illegal aliens sometimes must be, are inexcusable. Those lies have caused my family in its entirety, grave and irreparable damage. And for what?

~

All three women; my mother, my madam and my maid featured prominently in the saga of Chinelo the maid. Our children and I were not less involved. Neither were the other members of our family and those of Chinelo herself, immediate and extended. Scores of others indirectly involved by way of employment in our estate also deserve mention for their losses. All are victims of a single degenerate human virtue—selfishness.

Life has taught me that human beings are by nature, self-centered. The much celebrated among us who are recognized as selfless are often pretenders whose deeds, regardless of motivation, fall within the purview of nobility and humanitarianism. There exists, however, a few genuine humanitarians in all societies whose charitable deeds are unquestionably selfless, and their motivation unimpeachable. My mother was such a humanitarian in our provincial community of Amawbia, Nigeria. I will eat my words and give up the last scintilla of honor which remains of my battered image if any member of our community would paint a different picture of this good woman; including the maid and the very last of her relatives and sympathizers.

True to her nature, my mother made it her life's work to try and rescue the young of our community whose future wellbeing became imperiled by the pervasive poverty of the time. She set up Sunday school programs, educational programs and self-help programs to assist these unfortunates better their chances of escaping a future marked by hardship, deprivation and misery. She was an unrelenting advocate and believer in any cause which seeks to mitigate the sufferings of the poor.

Her children, I in the middle of the pack, at first queried the wisdom of her commitment to this cause, reminding her that we ourselves never had it easy and that while in the doldrums, found no rescuer. She acknowledged our protests but challenged us at every turn to rise above the selfishness of the present age. Her logic for her unusual nature was often so disarming that we always backed down in shame. We could see the rewards of her deeds all around her, enough to spill over onto us. I never met a happier person than my mother. Nor have I met one so at peace with God until her dying day. God rest her gentle soul… Amen.

I believe in spirits. I know that they inhabit the ethereal space which surrounds us. This is why I fear that my late mother, now one of God's angel spirits, feels the burden of Chinelo's act of betrayal, for it was my mother who brought her into the shadow of my household.

1996 was the year. Although already with failing health, my mother never gave a second thought to continuing with her commitment to charity. On this occasion, my wife had for the umpteenth time found little good to say about the labor of our fourth nanny from across the Atlantic. The nanny herself, after months of dejection, frustrated with my wife's unseemly attitude, snapped and took the fight to her. I witnessed only the tail end of that altercation. Quite naturally, the maid had to be shown the door.

I have been asked why I continued to indulge my wife repeatedly despite her uncharitable attitude. To this inquiry, I had no cogent reply. Most African male cultural chauvinists are known to rule as princes over their household. I was no exception—I, at least now, admit that to be true of me at that time. In response, I usually offered one excuse or another; love for my wife, well-being of my children, etc. The truth is, I cannot explain. The best I can offer now after years of much introspection on my repeated childlike indulgence of my wife's narcissistic demands is that I felt thoughtlessly compelled by a misplaced weight of obligation, perhaps linked to the welfare of our children, to act. My love and belief in family had also blinded me from exploring rational resolutions to my wife's excesses out of fear that it might threaten our family survival. Surely my handling of this singular aspect of my marital responsibilities reflects poorly on my judgment as the erstwhile head of my household. While I accept full responsibility for my woeful failure, I must again allude to the dangerous consequences of approaching and attempting to resolve issues from multiple cultural dimensions. In Nigeria, the engagement of community members in the manner which we practiced is a cultural sine qua non. Not one eyebrow is raised at what is part and parcel of our very survival and existence. It takes the entire village to raise a child especially the children of indigent members of that village.

~

Following the departure of the combatant nanny, my wife's radar again turned their laser beams on me. This time however, the usual panicked urgency was not there. We had two maids of Ghanaian descent who came in as daytime help only. Our children were finally growing up and needed less babysitting. Kimberly, our first born, was approaching 10, Adam was pushing 9 and Valerie nearing 7. They were all healthy, intelligent and precocious—our unquantifiable gift of God's blessing and mercy. We had few of the prickly issues which many less fortunate young couples are plagued with when one or more of their children come out handicapped. But instead of relishing this God-given good fortune, my wife's appetite for matriarchal status surged out of nowhere. I became overwhelmed with hard choices. From all directions, issues of the heart, complex problems fit only for the mind of one imbued with the Wisdom of Solomon, came hurtling at me. I was no Solomon, but I gave the situation the best of my mind's gift of prudence before I buckled.

I turned once again to my mother. I recall as if it was just yesterday, my mother commiserating with me over the telephone. Not an aorta of judgment or blame in her tone. "Call me in one week," she suggested, "let me look around and ask around."

When I called back one week later my mother was as usual pleased to give me the good news; "I am sure you remember the young girl Chinelo," she said.

"No, I don't," I replied.

"Well, your wife will remember her. During your last visit she was your wife's favorite among the kids jostling to babysit your children. Your wife took a liking to her and gave her a few gifts. I have always wished to assist her in a substantial way. I fear that it won't be long before she drifts away like her older sister. You know, she is my goddaughter and I would hate for her to fall prey to the vicious world out there. Just recently, her older sister was delivered of a baby as a result of an unwanted pregnancy. Their parents can hardly afford to feed themselves let alone provide for unexpected grandchildren.

"Is that so?" I remarked.

"Yes." She continued, "You know? A year ago, I could not rebuff the pressure for assistance from her parents, and so I sent her off to your brother Chiedu's home in Kaduna to help ease her parent's burden. But your brother's wife Ngozi felt she possessed some diabolical character traits which she found disagreeable despite her youth and beguiling innocence. She was returned from Kaduna and her parents are again stuck with the burden of her upbringing. Perhaps you and Stella can bring her to the United States. It would really be a major assistance to not only her parents but to me personally.

"Mama, how old is she?" I asked.

"I really don't know for sure, but she is in her mid-teenage years." She said.

"Oh no mama, she is way too young. It would be impossible to secure a visa for her travel. The U.S. Embassy has a policy of denying young people visas because they usually do not return once they enter the United States." I protested.

"Well I know nothing about that," she said. "It was just a thought since your children are now growing up and therefore require less babysitting and more adult companionship and coaching, I felt an older sister figure is more what they need now than a nanny. I believe Chinelo would be more likely to fit into the opening you described than another combatant nanny to duel with your wife. Think about it son, and call me back after you and Stella have talked it over."

We did, and I called my mother back.

Forty Eight

My wife Stella remembered Chinelo from our last visit to Nigeria particularly vividly. It turned out that my mother was correct about Stella's impression of her, for she described Chinelo as "that smart young girl." In my wife's opinion she was everything we needed. Someone who could supervise our children as they learned house chores—a big sister, just the way we traditionally raise children in Nigeria. It seemed an impossible dream realized. But I cautioned her that getting Chinelo into the United States remained an uphill task. No promises made.

The farthest thing in the minds of any of the whole lot of us involved in the issue of seeking passage for Chinelo into the United States was that she was to become a maid. First, she had neither the experience, nor the knowledge to make any kind of household help. She did not even know what a stove was let alone how to light one. The distinction between maid and ward from an African cultural perspective needs to be clearly emphasized because the issue has taken on a life of its own since modern day slavery took center stage in relationships between nations with diverse and sometimes opposing cultural practices.

Generally, when seeking to engage any individual as maid, babysitter or house help, there is no ambiguity in stating the facts. The employer is exactly who he/she is—the employer. The maid, babysitter or house help is who he/she is—the employee. The line between employer/employee is thick, not thin. Compensation for services is negotiated and duties are defined. Yes, even in Africa, especially in Africa, we understand the difference. Diplomas are not required or necessary for employees to know when their rights are violated.

These points are a necessary prologue to telling the story of how events turned and twisted a straight forward, age-old practice of helping your neighbor, into a crooked modern-day evil.

I cannot put a figure on the number of Nigerian adults who have passed through the tutelage of benefactors, such as the one intended for Chinelo, to become successful professionals, even leaders of society. I can only guarantee that the number is staggering. My parents both did. My siblings and I mostly did. A host of others are doing so now and even more will continue that legacy in the future. It is somewhat of a cruel twist of fate that whenever an unforeseen snag in progress develops as they did in my case, blames and accusations saturate the air. Truth and decency take a beating and evaporate while deceit and selfishness take center stage.

When Chinelo's parents were informed about the plan for their daughter, their happiness knew no bounds. They were aware of the potentials of such a proposal if it should succeed. Naturally, they went into prayer for things to work out smoothly. They knew it was a given that, if their daughter Chinelo succeeded in obtaining a passage to America, nothing would be spared in ensuring that her future would be bright. Their only contribution to the effort was their visits to my mother's home to receive word of progress and also their prayers. Many others before Chinelo had succeeded, hopefully, so would she.

It needs to be made clear that no offer was made and no request was received for salary on Chinelo's behalf. She was not meant to be an employee. Besides, no salary could come close to matching our planned investment in the young woman's future. If anything, we would be the party with the need to be compensated for caring for her and taking the burden of raising her off of her parent's lean shoulders. But that was indeed the whole point of accepting her. They needed us and we needed them. It was to be a win win relationship; as it always had been. In the process, an endangered young lady would have been rescued and given an opportunity for a better life while we would gain the honor and credit of having helped to reduce the pervasive poverty of our community. Even here in the United States, a student loan is considered a win win to both the bank which owes a duty to society, and the recipient who has a duty to pay the loan back with interest!

In hindsight, I wish Chinelo's parents had made demands for compensation ab initio. That would have halted the desperate effort and staggering financial exposure to which even her initial entry into the United States subjected me, and most importantly my family's current travails. My first effort to secure safe passage for Chinelo involved my request to the Immigration and Naturalization Service to grant her immigrant status as my daughter. This request was denied because she was not my biological child. I was then advised that it would take a long and convoluted bureaucratic process and there would be no guarantee of approval for me to have a shot at success even if I adopted her.

With that option for gaining entry into the United States eliminated, I gave up hope on any chances of playing any higher role in the life of this young lady, beyond the indirect assistance her family obtained from me through my mother just like other members of our local community.

Fate however, had designs of its own—thanks to an unrelated personal aspiration of mine, which for me had risen to the level of a lifetime cause;

I believe that the author of life designed every life form with specific objectives in mind. Among the existing life forms, there is the human being. Although we humans believe ourselves to be special— "created in the image of the creator Himself," we have foolishly divided ourselves into groups along every conceivable line in order to make the group to which we belong feel better by feeling superior to all others. This is perhaps part of the author's intention, but thoughtful leaders of society realize that human beings are inextricably tied together by a unified destiny and must therefore protect even those outside our own group. It is easy to rationalize this need; for example, if society fails to protect the weak, then the whole society—not the weak alone, becomes insecure.

My cause therefore was this; to avail my children the opportunity to live their lives in true freedom—an opportunity which I feel is denied most poor and underprivileged people of our unjust world. One of my ideas to achieve this goal was to steer them toward experiencing the world and understanding better that they do not have to always view the world as black or white, rich or poor, short or tall, beautiful or ugly. The natural place for me to begin was my country of birth, Nigeria.

This was the reason why in 1996, one year after returning to the United States from herding my entire family; myself, my wife, and our five children to Nigeria, I returned again—this time, to complete the process of securing admissions for our first two children, Kimberly and George Adam, at the Loyola Jesuit High School, Abuja, Nigeria. To complete this process, I had to take along with me the United States passports of my children for the purpose of identifying them, since they were to be administered the entrance examination far away in Washington, DC. The principal of Loyola Jesuit who himself is an American born Reverend Father required this to be done because entrance into the school is highly competitive. Only about 5% of tested candidates are usually successful. The principal had to ascertain that my children were the ones who actually sat for the test by properly identifying them. Absent their physical presence, the only sure method of identifying them was to view their passports. After completing the required identification formalities and paying a fee of USD $200.00 ($100 per child) for the test papers to be sent by courier to Washington DC, I was done with my engagements in Abuja. Shortly afterwards I made the four hundred mile journey to Amawbia to be with the most important person in my life—my mother.

⁓

The song and dance that usually followed my return to our ancestral home finally died down late that night. I then made the half mile walk to my provincial home which I had designated as Georgian Villa. The building which was nearing completion stage during my family visit a little more than one year earlier was now partially habitable and I chose to sleep in it as a sign of my arrival finally at God's destination for me.

The next morning was pregnant with fateful occurrences which were destined to alter the course of my life, but I had not the slightest warning as I walked the half mile to eat breakfast at my mother's dining table. Perhaps it was due to the heartiness of my mother's cooking, or maybe it was something else, but the decision I made that morning was my life's most ill-thought out decision. As I earlier noted, the excuses I have given for some of the sloppy events of my life deserve the derision with which they are greeted. But I challenge anybody to show even the slightest proof of mal-intent or selfish motivation behind any of my actions. I hold up my head today in the agony of prison confinement and the contemptuous regard with which I am perceived by many to say that I did it for the welfare of my family and even more for the welfare of the very soul that betrayed me.

⁓

After breakfast that morning, as I explained my mission to Nigeria and the success I recorded at Loyola Jesuit School on behalf of my children, my mother and I decided that Chinelo now depended on me for her future aspirations and as such qualified as my daughter. We therefore agreed that her last and only chance of gaining entry into the United States was if she returned with me as my daughter using my daughter Kimberly's passport.

Forty Nine

It is easy to get branded as remorseless when one has committed an illegal act and yet finds justification in taking a morally superior tone against his accuser. My accuser, in United States versus George Udeozor, was Chinelo Anyadiegwu. She however beguiled the enormously powerful government of the United States against whom I indeed trespassed to accomplish her life's ambition. The result is that on taking over as my accuser, the United States government ostensibly inherited a selfish cause which served only Chinelo's interest. Unwittingly, I became the villain and offender. The United States became the injured and accuser, while Chinelo won public sympathy as the innocent victim. In this capacity she is shielded from "attack" by the already branded remorseless villain.

Well and good so far for Chinelo the maid. But I now reveal the Chinelo for whom I risked and lost my honor. I do not recall the first time I met the young lady. But my mother said she was usually among the scores of young kids who every evening, gathered around several kerosene lanterns at our large compound. They each clutched onto one or more of the following prayer guides for the evening "Block Rosary Prayers" organized by my mother: a Simple prayer book, Catholic hymn book, a Bible, a Missal, or handwritten prayers and hymns, etc. The later part of my mother's life was devoted to caring for these youngsters. The cost of caring for them was of course indirectly borne by us, her own biological children who were already all grown up and been blessed with spouses and children. I am happy to share the good news that two young men who passed through this group went on to become ordained as Reverend Fathers and remain pious and in good standing today. Several of the others have moved on to become professionals; nurses, teachers, bankers, etc. Two young ladies from the group who subsequent to passing through the group, also passed through my tutelage and supervision, are today registered nurses and happily married to professional spouses. Both are blessed with children. I wish to point out that none of these success stories was achieved overnight and I do not claim credit for them. The credit belongs to God and the achievers themselves. Any remnants of kudos go to my mother. If anything is due me, it is just the words "thank you," for I did these not for myself but for my mother.

Chinelo's wish, just like those of the other kids was to benefit, like those before her, from my mother's benevolence. A wish she and her family rejoiced as mission accomplished, with the news that I wanted to take her to the United States. When the news of her imminent departure to the United States broke, my mother and I gained a number of enemies. Among them, neighbors and relatives who felt they had been betrayed by us in choosing others over them. They considered their kinship or closeness to my mother as loyalty worthy of reward—an entitlement to first right of consideration for a coveted offer such as the one now given to Chinelo and her family. They blamed my mother mostly for it.

But Chinelo was my mother's godchild and was above all, most in need of rescue. Her parents were among the most indigent in our community. Already, Chinelo had begun veering into the alleys of temptation which had consumed her big sister's innocence, thereby worsening the family's troubles.

The decision was already made and by the next evening, I met Chinelo and her parents, as I recall, for the very first time.

Looking back now, sitting by the steel bars of my cell window, a double barbed wire fence powered to electrocute would-be escapees as my view on the outside, I still have great difficulty believing that my reward for the choice of Chinelo, over all others, would be years in captivity and the permanent rerouting of my life's journey.

I had relied on my mother's assessment of her appearance when I accepted to present her as my daughter. But upon meeting Chinelo, I immediately hesitated and began reconsidering my decision. She was malnourished and unkempt. She reminded me of the media portrayal of starving African children on the various "save the child" advertisements back in the United States. When I expressed my hesitation, I inadvertently gave strength to my mother's emotional pleas on behalf of Chinelo. She said, "But son…that is the whole point. How does it feel to go on living your life in peace knowing that although you're not wealthy, still, your crumbs and spending on snacks alone could mean the difference between life and death for another person? By saving Chinelo, you would have saved a whole family and altered their lives for good!"

My mother's humanity... her love for her neighbors, was disarming. Like others in that mold, she was not great with making moving speeches or sounding off high-flown moral narratives about giving and receiving. It is in their examples that you get trapped. The way they live their lives—their simple, unassuming common sense outlook on fairness and goodness to their fellow travelers. By the end of our exchange on the matter, I relented.

Chinelo, who had dropped her shoulders in despair on catching wind of my hesitation, came back alive. She assured my mother that she would brush herself up and do the work to achieve the appearance of wellness required to pass for my daughter. And that was what she did. Her work on her appearance and her experiment with large portions of new, eye-popping nutritious meals, transformed the young woman within one week. By the time I saw her again shortly thereafter in Lagos, even I became convinced she could adapt herself to pass for the daughter of any parents of her choice.

~

There was no going back now. I was locked into a conspiracy with my own will. Nobody was at this point liable for any wrong doing. But even the fear of that liability could not surmount my will to rescue Chinelo. What my wife and I began as a search for a babysitter for our children, had now become an opportunity for me to open up a new and highly rewarding chapter in my life. The thrill of seeing an entire family's hopes come alive is quite exhilarating. Where there were previously stress lines, lines of laughter now blended with white teeth to form faces of joy and happiness. All based on hopes alone! And to be responsible for that transformation!

With firm resolve and a heart beating at several times its normal rate, I escorted Chinelo to Murtala Mohammed Airport, Lagos on the appointed day (October 1, 1996). I was going to make a difference in this family's destiny.

My head began feeling light and sweat trickled ceaselessly down my back on our final approach to the airport. All kinds of alarms of caution were abuzz in my head: "End this madness George," warned an invisible voice. "Stop now and send her back, and all will be well!"

Unlike me, the young lady, Chinelo was the picture of calmness where she sat on the front passenger seat. She clutched unto my daughter's passport as if her life depended on it. Her braids looked in place, just like the one worn by my daughter in her photograph displayed in the passport. She showed no anxiety at all which surprised me considering that she looked older than the image of my daughter despite her youthful make-up. It was her calmness and determination that strengthened my resolve. Although I still rattled with fear, I managed to stay on my feet as we went through check-in procedures. It was not the check-in counter staff I feared. They paid little attention to passport photographs. The terror that kept my feet off the floor and my stomach in turmoil as we coasted into the belly of the terminal building was the very counters we already had in our sight—the Immigration and Customs counters.

"Passports?" Demanded the officer looking intently into my face. I handed my passport to him and turned to Chinelo. "Give him your passport" I said in the calmest voice I could manage.

I had never been more thankful for broken air conditioners. The air conditioning systems in the departure hall were all broken. As a result, my open pores drained their salty water like several open taps in secret and I did not have to explain why I was sweating so profusely since all passengers were soaking in their own sweat, giving my more pronounced wetness plausible cover.

With his eyes focused on Chinelo's face, the officer asked, "Where did you visit while in Nigeria?"

As she turned to look toward me with a searching look on her face, I closed in, attempting with little success to block her from the officer's view. With my throat in my mouth, I said, "oh, we were at Abuja, Amawbia and Lagos."

"I'm asking the young lady," he protested, trying to keep her within view.

My panic became palpable. But all the same, it was show time, I thought. Do or die time. Speak up now or you're dead.

"Oh officer, my daughter does not understand the Nigerian accent. She has been trying but it isn't working so well. But I promise you, I will bring her home to Nigeria for secondary school. Surely then, she will have no choice but to learn the mother tongue." I finished with a gasp and looked on, now limp with uncertainty.

When his face cracked a grin, I belched out a gasp of relief.

"Sure, sure, Oyibo," he said. "I understand. It is very wonderful to meet par-ents like you, Mr. Udeozor. Others don't seem to understand that it is we who will develop our own country. By running away to America, we help them develop their already developed county even more, leaving our own in shambles. Here are your passports. Have a safe flight."

He stamped both passports and handed them back to us. Although I felt relieved, it was with much effort that I returned my whole weight back on my feet, away from the counter against which I leaned for support. "Thank you sir," I said weakly, "Stay blessed."

Across the metal detectors, just past the immigration counters, customs agents waited. As we approached, I swung my face from one end of their x-ray conveyor tables to the other searching the faces of the customs agents in effort to spot the friendliest looking among them. I decided on a woman agent with braids similar to Chinelo's braids. Her hairstyle was however not what drew me to her. It was the warmth she exuded as she processed her passengers amid smiles and conversation. All other agents appeared drab and unfriendly. My perception could not have been more accurate. Our customs clearance was a conversational walk-through. From the corner of my eyes, I observed as another customs agent grilled a passenger about some irregularity in his passport. The highly agitated passenger yelled and screamed about the agent's incursion into immigration duties. "You're a customs agent, not an immigration officer; he protested. The immigration officer found no fault in my passport! It is you who are adamantly trying to find fault where none exists. If you think I'll give you a bribe, better forget it. I will not!" The customs officer would not budge. He in fact felt insulted and was now poised for a real face off. I quietly slipped away, Chinelo in tow, toward the departure gate.

Believing that my troubles were over, I arrived at the departure gate unprepared for what happened there. Chinelo and I both handed our passports to the NAACHO (Nigerian Airways and Cargo Handling Company) agent in unison. The young man looked at both our photographs in the passports and frowned. The look on his face said it all. He knew that the girl standing before him was not Kimberly Udeozor. I had no time to react to what I felt was coming. It was one of those moments when you are incapacitated, frozen on the spot, anticipating the end. I held my breath and waited. After bouncing his glare interminably between the passports and our faces, he said, "This girl is not Kimberly. But since you managed to pass check-in, immigration, customs, and S.S.S. clearance, I will not be the one to screw things up for you. Here are your boarding passes. Have a safe flight."

Fifty

That my wobbly feet managed to carry me all the way to our seats on board the aircraft on that humid October night in the year of our Lord nineteen hundred and ninety-six remains in my mind today, a miracle which should never have happened. But it did.

Sitting in my seat now that we were airborne, I had nearly twenty four hours to brood over what uncertainties lay ahead of us. In my state of mind, nothing onboard was of interest to me anymore. My accidental dabble into the work of charity appeared right then as my albatross. The futility of any thoughts of changing my mind and reversing course was crippling. Even then I could not help toying with the idea... perhaps on arrival at London Heathrow Airport, if I walked up to the airline desk at the arrival hall, I could convince a British Airways staff to route us back to Lagos. To do this, our passports would come under scrutiny. How would I handle the possibility of British investigation should Chinelo's cover be blown? So far, Chinelo had not been required to utter a word. She could barely speak decent words in English and her accent was a dead giveaway, thick like rubber. Could it be arranged by one of my London based friends to take her in, and figure a way out of the trap I had unwittingly set, only to become its first prey? Or perhaps I should just walk away from her upon our arrival at Heathrow? Surely, the authorities would pick her up and return her to Nigeria...?

These thoughts were my delayed responses to the incident at the boarding gate a short while earlier, and I knew it. What or who prevailed on the young NAACHO agent to reason with such an uncommon rationalism for his job description? Surely, raising an alarm would have earned him reward and the envy of his colleagues for his alertness. So, why did he let us go, therefore forfeiting a golden opportunity to advance his career?

I could not yet fathom the answers to these questions or the reason for our good fortune but the real issue which kept my internal faculties in disharmony with one another was the certain knowledge that from the moment of our departure, if the secret of Chinelo's true identity was discovered, the chances of receiving the same treatment as with the NAACHO agent were lower than zero.

Of course there was a rational explanation for the entire event. The still, silent voice had moved ahead of my other faculties; the events of our lives have all been predestined. We are all actors on a global stage. Following a script previously mapped out by another who is infinitely superior to us. But then, the map gets tricky—especially at the crossroads. Now we are required to play a role in shaping that predestined destiny. Which road to follow?

That was when I decided. Hell or heaven? It was already decided, I thought. That decision was not mine to make. My decision was simply which path to take. At this point, I felt my heart rate begin to slow down. The weight had just been lifted off my back. Que sera, sera. What will be, will be.

I turned to Chinelo then and asked, "Are you enjoying the flight?"

"Yes sir," she replied, surprised to hear my voice.

"You look scared. Don't be afraid. The airplane will not fall off the sky." I assured her.

"Yes sir," she again replied.

"Relax; I'm sorry I've not said much to you. I briefly forgot that this is your first time in an airplane. It feels like you're in a big flying house, doesn't it?"

"Yes sir."

"You'll get used to it." I promised her. "Here, this is how you use the headphones. You may listen to music now. When the movie comes on, I'll show you how to change to the channel where you can listen and enjoy the movie."

"Yes sir." She again replied.

I was once more quiet and contemplative. Only this time, I had completely calmed down. From the good book, one of my favorite lines slowly played in my mind; *happy is the man who finds refuge in himself.*

Through the terror of the last several hours, a lucid calmness had come over me, and now, I found myself almost cherishing the moment. Strangely, I felt no more fear. No more anxiety. Out of nowhere I received assurance that all would go well. At that moment, I felt the warm breath of God on my skin and then I heard the still silent voice say: "Remain steadfast and follow your heart." That was what I did.

One of the rewards of midnight flights to London from Lagos in those days was the early morning arrival. I always looked forward to the few hours I got to spend either visiting friends or pacifying the strong hedonistic urges of success-driven young adults. Since I was a young adult myself, I found that those urges surged to the surface every time I was in London. However, on this particular early morning arrival into London, I had neither the urges of self-indulgence nor the illusions of a success-driven young man.

I was sober, even somber as we began our final approach. There was no resurgence of anxiety. Far from worrying, I was reflecting on how I had led my life so far. My accepting to bring the young lady Chinelo to the United States and attempt to assist her and her family transform their legacy of perpetual misery and dearth appeared to be returning me home like chicken to roost. I had known Chinelo's condition of birth and upbringing in my own life. My parents simply did a better job than many other parents who shared our predicaments, of motivating us against all odds to shoot for the skies. My mother especially taught us, her children, to believe firmly in the love and good intentions of our Father in Heaven. "Cling onto His apron strings, and He will never cut you off." These were her favorite teachings.

With those thoughts I felt a firm conviction that although I was breaching some laws, I was doing so for a purpose which the law makers failed to address in making those laws—a purpose justified by the underlying good intentions. The inner peace I purchased by this reasoning was, if nothing else, very reassuring to me. It motivated me to carry on.

As if an endorsement of my conviction, our arrival and check-through process at London Heathrow Airport was the smoothest I had, so far, ever experienced. Both the British Immigration and Custom personnel were particularly courteous as they processed and checked us through. I had always admired the Englishman's brand of humane courtesy: "This way Mr. Udeozor, run along. You may be able to catch the next coach to Gatwick, if you hurry."

What I did not disclose was that I had a crucial, long overdue errand to run at the center of London before heading for Gatwick. We had a nine hour layover in London before our connecting flight to Washington Dulles Airport—enough time to get a lot done.

After Stella and I ate the vulgar strawberries which resulted in the conception of our daughter Kimberly, a related event which came close to scuttling our planned wedding in Nigeria happened. My longtime girlfriend had taken in shortly before I met and fell in love with Stella. Our relationship had however hit the rocks when she was caught red handed in a steamy affair with another man. As a consequence, any discussion of doing the respectable thing for her unborn baby even in the absence of affection by taking her to the altar was also out of the question. When she decided to carry the baby to full term, I offered as the father, to give her my full support and to be there for the baby. What transpired between us did not diminish the love we shared for a long time and the fruit of that love affair would not need to suffer the psychological wounds of an absentee father in a situation in which he was completely innocent.

Before the baby was born, I informed his mother about my fiancé and our impending nuptial voyage from our base in Los Angeles to Nigeria. She expressed her hurt and dismay at the news but showed no sign that she would try to disrupt or scuttle our wedding. Meanwhile the baby she bore became instantly my heart's greatest craving. He was the first real miracle of my life. I was at his mother's side at the hospital for his difficult delivery. The moment he was born, it was love at first sight. I named him Jeffrey.

My love and doting over Jeffrey was not lost on his mother, and she soon devised a plan to take advantage of my growing attachment to the baby to inflict maximum hurt on me as a foil for the hurt she was feeling. She moved with the baby to London, far away from my reach. It is not possible for me to tell whether she drew any sense of accomplishment from her action at that time, but I felt an indescribable sense of loss. I was devastated—a feeling I shared with no one else, not even my soon to be wedded love. There was no reason, I felt, to spread the hurt even more by weeping on her shoulders knowing as I did by then that at that moment, inches away from the shoulder bearing my head, another miracle of my life was waiting to happen.

Fortuitous occurrences seldom happened in my life, but eight years after Jeffrey was torn away from my life, I was sitting across the table from a great friend of mine when our casual conversation dovetailed into a shocking discovery. My friend was at the time, the Defense Attaché at the Nigerian Embassy in Washington, DC. We had known each other and exchanged family visits with one another for a long while. But mostly, I visited him at the Embassy. During the visit of that fateful day, our jesting veered into a discussion of our premarital relationships and their associated heartbreaks. He shared some of his, prompting me to share mine as well. But as I progressed with my jesting, his demeanor began changing. He shifted a lot on his seat and his facial expression held a look of incredulity. I was forced to pause and ask if he was alright. He said he was and urged me to finish my story. I did.

His first words after I completed my story were the question: "Was the name of this girlfriend of yours Julie?" It was now my turn to fidget on my seat and contort my face into a scowl. "How did you know?" I asked in confusion because I had mentioned no names. But he ignored my state of bewilderment and further asked, "Is your son's name Jeffery?" That did it. I got up from my seat and began pacing around in his office. That was how I discovered that beyond our friendship, and unbeknownst to either of us, a deeper bond existed between us. His wife was Julie's older sister! My son Jeffrey and his children were cousins! Before I left my friend's office later that evening, I had spoken with both Julie and Jeffrey in London.

From the arrival hall of Heathrow Airport, I placed a surprise telephone call to the number I called so regularly that I had memorized its eleven digits. In her husky voice, made even coarser by sleep, Julie answered, "Hullo?"

"Hi J, I'm in London, is there any chance I could see you and Jeffrey?"

"You're in London? You're not kidding?"

"I wouldn't kid you Julie!"

We met at Victoria Station and all my machismo could not hold down my tears when I beheld my son for the first time in eight long years. With deftly practiced cunning, I hid the tears from all, but Jeffrey. I believe he appreciated the emotions because he knew where they came from. That was how the union between father and son was re-established.

I floated in a Spiritual Trans as the speed rail bumped and squeaked in its metallic contrast with the train to ferry us to Gatwick Airport, London. The train got us to the airport on time to catch our uneventful flight to Dulles Airport, Washington, DC. We each presented our passports and were cleared at immigration and customs without incident. What *will be, will be.*

Fifty One

I do not intend to repeat what I have said before, or to retell other people's tales which I did not myself witness. It is from my direct encounter with the entire details of the events that followed my arrival at my family home in Darnestown, Maryland that my narrative emanates.

My madam was busy attending to the infirm at the clinic when we arrived from the airport. It was about 4:30 in the afternoon. I believe the two house-helps who took charge of house duties daily after the children went off to school and my wife and I departed to work were the ones who greeted and welcomed us upon our arrival. Shortly afterwards, my eardrums were entertained by the thunderous stampede of little feet bounding upstairs to where I had just laid down my head on the pillow in an effort to shake away the drowsy sensation which had assailed my entire body. They had just returned from school.

"Daddy's home! Daddy's home!" They cried as they raced against each other until their little soft bodies were piled on top of my exhausted prostrate body. I made sure each one of them felt my highly inflated body temperature before I explained to them, "I have jetlag fever. All I need is a little rest and I'll be alright. Then we'll talk. We have a lot to talk about." I promised them.

"Okay Daddy, this jet rag, where did you get it from?" My son George Adam wanted to know.

Too fagged out to laugh as hard as the question called for, I explained to them for the umpteenth time what jetlag meant.

"Okay, okay Daddy," they chorused as they filed away slowly and reluctantly.

I had barely shut my eyes when, with a bang, the door to my bedroom opened once more. My daughter Kimberly stood in the doorway and unapologetically demanded, "Daddy, who is that girl downstairs? What is she doing in our house?"

I gave up my effort to tackle the jetlag. I knew that until I did the duties I owed to them to their satisfaction, my fever could only get worse. These harassments were by the way, the activities that gave me the highest feeling of satisfaction as a father. I lived to be harassed by my children. I knew that without them my life would've been devoid of balance.

"Easy Pumpkin," I whispered. "I will tell you. But first, come take a look at what I got for you!"

At that moment all four of my other angels wrestled their way into the room, almost sending Kimberly to the canvas. They had hidden their bodies behind Kimberly while they eavesdropped into our conversation.

From my carry-on luggage I began sorting their presents. Swiss chocolate candies, various toys, assorted candy bars, children's clothing, etc.

It was my children who demonstrated to me that although they're made by the same company, Cadbury's Chocolate from London tasted better than the ones on sale locally in American stores. Their discerning taste buds even had me visiting Self Ridge's Confectionery stands where I bought items as ridiculous as sausages for export into the United States.

I honestly believe that part of my wife's discomfort as our children enlarged in number and size could be traced to her frustration with getting our children to show her some measure of the same robust romanticism with which they regarded me. What she failed to see was that our roles in their lives were different, as they should be, for whereas they may be children and therefore given to self-centeredness in their choices, they were smart enough by virtue of their natural endowments to discern what role is to be played and which parent to approach for it.

Thanks to our early arrival, my wife was away at work, leaving me alone to thoroughly enjoy the role and love of my life—fatherhood.

"Now, sit down Pumpkins. Sit down Rangers." My girls, including their mother were my Pumpkins, while the boys were my Rangers.

"Don't any of you recognize the girl downstairs?" I asked the lot of them who were still hugging their gifts while busy coveting their neighbor's gifts.

"If you were not going to listen to me kids, why did you come and wake me up from sleep?" I protested seriously. "I thought you wanted to know who the girl downstairs was," I concluded in a faked, loud and angry voice.

"Sorry Daddy," Kimberly replied in a low contrite tone as the others sat up wide eyed and nodding their heads to indicate that Kimberly spoke on behalf of them all. "Yes, we want to know who she is. I don't remember her." The others promptly supported their big sister with emphatic shaking of their heads—no.

"Okay then, let me ask you this: does any one of you remember our trip to Nigeria last year?"

Their little hands flew up into the air. "I do, I do, I do, me too!" They chorused, and I continued. "Does anybody remember any babysitters… I mean, the people who helped babysit Stella Georgina at Amawbia?"

"Yeah, yeah, yeah, yes I do, yes, yes, me too" rang out from their adorable lips. Kimberly, who remembered better than the rest added, "There were many of them Daddy."

"Thank you kids. The girl downstairs was one of them. Do you remember her now?" I asked expectantly.

Flashes of recognition spread across their faces, some of them not quite confident. But the big sister came to the rescue of the others. "Yes Daddy, now I remember her." She said. "She looks a lot different than I remember—a lot older and better looking. What's her name?

"Chinelo."

At this point Adam's face cracked into a grin and he said, "Daddy, she used to follow me around at Amawbia asking me to show them the ninja turtle kick."

"Is that so? Well then, now you can also teach her the kick, okay?" I joked.

"Never," my son yelled in protest.

~

As boisterously as they had been coming up, they all descended the spiral staircase chanting, "Chinelo, Chinelo, we know your name!" I was relieved to have the commotion shifted to another location and to one with more of their kind of stamina than myself. But out of curiosity, I leaned over the railing to spy on the crowd for a while.

Chinelo's timidity seemed to embarrass her as they slugged her with a barrage of questions, most of them rhetorical.

"Wasn't it a very long flight from Nigeria? I bet you thought you'll never get here. Wasn't it your first time on a plane? Are you going to live with us? It is real cold here, isn't it?"

As Chinelo smiled sheepishly, nodding her head intermittently, I knew that at the rate they were going, it would not be long before she was forced to adapt to the American way. With that degree of pressure on it, even an emu could learn to fly. I turned around and went straight into bed with a smile of contentment on my face. Finally, I was free to relieve myself of the malady of jetlag fever.

But I was not yet off the hook. Just as I drifted into the initial trance-like stupor which is characteristic of jetlag sleep, the voices of my little angels were back at my bedside. Valerie and Stella Georgina, the last two of my Pumpkins, were tugging the bed cover hollering, "Telephone daddy, mom is on the phone."

It took a while for blood to rush some reason into my head. "Okay Pumpkins," I managed to smile at them. "Thank You," I said as I took the telephone handset from Valerie.

"Hello Big Pumpkin!" I murmured into the mouthpiece.

"Sorry Darling," she whispered apologetically. "They told me you're 'jet ragged' and sleepy. But I had to speak to you. *Darlin*, you're incredible. They told me you returned with Chinelo! You're something else! Are you crazy or what?"

"Only crazy in love with my family." I gloated.

"I don't even know where to begin my questions. I wish I could take off right now. Oh, I've missed you!"

I could sense the vulgar strawberry talk coming. "Really" I teased, "can you prove it?"

"Sure," she returned, "How do you want me to prove it?"

"With you spending all those hours at work, I do not think you'll have the energy." I challenged.

"The way I am feeling now, I'll be equal to your demands. Besides, I can always let you do all the work."

"You mean, as in, you'll not participate?" I quizzed.

"Yes, as in, I'll be your sitting duck."

"You're crazy." I said.

"Only for you" she reassured me.

"Alright, I'll go back to sleep now. I think I might need a good rest to get me ready for you."

"Before you go *Darlin*, have you eaten?"

"Not yet. We had lunch twice in the air. You don't want me fat and lazy, do you?"

"Sure, that way I know you'll be mine alone. Because then, all those sleazy flirts would not want you."

"Good luck to them, I'm already spoken for."

"I love you."

"I love you too."

Fifty Two

Stella, my madam, is a creature of habit. At the beginning of our relationship I sought without success to curb her one habit which I found the most objectionable; her carefree and welcome attitude to tardiness. With Stella, nothing got done unless it was done late. Bedtime ranged from 1:00 AM to 5:00 AM. Wake-up time was usually 11:00 AM to 2:00 PM. Arrival at church, usually thirty minutes to one hour after normal opening. Major events of celebration were her most notorious casualties. She had to arrive just before closing. The more serious activities such as education or paid employment were not even sacred ground for her. But being book-smart and skilled in her field, the consequences of her bad habit usually came slow. But there were always consequences.

It was therefore not a surprise when I recovered my lost consciousness at about 1:00 in the morning that I found her relaxing with a cup of tea on the table and the telephone to one ear. She was as alert as any nocturnal creature could be at that hour. For the first time in our lives together as a couple, I was glad to find her that way at that ungodly hour. I had been rendered nocturnal also, thanks to my jetlag. We only needed the lights off to transform ourselves into bat-like creature which naturally led to bat-like behavior. But since only one of us was truly nocturnal, that behavior only lasted until about 3:00 AM before, just like all other normal humans, we both helped each other up the spiral staircase and into bed.

True to her nature, my madam was just beginning to savor her slumber when our five angels converged in on us, their gifts in tow. A sight I still miss to the present day. The bedroom was given a new look before the older four stormed away to Mary of Nazareth Catholic School only half a mile away. After tranquility returned, I slipped out of the bed and bedroom to find Chinelo already engaged in conversation with the two Ghanaian ladies who kept watch and catered to the children's needs in our absence. The two ladies were already schooling Chinelo on how things worked around the Udeozor household. It was not unlike the kind of maternal coaching administered to every young woman of our cultural origins back in West Africa. My two young daughters, although still pre-teens, were already quite well schooled in this art of home keeping.

It was time for me to play the role which I felt the good Lord designed me for—fatherhood, my way. Our last baby Stella Georgina, born May 11th, 1994 was to be our very last bundle of joy, my last pumpkin. That was the reason I named her Stella-Georgina, a coinage from both of her parent's first names, Stella and George. When she came into the world, she arrived with pizzazz. It was such a swift delivery that it was the testiest challenge I've ever tackled—to catch a slippery 10lb baby at the tail of a delivery table! At 9 pounds, 9 ounces, she weighed more at birth than her other siblings. After it was all over, I assured Dr. Nixon Asomani, our OBGYN Doctor, that I would've had his head if the baby had slipped through my arms. He mused that he was good at what he did; only giving a chance to daddies who had proved their mettle.

It was hence this baby that I marked as the one to cater to me when my bones began to creak and rattle. I reasoned that she would owe it to me since I did such a good job of showing her into the world. One turn, they say, deserves another.

I picked Stella Georgina up. "Mommy," I whispered in her ear, "someday I will tell you why I love you so." I played with this baby until, out of exhaustion she passed out in my arms. When we got into my room, the baby on my shoulder, her mother was wriggling under the cover and moaning with pleasure and satisfaction. It was her wake up time.

~

It is somewhat of a strange logic in my opinion that some people choose in their relationships that there be no rules made. But when the other party in that relationship behaves in a manner deemed inappropriate, accusations are raised from the earth and all manners of rules appear which the aggrieved seeks to enforce.

When I finally sat down with my wife to share with her, the hair raising details of our journey out of Nigeria, I had a hidden concern in the back of my mind. That concern had to do with the manner of kinship we must extend to Chinelo in relation to both ourselves and our children. It amounted to stating the obvious for me to remind her that the young lady was no blood relative of ours but I felt it was necessary for me to do so if we were to begin on good footing. I cautioned her to set a motherly tone from the beginning and to lay down her law as she saw fit, as a mother would for her child, but not to ignore the necessity altogether, as she did in the other failed instances.

We were bringing a young woman who was not our biological child into the closest possible proximity with our children, with the intention of treating her like one of ours. Children understand certain things by natural instincts and they need to be accorded that respect. If distances were not properly defined, I cautioned, problems might arise out of an unexpected source or out of nowhere at all. I always found it greatly distressing when my wife interpreted my insistence on dialogue first as an overreaching attitude on my part. Yet whenever it turned out that I was right to begin with, she loathed the blame, "I told you so." Or, "I warned you."

I failed to see myself as overreaching in the case of Rita when I suggested to Stella that a meaningful distance must exist between madam and maid. I had nothing against the maid in question, for she was my second cousin. My wife instead, used my caveat as a means of cementing her mismatched friendship with the maid. While the going was good between them, I was held in disaffection by my second cousin because of my belief. My wife saw nothing amiss until she ran into hot water with the maid. I was not present when the strife began, but as I later learned, whatever my wife said or did failed to meet the maid's approval. So hands akimbo, she refused to bend. When madam advanced on the maid, shoe in hand, the maid made it clear that if madam so much as laid a finger on her, she would thrash her even harder. Sadly, she made good on that threat. Although the incident would not have happened, had I been there, I believed it was necessary that it did. Maybe madam did learn a lesson from the incident. It remained to be seen.

My role thus concluded, I left my wife to run the home. When it comes to family, I am a firm believer in role playing. This was not a secret to my wife. From the wording of our wedding vows to the Christening of our children, I expressed my brand of conservative idealism. Role playing was its central mantra. If she had any objections to this, my wife did not verbalize it. On the contrary, she wholeheartedly endorsed it. Or so I naively believed. In any case, I still suffered from the hangover from my presumed authority as the head of my household—a pure fantasy which was already in its final tail spin. I just did not know it yet.

It is sad that it took the slow collapse of my marriage, a catastrophic event that seems unending for me to become exposed to the skills and information which would have prevented my family's demise. In retrospect, I lay no specific blame on either the cultural values of the United States or those of my birth country for the unnecessary anguish my family has had to endure. I however, find great flaws in the judicial systems of both countries for failing to deploy their most sensitive and most sagacious assets to this human relationship puzzle rather than the desensitized scholarly, political approach currently in practice worldwide. It has to be recognized that the United States, as the undisputed sole superpower of the world has a much higher responsibility in this matter. I wish to be clear on my opinion on this particular issue:

I have not a single doubt that if my situation were played out in reverse order, in which case I was a United States citizen by birth and only a naturalized citizen of Nigeria, my conviction for the offense of involuntary servitude would have been unthinkable. This claim is in reality not a mere opinion or speculation. Documented cases saturate the airwaves where United States citizens are caught in the same humanitarian tight rope in which I find myself, only to be rescued from the legal system of the second country using the same culture-based defense which failed me in the United States. Ironically, it is the machinery of the same State Department that ensured my extradition and conviction which usually guaranteed (brokered) the rescue of the maliciously accused United States citizens.

The point of my circuitous discourse on culture is to draw the attention of others who go about engaging in their alien cultural practices right here in the United States under the mistaken assumption that naturalized American citizens enjoy the same freedoms as do natural born U.S. citizens to practice customs which are engrained in their culture of birth to the danger they face. Granted, I possess neither the natural grounding and authority, nor the academic credentials to illustrate why offenses committed in the act of practicing one's culture must be judged with some degree of difference. What I do have is a conviction based on common sense and the moral sense of justice that hypocrisy and double standard do not belong in the laws of civilized society. If the government of the United States is sensitive enough to cross cultural woes of its citizens overseas, then it must show a minimum of the same amount of sensitivity to the cross cultural woes of United States citizens at home regardless of the country of their original birth.

I believe that unless and until enough voices are heard and harkened to, an untold level of cruelty and unjust convictions will continue to be routinely recorded as matter of fact, business as usual practices in America's numerous halls of justice. To those adversely affected, these halls are easily seen as halls of injustice—a sad and poor reflection of the true sentiments of these misunderstood United States citizens about their adopted country.

By handing Chinelo over to my wife for the purpose of mentoring and assimilation into our household, I had followed our cultural traditions. It is the wife's duty, not the husband's, and not even the joint responsibilities of both, to cater to this important role. Our culture does not mandate an official adoption to raise Chinelo as we would our own child. Besides, it would have amounted to a criminal act to pursue an adoption process without her parent's expressed consent. My family had been helping raise her, which clearly implied that I had been indirectly involved in raising her all along. The difference was that my wife and I were now to become her sole benefactors and our roles had become more direct. We had become her alternate parents.

I cannot point at any action on the part of my wife in the days following Chinelo's arrival that would suggest that she planned to treat her like a maid. Neither I nor my children looked upon Chinelo or treated her like anything other than a relative. As a result, no incidents to alter this status quo occurred while my family lived as we did, in amity until the unfortunate deterioration of my marriage to Stella. For this reason, all I recall is the gradual and incremental assimilation of this young woman into the lifeblood of my immediate family until no visitor could discern her from my biological children.

My madam's high intellect and gregarious, outgoing personality belies a deep seated insecurity. I ought to know, we were married for over thirteen years. I made it my duty to try and discover the origin of this animal that hid within her, causing us no trouble at first, but nevertheless issuing threats from time to time. This animal—the shrewd and crabby devil that it was, avoided direct tango with me. He knew the depth of my love for the madam. To soften all of her defenses, the animal co-opted the joint alliances of my madam's double childhood alter egos—her mother and her brother. Just like the serpent in his play for Adam's soul, this animal was a master of deception. He needed only one device for his wicked act—human greed.

With the arrival of Chinelo and her assimilation into the family, it appeared the animal determined that the hour had come to go for my jugular. Her successful arrival into the United States accomplished, it was now time to plan for her future. The role fell on me to take the lead and attend to the details of the promised transformation of her life. My first project toward achieving that lofty goal was to try and re-establish her proper identity. To this end, I undertook yet another costly journey back to Nigeria. During this trip, the first of the two which was required to fulfill the task, the animal went to work.

Insecurity as an animal is the ultimate wrecking machine. The coward that he is, he operates from the secure comfort of his victim's medulla. In my case, it was my madam's guileless and trusting heart. With his fail-safe allies; my wife's most trusted, flesh of her flesh, and his signature pitch fork, the animal went to work. His allies, mother and son had an easy assignment; nothing to it—it was to simply scare all reason out of my wife's senses.

While I was away in Nigeria trying to obtain a passport for Chinelo as proof of her identity, the alliance went to work on my madam. Upon my return, the alliance had left their mark in the heart of my other half. The seed of discord was budding. When she demanded to establish a separate bank account for the first time in our ten years of marriage, I knew she was repeating the demands of others.

The demon knew his game and the route to success, so using his allies he applied the pressure directly on me. What manner of husband, father and provider would I be if I failed to return fire for fire in defense of my family? Lo, but with some adversaries, the rules of engagement must be ponderously and collectively decided. That was why I turned to my madam for alliance. At first she embraced my fight as our joint responsibility—a duel for the life of our family. She even brought some vulgar strawberries to the room that doubled as our bedroom and war room.

Sensing the possibility of defeat, the animal backed away—but it was only a tactical delay. Then it was time for me to journey overseas once more. The first leg was to Nigeria to complete the process and secure proper identification papers for Chinelo. But first, the strawberries resulted in the arrival of my warrior from the stork. I delayed my journey and the quest for Chinelo's identity for the reception of my son. I named him Malcolm Christopher (or Malcolm Xtopher) after my favorite warrior for justice, and promised him to the Creator as the warrior for my family.

A few months later, after the christening ceremony of my warrior, the animal fired his most devastating salvo yet.

Fifty Three

I try never to wear my scars as badges of honor. But how can I conceal them? They are not few and far apart. Instead, they are many and gathered in one spot. They are not healed and blended to an even texture. Instead they are gaping and festering. I try and I try, but I don't succeed. I guess these scars of mine are meant to follow me forever. I guess they are meant to remain forever: My Badges of Honor!

When strife has first entered a marriage, it almost invariably returns at will—just like policemen to the scene of a crime. The fingerprints of strife were already all around me but I naively ignored them, allowing the animal enough time to reload and then fire the salvo.

Those deadly shots first sparked quarrels between my madam and me. The quarrels then were few and far apart. Then, bit by bit we began working each other up, taking a little step at a time toward each other. Edging toward the point where words ceased and assault began. Foul words which usually hurt were hauled between us almost unnoticed, as if neither of us listened anymore. I knew then that we had arrived at the threshold of violence. It was time to put a distance between us.

~

They say that vision in hindsight is 20/20, yet today, over a decade later, I remain at a loss how I could have handled things differently.

First, my madam demanded to begin operating a separate, private bank account. Ordinarily this demand would have been a non-issue. Every working adult, married or single has the right to do so. But our money management was not ordinary as in the cases of many couples whose household income comes from the same source as ours did—a partnership in the family business. We both trusted each other's judgment from the beginning when only one of us brought home the bacon. Because that income was single handedly generated by me overseas, we agreed to maintain only joint accounts where I deposited all my earnings for the purpose of meeting the family's financial needs. We bought our first home and supported both our extended families from those joint accounts. Our children's needs were similarly met. So also were our own needs.

After my madam completed her residency in Family Practice, she and I agreed that she only needed a daytime job which had some flexibility and sensitivity to family demands. Her income would only serve to support mine and although we operated joint accounts, the checkbooks were usually in her custody. Everybody was happy. My in-laws were extremely happy. Their daughter and her husband were mega stars.

Then in 1991, in the summer of that year, we took our first family vacation. Nigeria was our first choice for this August occasion. Our three children got a grand tour of their ancestral homeland. But it was at a very high cost. My madam's three month old employment at a medical center located conveniently near our residence was our price for that summer jamboree. Her employers were very adamant about the finality of their decision to fire my madam on account of her late return from vacation. Dismayed by this insensitive, unbending stance on a situation which I felt my wife could not help—her late return was caused by the sudden illness of our third child, I paid my madam's employers a visit. It was with shame that I read the time card maintained by this medical center, of the catalogue of my madam's three month history of daily tardiness in her three month employment with them.

It was therefore an easy decision to make for my madam to go into private practice knowing as I did that further attempts at paid employment would result in the same fiasco of termination.

That was how the family brand "Optimum Care Medical Center," our family business was born. I funded this project in its entirety. No loans were secured for the founding of this medical center. I breathed a sigh of relief in that this budding one-office medical center would finally provide my madam with a safe employment and the ultimate job security. For a short while, this was indeed the case. My madam was happy. I was happy. She was the boss. And life was good.

I should never have taken my madam's bait. But I sadly did. With her need for house help met, her struggle with tardiness neutralized, and our financial situation promising, it all seemed too good to be true. It is often at this juncture that the insatiable nature of humans drums up new agendas. Now my madam's problem shifted focus. She latched onto my long absences from home. That became her family cause célèbre. She put everyone on notice that I was an absentee father and suggested that I was gallivanting the globe and having a blast. When reminded that my job as Defense Contractor and Revenue Consultant required such travels, she became inconsolable, crying "you mean to tell me that our children are worth less than his trips overseas? Can't you see that I'm nervous raising them all alone?" When reminded that my trips only took me overseas for short periods and that I really made supreme efforts and sacrifices for my family, she'd reply, "So then, when I die, his sacrifices would be justified?"

To win sympathy and support, my madam threw me the bait. "You have started this medical practice for me," she would say, "You are a business man, an accountant, why don't you stay here, at home with me and the children. Take over as manager and run the medical practice?"

At first it was unthinkable to me. I waved away any chances of taking this bait. "And then you and I will start running around each other in circles. From home to the clinic and back again and again, day in and day out!" I would scoff at her. But her pressure got more intense. My mother, my oldest sibling, and my sister Chinwe all got drafted by my madam. They each began reciting the merits of my madam's viewpoint. I would challenge them, "What did she give you? Whose side are you on? If I quit my work how will we pay our bills? How much do you think this medical center can generate?" They would back off at this point with a caveat. "Your wife is highly tensed up. If anything should happen to her, your logic would be meaningless!" That was how my mind, body and soul were won. I began exploring the possibility of working with my wife.

My first assignment was to change the medical center from its status as a doctor's office to an LLC, a limited partnership. Next, I expanded the medical center initially to a two location practice and finally to a three office medical center. I was the Chief Executive Officer and my madam was the Medical Director. As the CEO, I was allotted 51% ownership while my wife got the remaining 49%. At its peak there were four medical doctors on permanent staff payroll and three part-time visiting physicians.

It was while in the middle of these fantastic endeavors that I first noticed the hand of Esau. For while I was busy engaging insurance companies, the Medicaid/Medicare programs, healthcare organizations and ambulance chasing attorneys, my madam's relatives and apologists had gone off on a campaign, working on her weakest personality flaw—her acute sense of insecurity.

As I already noted, it was clear to me when my madam made her demand to break up our accounts and to begin operating a private one, that that idea originated elsewhere—surely not from her. Even then, the implication of the request did not hit home fully right away and so, I shrugged it off. "Why would you need a new account?" I asked her. "You already hold all our checkbooks. I only keep the business account because of the daily operations and payroll. Even then you have complete access at any time of your choosing. So why do you need a private account? We are both equal signatories to the accounts. So what is the problem?"

It was evident from her responses that she needed better coaching. She had no answers to the questions I raised. But from the way she struggled with her thoughts, it was clear that others put her up to this ugly campaign. What I found strange was that at that particular moment in time, the medical practice which we jointly owned and now depended on had come under intense scrutiny by agents of the State. Reports had been filed against the medical practice accusing the practice of illegal billing. In the middle of the allegation was my madam who had been cited as signing off on services which were allegedly provided by physician's assistants in our employment and thereafter billed as if my wife had provided the services. With my madam nearing full term to the birth of my warrior baby, I shielded her and attended meetings in Baltimore and a grand jury hearing convened to determine whether indictments should be issued against Optimum Care Medical Center. My sincerity and truthful responses to those investigative hearings must have convinced them of my honest intent to serve my community in an honorable and fair manner, they therefore backed away. To my utter consternation, instead of the kudos I knew I deserved from my madam, she got even more cynical, accusing me of exaggerating the extent of the fed's allegations and investigation. But I was already deeply committed to making a success of the medical practice. I therefore consigned her grouchy and snide attitude by way of an explanation to the mood swings of a full term expectant mother.

The delivery of my warrior baby provided only a brief respite. To me, this was most unfortunate as I had put my entire hopes on the wonderful joy that follows the birth of a new baby. So, while I intensified my role as a father with the birth of our new infant son, believing his birth capable of renewing and reinvigorating the sullied passions of his parents, the demon was hard at work with his allies, even recruiting new allies. One of his new allies was the medical assistant who had been fingered as practicing medicine without a license. Upon discovering that he did not intend to give up his elevated status as Dr. Randmat, and so continued to treat patients in place of their assigned physician—my madam, I showed him the door.

With my termination of the rogue doctor, for whom I had already faced federal scrutiny and grand jury investigation in order to clear my madam and the good name of our medical center, I incurred my madam's unqualified wrath. She immediately commenced a daily nocturnal conference with the new allies. The animal was busy. He worked best at night and thrived in the assemblage of the manner of home wreckers who my madam attracted in droves.

What purpose will it serve to keep a tally of these meetings, save to say that they were many. God! What I would have given to be at the venue of these assemblies of depravity.

Those were the days when night after night, I was greeted by our empty matrimonial bed no matter what time I returned home. The thought that my madam's mother was one among the gamut of designers of evil plotting to bring down her own star baby Stella, is a testament to the potency of human greed. I became so incensed with her that on one occasion, I could not resist throwing her out of our home. She belonged more to the venue of their nocturnal gatherings and I let my feelings be known to her. The fact that before she died, we were able to sit side by side and forgive each other remains one of my happiest memories, for that was one of the most regrettable actions I ever took.

By late 1998, things had completely fallen apart between my madam and me. The center had come unglued. The only life left in the marriage hung suspended in the lives of six children and one maid. When the names of those six plus one lives showed up on court documents in the form of a court order barring me from within two miles of my home, those names included, I knew that the marriage had taken its last breath. It was simply a matter of time. But because we both loved our children, and I was raised never to give up, and because I felt deep down that my madam and I still loved each other, I decided to try the last treatment, a shock treatment of sorts—separation. If separation was what was needed to save our children from doom, I'd try it.

Fifty Four

Far from being in a state of inviolate chastity, Chinelo the maid was all woman when she arrived in the United States in October, 1996. This was the primary reason my mother thought it urgent that she was taken away from her environment which had exposed her early to the loose lifestyle that had doomed many teenage girls before her. Her older sister, who she looked up to, had already set a bad example with her unwanted pregnancy. It was not my place to x-ray her past, or monitor the development of her sexual morality because she had already crossed the line for such engagements when she tasted the forbidden fruit. My duties to her and her parents were first, to provide her a healthy environment for her physical and emotional wellbeing and second, to try and avail her opportunities to educate and improve herself. I was fully committed to meeting both of these goals, until the hands of fate dealt me the most unforeseen and cruelest obstacle to progress, thus freezing all actions on my plans for Chinelo and crushing my dreams to build a socially, emotionally, and financially secure family for my children.

Much has been said and written about my alleged immoral and amorous involvement with the young lady Chinelo. What I find curious is that nobody—neither even one of those assigned to bring a case against me, nor any of those employed to defend me has asked me to explain or confirm the veracity of this ugly allegation. Yet, although the charges against me did not include any count of sexual abuse against this young woman, the government prosecutors and the courts alike focused on the sensational and lewd imagery which the thought of illicit sex invoked in their pursuit of my conviction.

I have as a consequence of this relentless emphasis on the subject of illicit sex, given the matter a great deal of my time—researching, enquiring, and investigating, trying to discover why it has gotten to this: that the subject of human sexuality has taken ownership and now possesses the minds of many a highly paid public officials. It appears that the world has lost its highly prized sense of proportion. That was when I began wondering; am I imagining these things? Or have these things narrowed the minds of thinking men and women to viewing sexuality only from a lewd aperture? Is this a worldwide affliction or is it just a localized American phenomenon?

Then, the answers I sought began to crystallize. After pouring so much of my time into the subject, I have made a few discoveries: without the backing of statistical data, I am convinced that just like the United States leads the world in pushing the boundaries of discovery in most fields of human endeavor, the country also leads humanity in pushing the limits of exploration into all forbidden sexual practices. No area of this subject is left to fantasy and imagination any longer, thanks to the American spirit of discovery.

But this portends terror for the likes of me. Because America's supersized interest in illicit sex now transcends, it seems to me, the country's interest in all other unlawful afflictions of the mind combined, and the nation having lost its sense of proportion, all allegations of lewd conduct are treated with the supersized whip of law enforcement. Even for the innocently accused!

My heart is attacked every time I watch television and stories unfold where young women, some of them so young they have not even attained puberty, are subjected to unprintable acts of perversion. As a father of children who fit this age description, this poses a nightmare scenario. My sensibilities go berserk. I fancy the necks of those who sacrifice the security and wellbeing of these kids, ruining them . . . I fancy their necks laid on the guillotine and....

But not so fast! Alas, mischief is still a faculty of human nature. I would not have known this and would have remained an avowed advocate of the guillotine treatment had Chinelo not crossed my journey through life.

Chinelo has become to me, not just the name of my tormentor, it is the face of every traitor who elected to cash in rather than endure a period of test by receiving a price for the betrayal of him who delivered them out of consuming bondage.

You, my reader having followed the odyssey this far, have become familiar with how the young woman named Chinelo came to reside in my home in October, 1996. But that is perhaps the extent of your familiarity with her. You have not been told how hers became the face of perfidy.

It all began with the animal. Remember that animal named insecurity—the one that embedded himself deep in the medulla of my madam? Yes, that animal. Under the controlling influence of this demon, my madam turned against me. In my struggles to save the medical center, I was all alone. In my duties relating to our staff, some of whose jobs I knew little about, my wife withheld her role. In the daily running of our home and the office she showed no interest. In my myriad struggles with her brother over his delinquent debts to us, his incursion into our family affairs, his sabotage of my efforts to grow the medical center, my madam kept mum. Regarding our finances, my madam was determined to spend every penny and render us bankrupt to justify her concerns about insecurity. Her nocturnal conferences intensified. My madam deserted our matrimonial bed and began sleeping in my daughter Kimberly's bed. Among her most despicable acts was the unprovoked filing of an ex parte motion praying the court to restrain me from within two miles of our home and our children? She maliciously cited as one of her justifications for this cruel request, the sinister charge that I planned to kidnap our children following our planned trip to Los Angeles, California for the wedding of my youngest sibling, Bernard Udeozor. In an act of calculated wickedness, the demon deceived my madam into claiming Chinelo as one of her own, urging her and our children in their entire numerical strength, seven in total, to stay clear and away from my side of the family. This last act which she would come to regret, along with her other acts of subterfuge and depravity, all told above, and many forgotten and untold, form the barrels of the animal's last salvo.

At the county courthouse of Montgomery County, Rockville Maryland, it took the judge only a few minutes to determine that there was no basis whatsoever for the order sought to be imposed against me by my madam. She immediately threw out the order which had been in effect pending the hearing. There was however a caveat from this female judge who appeared seasoned by experience. She advised my wife that if it was divorce she was seeking, she should find the right court since the rules of that court were different and might entertain her complaints. I left that court in utter disgust wishing that this judge had known the source of my madam's quibbling. Two of them sat in that court, ensconced in one whole row of the mahogany pews unnoticed by the judge. My brother in-law and his wife had come as the main allies of the animal to oversee their handiwork. Without a doubt, their expectations had been dealt a blow. But I knew that they had succeeded beyond their dreams because it was on that day that I took the decision that effectively terminated my conjugal ties with my madam.

Upon returning home from that court hearing, my head filled with tears and confusion, I packed my personal belongings out of our matrimonial sanctuary and moved into our guest room in the basement of our house. This move, in the middle of 1999 marked the first time in our thirteen years of marriage when my madam and I both slept on different beds by choice. It was also during this period that all the devices of Chinelo's devious mind caught my attention.

It seems a real pity to me that due to their own personal weakness when it comes to sex, those appointed or elected to protect the weak and vulnerable in society from the predators among us are fast losing their moral claim to the offices they occupy. This reminds me of the legal doctrine that suggests that defense attorneys adopt the great octopus strategy when in a losing battle. In their conflicted roles as sexual beings on one hand and legislators of sexual behavior on the other, they make laws pursuant to political expediency, not necessarily giving consideration to any immoral or unjust exposure to which they might subject many who would become trapped in the web of such laws. In their selfishness and narcissism, they believe themselves above the laws they make. So, they go right along embracing the octopus and by spewing out draconian laws, codes and rules, they keep the proletariat engaged and confused. The proletariat themselves in their anguish over their endless suffering at the hands of predators appear insatiable for more draconian decrees while staying long distances away from mirrors lest they are forced to face some predators themselves. I observe many of my fellow citizens and co-travelers through life who clamor for justice without due process and wonder if they know how close they expose themselves to self-destruction.

Fifty Five

I look in the mirror every day and see no predator. In all the mirrors I look, all I see is a father denied his role and cut off from many who have need for him. That is what I am—a father who made mistakes, unjustified mistakes which ran afoul of the law. For my mistakes, I asked not for forgiveness but only that I pay for my mistakes and not for the political aspirations and job security of some office holders. Most importantly, I asked not to be labeled public enemy for the spurious claims of a young woman who is unfortunately representative of many youth of today and who have been molded into little tyrants by a society that has chosen to leave nothing to the imagination. A society that by choice groups good and evil in the same category, glamorizing both, while hoping that somehow the young and still impressionable among us have their heads, like ostriches, buried in the sand or that after viewing the mixed messages they would be able to make their choices from the right category.

Chinelo made choices from the wrong category and today I am paying for her choices and also for giving her the opportunity to make those choices. I have tried searching my memory beginning from the precise moment I moved out of my matrimonial bed to the guestroom bed in my house back in 1999 to see if I can spot anything I did which in hindsight I would wish to take back. Every time I engage in this search, I fail to find anything. The things that I would do differently in hindsight had nothing to do with what transpired in my home between 1996 and 2001. Those things, the events that led to Chinelo's arrival in the U.S. and her becoming part of my family are the things I wish I had never allowed to transpire. But those events transpired and here I was, accused not seriously of those events, but of made-up, spurious and treacherous allegations that were concocted for the self-serving pursuits of the very young woman Chinelo who I had gone out on a limb to rescue from the ire of consuming poverty and wretchedness.

Even merely reading the charges in the indictment which Chinelo caused to be issued against me was always enough to trigger shivers through my entire body. To think that this young woman herself and not some malicious, scandal-seeking looser would instigate these charges against me always brought me to the crest of despair.

INDICTMENT

The Grand Jury for the District of Maryland charges that:

1. Beginning in or about September, 1996 and continuing through on or about October 28, 2001, in the District of Maryland, the defendants;

ADAOBI STELLA UDEOZOR
AND
GEORGE CHIDEBE UDEOZOR

did knowingly and willfully combine, conference, confederate and agree with each other and with others known and unknown to the Grand Jury to commit certain offenses against the United States, specifically,

a) knowingly and willfully holding a juvenile alien to involuntary servitude for a term in violation of 18 U.S.C. § 1584;
b) knowingly and in reckless disregard of the fact that a juvenile alien had come to, entered and remained in the United States in violation of law, attempting to and harboring such alien in any place, specifically the defendant's residence in the District of Maryland, in violation of 8 U.S.C. § 1324(a)(1)(A)(iii); and
c) knowing and in reckless disregard of the fact that such coming to, entry, and residence was in violation of law, encouraging and inducing the juvenile alien to come to, enter, and reside in the United States, in violation of 8 U.S.C. § 1324(a)(1)(A)(iv).

COUNT TWO

The Grand Jury for the District of Maryland further charges that:

1. Paragraphs 2 through 3 of count one are incorporated here.
2. Beginning on or about October 1, 1996 and continuing through on or about October 28, 2001, in the District of Maryland, the

defendants; did knowingly and willfully hold a juvenile alien to involuntary servitude for a term.

COUNT THREE

The Grand Jury for the District of Maryland further charges that:

1. Paragraphs 2 through end of count one are incorporated here.
2. Beginning on or about October 1, 1996 and continuing through on or about October 28, 2001, in the District of Maryland, the defendants;

   Knowingly and in reckless disregard of the fact that the juvenile alien had come to, entered and remained in the United States in violation of law, attempted to and did harbor the juvenile alien in a place, specifically, the defendant's residence in the District of Maryland, and did so for the purpose of commercial advantage and private financial gain.
   8 U.S.C. § 1324(a)(1)(A)(iii) and (B)(i)
   18 U.S.C. § 2
   Indictment Signed by:
   THOMAS M. DIBIAGIO
   United States Attorney.

Reading these charges, you would think that for someone who had never committed any illegal acts, not even minor illegal acts, these were some pretty ominous charges. You would be quite correct, because although at the time the charges were first read out to me, they sounded like the lyrics of a rap war song, thanks to my obtuse schooling in legal knowledge, I failed to recognize the weighty implications of count two (2) of the charges.

As I have now come to understand and appreciate, ambiguity is not necessarily an error in the construction of laws. They are also artfully and purposefully built into judicial procedures in order to provide the operators of the judicial systems room for the adaptation and manipulation of the process to allow them to achieve the goals they desire.

I grant that the nature of the prosecutor's assignment calls for him or her to demand that investigators strive hard to uncover evidence of crime so as to ensure a conviction at trial. Had the investigator's overreaching actions during their investigation of my case been the only corrupt manipulation of due process, then I could easily live with the outcome of the entire parody which United States versus George Udeozor represents. But their actions only marked the point at which manipulations began—the tip of the iceberg.

Had the prosecutor not smelled conviction and pounced like a shark does when he smells blood and attacks, then perhaps the government would have given the matter a little more due diligence. But the cry of rape by a young woman in the age of rampant perversion of human sexuality can be counted upon to sound better than music in the ears of any ambitious prosecutor. What with the fact that there was a clear case of physical abuse of the complainant by the wife of the alleged rapist.

Here is how it happened: Two years after I broke up with my wife and consequently separated from my family, including our children and Chinelo, confusion and insecurity set in, replacing the umbrella of calm with which divinity protects every blessed marriage. With that umbrella collapsed and gone, all of us within that household became insecure and easy targets just the way the animal had planned it. From my location in Nigeria, I could offer no protection, no actionable assurances and no way forward as I formerly guaranteed the young woman Chinelo. My continued reassurances over the telephone and through her parents in Nigeria became to her, empty promises after my long two years of absence. In due course she ran out of patience. From her own words to me, I could sense rebellion and treachery, but I was powerless to do anything then. My estranged wife compounded the looming sin in the family by sinning in the most audacious and impious manner for any mother who has the fear of God in her—she moved the hateful man-reptile Anuofia Adoga into our matrimonial bed and commenced living in mortal sin with him before our poor little angels! And Chinelo too!

Chinelo quickly formed alliances with readily available sympathizers at every turn; the internet, new friends, boyfriends, children's rights advocates, any and all sources possible. She sought out all who would offer assistance and advice although they knew absolutely nothing about her background.

With the divine umbrella lifted and withdrawn, my family became marked for destruction by Satan. This is what I believe. I ask to be trusted with this belief because I know in my soul that I would have been charged with a more grievous offense—one that tops the list of all offenses, had I returned in my state of mind immediately upon receiving the news of my wife's sin. But the hand which removed the umbrella restrained me—urging me to forgive. That is why I believe we have been marked—as an example to warn those others who suffer more or less, for there are certainly both, than we have and continue even today to suffer.

As a sinner myself, I know the implications of finger pointing. I am well aware of the number of fingers which point my way each time I point toward another, away from myself. As a result, I have reasoned and believe myself to be just when I accepted responsibility for my own failings. By accepting responsibility for my actions I had told the truth and so I felt I could now forgive myself in order to move on. But not so with the rest of the world—truth telling is either out dated or unimpressive nowadays. I am befuddled by this modern day phenomenon. My accuser, her family and the prosecutor appeared to not care anything about the truth but were rather intent on destroying me despite the truth. Perhaps that is why it has taken this long and all the suffering, and the writing of America Gives and America Takes, for me to be finally heard. I had accepted responsibility for the wrongs which I did and for the wrongs of which I had been maliciously and falsely accused, I had denied. What remained for me now was my day in court. After that, then the much more significant issues of what my debt to society ought to be and what the future held at the end of it all.

While I waited for these upcoming events, my mind gradually migrated from thoughts of the women in my life who, for good or bad, ruled my life for the period which gave rise to the anticipated events; my mother, madam, and maid, back to my condition of confinement at Montgomery County Detention Center. One week after I arrived at the detention center, I received news that I was to be transferred to Clarksburg, a distance of about ten miles, to Maryland Detention Center (MDDC). On the day preceding that transfer, I received a letter from the Clerk of Court at the United States Court for the District of Maryland appointing Attorney Michael Citara Manis, Assistant Federal Public Defender for the District of Maryland as my defense attorney. As directed, I telephoned Mr. Citara Manis and set up an appointment for our first meeting two days later.

PART FOUR

United States Vs George Udeozor

"Summum ju s summa injuria
(Extreme Justice is Extreme Injustice."
~CIERO in De Officiis; Legal Maxim

"One could even say
that the U.S. Criminal Justice System
is no longer concerned
with innocence or guilt,
only with ruining as many people
as quickly as possible
in order to justify
budgets and political ambitions
with high conviction rates."
~Paul Craig Roberts &
Lawrence M. Stratton,
The Tyranny of Good Intentions

Fifty Six

As dawn began its approach, my internal clock kept me abreast of what time of the morning it was. I did not need to see a clock. At about 3:00 AM, I was all nerves, twisting and turning underneath two blankets. It was no use lying in bed. Sleep had departed my constitution hours earlier. It was the day for the move from MCDC to MDDC. I could already feel my veins twitching in protest. Those chains and handcuffs were only a couple of hours from being wrapped all around me once again.

There was no denying the obvious. I knew that the U.S. Marshals considered me fastidious and temperamental about the tools of their trade. But how could I help myself? The thoughts of their cold metal implements, the vice-like feeling they convey—like a plank between the jaws of a clamp. If only planks had life like I had. The fear of getting thrown behind the steel mesh security screen of their cruiser or van with all those steel gadgets in place and racing past all other moving devices as if they stood still, to another strange lock-up facility, being booked, fingerprinted, photographed, and processed, and again getting cooped in one freezing cell after another like a product at various stages of manufacture. Those thoughts were enough to keep sleep at bay for quite a long while.

~

It turned out that my worries were not misplaced. If anything, my fears were inconveniences much less traumatic than what transpired shortly after dawn.

Beginning at about 4:30 AM, those of us who were to be moved to MDDC under supervised instruction had to fold our beddings, pillows, issued uniforms and mattresses into one large bundle. We had to queue up and return the bundles to the same point from where they were issued to us about two weeks earlier. We were thereafter processed and given the bend-over-squat-and-cough treatment. All this while, the sound of metal chains, to which I had become desensitized by this time, went on clanking all around me almost unnoticed. My attention only detected that for the first time, we were being processed, not by the usual United States Marshals, but by the Sheriff's Deputies.

Then, almost as if by design, to drive home the message of our diminished, dishonored and degraded self-worth, we followed the Sheriffs orders into the vestibule of the prison intake wing where I froze on the spot upon entry. Only a few scenes in life are capable of invoking the kind of emotions that came surging into every living cell of my body.

It's been years since that first experience, yet I see that scene still. I open my eyes daily and I see it. It is still hard to find the words to describe it. It is nauseating. It is cruel. And it does not befit the image of the United States of my dream and the dreams of many around the world who would undoubtedly find that scene as offensive as I did on that early winter morning.

I had only seen caricatures of chain gangs in pictures or pictorial depiction of slaves bound and shackled and thereafter linked by chain one to another and lined up in rows. Until I walked into that vestibule, I never realized that today, in the twenty-first century United States, this practice of cruelty remains alive. I had only a few seconds to observe and absorb this spectacle before I became the sixth inmate in one row of six miserable souls.

Without much ado, as if a normal routine with which we all should be familiar, they began marching the inmates by rows out to their waiting vehicle. The row to which I was attached did not get to be marched out with the first groups to leave, and had to wait for over one hour, bound and linked as we were, until the vehicle returned after discharging its first load of inmates.

The vehicle was a large metal box. By the color and feel of it, the box was almost assuredly crafted out of panels of one variety of aluminum alloys. There were no windows on any side of the box, just a double door at its tail which swung outward to admit or discharge its human cargo.

Without being told, it had to be understood that walking with handcuffs and chain restraints in place was impossible. So, when the Sheriffs Deputies ordered us to march to their "Paddy Wagon," they fully expected that we would wobble and stumble in the process. As far as they were concerned, it would be a great pity if we marched safely to the vehicle without incident.

Just as I thought, they were prepared for our follies with their chains. They walked alongside us cajoling and "assisting" as we stumbled and cried from the crushing pains inflicted on our veins by the handcuffs and leg chains. "Here, let me help you, you cry baby," they would joke. "Hey, what's wrong gangster? Got a problem? Aww, maybe I should call mama . . . yes?" I could see that our ordeal was pure entertainment for these law men. My mind could not resist traveling three hundred years back in time for quiet meetings behind the clouds with my kit and kin to share their misery from that time, when these cruel practices first began.

Maryland Detention Center (MDDC) presents a vastly distinct environment from the Seven Locks facility (MCDC). Perhaps because the facility was significantly newer than the Seven Locks facility, it appeared as if time spent here would leave less harrowing memories on a soul in despair. Although the manner of humiliation suffered during what they term "routine" processing was the same as they had been at first experience, I had begun to numb my mind to the feeling of being defiled. I had begun growing weary of feeding the sadistic pleasure which some of the officers derived from witnessing the horror in my eyes as I bowed to their command and authority.

After the usual several hours long session of booking, fingerprinting, photographing, processing, and, don't forget, getting cooped in about three different cells, we were handed large plastic tote bags and directed to the pods designated on the tags attached to our bags. It was like wading through an airport departure lounge in search of your boarding gate. An electric door was popped open at one end of the intake vestibule and we were waved into a long, long hallway. At intermittent intervals, we were halted at a glass door and the leader of our group, an inmate who was a revolving door offender guided us through several security stops, each one manned by an officer, some of them male and others female, until we got to a security stop where we split up, each inmate to his assigned pod. The entrance to each pod was clearly marked with the pod number and had a call button beneath it which we were sternly warned not to push or even touch. After a few seconds, the sliding glass door opened to one side and I followed other inmates into an enclosure which was much like being inside an elevator. The door slid shut. But instead of riding up or down like an elevator would, another sliding door opened on the opposite side of the first door. We were at that point ushered into a large lounge arranged like a party lounge or game room in a sports bar. Right outside that door, a correctional officer who appeared bored and sleepy got on his feet and began recording and assigning us to pre-designated cells. I was assigned to cell C16. As I followed the correctional officer's directions to try and locate cell C16, I made a 360° sweep of the facility described as a pod and noted the closeness in design and layout of this enclosure to a modem motel lounge. Even the color scheme fit that of a modern La Quinta Inn. Cell C16 was on the mezzanine floor. As I approached the door, I looked down and observed that the correctional officer was trailing me, as well as other inmates with his eyes. He waved at me to open the door. Just as I gestured to do as told a loud click sounded which popped the door open. It was an electric remote control operated door. It felt heavy to touch and once inside and locked down, that dreaded feeling which is suggestive of an animal in a zoo cage returned. I was all alone in a cell enclosure measuring no more than seven feet by nine feet with twin bunk beds, one steel toilet, one steel water fountain and my plastic tote bag.

I unpacked my plastic tote bag to discover two white bed sheets, two towels, a mini tooth brush and a matching tooth paste tube. There were also in my tote bag, one blanket and two extra green jump suits which were the official inmate uniforms for my designation at MDDC.

Because it was so cold, you'd think you were in a dairy cold room, I put on my jumpsuit over the one I already had on. I then wrapped myself in one white bed sheet, having spread the other over the styrofoam mattress; I covered myself in one bundle with the blanket and laid on the bottom bunk bed and was soon coasting the playgrounds of the living dead.

Fifty Seven

I do not know whether it was the approaching trial or the knowledge that my children who I last saw nearly ten years earlier were just a few minutes' drive from where I was, but after the long, all morning, all afternoon sleep on my first day at MDDC, I woke up in a dreamy, nostalgic state of mind. Just as if at the snap of a finger, the low feeling of depressed anxiety was gone. My memory carried me backward in time, into the moments of blissful family life which was once mine. Moments I knew could never be recaptured but which made me more determined than ever to survive my current ordeal, no matter how difficult, in order to re-unit with the wonderful children who made these nostalgic moments possible.

I quickly surveyed my new cell and noted the location of the light switch and a call button on the wall. No longer feeling the chill of earlier that morning, I untangled myself from the sheet and blankets which held me down like a strait jacket. I had no idea what time it was and there was no immediate way of finding out. What I had was a clear head and an understanding that the journey ahead was going to be a difficult one but with my renewed sense of optimism and strength, I would come out stronger at the end than when it all began. No barriers were too strong, no obstacles too tough and no mountains too high for me to overcome in order to become a father to my children once more. At this point, I got up from my bunk bed and walked to the door. Running down the middle of the door was a thick reinforced glass strip through which I could see the correctional officer sitting in the middle of a work station. Just then two large carts were being wheeled into the area adjacent to the work station with trays stacked high on them. I assumed those trays contained the lunch for the pod inmates. Above the entrance doors was a clock which I could see clearly but could not believe. Was it possible that I could have slept this long in the daytime? It never happened before, as far as I could remember, 4:30 PM? I was still lost in wonderment when a string of clicking and popping sounds rang across the mezzanine floor doors and as I looked on through the glass strip, about forty inmates in their green jumpsuits bolted down the stairs as if in response to an emergency call and immediately queued up before the stack of trays. No instructions or special calls were necessary to send me crashing through my own door to pick up my tray before those wolves in green devoured it too.

Before I was moved from MCDC to MDDC, life had, as usual, settled into a routine. From what some of the frequent flyer inmates who had revolved around the system a number of times said, MDDC and MCDC were like twin sisters born two generations apart. If that turned out to be true, then it would be a welcome development as far as my need for readjustments. I had come to understand that in confinement, whether in prison, jail, detention center or a holding cell, life is all about routine: prison authorities mandate this to be so. They need the uniformity in order to quickly and easily spot any departures from the established routine. As a result each new day is like the one before; each week like the one before it, this way the months blend into each other which all blend into the years like yarn with no beginning and no end.

Although designed to punish and deny inmates such as I now was the ability to exercise control over our time and the activities we engage in, I was determined to manipulate that design intent to suit my purpose. To build my own control of their routine into as much of my private time as possible. In order to achieve this, I needed the authorities to be both efficient and rigid in the discharge of their duties. The adjustments were many, but with discipline, consciousness and focus, it was possible to tune my brain to believe that I had control over my time. For example, it was not mandatory to eat any meal unless you're put on suicide watch. So, by choosing which meals to eat, one is able to put himself up to a level of control. Exercise, studying and worship also break the sort of total control which the authorities would prefer to exercise over inmates. I was determined that I would take maximum advantage of these opportunities which are inbuilt into the system, and use them for my own benefit as against the intended purpose.

It was therefore pleasing to me as I rounded up my supper at about 4:50 PM that I could continue to build onto that routine which I was already acclimatizing myself to. Although surviving through the first few nights was the most grueling such experience of my life, these routines were to become the foundation from which I would begin to reconstruct my life. Breakfasts were served at between 4:30 AM and 5:00 AM. Lunch followed at between 10:30 AM and 11:00 AM. Supper was eaten at between 4:30 PM and 5:00 PM. Between meals, we were allowed 45 minutes or 60 minutes of television and phone time. Once a week, we got to spend one hour at the leisure library and another one hour at the Law Library to research and work on our cases if we knew what to look for.

We were allowed to check library books out for two weeks at a time and a maximum of six books could remain in our custody at any time. All together we were locked down in our two-man rooms a total of approximately twenty one hours every day. Visits from family and friends were allowed but limited to three visits per week and a maximum of four visitors per visit. This visit which was anxiously anticipated weekly and which made the difference between sobriety and insanity for many inmates lasted for only forty five minutes at a time and was conducted strictly without any form of body contact. In fact, body contact was impossible as the visit only allowed eye contact through a thick plexiglas window and muddled up conversation via telephone intercom. No prison official has been able to explain to me yet why at both MCDC and MDDC, inmates were routinely body-searched following every family visit even though the entire visit was conducted under correctional officer's full supervision and without any possibility of physical contact whatsoever between the inmates and their family members! Could it be that they believe some inmates possess extra sensory powers?

Within 48 hours, I had begun settling down to a routine and getting used to the rare good fortune of sharing cell C16 with nobody but roaming spirits and library books. With nothing but visits from my sister Chinwe and the upcoming visit from my newly appointed attorney to look forward to, I could not have asked for better punishment.

I knew I had my work cut out for me in the days preceding the pretrial hearings in my case. Topping my to-do list in readiness for my first meeting with my appointed attorney and the pretrial hearings was to finally get down to reading the indictment and other charging documents which had been made available to me. In my denial and reluctance to accept that a truly genuine attempt to offer a helping hand could be rewarded with a prison sentence, I had deferred continuously, the crucial task of outlining my responses to the serious charges hanging menacingly over me. I do not know how others in my situation cope, but even at my most sober, clear-eyed moments I was still hoping to wake up from the ugly nightmare which refused to go away.

Now, I found promise in the fact that I was finally feeling ready to face the inevitable. One good thing that can be said about incarceration is that enforced isolation is very conductive to study and meditation. I was coming up to the fight of my life and nothing could do more for me than an in-depth study of the laws relating to the charges against me and a rediscovery of my fighting spirit through meditation in solitude.

The performance of the prosecutor during the preliminary hearing before the magistrate on my first day in court, on the very day I arrived from Nigeria, had so jolted and disillusioned me, I found it difficult to look into the details in the charging documents. My paid attorney's dismal responses, almost as if whimpering an entreaty for the bully to show some mercy, completely let the air out of my fighting spirit. While I shook my head in protest, scribbled my objections on paper, expecting her to stand up for me, she shrunk further and further away from me, at the same time reminding me that I was not to speak during these hearings unless prompted by the court to do so. I was therefore forced to listen to a depiction of my person which sounded and appeared like a nightmarish fiend, a criminal without redemption. I finally came face to face with the image of myself which the prosecutor wanted the world to see and believe and which she would spare no resources to ensure that no defense attorney could erase or even mitigate.

The prosecutor's strategy succeeded, I believe, beyond her wildest dreams. She read from her records, accounts which suggested I had numerous aliases, numerous identities, numerous social security numbers and even prior record of conviction with the law. At the time, it was startling to me, for I believed the government to be infallible. Although I had never even visited some of the venues where her allegations attempted to place me, I nervously entertained some degree of self-doubt. Was it a case of multiple personality? Was there a version of myself which I knew nothing about? But of course I knew it was a fruitless fantasy. If this prosecutor really dug such information up, then she knew they were false, but deliberately decided to tap into the prejudicial value it would provide. When I later discovered that one of the social security numbers entered into record belonged to my son, George Adam, it confirmed what I already suspected—there were similar explanations for the other false information used by the government to obtain an easy indictment against me.

A few days before the meeting with my new attorney, Michael Citara Manis, I had made a brief mental summary of what really happened in the case now known as United States Vs George Udeozor. Now, I decided to put those thoughts down as I would present them to Attorney Citara Manis:

> *"Early in 1996, I made my mother a promise which I should not have followed up on but which later events tricked me into fulfilling. I assisted* a *very*

poor young woman named Chinelo who was also my mother's god-daughter from my native African village to enter the United States illegally using my daughter's U. S. Passport. The object was to assist her family in raising her and by so doing, better her chances of success in life. She resided with my wife, me and our six children for a few years. Three years after she arrived, I separated from my wife as a result of marital difficulties. I then returned to Nigeria and resumed my earlier discarded consultancy business with the government. In my absence, the young lady at one point argued and fought with my estranged wife who threatened her with deportation back to Nigeria. Fearing that the threat was serious and portended dire consequences for her future in the United States, the young lady solicited from her new friends and other sources and decided to preempt my wife by contacting the police first. She falsely claimed that she was a victim of abuse and enslavement. Without proper investigation, the justice system descended heavily on my family, destroying it.

Today, my estranged wife sits in prison, her career as a medical doctor ruined. I, myself, after suffering a humiliating arrest and detention in Nigeria, am again now sitting here in detention, awaiting an apparently already pre judged trial in court. Our children, totally unprepared for their uncertain destiny as fatherless and motherless are now forced to endure some untold and unfair developmental pains on their own."

Fifty Eight

After attentively listening to my tale, his calm demeanor intermittently punctuated by low grunts and the narrowing of his eyes in flashes of surprise, he heaved a long sigh and said, "Kindly allow me a few moments to review my notes." He had been taking notes and while I spoke and from the look of things, his prior notes and what he thought he knew coming into our meeting did not look or sound like they emanated from a common origin with the notes to which he was putting some finishing touches.

Attorney Michael Citara Manis' concentration was suddenly broken by a phone call from his secretary reminding him of another one of his appointments which was already past due. Because he had arrived a bit late to see me, he now risked disappointing another client who had waited long to see him in reference to her hearing on the very next day. He apologized and rescheduled another meeting with me for two days later.

Although it had been a very brief meeting, the visit of Mr. Citara Manis felt like a booster shot in the arm to me. In very few words he gave me the indication that he believed my assertion that I had already been convicted by the court of public opinion and that I was a classic victim of vicious gossip and innuendo. His body language as he got up to leave revealed genuine determination to assist me. He backed that body language up with his parting words; "George, go and get you a long rest. It appears you have a long battle ahead of you. I believe your story and I will do everything in my power to fight for you."

"Thank you Attorney Citara Manis. Your belief in my story means the world to me. God bless you." I said. We shook hands and he exited Pod C.

Whether he knew it or not, Attorney Michael Citara Manis left me in a much happier mood than he found me. After he left, I became more aware of my surroundings. I did not run straight back to my cell as usual, but decided to spend the 60 minutes television and phone time with other inmates who were already either scrambling for one of the four telephones available or to decide which channel of the television all other inmates must watch along with the winner of the tussle. It was during this battle of the pod bullies that I formally met two inmates who were the designated pod representatives with whom I had, on other occasions made light hearted conversation.

We introduced ourselves by each stating our full names. As far as I remember, that moment marked the beginning of my true emergence from the protective shell in which I had encased myself from the first day I arrived back in the United States.

"Hi, my name is George Udeozor," I began, "I've been meaning to introduce myself. I hope I can count on you guys to help show me how things work around here."

"It depends on what you need to know," replied the dark smooth and slender one of the two. "Oh, I'm Ed, Ed Brown, nice to meet you George."

"The pleasure is mine," I replied, and we both turned to the third among us.

"Okay, nice to meet you George, my name is Oladepo Olafumiloye." The twisted, knowing smile on his face meant that he knew he had hit a home run with me.

While Ed's face contorted into a quizzical scowl at the strange sound of his friend's names, names he apparently heard for the first time, I jumped onto my feet to lock into a manly hand shake with the same fellow. We both exclaimed, "You be Nija too?" Which meant, "You're a Nigerian too?" Before the introductions, we had acknowledged each other from a distance, little knowing that we shared a common national ancestry. "Ed here only knows me as Ola. I bet that was why he thinks that my name sounds like that of an alien locomotive," Ola jokes.

"This is why we must always be good to strangers," added Ed, "you never know who the devil might send up your alley."

Meeting Ed and Ola changed my entire outlook on our shared classification as awaiting trial inmates. Prior to meeting them, I had been wrongly informed that only convicted inmates were entitled to secure jobs within the facility—a situation which I found very distressing as it was only by securing a job that one got a shot at the luxury of exclusion from the long twenty one hour lockdown every day. It was bad enough that the institution as a whole operated 100% under one roof, with no access to natural sunlight for as long as one remained incarcerated at MDDC, but it was quite another animal altogether to be cooped up in a tiny cell for 21 of every 24 hours!

Through Ed and Ola, I got a friendly introduction to the unit counselor of pod C, Kevin. A beefy ex-cop, Kevin was full of life. His jokes always had me laughing and shedding tears until I could not stand it anymore. He referred to Ed and Ola as his "dogs," making sure to clarify that his fondness was not amorous. He also told more dog jokes than anybody I know.

One month after meeting Ed and Ola, Ed was sentenced to a term of imprisonment and was transferred to a different institution. I was the natural heir to his position and it was so ordered by Kevin. I also quite naturally became one of his "dogs".

The beginning of any new routine is most often awkward. But with time, a pattern develops which becomes almost a habitual part of a prisoner's life, especially in a situation where regimen is enforced as a way of life. When I was first assigned my duties as a pod representative (Pod Rep), my enthusiasm about the associated fringe benefits of the job took a major hit because then I was required to break my established routine by having to wake up one full hour earlier than usual at about 3:00 AM. At that ungodly hour, Ola and I had to prepare the dining tables and ready the garbage containers before our breakfast was wheeled in on a cart stacked high with hot trays. It was part of our many duties to hand these trays to inmates, clean up the pod and wheel the empty trays back to the kitchen at the end of the breakfast "party". I call breakfast a party because the inmates acted in that manner at the table. I usually wondered whether they ever ate meals at dining tables before. They played with their food; complained about every little irregularity they could come up with; blamed the Pod Rep for hair in their food mostly inserted by themselves or just made up lies. Our job included chores I would have preferred not to be aware of let alone be assigned with the doing. Chores like cleaning the bathrooms every evening before the lights were dimmed for sleep. The rewards of those duties were on the other hand, simply too tempting to pass up, and for good reasons too. While other inmates were under locks, we watched any choice of television programs we preferred. We had unfettered access between the two of us, to the four telephones which were normally shared by 64 inmates. We got our choices of the best side dishes of fruits and dessert and we also got the best of any extra trays. Above all these perks, we got to spend as much time outside the confines of our cells for enough hours to feel significantly unburdened from the claustrophobic cruelty of extended, day long lockdowns.

As Pod Reps, Ola and I, both immigrants and also both having our first and surely, last tour through the world underground were unwittingly placed to oversee the affairs of very hardened and sophisticated gangsters and criminals. It was during this period that I experienced some of the most bizarre codes by which prison inmates relate with each other. Although I may never learn the whole lot of these codes and rules, it was at MDDC that

I learned how inmates placed each other in various social categories based on subtle traits and flags which may not be obvious to the ordinary "fish", as we were known, but are trite cultural norms to the career offenders. Therefore, **whereas a tight-fitting pair of trousers held no special meaning to me, most of the other inmates understood that that signaled a come-on to inmates who were homosexual. As a rule, acceptance of a gift carries the implied acceptance of debt which payment is up to the gift giver. I also learned that it could be a fatal mistake to be caught off guard, which made it a rule to wear solid shoes always when in the common area, as bloody fights or riots can happen at any time.** Ola and I simply prayed for divine protection through our tenure as Pod Reps, a prayer I am glad to report, was thankfully answered.

When Attorney Michael Citara Manis returned for our second meeting, I was ready. Following his first visit, my family and I held a few deliberations during which we decided that it had fallen to Mr. Citara Manis to represent me. Unknown to him during that first visit, we were still in negotiation with a highly reputable attorney who had garnered national and international exposure in a landmark police brutality case which involved Los Angeles Police Department. My brother had offered to pay a deposit of $50,000.00 demanded by the highly rated attorney. I had however, requested that he give me a summary of his defense strategy for my trial after he received full briefing and some of my charging documents. When he candidly informed me that he would pursue a plea agreement as a preferred option for resolution rather than go to trial, I became distraught and asked him why. He confided that my wife's trial and conviction was my albatross. He reasoned that although it was remotely possible that I could run into luck if my case were transferred to a jurisdiction different from the one that convicted my wife, the chances were stacked high against that possibility because of the high publicity the case had already received. But even more troubling was the fact that after having already convicted and sentenced my wife, both the government and the court would spare no resources to bring a similar result in my case. As a consequence he offered his unwavering conviction that based on the quantum of information available to him, he was all but over 100% certain that he could negotiate a plea agreement with the government that would have me sentenced to a term that would correspond with the time which I had already served in detention both in Nigeria and the two Maryland detention centers.

On the strength of three reasons which we considered sound, we elected to drop all plans of engaging the paid attorney and opted instead to work with Mr. Citara Manis, the government appointed attorney. First, after my three-year-long extradition proceedings in Nigeria, I was financially strapped and did not wish to place undue financial burden on my family which had suffered greatly on my behalf. Second, the paid attorney had chosen to adopt a defense strategy which, I was convinced would likely yield the same outcome regardless of who I selected as my defense counsel. Finally, my first meeting with Attorney Citara Manis left me with a very positive impression of him. He was certainly not a newcomer in the arena of complex political/cultural issues which fall in the grey areas of criminal behavior. But to me, the strongest point in favor of choosing him was that he believed me. He was the first outsider from my family to bother to look deeply into the circumstances of my legal woes, after which I intuitively knew that he believed me wholeheartedly.

After a detailed meeting which lasted the whole of 3 hours, we arrived at a tentative agreement to try and enter a plea agreement with the government, depending on the terms which they offered. He vowed to fight aggressively on my behalf should the terms turn out to be unfavorable to me.

Fifty Nine

During our meeting, I made it clear to Attorney Citara Manis that I did not intend to approach either my trial or plea deal as a supplicant, but as one whose cultural beliefs ran contrary to the laws of my prosecutor. The charges against me were largely based upon actions which would be considered honorable in the context of the environment and circumstances of my cultural origins. I took actions fully knowing that I risked exposure to serious legal consequences should Chinelo's illegal status be discovered. I have always believed that sometimes, in the contest between man's conscience and society's laws, conscience compels man in a direction which violates society's laws, but nevertheless yields victory for both the guilty conscience and society.

My actions were motivated and driven by the conviction that although I would be breaking the laws of the United States in aiding Chinelo to enter and reside in the country illegally, humanity at large stood to benefit rather than lose as a result of my action—a win against poverty and misery anywhere on the planet earth is a win for humanity. I consequently would not be seeking the courts forgiveness but would rather ask that the court administer only fitting punishment for my offense. I would accept responsibility for my actions and pay America's asking price for them.

That was indeed the puzzling aspect of my dilemma. What would constitute a just punishment for my actions? Although I refrained from concerning myself with Chinelo's act in betraying me, I rejected, denied and rebuked as satanic, her fiendish lies whose sole purpose was to deceive an unsuspecting and protective judicial system into approving her request for legal status the dreamy path to United States citizenship, the green card. What she did with both her statements to the police and her testimony in court was to tell something of the truth in everything, but wrap each little fragment of veracity in layer upon layer of falsity. Had I not known the truth and been unconnected with the case, even I might buy her story as gospel truth.

But I knew the truth. And I was involved. And, the fact that the jury had already accepted some of her lies as the basis for convicting my wife and sentencing her to a stiff term of imprisonment was unnerving as I pondered out loud what it would take to expose this young lady's deceit and callousness—her Judas perfidy.

After I concluded pouring out my worries, Attorney Citara Manis sat back in his chair and stroked his bearded chin, his brow furrowed as he tried to come up with a well-reasoned response to my concerns.

"First thing we've got to do is withdraw your request for a speedy trial. I have just received your files from your former attorney and have yet to fully study the documents in it. Secondly, I have not received the discovery materials which I've requested from the prosecutor. Those materials will play a crucial role in my advice to you on strategy. Until I know what the prosecutor has in his file against you, I cannot wisely comment on any defense strategy." Attorney Citara Manis was very thoughtful as he spoke.

"I understand," I replied. "I'm only sharing my grief and disbelief at how rapidly the public bought this young woman's story. Especially considering how ridiculous some of her allegations are. Why is this so? I inquired.

"Don't ask me," he said, "I am the wrong person to bring such questions to. In my over twenty years as a public defender, I have seen the most innocent looking individuals come out guilty and some others who were already certified guilty judging by their appearance surprisingly turn out innocent. In your case, I can tell you that it was not your appearance or your charm that convinced me of your innocence. It is your acceptance of responsibility for your actions and your feelings for your children. Your love and commitment to them is obvious. But I can assure you, after my endlessly long experience in the judicial system that I am less of a good reader of people's minds now than I was when I first started."

I found the statement incredulous. "Why then have the government, the media, and the American people condemned me even though nobody has given me a chance to utter a word in defense of myself?" I demanded.

"Listen George, if we spend the next few months fishing for answers to your questions, we will get nothing done in your defense and we still will not have any answers to your questions. Please save these questions. The answers will come from sources you least expect," he admonished.

"I am gigantically sorry," I apologized. "I have often foolishly assumed that to all people 2 plus 2 always adds up to 4. Hell, Democrats and Republicans cannot even agree on how tall the president is!" I said.

"There you are." He had the last word on that subject.

Over the next few days, I began putting together, piece by piece, the events, detailing names, places, circumstances that had anything to do with Chinelo, the maid. My attorney felt that my presentation to him, while convincing to him about the veracity of my story, was too sketchy. He felt I should focus on the detailed account of our family life before and after Chinelo came to reside with us, giving account of the issues, if any that could prove that we did not prevent her from leaving our home or "escaping" if she had chosen to do so. His premise was to attack the government's allegation that Chinelo was forcibly kept in our residence and involuntarily worked as a housekeeper and maid for the coconspirators - my wife and I. As I applied my mental faculties to that task, memories of those days began flooding into my head.

From the early days of my marriage to Stella, family was everything to me. We had not everything, but we had love. Besides the love I had for my wife and my family as it grew, I had also, love for nature. Everything in nature seemed created with undoubtable and mesmerizing logic. The why and the because were always balanced. The dawns were made to rejoice you upon waking, the days to ripen the harvests, the rains to water them, the evenings to prepare for sleep, the nights dark for sleep, the father to feed strawberries to the mother, the mother to return the favor and the children to flutter from heaven's manger, to stretch the love forever. With the addition of Chinelo, the love in the family maintained its growth but suddenly took a pause and then abruptly screeched to a stop. My in-laws made their entrance. Then the troubles began.

The details of what followed, I had already lived and relived over and over for the last nine years. Now, I had a duty to pen them down, and do so in a manner that could convince a public which had judged and convicted me in their minds. It was a daunting task but I knew that any chance I could dream up for a fair trial depended on this assignment. Going by the contents of the transcripts from my wife's trial which Attorney Citara Manis availed me with, I had already begun to dread the prospect of sitting before the trial judge in those hearings. Judge P.J. Messitte demonstrated his clear tilt in favor of Chinelo in the way he ruled during the testimony phase of the trial of my madam, Stella. His admission of a tape recorded conversation between me and the alleged victim in which statements were made between us into evidence was a clear judicial error. The tape which was illegally obtained under the backing of a bogus legal doctrine known as the color of law was, if nothing else, underhanded and below the esteem of the court's exalted ranking. That tape which the prosecutor was now dangling before me, as if it contained damning evidence of my guilt was in truth a disingenuous effort by investigators who had no reliable evidence to present to their employer, to extract a conviction from a trusting public should I elect to go to trial. I knew, Chinelo the maid knew, and the investigators also knew that if my earlier conversations with Chinelo, which I believed were also recorded, were to be presented, then the prosecution would have been shamed, and Chinelo would have become the subject for immediate removal or deportation. It was her threats during those earlier phone conversations, threats of what she would do to Stella and my children, threats that would have exposed her for her plot to secure a green card and remain in the United States that prompted me to plead with her for a return phone call. As the transcripts of my later phone conversations clearly reveal, my overriding concerns were for the welfare of my children and Chinelo herself. Even though I made statements, true though, they entirely were, and damaging, definitely, they were to my madam's defense, they were not intended for any other listener other than me and Chinelo the maid. The government violated my right to privacy. They taped my phone conversation illegally and lied about it!

Sixty

The first pretrial hearing before Judge Peter J. Messite lasted less than thirty minutes once he mounted his judicial throne. Just like the proceedings at the preliminary hearing, the entire process was concluded just as quickly as it was started. I only managed a snappy gesture of appreciation in the direction of my sister and her friend who were the only members of the small audience in the courtroom with favorable disposition toward me. A stern faced marshal quickly admonished me, reminding me that I had been pre-warned of such infractions. I silently wondered what he might do if I ignored him and flouted his rules even more. Perhaps, he might wring my neck? I was already in prison for crying out loud!

The other members of the audience were simply a few press people and a handful of strange looking women who appeared like mystics or some form of fortune tellers. I never was able to piece together who they might have been or what their interest in my case was.

For a proceeding which lasted a mere thirty minutes, with nary an input from me, the accused, the system it appeared, couldn't care one bit if I was awake, conscious or delirious, as long as my form was seated in the courtroom. Early that morning, I was awakened at 2:30 AM after about 2 hours of sleep. Along with other inmates who were also bound for court or transfer to other institutions, I was cooped in one cell after another for apparently no reason at all. After waiting down the clock to 8:30 AM, the Marshals arrived. This time, I was the only inmate bound for the District Court at Greenbelt. I was again cooped in the chilly holding cell underneath the court building. It was not until 3:30 PM, while I was feeling comatose with hunger, that the Marshals came hurriedly to fetch me. When I complained about hunger, they said I was passed out, asleep, when they brought me a sandwich and soda. "You cannot eat now, the judge is already seated!" They exclaimed. They ignored my whimpering about the harshness of their handcuffs and leg irons and slapped them back on anyway. Without feeling, they led me to the elevator and on to Judge Missette's courtroom.

He was indeed waiting. So also, were my attorney, the group of prosecutors, and the courtroom audience. I sank into my seat and listened as words began flying in all directions across the courtroom and over my head all of which were at that time, nothing but a lot of legal mumbo jumbo to me—rituals which only summed up to what they intended to do with me. I remember thinking, even in my state of delirium, "Judge Missette, what in heaven's name is this entire charade about? Why don't you cut to the chase and pronounce your sentence? Lynch me, if that is what you intend! All this drama is nothing but acting—mere rituals before the hammer is brought down."

My thoughts during those proceedings were to be replayed over and over again inside my head and were soon to form the basis upon which I made my final decision on my trial strategy. At the conclusion of the hearing, nothing was said which I did not already know as I came into the court. One is left to wonder why all the show is put on anyway. My request for bail was denied. My application for expansion of time prior to trial was granted, although it seemed the prosecutor needed the time expansion more than I did. If any other issue of high value was addressed, then it must have flown over my head, for I was mostly not functioning mentally.

After the proceedings ended, I began dreaming about the sandwich and soda. I was starved. As we walked, all sounds—shoe steps, closing doors, echoes from voices in holding cells, all made ringing sounds in my head. You would think the Marshals would understand and show some compassion, but no. They had set the probation officer up in a room that felt as though it was refrigerated. The room was divided in two by plexiglas, with telephone handsets sitting on the table benches next to the plexiglas partition. Sitting next to the probation officer was my attorney Michael Citara Manis. He explained to me that the U.S. probation officer Ms. Manisha S. Gardner was going to ask me some questions. That her questions were very important as she would prepare a report, known as a Pre-sentence Investigation Report (PSR), based on her interviews with me. He said that her questions were to be a sort of prelude to her main appointment with me during which she will complete her investigative work. For that appointment, she would be paying me a visit at MDDC. Having made his input Mr. Citara Manis turned to Ms. Gardner to begin her grilling of the defendant.

Still near the crest of hysteria with hunger, I began responding to her questions which were in the order of, State your full name. State the names of your siblings, living and deceased? Parents names? Schools attended? They were mostly bio-data questions and I supplied the answers to her questions as best as I could in my condition. Despite my attorney's speech about the role of Ms. Manisha Gardner, I saw no reason to take her questions or her role very serious. The hunger pain in my stomach demanded attention and absent real food, I could at least dream about the sandwich waiting to resolve that serious problem. Several years later, I am still in shock that it was that probation officer's report and not a jury which sealed my fate in the matter of United States Versus George Udeozor.

I got my sandwich, and soda, and the much needed relief from the fire in my stomach, but Ms. Gardner's promised visit at the jail never happened and her Pre-sentence Investigation Report which she based on mostly information that did not originate from me, started a Tsunami in my life that promises to never end.

Back at MDDC, I quickly devoured my dinner which was saved for me by the correctional officer on duty. When I shared my experiences of that day with my buddy Ola, he acknowledged them as the norm with pretrial hearings. He said I was lucky to be the only inmate from MDDC scheduled for that court on that morning. If we had been up to ten inmates, he said, my story would have been grimmer. Lighten up George, he teased. I agreed with him and repeated a sage aphorism which I had learned from one of my mentors in business, "I was complaining about my ill-fitting shoes until I met a guy who had no legs." Ola agreed; "That's the spirit George," he said.

Ola and I gradually grew very close and very protective of each other. We both began to share our life stories. Before long our relationship with the loves of our lives, our madams, became the point of convergence for our nightly tete-a-tete. We began telling each other the most intimate affairs of our hearts. We shared information about how very much alike my family troubles were with those of other Nigerian families in the United States. Indeed we were much like many families from other far away countries like India, Pakistan, Indonesia, Philippines and a host of Middle Eastern families. Like them, our conservative cultural values often pith us into situations where we are forced to take positions which are legally unacceptable to our adopted nation.

During those moments at MDDC, Ola and I were scarcely separated. We lived, thought and dreamed together. We read, ate, watched television together and shared a cell. It was then I discovered that he was writing a book. He similarly found out that I was assembling a detailed diary of my journey through our new lives in the world underground. We began to encourage each other. I found that Ola's passion was in motivational work and I encouraged him and supported him with all the information available to me in that field. He similarly encouraged and provided me with information as best he could. Incarceration provided us both the kind of perspective on life which we would otherwise most certainly not have pursued on our own. Writing a book never seemed part of my life's karma. Ola himself confided that he also never entertained or planned any such endeavor. But here we both were, digging into our souls, exposing all the secretes we once harbored and protected, sharing them so that others may not get trapped like we were in a world to which we both clearly knew we did not belong.

According to Ola, he arrived in the United States with dreams of partaking in the American dream by reaping bountifully from the work of his hands. His years of stagnation in his chosen trade—building construction and sales, finally ended about 2002 following the upsurge in the real estate market. Through private finance companies he qualified a good number of his clients for upward movement into choice properties. When the real estate crisis began, he became one of the industry's earliest casualties of the most massive systemic failures of our generation. "While those who crafted the schemes that put homebuyers into homes which they could not afford were being bailed out by tax payers, thanks to Uncle Sam, little dreamers like me are being shown into the slammer," Ola complained bitterly. Although I had purchased homes spanning the period of my youth in Los Angeles and my middle age years in Maryland, I never really understood the grand money bonanza schemes run by the operators of the real estate market, until now.

While Ola was dealing with the legal ramifications of his real estate deals, I was preparing for my next meeting with Attorney Michael Citara Manis. He had already met with the prosecutor in my case and talks had begun between them on a possible plea deal. In a telephone conversation which I placed to him to confirm when he planned to visit and update me on progress so far made, he informed me that he had succeeded in securing the services of an investigator whose job it would be to verify the claims and allegations against me. I immediately expressed my pleasant surprise at that development.

"Really?" I asked, worried and confused. "I hope this will not cost me too much money. I've already explained my unhealthy financial situation to you," I complained.

"Not to worry George. She is our investigator. By the way, it's a woman, and she is good at her job. If anybody can uncover any useful evidence, she is the one to do it and you do not have to pay her for it. She is already well paid. Matter of fact, she will come along with me on my next visit to see you," he assured.

"Thank you so so much. God will reward you richly for your help," I thanked him, truly grateful for his calm reassuring tone on the phone.

~

It remains a source of conflicting emotions to me, puzzling and perplexing to boot—what America represents to the world. The undisputed home of the brave—the leader of all who fight against oppression and the defender of the rights of all. Yet at the same time, home of the cowardly and father of the greatest bullies, celebrated and obscure. America is the author of the greatest Constitution known to man and some would argue has become the greatest violator of the articles of her own Constitution and those of other nations. The United States of America, the world's last remaining true believer in the divinity of God and yet the host of the world's most loyal Satanists and religious bigots.

The government of the United States would spare no resources to convict me, yet it was the government of the United States who was paying for my defense. I was wondering if this view of the United States was just a figment of my imagination or if anybody else noticed a conflict in this arrangement. Should I revile America for trying to convict and punish me unfairly, or should I thank her for standing by me to defend my honor?

Well, for starters, my country of birth had not even shown concern about her duty to defend her very own Constitution in the first place, let along defend the honor of her expendable citizen. Did the Nigerian government even realize that the Nigerian culture was on trial? Would it have made a difference if they had been aware? I found it doubtful. After all, since being handed over to the United States authorities, not one soul from the Nigerian embassy in Washington DC, barely thirty minutes' drive from the venue of my trial had followed up even with a simple phone call to ensure that my trial followed the letters of the treaty based upon which they surrendered me. What is the value of Nigerian citizenship? Are there cultural values unique to the people known as Nigerians and are there benefits accruing from those values that are worth defending? Are we Nigerians in existence merely to fill in a void in humanity or are we here to be counted? If the government of Nigeria cannot speak up for Nigerians in the international arena, who then must that duty fall on, considering that Nigerians are among the world's most traveled folk?

Allow me please to clarify my bellyaching about Nigeria. I found myself in love with my tormentor. You may ask why the foolishness? Why disagree with myself? Why love my tormentor? I reply, why not? Have I not bankrupted myself trying to prove a point to the world on behalf of Nigeria? The point that we Nigerians, possibly even all of we Africans, have not been successful in our efforts to adopt wholesale, the sociocultural values of the West. And, did not Nigeria's Attorney general after giving my supplication the deaf treatment finally command that my "person" be handed over to him who I portrayed as my tormentor? Now, in the hands of my tormentor and at his mercy, has he not fed me, fixed my broken spirit and despite my grievances, offer me a chance to defend my honor?

Is there still any wonder why I decry the shameless antics of Nigeria's government men? Men who hold propped-up, the discredited relics of colonial systems of generations gone by—systems that only served the interest of the master. Must an endless list of Nigerians continue to roam the globe like sheep without a shepherd or will their country finally acquiesce to her statutory duty as shepherd to the multitude of Nigerian citizens the world over? I challenge Nigerian youth to demand that Nigeria's government men play their proper roles or else!

Two days before my scheduled meeting with Attorney Citara Manis and the investigator, I was called to report at the visiting area for family visit. As usual, it took me under five minutes to freshen up and travel the long corridors to the long plexiglas partitioned visitation hall. The booths numbered A to Z had dwarf walls between them, each with two-way intercoms for the no-contact communication between inmates and their visitors.

As I strode down to booth "Q" for my visitation with my sister Chi—my usual lone guest since I returned, I noticed three young women who, judging by their innocuous appearances, I thought at a glance, nubile goddesses. On my side of the glass partition, the inmates were going gaga like starved zoo animals at the sight of prey. My excited sister was at that instant waving at me to pick up the telephone handset and gesturing toward the three girls and their male companion. Her first words into the mouthpiece were, "it wasn't me who brought them." She paused and then exclaimed, "You don't recognize them? They're your children!"

Sixty One

For a brief while I was frozen in disbelief. Impossible! It was like coming face to face with strangers who yet remind you of yourself in another life! "No! No! No!" I lamented, "They cannot be my babies. No way!"

"What are you talking about?" my sister challenged me. "That's Adam over there, and Kimberly, and Valerie, and Stella Georgina!"

"God, give me strength," I prayed aloud. "May I please speak with the first one, Kim."

Kimberly came forward and took the handset from her aunt, Chinwe.

"Hello daddy" she began.

"Hi Pumpkin, will you please say a prayer with me?" I pleaded, and without pausing, "I believe in God, the Father Almighty. Creator of heaven and earth . . ."

I could see that I was embarrassing her but I needed to know that this was not a dream that I was having. It was not a dream! One after the other, I spoke to these young souls— extensions of my body and my own soul! With the greatest reluctance I let the youngest and the last of them off the phone. I could feel the weight of my heart as it measured this moment in time. None of them across the partition knew the violent emotions boiling in my chest at the scene before me. My infant puppies had grown into cubs! For nine years I had waited. But this was not the moment I was waiting for; not for bland words across telephone cables, not for longing gawks through reinforced Plexiglas, and certainly not for grown cubs too heavy to lift!

What happened to my puppies? I lamented sorrowfully in the secret cover of my thoughts. For nine years I compensated for our separation by remembering details of our lost lives together as a family—the exact feel of the skin of each one of my six puppies; three pumpkins and three rangers. I had longed to feel the temperature of their hands at any time of day, the warmth and softness of their lips on my cheeks during their off-to-school goodbyes and their eagerness to give the right answer first at the weekly family meetings between Udeozor children and their father. We shared the fellowship of the bonded children to their father. For nine years in Nigeria I felt their absence acutely, like a deep hunger for protein. I despaired for the sound of their voices, and their footsteps whether in harmony or disharmony. I missed them with the passion of David for his son Absalom.

For a while, I studied their faces and forms in disbelief. I had in one instant become forced to confront my mind's folly. As if drugged with delusion, I had taken a nine year period and had frozen that span of time into a blink of an eye. Now, with my eyes open, I expected to find my little angels the same way I left them before my eyes blinked nine years earlier—still my little puppies, still my girl puppies that I called my pumpkins and the boy puppies I called my rangers. I must have been insane, for only the insanely in love would do as I did in 1999. Only the insane would leave everything he worked for—a way of life, and all the blood, sweat and tears spilled in the process to walk away, into a life of stagnation and uncertainty.

What was I to do now? How could I convince my puppies after the long blink which turned them into cubs that it was not I who transgressed? They are not cubs in the wild. On the contrary, if cubs were ever tame, they are those cubs. They all believed I abandoned them! I became dumbstruck and decided to let time do what it does best—bring a higher wisdom to work things out.

After spending the next two days in the doldrums over what language and manner with which to explain the apparently inexplicable, I applied shaving cream to my neck, chin and cheeks in an effort to remove the jagged stubbles which had germinated all over my face, disfiguring it. I had to clean myself up and look less like a prisoner before the arrival of my attorney and the investigator who were scheduled to visit me at 2:30 PM that afternoon. I had learned that rough appearances equate to guilty in the minds of even the most liberal observer. Fair or not, human beings are given to judgment by stereotype. That is just the way it is.

When they arrived, I was ready. I was also nervous. It was going to be a particularly revealing pretrial conference. It was likely the day on which I would make the crucial decision whether to enter a plea agreement with the government or proceed to a legal duel with forces against whom my best effort could not manage even a scratch.

Attorney Michael Citara Manis and his companion, the female investigator, whose name I do not recall, arrived at 2:30 PM on schedule for our meeting. Thankfully, attorney visits, unlike family visits were full contact visits. Nothing compares to the feeling of apathy experienced during family visits conducted on opposite sides of a partition.

"Good afternoon," I offered as I sat in the chair opposite Attorney Citara Manis and the investigator.

"Good afternoon George," he replied. "Please meet the senior investigator for the U.S. Public Defender's Office. I spoke to you earlier about her."

"Yes, I remember, good afternoon ma'am." I shook her outstretched hand.

"George, she is one of the only two investigators who work on our cases. She is one very busy lady. Her work load is very demanding but she still manages to do a thorough job of every one she accepts. Because she has to leave soon for another appointment, we will have to conduct her interview first so that you and I will then sit back and get to work. We have a lot to talk about." Citara Manis said.

"Sure, I've got nothing but time on my hands. I'm grateful to spend it all with you both," I replied, drawing a lot of good natured laughter from all three of us.

"Alright George, we sure don't have that much time ourselves. We have to get on with it." Attorney Citara Manis gestured toward the investigator who then began speaking.

She began her interview by first explaining to me that although she had received some scathing briefing on my case, she needed to hear the details in my own words, of my relationship with my accuser, the maid and also my children. She said that these were the parties who could influence the outcome of my trial, for good or bad, during either the trial or negotiations of a plea agreement.

"They were here to see me two days ago!" I announced in a cheerful tone.

"Who?" They asked in unison.

"Who was here to see you?" my attorney continued, excited and expectant.

"The children," I responded excitedly, "The first three of them; Kimberly, Adam, Valeria and the last of the girls, Stella Georgina."

"That's good, very good, George. We're going to need their cooperation if we have to take this case to trial. So, how did they react to seeing you after such a long time?"

I proceeded to tell both of my visitors about my surprise family visit of two days earlier. The trauma I suffered at the sight of my children. How I expected to find them still like the puppies I separated from only to now find them as grown cubs, even if the most beautiful cubs of the human species. There was still a lot to tell about a father's heartbreak dating back to the best days of our lives together, mother, father and children, to the beginning of discord and the sad disintegration of the family. Midway through my tale, I could not hold my tears back. As I tried to choke back the free flow, I noticed the investigator doing likewise, but she was better at controlling her own emotions than I was. I was forced to pause for a while. It was one of the rare moments in my life when I was certain that I had figured out how God works. I bet my guests were unaware of it, but I chuckled. A stolen moment of gratitude to the angel spirit in this woman that made her connect with me in such a spiritual way, a tear drop that showed me that all would be alright, that my heart was in the right place.

By the time she left me and my attorney, she had heard an earful more from me. She promised to give my matter her best effort and wished me well. She also unwittingly, through her good nature, left me much stronger and much more determined to survive my ordeal and exit it in better form than I entered into it.

Attorney Citara Manis came into this meeting with far more materials than I expected. He began our meeting by congratulating me once again for the reunion visit I received from my children, stressing how valuable their testimony might eventually turn out to be. From his tone I believed that he had come to the conclusion that we were proceeding to trial. But his next presentation completely contradicted that notion. He handed me two sets of documents which he explained to me were proposals for an alternate solution to a long drawn-out legal battle between me and the government. The first document, he explained, was a proposal from the prosecutor which was an offer that if I pleaded guilty to one count of the three count indictment against me, the government would be willing to dismiss the remaining two counts and sentence me only on the basis of the one count. The second document, he continued, was the draft copy of what he termed the Pre-Sentence Investigation Report (PSR). This report, he explained, owed its significance to the reliance placed on it by judges in determining the appropriate sentence to impose upon conviction. After handing me these documents, Attorney Citara Manis, apparently sensing my fits of nervousness, spoke in a calm reassuring tone when he informed me that these documents were not in their final form. He stressed that there were unfavorable and unsavory clauses or segments to which he had already raised objections, which he was certain to get corrected before any final agreements or reports could be acceptable. He suggested I read the documents and register my remarks and objections which he would incorporate into his own observations to draft a counter offer to the government.

Shortly after I started reading the first document, I felt the breath of God slowly grow cold on my skin. Goose bumps quickly spread all over me like a cloud over a naked sky. Emotions unlike any I had ever felt began to swell up inside me. My first thoughts were of self-blame. Why did I have so much faith in the justice system? Why had I ignored the complaints of so many who recorded their grievances against a justice system which relentlessly pursues victory in court even at the expense of the truth? What happened to the doctrine of presumption of innocence?

In spite of indications that the government was intent on making me pay a heavy price for the allegations against me, I had remained certain that when the time arrived, I would finally be given the opportunity to try to prove my innocence. The two sets of documents presented to me by my attorney not only presumed me guilty of the offenses with which I was charged, they declared me guilty of despicable acts of which I never imagined or contemplated in all of my years as a man. What was the most disturbing of the government's proposal was that it was those acts which were not part of the charges against me that they appeared most interested in.

When summed up in brief, unambiguous language, the charges against me were as follows:

(A) Knowingly encouraging and inducing a juvenile alien to illegally enter and reside in the United States in violation of law.
(B) Knowingly attempting to and harboring an illegal alien in my residence in violation of law.
(C) Knowingly and willfully holding a juvenile alien to involuntary servitude for financial gain for a term in violation of law.

Of these charges, there was no doubt in my mind that I had transgressed some aspects of the first two. Even while in the process of convincing myself that although my actions violated laws which were at the time unknown to me, I felt that saving Chinelo from the bleak prospects she faced was worth risking some retribution. Surely, I would not have taken the costly actions I did if I had not thought of them as honorable. In my years living, studying, working and socializing with the everyday, average American citizen, I cannot claim knowledge of a more giving and more forgiving people on planet earth. Yet again, I now find that I cannot recall in my travels ever meeting a more vindictive and intolerant people anywhere.

The third charge against me bears out my opinion. By no stretch possible was it even plausible that Chinelo was brought to the United States for any kind of financial gain, nor was it even thinkable that she resided with my family in involuntary servitude. Adding to these whacked out charges, the suggestion that this young woman was both physically and sexually abused, and even raped by me, is beyond preposterous!

Yet, both documents bore these bleeding heart allegations against me for which the United States government was now seeking, without the due process of law and in accordance with the United States Constitution, to punish me to the hilt.

My reaction was instantaneous and emotional. From the somber look on his face, I could tell that Attorney Citara Manis understood and sympathized with my discomfiture. "Disgusting," I practically spat on the floor, which would have terrified my attorney more than the acts which drew that feeling of repulsion.

He had been watching me squirm and writ in pain as I read those documents. Finally he spoke out and showed his understanding; "George," he said, "Don't expect life to work out like a math equation with everything coming out equal. I know that injustice happens. When you are good, bad things can still happen to you. Sometimes, even bad people get lucky and good things happen to them. But I assure you, I will do all within my power to help you with your problems. There is no doubt that the picture is ugly but we can make it better so that at the end you can go on with your life and repair your family. I believe that's what you want at the end of all this mess. Am I correct?"

My response did not come right away. I was still anguished over the unprintable allegations for which the government was seeking to obtain a guilty plea from me. "Yes," I responded in a subdued tone, "but you cannot make this matter go away, can you?

"No. Unfortunately, I cannot do that. But I can sure give them a good fight. Who Knows? Maybe you will end up not serving any additional time in detention. Do you think you can comment on the government's proposal now? Or do you need time to think it over, or perhaps discuss it with your family first?" He inquired in response.

"There is nothing to think about," I said disconcerted, "there is no way I would even consider a plea agreement with these charges standing. They're outrageous lies! Barefaced fabrications motivated only to deceive the authorities into allowing the alleged victim remain in the United States.

We'll just have to proceed to trial because I cannot accept this agreement as is." I emphatically protested.

"I understand George," my attorney said with genuine emotion. But, as I've already told you, this is not the final form of it. I will return to the prosecutor with a counter offer and I'm sure we can get some of the points removed and the language of the allegations tempered and made less hideous."

"But these are not the issues I'm concerned about! The language does not matter to me, hideous or tempered. They're all lies! I will have no honor if I admit these falsehoods as true! Does the government not care about the truth? What is the government's ultimate goal here? Is it no longer to see that justice is done?" I demanded in frustration.

"Calm down George. There is no need to work yourself into frenzy with worry. Remember that you need your health if you plan to reunite with your family, your children I mean. I've already told you. Life is not a math equation. It does not always balance out. I'll tell you what. You can go ahead and keep the documents. Call me in three days so that we can set up a new meeting. By then I would have contacted the prosecutor. I should have additional news for you then. Take it easy George." He said.

"I know you're trying to help. Please be patient with me," I said with a shaky voice, holding his steady reassuring eyes. "What about the probation officer's report? You said she would visit me but she never came. Now, she has prepared this damaging report. What are we going to do about that?" I queried, wishing he would stay a while longer.

"She sent that report over to our office. I have not seen her since she sent it. When I do, I will raise your concerns with her. I believe she will still visit you. She can always correct any errors. As you can see, she has not received feedback on her various investigative inquiries. She will correct all errors as she receives feedback. There should be no problem there. I must be leaving George. I've got other appointments."

"Sure, please accept my thanks. I am truly grateful for your efforts. God bless you."

"And you too. Good luck George."

"Goodbye."

Sixty Two

A thousand thoughts converged in my head, all of them disquieting. I sighed and turned away from facing the wall and felt under the pillow for my headphone radio. I put the headphone over my head and returned the dial to WTOP in the AM dial. The twenty-four hour news radio station came on. The time was about 1:00 AM and I was unable to fall asleep.

Attorney Citara Manis had not categorically said that he preferred the plea agreement as the best approach for addressing the case against me, but there were subtleties and nuances in his statements that clearly indicated that as his preference. It was clear that he wanted me to accept the plea agreement, and avoid proceeding to trial. I was also not sure that I had the stamina for that battle either. But my mind was made up. I would not be led like a lamb to slaughter. Even though I had been stripped of my identity, my dignity and my freedom, the truth was still on my side. I therefore resolved that much as it was preferable to resolve the matter without having to engage the United States of America, the country that made me what I was, in the costly battle which I had all but lost, I would only plead guilty to one or both of the two offenses of which I was partially guilty. I did not subject Chinelo to involuntary servitude, did not in any way gain financially from my relationship with her and her family, and I did not violate my position of trust or authority over her. If anything, despite my inability to provide her all I had promised her family due to circumstances beyond my control, her presence in the United States had transformed permanently, her prospects for a successful future for good. I would take my chances at trial with the truth, believing and trusting in God for redemption rather than plead guilty to an offense which I did not commit. Once I took that decision, calmness settled over my prostrate form and sleep relieved me of the feeling of hyper anxiety that had kept me awake all night.

My awakening to the true nature and practical application of the law to the lives of common citizens such as I came home late and in little drips to me over the span of my life. As it came, it was difficult to immediately accept, for I had planned my entire life on the assumption that in the United States of America, the law applied to all persons equally, regardless of their social status or official position. But now, I had begun to see that there exists a wide difference between what I had chosen to believe and what I was confronted with.

Nobody brought home the realities confronting me more than my sister who had been in court for most of the hearings that were held during my wife's three month long trial. The outcome of that trial had proved to my sister that despite the pontifications of the court about the presumption of innocence, in a situation where the minds of the jurors or the judge had been made up, no amount of evidence or testimony is enough to assuage their thirst for conviction. In her case, according to my sister and many other observers, although my wife did nothing to help but a lot to hurt herself, the minds of both the judge and jurors appeared to have been long made up while they waited for the testimony and the evidence to be presented. According to most who observed the hearings, the verdict of innocent would have surprised many who sat through the entire proceedings.

Neither my sister nor any other person to whom I spoke claimed to know firsthand, the veracity of my wife's testimony in court as my wife and her attorney declined my sister's entreaties to join hands with me by including my testimony during her trial or arranging for the joint trial of both of us. Had the suggestion been accepted, perhaps certain evidence and testimony which I am now able to reveal only through this medium would have been compelling enough to the jury or the judge to save the family the calamity of total collapse.

Now, I had a decision to make. Should I accept a plea agreement with the government even if they insisted that I plead to an offense for which I was innocent—if the government decided to offer me a deal which precluded serving further time in detention? Should I stick to my vow to accept only a deal that excluded all the bogus and ill motivated charges against me? What do I do should the government insist on their offer alone? Was I mentally and financially ready for the prolonged legal battle that the case promised if we failed to negotiate an agreement acceptable to both me and the government?

Unless you are the accused, facing the awesome machinery of the United States Justice Department, it would seem a no brainer figuring out which choice the best is. Why should any sane person choose to plead guilty to an offense he did not commit? You plead "not guilty," Right?

Well… maybe so. But, how many times has any adult managed to convince a biased jury or a judge of his innocence when wrongfully accused by a juvenile who they already considered a "vulnerable victim?" In my case, I had no video, audio or pictorial proof of my innocence as far as the charge of involuntary servitude. All I had was the truth—my word. But the prosecutor had managed to convince the court in my wife's trial that she was guilty as charged. Since we were jointly accused as co-conspirators of the same offense, what were my chances of convincing the court that I was innocent while my wife who was already convicted and imprisoned was the lone guilty party? I was not in a state of delusion despite my longsuffering journey so far. I had to admit that it would be easier for a camel to pass through the eye of a needle than to find twelve jurors in Montgomery County Maryland that would find me innocent of the offenses for which my alleged co-conspirator, who also happened to be my wife, had been convicted and imprisoned.

With these stark realities weighing heavily on my mind, and considering that no member of my family was favorably disposed to a drawn out legal battle with the government, I made up my mind to drive for the quickest and most favorable plea agreement as a means of finally finding a terminal date for this nightmare from hell.

Three days after his last visit to see me, I called Attorney Citara Manis. When I informed him that after a deep introspective review of my options and also following consultations with members of my family, I had decided that my best interest would be served if a fair plea agreement could be negotiated, he sounded happy and relieved at the same time. He reiterated his pledge to do all that was within his ability to end my suffering as quickly as possible. On that note he set up another meeting between us for the following week. As usual, after speaking with Attorney Citara Manis, my spirits became significantly lifted from the depths of despair thrust on it by the seemingly inescapable snare of a programmed judicial system.

When he arrived one week later for our meeting, merely examining the documents he brought along with him and the manner of his speech, I knew that the march, the final march toward freedom or further time in prison had begun. He methodically laid out the documents on the table as I kept stealing glances at those easily visible; trying to see what good or evil news they bore. It was, after all, my life that was being written away—at least what remained of it. The State's Attorney, Probation Officer, Investigators, Agents—people I had never had contact with and who did not know me, were dealing away the years of my life and my reputation while building theirs. Sadly, their work was based on allegations made by an accuser whose intentions, as against mine, were selfish, ill-motivated and ill-conceived.

Finally, it came down to this; the government did not wish to go to trial with me but would equally not give in to my offer to plead guilty on either of the two counts of the indictment. Rather than accept my offer, the government was willing to proceed to trial and let the chips fall where they may. Now, if my assessment of the various options available to me were accurate, then we all already knew where the chips would fall. The question was: "what price was I willing to pay for my honor?" As if to offer me a face saving way out, my attorney followed up with a reassuring narrative; "Look George," he said, "in a plea agreement, pleading guilty does not automatically imply that you accept that you are guilty as charged. It means rather, that you accept the terms of the agreement as a means of resolving the conflict. By pleading guilty you are not accepting that you did all the things the victim is alleging. I assure you, if you accept the offer, then you may end up serving no additional time or perhaps just a little more time allowing you plenty of time to attend to your family matters. I think you should accept the offer."

On that note I signed the government's offer and accepted to be bound by the terms of the plea agreement.

Sixty Three

Attorney Citara Manis' legal narrative on plea agreements had a galvanizing effect on my thoughts toward how I could regain my honor which had suffered many crushing bruises. I realized right away that I could only look forward to a new future now. It was the future alone that mattered henceforth. Whatever reputation I had built in the past had been erased and there will be no road back from the direction in which I was now headed. The future was mine to shape. At over fifty years of age, with three years already spent and a possibility of further time to spend in detention, many would undoubtedly give up on life. I knew it was my duty to resist resigning to such fate. The only caveat was; there was zero time to waste.

It was time to fashion a response to the government's allegations against me. Although I was not a lawyer, and the prosecutor had leveled the government's charges against me using intricate legalese, tangled in booby-trapped rules, I will articulate my response in the common man's guileless language. I will be truthful and I will tell it to the court regardless of the court's negative disposition toward me. I had hurt myself enough protecting other people. I had naively misrepresented facts in the past, intent on protecting those I considered disadvantaged or weak, because I believed that to be the path of the noble. Now, I have learned the lessons which, in my thinking, few people in life are given the opportunity to learn. Among these lessons is this one which every well intentioned benefactor of the needy must bear in mind when offering to help: "if the truth cannot help the needy beneficiary, then that beneficiary does not need help." In other words, if I had to lie in order to dig out a person trapped in a hole, then that person rightly belongs in that hole. From here on, the future—my future, will be based entirely on truth telling, and nothing short of my death can alter that resolve.

Because it is a great deal easier to tell the truth than to run a false spin, out of which one is usually unable to untangle one's self, truth telling is both clever and fruitful. For that reason, it took me little time to pen down the entire saga of Chinelo the maid. My intention was to find a way to get this documented account of Chinelo's sojourn in my home to the presiding judge in my case; Judge P.J. Messitte. But first, I must have my attorney review the documents and offer his opinion and advice. For that purpose and also to prepare for the hearing before the judge, I contacted my attorney by phone and set up an appointment for him to pay me a visit.

When Attorney Citara Manis arrived for that meeting, I caught a foreboding gleam in his facial expression, but knowing him as a man of duty and solemnity, I did not push him for explanation, but allowed him to address his mind's troubles as he deemed appropriate. He wasted no time, much to my surprise.

"George, I have good news and bad news for you," he said.

"I hardly know the difference these days. Begin with either one," I replied jokingly.

"Well George," he said pensively, "the investigator was able to make contact with Chinelo and . . ."

When he paused mid-sentence, I interjected, "That's great! Will she be at the hearing then?" I queried.

"No, no, no, George. That is the bad news, Chinelo refused to speak with the investigator at any length. She in fact only spoke to her from the fourth floor balcony of her apartment building. She would not let the investigator into the building. When the investigator requested that she show up in court to be interviewed about her charges against you, she said she was done with any issues that had to do with the Udeozors. She was very uncooperative."

I was disappointed, but not surprised. "I told you that she will not submit willingly to an interview or cross examination," I said. "If I were in her shoes, knowing how many lies I had told and the contemptuous way I had betrayed my benefactor, I would also dodge. No amount of pressure would force me to cooperate."

"I'm afraid that is the position she has taken" Attorney Citara Manis agreed.

"But, can the court not subpoena her? Can she refuse the order of the court for her to appear?" I enquired.

"You cannot make the court order her appearance because you're pleading guilty. Unfortunately, that is how a plea agreement works," he answered.

That was the nature of my quagmire. For the first time in my fifty-two years of existence, I wished the future was less predictable—that is, the future outcome of my ill-fated court battle. Anguish imperiled my soul, for I knew with certainty that the judge's mind was made up, and all the nitpicking courtroom dramas were only meant to fulfill the court's obligation to avail me my due process rights. Or to at least appear to have done so. Do not ask me how I could be so certain. I believe I already risk being found in contempt of court for daring to hint at judicial misconduct, even if post-conviction.

"So, I'm screwed either way," I complained. "If I rescind my decision to plead guilty and elect to go to trial, you and I both know I would be convicted for one or both counts of the indictment for which I've accepted responsibility. The court and the government, of course, will show little mercy for my 'impudence' in taking up valuable time and wasting tax payers' resources on a trial and would reflect that feeling during sentencing. On the other hand, if I plead guilty, both parties would pat me on the back and possibly reward me with a milder Sentence for making them look good to voters, and being tough on crime. Too bad if my reputation is damaged, my family is ruined and above all, my right to justice is trampled. I ask you Mr. Citara Manis, why does the suppression or selective release of truths not disturb people's sense of justice and fair play anymore? Why has service to the people taken a back seat to manipulation for the control and dominance of the system in the eyes of those entrusted by society to serve?" From the look on his face, I could tell I was taking my attorney in a direction he did not wish to go, so I concluded my tirade on a somber note. "I'm sorry Sir. It's just that I cannot help myself. Despite my resolve to not let my emotions run in circles, I find myself caught in my humanity each time I think about my problems. Please tell me, what is the court date for the plea hearing? Has it been set? And how is it conducted?" Relieved, Attorney Citara Manis went on to explain the procedures of court during a plea hearing. Again, I would be required in court.

"Alright George," he began. "First, I want you to understand that I sympathize with you on what you're going through. Your emotions have not been misplaced. Having said that, I believe the time has come for you to man up and face the inevitable. Despite how undesirable the situation is, it has happened and there is no going back now. I've already submitted to your position that the system is not perfect and sometimes people are punished unjustly. But that is the best the society has evolved and more often than not, it works. This is why we must work hard to ensure that it works in your case. Now, the court date has been set for July 16th, 2008. On that day, just like during the bond hearing, the marshals will bring you to the court. This time however, it will be a lengthier hearing. The prosecutor will inform the judge that both parties—the government and the defense, have arranged a plea agreement. I will also affirm the prosecutor's statement to the court. The judge will then briefly interview you. He will ask you many questions whose aim is to ensure that the plea agreement meets the requirements of law. His questions will address the decision to plea bargain instead of going to trial. The court must be assured that the decision was voluntarily taken by the parties involved. He will discuss the process and principles of entering a guilty plea to ensure that you understand what you are getting into and that at the time of negotiating the plea, you were competent to do so and were not forced or induced to do so. Finally, he will explain your rights and opportunities to withdraw from the plea agreement. Once the judge determines that the deal meets the requirements of law he will set a date for sentencing. At that point, if no objections or issues arise, the matter is adjourned until the sentencing date."

A long silence followed Attorney Citara Manis's equally long explanation of the process to me. I cannot claim that I was incompetent to enter into a negotiated plea deal at this stage of events in my case, but in hindsight, there is no question that I was, at that same time, a teary eyed believer in the good intentions of every letter of the law. It is only now as I live day to day, through the days and months resulting from that plea agreement reached in September of 2008, that I appreciate the need for and the value of a good understanding of how the law works—the way codes, procedures, and ambiguities are built into the process and the uses to which they are put in order to achieve the wishes of those who run the system.

During the plea agreement hearing proper, no special incident occurred. My sister Chi came to the court accompanied by two of the most special friends of our family. The media representatives of local radio and newspapers were present. A few other small groups sat in their seats spaced out in various parts of the courtroom. It was eerily quiet and freezing. Shortly after I was seated, the court proceedings which were already in progress, was resumed. It went strikingly according to Attorney Citara Manis's earlier lecture lines to me about the process. I was prepared for the harshness of the language of the prosecutor because I had heard them before. My skin was growing thicker and my senses were quietly developing immune responses to verbal abuse. When asked if I was pleased with my attorney's handling of my case, I responded in the affirmative, "very pleased, your honor." Again, when asked whether I was in any way forced, induced, or coerced into pleading guilty, I responded, "no, your honor." After a series of questions to which I responded in similar fashion, my part in the process was over. No one else could see, nor could notice the disquiet between my attorney and me. Throughout the proceedings, I was writing him little notes, whispering to him my feelings of anxiety and foreboding about the admissions I was making under oath. He was in turn reminding me of the possible consequences of toeing a different line. All said, I was glad and relieved when it was all over. Our heads bowed in resignation and uncertainty, my family and I exchanged glances acknowledging each other as the marshals led me through a side door back to the holding cell where I waited in the cold discomfort of a room formed out of concrete and steel until the marshals were ready to transport me back to my life at MDDC.

Back at MDDC, as I walked the long hallways leading to my pod, I was aware of a number of long, sustained glances coming in my direction from familiar inmates and correctional officers. Each time, I looked back over my shoulder to try and discover the object of their interest. Failing to find anything attracting such glances, I would continue along, feeling awkward and berating myself for reading too much meaning into people's actions of which I was in the past, usually obvious. But that feeling of paranoid delusion was hardly misplaced as I found out on arrival at my pod. The correctional officer on duty called me to his workstation the moment I entered my pod. "George, George," he said, "I'm shocked you did not tell me anything about your case. Why in the world would you plead guilty to such charges? I remember this case from two years ago. Your wife, Dr. Udeozor, was my family doctor. We all know that the maid was a liar! It was unfortunate the judge refused to believe your wife's testimony. That girl thinks she has escaped with her lies but she seems to forget that God sees and knows all things. She will reap as she has sewed."

I was taken aback. "But you've known me for a few months now and never mentioned anything about my wife. When did you become my wife's patient? And for that matter, how did you discover all of a sudden that I am her husband?" I asked, still stunned.

"Oh, but the news of your guilty plea has been playing all morning on WTOP radio. Everybody around here has heard about it," he responded as a matter of fact. "I became Dr. Udeozor's patient from 2000 until she was sentenced. My family still misses her. She is a really good doctor and a very kind person."

"Thank you," I said, not knowing how else to respond. When I began to step away from the workstation, he called me back. His face wore a new solemn expression on it. "Mr. George," he said, "It was that evil man who put your wife in all this mess. The moment we saw him, we knew he was up to no good. He was always hovering around your wife like a jealous coach. We could never see what your wife found in him. At first we thought he was her husband. Then we learned from other patients that he was just a gold digger. Now that I've met you, I think Dr. Udeozor had to be crazy to let you go. Look at me. I am very serious about this. Something must have gone wrong with her. Do not blame her. Try and forgive her so that when this is all over, you can repair your family. You owe it to your children. Do you hear me?"

How else does a weary man respond to such unsolicited, yet well intentioned advice? "Thank you very much for your concern and good wishes," I said weakly. He then let me return to my cell where my knees gave way and I dropped into my bunk to join the hundreds of men sleeping away their lives at that same hour all around the facility.

~

Trying to sleep was an exercise in futility. How could I? Had I not already broken my vow to live by the truth for the rest of my natural life? How long had it taken me to break my own vow? Just a few days! Now what? Do I make a new vow or do I pretend I had not broken the original vow in the first place? Would that not be insane?

But, wait a minute. Is not the entire world insane? Is it not insane that I suffer so horribly for action which was good but was also a crime? Is not society insane for operating a system based on falsity which was initially founded on truth and fair play? Is not that what the justice system of today is? The system was asking of me, to plead guilty and perhaps it then might be merciful to me although I might be untruthful? On the other hand, the same system challenges me to proceed to trial and risk certain conviction, and punishment severe enough to knock the wind out of the remaining productive years of my life! Tell me, if that is not insanity, then what is?

It was while I debated the insanity of our impure and treacherous new world in my head that the silent voice spoke again to me. The voice assured me that I had not broken my vow at all. "Following your lawyer's counsel is not being untrue," the voice said. "Quit beating up on yourself. Get up; begin today to prepare for your sentencing. It has been set for October 7, 2008. Begin now to do what you must to get ready. At sentencing you must tell the whole truth. You will not be interrupted. You will not be questioned by anybody. That will be your day. For fifteen minutes, you will have your chance to tell the world the truth. You will have nothing to lose. Get up and go to work now!"

I harkened to the voice, for it had never lied to me before. Surely, I had merely followed my attorney's counsel and I had simply responded as advised. No doubt I wished to end my ordeal in the hands of the legal and judicial systems. Only then could my new life truly begin. It was not my wish to blame my attorney for my troubles. If anything, I had answered truthfully when I said that I was very satisfied with his handling of my case, because I knew he was trying to assist me within the framework of the only judicial system in existence—a system that neither of us had the power to influence or change.

It immediately occurred to me that Attorney Citara Manis had not returned the copy of my response to the government charges and Chinelo's allegations against me. I had given those documents to him to study and advise me from a legal perspective on its tone and also to advise me on what was more appropriate—to send it to the judge or to read it out as my address to the court before the judge pronounced his sentence. I now needed the document back to put finishing touches on it before October 7, 2008, the date of my appointment with destiny. I made a phone call to Citara Manis a few days after the plea hearing and he promised to return the document in plenty of time before the seventh of October so I could make all the necessary adjustments that I needed to. During that call, I enquired about the investigator's progress but learned that very little else had been done subsequent to our last discussions on the subject. I was particularly interested in finding out whether the investigator had obtained the promised videotaped interview of my children about our family life prior to my departure in 1999. That interview, had it been done, would have been worth the world to me. But it wasn't.

One week before the 7th of October, 2008, Attorney Citara Manis visited me. The story was not much different from where they stood during our last telephone conversation. I got the distinct impression that my attorney had such a heavy work load that he had therefore no more time to spare for my case, on which he had expended a lot of resources and his personal time and energy. I decided to withhold any further pressure on him. Que sera, sera.

The weekend prior to the seventh of October, 2008, my sister Chinwe visited me. She brought with her, cheerful news and information of the deluge of letters being sent by family members and friends, all of them support, wishing well and testimonial letters about my character. She also brought news that my brother Chiedu, Cousin Helen and her husband, and many others will be in court to support me.

Sixty Four

At 2:30 in the morning of October 7th, 2008, the correction officer on duty woke me. In ten minutes, I was dressed and ready. After having swallowed two cups of scalding black coffee, followed by a large glass of lukewarm water, I rejected breakfast and began the long walk to the intake area. After the long hours of processing, I was cooped up in one cell where I waited for the marshals, occasionally drifting off to sleep in a sedentary position on the bitterly cold concrete bench. At about 7:45 AM, the marshals finally arrived.

From the moment we got outside, I felt chilled to the very marrow. It was one of those early dawn mornings in the fall when the earth seemed dead with cold. The frozen air felt palpable, causing me pain at all points where the marshal's handcuffs and chains gripped my limbs, biting me, piercing through me, and killing me under its invisible vice-like power. It was clear that other forces were also at work—the powerful forces of fear, for my heart rate had skipped into overdrive.

My fear was not without provocation. I was heading to court for sentencing. Although I did not share my sister's unrestrained, unyielding optimism about the ensuing judge's decision, the possibility did exist that my ordeal could come to a dramatic end. It was within Judge Messitte's power to turn me loose and set me free. After all, if the whole truth had seen the light, I might not have been put in prison in the first place. But during the plea hearings, something in the judge's manner seemed odd to me—a distant look, eyeballs that told volumes about the contents of his mind. I could not accurately interpret that look; however, I knew it was not good. But how could I verbalize my fear? Upon what facts could I base my distrust and suspicion of this judge? A United States Federal District Judge who I did not even know, but who had scaled hurdles upon hurdles, passing the various tests required to arrive at his exalted office?

And even if I had concrete evidence that the judge's mind was already made up, for whatever reason that I had to be severely punished, to whom could I turn with my complaint? He was after all, the judge, and at that moment, the highest judicial authority with jurisdiction over my case.

And so, bound and shackled, under the caustic attack of severe weather and fear, I willed myself to walk tall as one with no worries in the world. I reminded myself over and over that even in my state, I could still summon courage to the surface such that my observers were blinded to the rumble in my stomach and the quake in my chest. Thank God Almighty. I read it someplace, in some book, that courage is fear that has said its prayer, and God knew that I had said many prayers.

No institution erected by man ever did, do now, or ever will compare to the institution of family, for therein lies true love, loyalty and devotion. From Nigeria, my brother Chiedu, my cousin Helen, and her husband journeyed across the Atlantic. From Los Angeles, my sister Christine, my brother Benard traversed the vast breadth of the United States. From the south, the sprawling city of Houston, Texas, Arize Ogudo jetted into Washington. From their homes all around Greenbelt Maryland, Drs. Cecilia and Christian Nwankwo, Attorney Maryrose Nwadike and a host of others converged around my sister Chinwe and my daughter Kimberly in Judge Messitte's vast frigid courtroom for the occasion of my sentencing.

For the first time since the beginning of the series of court proceedings leading up to my sentencing, on this foretoken October morning, I walked into Judge Messitte's courtroom and gave a broad smile. The warm, friendly faces of my family members, and the energy radiating from within them felt like the hand of God on my skin. I had long seen the resolve in the judge's eyes to ensure that I receive no mercy. That decision had been made before he laid eyes on me. At that moment, in the presence of my family, thoroughly doused and inebriated in the magic of their love, the judge's imminent decision seized to bother me. I became ready. Freedom or prison, I was prepared for both.

Under the watchful and restraining eyes of the marshals, I managed to exchange a few greetings with some of my family members before the marshals decided to withdraw their generosity and disallow further contact between us. Shortly thereafter I was called to rise and be duly sworn under oath.

The court proceedings attracted little interest from me until it was time for my attorney to make his case for the reason the judge should disallow the major contentious issue of the plea agreement—the prosecutor's recommendation that I be punished for inflicting serious bodily injury on the "victim." To me, conviction was already a *fait accompli*. There was no need to listen attentively to verbose legal narratives which I scarcely understood, and whose purpose I saw as justification for the lucrative careers of the learned professionals in government employment. No recriminations, no matter how truthful would do for Judge Messitte to backtrack on his decision. But due diligence had to be done. I therefore paid close attention particularly to the judge's body language as my attorney laid out our argument against the requested enhancement of my sentence due to "serious bodily injury." Even to the lay person, my attorney's argument sounded straight forward. He stopped short of calling the government's recommendation illegal, which was what it was. Then he rested his case.

From his physical responses, I could tell that the judge had no intentions of altering the decisions which he had already made—he took no notes, asked no questions and sought no clarifications. He sat motionless, and appeared a bit impatient for my attorney to get to the end of his presentation. One of the few good things that result from incarceration and association with hardened offenders is the opportunity to observe them up close. This way, one is able to overcome the mythical fear one has of these mostly ordinary people, evil as they may sometimes be. In that same breath, one is also able to extend that newfound freedom from fear to include some authority figures that inspire fear and consternation unnecessarily in ordinary law abiding citizens. I no longer harbored fear for this judge and his intimidating office. I felt he owed me a fair hearing but had decided not to avail it to me simply because he did not have to. He had both the authority and power to do as he pleased. I was not afraid but frustrated that even though I had taken responsibility for my unlawful actions, the system had apparently chosen to punish me, not for those actions, but for made up meaningful options left for me to work at developing a thick skin, to harden my heart, strengthen my patience and endurance and submit myself to the will of God.

With the due process of law satisfied or the appearance of it fully addressed, the judge reluctantly acquiesced to the clamor by my very passionate family members and friends to give oral testimony about my character. They still believed that there was a chance that the judge had room for appreciation and sympathy for the tragic human condition which led me to act in a way that contravened United States laws. Although, his reluctance seeped right through his judicious posturing, he decreed that only two of them could speak, each one to speak for no more than five minutes. Looking back at the spirited efforts made by the two who were selected to speak—my senior brother Chiedu, and a close family friend,

Attorney Maryrose Nwadike, it still mystifies me why this judge allowed them to address the court when he knew he had no use for what they had to say. Like two teary eyed pre-teen youngsters with strong convictions that the tooth fairy is alive and well, they gave the most moving testimony of some charitable activities from my past, of which I can honestly say that I did not know they had taken notice. They candidly tied the motivations which prompted those deeds to the one that brought the Chinelo saga to bear. These two knew my heart, if anyone did, and they let the judge and all in that courtroom know it too. Through most of their testimony, the whole lot of my family and friends were sobbing. Despite my determination, I failed to hold my own tears back. When my brother choked mid-sentence, unable to further properly articulate his thoughts, I cursed the devil that visited this evil day upon us.

Judge Messitte was unkind to both my brother and Maryrose during their address of the court. He intermittently interrupted them to instruct that they limit their testimonials to what he, the judge, considered relevant, such as my habits rather than any acts of charity in which I may have engaged. Despite his interruptions, the testimonies evoked deep feelings of sympathy among other observers, even those who were unconnected to the court proceedings. Since I was not asking for forgiveness but rather for fairness in accordance with the law, I did not deem their efforts a waste of time and energy although the judge apparently did. It appeared to me that he did not wish to hear testimonials which he could not ignore in good conscience. Only he can attest to how effective that strategy worked for him, for he did not strike me as fully confident in his convictions when he indicated that I could now address the court.

Even before I became aware that I had broken the law, I was already paying a price for it. Only people who have been wrongly accused, wrongly convicted and wrongly punished can truly claim knowledge of the emotions I was feeling when all eyes and ears focused on me for my address of the court. I knew that I was not skilled in speech making but I did not realize that it was an art that required more than merely reading a prepared text, quite distinct from classroom reading or perhaps participation in interactive conferences, both tasks with which I was familiar.

Once given the opportunity to address the court, I had estimated my plea in mitigation to last about twenty five minutes. It was not meant to be a judicial appeal—I had already pleaded guilty. It was rather an appeal to the conscience of the court to consider three crucial issues before imposing a sentence on me:

(1) The motive behind the "victim's" sojourn in my home which was to receive humanitarian assistance. Despite the regrettable incidents which unavoidably slowed the process of delivering the assistance, the "victim" was light years better off in my home than she was in her parent's home and her future prospects were that much brighter.

(2) From a cultural standpoint, the arrangement between my family and the family of the victim is the practicing norm even in present day Nigeria. Although I pleaded guilty to this offense in order to express acceptance of my responsibility subject to the laws of my adopted nation, the ramifications and complexities of this issue does not need to claim more victims before a middle ground is found. Perhaps my country of birth will step up to its own responsibilities to her citizens who suffer rejection and abuse needlessly and shamefully.

(3) Finally, my children who were caught in the middle of the entire saga also had rights which the system appeared to overlook in their professed duty to protect the rights of an "alleged victim." I felt that the court had a duty to my children who deserved the same level of care and consideration given to the alleged "victim," at the very least. Clearly, from the interest shown by the government, my children had received zero consideration. I found that fact befuddling and out rightly alarming.

By addressing these issues in my speech I hoped to explain to the court how and why I acted the way I did and why, if broader consideration is given to the humanitarian and cultural reasoning behind my actions, society would be better off and justice would have been served if I was not subjected to further punishment.

Although I maintain my conviction that the judge's mind was fully made up coming into the court for my sentencing on October 7, 2008, if I were to address Judge Messitte's court today, I would have chosen my words differently. I have since then learned more about the delicate relationship between selfishness and selflessness. At the core of that lesson is the fact that in any verbal exchange, it is usually counterproductive to sound overtly altruistic or take a morally superior tone to the other party or to one's audience. People, I have discovered, react negatively to too much virtue or even a perception of it. Generosity and selflessness are as equally hated as mean-spiritedness and selfishness. In articulating my speech, which was actually a letter to the judge, I clearly came across as though pontificating. My emotions focused too much on the noble virtues of my actions as though I was suggesting that they were enough to override the things that I did do wrong. Had I known then, the things I know today about the human side of judges, which is that they find virtuous sounding defendants too irritating, I would have tried to weigh my words more on an earthly balance than I did.

I present the full test of my speech for my readers' scrutiny. Perhaps some may not judge me as harshly as Judge Messitte did after reading it:

> *Thank you Judge Messitte,*
>
> *For the opportunity, the first I have had through my ordeal to speak at any length on the issue that has had the greatest impact in my life, and in the lives of most members of my family.*
>
> *I begin by offering my profound and unequivocal apology to the American people for my actions in this matter of the United States government versus my humble self.*
>
> *I deeply regret my actions and hope that the mistakes that led to these actions are seen and taken for what they truly are; mistakes of the head but not of the heart.*
>
> *Your honor, the portion of my life's journey which I have spent here in America has become twisted into such a conundrum of cloak and dagger tales that I often pinch myself with a silent wonder in my head; "who are you?" I so wonder because it is clear to me that these tales do not describe me. They are mere fables.*
>
> *The truth is that I am a man who dreamed, hoped, and prayed to God for deliverance from the hardship into which I was born. A man who was given a chance to share in the dream that only one nation on earth would freely offer a person such as me. Above all, I am a man perhaps of feeling and sympathy, but still a man, with all the traits and weaknesses of self-indulgence and imperfection.*
>
> *When I landed on U.S. soil for the first time about 31 years ago, I was armed only with the armor of my mother's blessing and abiding love. You see, your Honor, when this journey was merely a dream to me, she was the only person who believed I could make it.*

When it became certain that I was to come to America, she was again the only one who provided me with both the spiritual and financial support necessary for such an epic journey. How could I harbor any feelings in my heart for her but for feelings of gratitude and adjuration?

With no tutoring on what to expect and how to solve the many testy problems and obstacles I was to contend with growing up alone in the United States, my new home, I relied solely on my mother's counsel to always follow the straight and narrow but difficult path rather than the winding, wide and easy road. Your honor, any honest immigrant who has travelled the narrow path will tell you that it is impossible to reach your destination without straying at all. But by God, I did my best to stay on course the difficult path. I admit that I strayed from it sometimes, but I never lost sight of the path.

We are here today because sometime in 1996, I strayed from the path, and unfortunately for me, my punishment for straying will be determined today, not by my mother but by you your Honor. My mother would certainly have been totally befuddled by that duty since it was her altruism that gave birth to the chain of events which has brought this moment about. I'd like to point out here that it would be disingenuous of me if I tried to pass the blame for my actions to my late mother. Far be that suggestion from me. My alluding to my mother serves only to illuminate your Honor on the difficult choices which I was confronted with and most importantly to tell your Honor the whole truth and nothing but the truth.

Neither I, nor my mother, first approached Chinelo's parents with a proposal or request for their daughter to come and reside, work, study, or become a servant for me or my family. I reiterate that I am not trying to justify or exonerate myself from any actions or any shabby treatment she may have received while residing with my family. I am merely alluding to the honorable intentions behind her coming to the United States because I am certain that all sides to this sordid tale would be best served by the whole truth and nothing less.

Even before I came to the knowledge of Chinelo and her family, they and many other families in our community in Amawbia were regular solicitors of my mother's assistance. My mother's work as a philanthropist is widely known in our area. She was recognized by churches and community organizations for her invaluable contributions. So appreciated was her work that the Catholic Church nominated her for a prestigious papal honor. When His Holiness Pope John Paul II visited Onitsha, Nigeria in 1990, my mother was one of the few who received the honor of a papal handshake and a kiss of His ring in gratitude for her work of charity.

The story of how Chinelo came to reside with my family certainly sounds corny or perhaps like buck passing on my part but lying to the court is not even an option for me. By telling her story, I believe I am fulfilling my obligation to society by exposing the truth about a situation which many who are similarly accused shy away from because of the offensive nature of the subject.

Chinelo had lived in the homes of both of my elder brothers (Paul and Gilbert), as well as in the home of my mother at various points in her life before my mother suggested I bring her to live with my family in the United States. During these periods, the arrangement had been made, not to utilize her labor, but to assist in feeding and educating her since her parents could not afford the financial burden of that duty. The first time my mother brought that request to me, she convinced me that Chinelo's only chance of making something out of her life rested on me. My mother was her godmother and intended to lift her up in life. Her chances for self-improvement in Nigeria were badly obscured by extreme poverty—the kind of poverty not known in the United States. My mother's request coincided with the advent of my final interview for full United States citizenship in 1994. Even though I had never met her, I initially included her name as my daughter in the paperwork. This act was not meant to deceive as it would be interpreted here in the United States. It was in keeping with our cultural traditions which do not require any paperwork for transfer of guardianship. Even though she would pass as my daughter, she remained the legal child of her biological parents. I had no stake but those of a benefactor in her future. When the INS official who interviewed me informed me that only my biological children could qualify for immigrant visa under my application, I crossed her name out and gave up the idea of claiming her as a daughter. My mother did not however, give up hope when I informed her that our cultural traditions are a hard sell to U.S. Immigration.

In 1995, I visited Nigeria with my family for summer. During that visit, I was informed that Chinelo assisted in providing care for my children among various other youngsters who scrambled to be of assistance. My mother singled her out and praised her as bright and promising. Her endearing remarks were calculated to keep me reminded of the need to help rescue Chinelo.

After we returned to the United States from that visit, I telephoned to inform my mother of our safe return. At the end of our conversation, she reiterated the urgency of the need for assistance for her godchild, Chinelo. I promised her that upon my return to Nigeria in a few months on business, we would discuss the matter again. Coincidentally, it was during that same period that my wife and I had the conversation about suspending further recruiting of fulltime nannies. Since our children's needs had changed as they got older, we decided they would benefit more from an older sister than a full-time nanny. I also had begun making plans for our two oldest children, Kimberly and Adam, to eventually enroll at Loyola Jesuit Secondary School in Abuja-Nigeria to begin learning more about their ancestral land. The principal of that institution who is also an American Jesuit Priest, had required my children's passports in order to properly identify my children before considering them for admission.

When I returned to Nigeria for my planned business visit, I therefore took along with me, the passports of Kimberly and George Adam; my two oldest children.

Nothing could have prepared me for my mother's suggestion upon seeing my children's passports, but knowing her and the greatness of her heart, her suggestion did not surprise me. She believed that because I was already indirectly instrumental in the financial upkeep of Chinelo, she qualified as my daughter. I also knew that as a father and a contributing member of our community, tradition had already designated me as a father to any and all children born into our community. This cultural practice which also validated my mother's reasoning was the reason why she suggested that I return to the United States with Chinelo as my daughter using my daughter's passport. It is important to understand the psyche of a mother in my village community during the generation of my mother. At that time, and even today, articles of clothing, text books, food, jewelry, in fact all materials of value are passed along to other members of the family for use. Siblings also represent other siblings as if their identities were interchangeable. My mother's suggestion while not the norm would not raise even a stir among her own peer. To her, as well as her peer, the question would be; "What difference does it make if the passport belonged to Kimberly, so long as they feed out of the same pot?"

As I considered my mother's suggestion, I was crest fallen with worry because I knew the dangers involved, and also because I was yet to ever refuse a request from her. I was not about to begin turning her down with her plans for Chinelo. For one thing, Chinelo was exactly the sort of 'big sister' my wife and I needed at home with our children. Secondly, my mother's altruism and sense of right and wrong were delicately interwoven. Also, that peculiar sense of justice had been firmly established before even the adoption of Western legal practices as part of Nigeria's legal and judicial systems. Refusing her would impugn that sensibility which even I held as sacred. In the end,

I succumbed to my mother's request and agreed to give the plan a chance. The caveat was that the young girl Chinelo and her parents understood the risks involved and were willing for Chinelo to temporarily assume my daughter's identity. In other words, I was not giving a guarantee that she would be admitted under the assumed identity. Your Honor, the young lady and her parents did not only accept the proposal, they eagerly embraced it.

That, Your Honor, was how the idea was conceived. No more, no less. The allegations that I promised a salary to be paid to Chinelo's parents and that I would enroll her in school, etcetera, are all practiced and rehearsed lines concocted to enable the 'victim' to obtain favorable consideration for a green card. Indeed, the truth is that I assumed, along with my wife, the duties of parents to Chinelo. Naturally, those duties included providing for her education. Your Honor, God knows and Chinelo does too, that I began planning toward achieving that goal from the moment she successfully arrived in the United States. Unfortunately, circumstances beyond my control put a temporary delay to progress in that effort.

I believe that Chinelo's successful manipulation of the system falls perfectly within the well-known litany of ploys employed by most aliens living illegally in the United States in their quest to qualify for the elusive green card. Chinelo obviously believed that betraying me was a worthy sacrifice for that lofty price. Unfortunately, when I succumbed to my mother's request and enabled Chinelo's travel to the United States with my daughter's passport, knowing the risks involved, I opened myself up to all the possible consequences including the one with which I now grapple, and for which you're about to sentence me.

As you are about to take a decision which is bound to have a profound impact not only in my life, but also in the lives of my family members, particularly my children, I believe it is important that you consider other related events which influenced my actions during the period under review. For most of the period during which the allegations against me purportedly occurred, I was away overseas. My relocation overseas was completely involuntary. It was a move to avoid further degeneration of communication between my wife and me which resulted from the intrusion of my in-laws into our family affairs. The main intruders, Chuck who is the younger sibling of my wife and their mother had encroached into our family life beyond acceptable limits—to the point of dictating to me and attempting to direct the daily running of both our home and business. Their actions were unacceptable to me and I promptly rejected them and sought to find a peaceful resolution of our differences. Unfortunately, my rejection of the activities of my wife's closest relatives pitched me against her on most issues. The resulting disquiet between my wife and me appeared too unhealthy for the emotional and psychological wellbeing of our children. This too was unacceptable to me and it was in a bid to avoid this negative spillover of strife onto the loves of my life that I relocated to Nigeria in 1999.

Your Honor, my extradition back to the United States is my first re-entry into the country since departure nine years ago. This clearly shows that a bulk of the allegations against me which purportedly occurred during the period between 1999 and 2001 could not have possibly taken place but were in fact fabricated. The same goes for others which purportedly occurred during some of my overseas travels between 1996 and 1999.

It is also significant for me to make a brief mention of another related issue which impeded progress toward providing the intended assistance to the 'victim.' Shortly after my separation from my family, the 'victim' informed me in a telephone conversation that my wife had taken in a lover and had brought that lover into our matrimonial home. This devastating news was incredibly exacerbated when the man identified as my wife's lover showed up in Nigeria and made an unsuccessful attempt at my life. The individual in question, who Your Honor must agree with me, is very dangerous, went on to jointly, with my in-laws; foreclose any chances of reconciliation between my wife and me. Would you believe, Your Honor, that this individual was the orchestrator of my wife's lie-ridden trial strategy which sought to point every conceivable false and malicious accusation toward me. Their belief was that by pointing the finger at me, they would secure my wife's freedom.

Here we are, Your Honor. Please do not oblige them. Take a good look at me. Also, take a good look at my children sitting over there and are hanging their every hope on each letter of your judgment. After a long and perilous journey, we are weary. We need a chance to become a family once again. We've never needed that chance more than we need it now. I am pleading for mercy in your judgment because nobody else would willingly give his freedom, and if necessary, his life for their safety. I would. Every man needs a cause to keep him sane in this world. My children represent that cause in my own life. I know them individually like no one else does. I felt what my son George Adam felt when you delivered the judgment in the case against their mother. Although she refused to see the light, my aversion for conflict has never been about me but about them. As long as it pleases God that I live, my actions will be guided by their welfare first. If you send me to prison, that will simply add more time to my nine years already spent in delirium. I will survive it, God willing, but what about them? Sure, they will live, God willing. But who except God would be able to see the extent of their emotional hemorrhage? Who else would be there to shepherd them through the misery and treachery of our unsafe streets and the savage snares of the devil? Their mother, in spite of my differences with her, was a good mother to them. But she is not now with them. Even though she underestimated the insecurity which my absence eventually created within them, I have observed every bit of the ill effects of that condition in their hearts, like land mines tucked away in unplowed fields. Your Honor, I am the right person to de-mine

> *their hearts. I love them more than words alone can express. They're my summer roses. If I bloom, they bloom, if I wither, they wither. Every minute I spend away from them, there is a net negative impact against their future wellbeing. Please give me another chance with them. Society has nothing to fear from me. On the contrary, society will indeed incur a loss by my further incarceration.*
>
> *Remember, Your Honor, as a father, I owe many sacred obligations to them, not the least of which is to ensure that they are properly educated. It would serve society poorly if by investing in the effort to punish one harmless individual; six young souls are sacrificed in the process. Please chew my words over thoroughly and consider the fact that in the period I have already spent incarcerated, I have come to terms with what is required from going through the process. I have learned my lessons. Please temper justice with mercy.*
>
> *Thank you, Your Honor.*

Midway through reading my testimony, I was stunned when Judge Messitte broke in, interrupting me. "How much longer do you think you need?" he inquired, showing both impatience and disdain . . . "By the way," he continued before I could answer, "I do not know if you understand the plea agreement you signed. But . . . how much more time do you think you need?"

"About fifteen more minutes Your Honor," I replied.

"Okay. We will recess for ten minutes and reconvene for your conclusion. The court is in recess."

When the judge returned, I went straight to my resolve. While the court was on recess, I had decided to toss my written testimony aside and address the judge directly for a minute and thereafter conclude my speech. It seemed pointless to continue with the balance of my oral presentation when the judge had made it clear in more ways than one that I was beating a dead horse. His attitude while I was reading my written speech had confirmed my belief that his mind was already made up and that signaled to me that his ruling would be unfavorable.

In my state of mind and without the aid of my written testimony, it was difficult for me to recall the issues in orderly sequence. I therefore simply made the point to the judge that I had chosen to withdraw my court battle in the Nigerian court and had given myself up to be extradited to the United States for two reasons; first, out of my sense of responsibility as a law abiding citizen, and second, out of my sense of obligation to my longsuffering children. I then urged Judge Messitte to temper justice with mercy.

Judge Messitte took only a few minutes to explain that he did not believe my testimony. He indicated that if I had read the Pre-Sentence Investigation Report, the basis of which he was sentencing me, perhaps then I would not have wasted the court's time making my self-serving speech. He concluded by giving me the high end of the recommended range of prison sentence for the offense to which I had pleaded guilty. By sentencing me to 97 months in prison, he ensured that I would spend a little more than three more years in prison as against sentencing me to the lower end of 63 months which would have meant that I had practically served all the time required and might have seen me exit the courtroom with my family.

His assignment concluded, the judge rose, leaving the courtroom full of my family members stunned and sobbing uncontrollably.

It was supposed to be the end of me. It had finally been made official. The years of waiting had ended on October 7th, 2008 only minutes earlier. Judge Joseph L. Messitte had, by his ruling, declared me a felon. So how come I felt no pain anywhere in my body? How come my tears dried up at the moment the sentence was pronounced? Was there a plausible answer to such a bizarre response?

As I sat alone in the prisoner transport van with the only other occupant, the Marshal who was driving me back to MDDC, I felt unusually energized. Only a few thoughts were in my head. Surprisingly, those thoughts at other times would have rendered me sullen, but not this time. Instead of feeling depressed, I felt relieved, even happy.

That is the way it was meant to be, I thought. Otherwise my mother would not, could not, have foretold of such tragic crossroad for my life. Upon her visit, her last visit to my home before she was claimed by heaven, she had wept. She told of a dream she had—a dream to me, but she was convinced it was not a dream but a revelation. It had been revealed to her that her son, which was me, for her vision was specific to me, had trouble with the law. She lamented and grieved over the revelation. In spite of her failing health—she was dying from cancer; she was daily bowed in prayer for my redemption. But I believed she was being a worrywart and I reassured her over and over that all was well and will stay well. She confided that she was not worried about me but about forces outside of me and against which I had little control. It was those forces' resolve to do me harm which troubled her. My reassurances did nothing to assuage my mother's fear. But when I gave her my word that I was not afraid of anybody or any forces except God's displeasure with me, she relented. That was at the point where she spoke to me with mettle, mother to son, exhorting me to live the balance of my life by the truth and to fearlessly and courageously accept any outcome. "Son," she said, "if things go wrong in your life, stay strong and do not go wrong with them. If your conscience is clear, fear no accusation."

It was this reason—the dream-like playback of my mother's words that strengthened me, relieving my heart of the weighty implication of a tagged life—Yes; My novel name tag; Felon—a much detested, terrifying word. But now applied to me, it suddenly shed its ugliness. It might as well have been another fancy English word whose meaning I was yet to discover.

Suddenly, out of nowhere, only minutes away from MDDC the Marshal broke the silence which had been hanging between us like a frozen sheet of ice;

"If you are innocent like you claim, why did you plead guilty?"

I was startled by his question which was clearly unexpected, but I managed an answer; "What do you think? I mean… after all you heard, what do you believe?"

After another lengthy silence he said, "I agree with the judge's ruling."

"Then, your question was uncalled for," I replied light heartedly.

The marshal turned on his seat, took a long look at me, eyeball to eyeball, and then said, "I wish you luck."

Then he delivered me to my jailers at MDDC.

PART FIVE

Seeking Justice While Serving the Time

"Justice Too Long Delayed
Is Justice Denied."
~ Martin Luther King, Jr.

Through this toilsome world, alas!
Once and only once I pass;
If a kindness I may show,
If a good deed I may do
To a suffering fellow man,
Let me do it while I can.
No delay, for it is plain
I shall not pass this way again.

"The law hath not been dead,
though it hath slept."
~ William Shakespeare

Sixty Five

Less than twenty four hours following Judge Peter J. Messitte's pronouncement of his 97 month sentence on me, my chaotic spin toward the Federal Institution in which I was destined to spend that time was kicked off by the United States Marshals. However detestable I found their job, the United States Marshals' jingoist impulses toward service to their country is without reproach. They got you from point A to point B alive. It is clearly not part of their job description to account for what shape you are in, between those two points, or following your arrival at point B. Those small details always take care of themselves. The important thing is for the numbers to add up, for the tees to be crossed and the eyes to be dotted.

As an inmate in federal custody, you must be prepared for the Marshal's call at all times, and woe betide you if you made any momentous plans longer than one minute into the future. Uncollected debts, planned phone calls or even suspended answer to nature's call must be forfeited or jettisoned. When the Marshal calls, his plans must be implemented. All other plans are canceled.

When they came calling for me, I was totally unprepared. There was good reason for my tardiness in packaging myself for the U.S. Marshals. In the few months that I had resided at MDDC, the Marshals usually called to claim their convicted inmates about two weeks after they were sentenced. My mistaken assumption that that practice was the norm and would apply to me as well, revealed that I had yet myriad lessons to learn about the system of American Bureau of Prisons, my eight month sojourn at Maryland Detention Center notwithstanding. That lesson—the lesson that the Marshal could call at any time of his choosing to pick me up, ready or not, was rudely rammed into my throbbing head at the ungodly hour of 3:00 AM on the wake of my sentencing.

Still smarting from Judge Messitte's judicial assault on me, I had managed to force enough food down my throat to ensure that the night would not be exceedingly restless for me. At about 1:00 AM, I laid my head on the pillow feeling that rest would be good then. An hour or two catnap to clear my mind before doing the inevitable mental review of the worst day of my life. Minutes into my rest I was certain that I was still awake. But I knew that something about me had changed. I knew that something was wrong; I could feel it like I could feel the hardness of the bunk under my body. I could not place this feeling or understand it, but it was a feeling I had experienced before, sometime in the not so distant past . . . There she was at the door. A slender figure with her face concealed behind thick strands of golden false hair. She had a tray balanced on both hands. I caught a whiff of my favorite early morning breakfast dish of fried plantain, sausages and cheese omelet.

"Who are you?" I called out to the figure. "Let me see your face."

She shook her head, keeping it bowed over the tray.

"Pumpkin? Kim Pumpkin, is that you sweetheart? Did you fix daddy some breakfast?" I queried.

"Ha ha ha Kim Pumpkin indeed! Well, if you don't recognize me, then I do not know who I am as well."

It was not my daughter Kimberly at the door. It was Chinelo.

"What day is it today Chinelo? Where is Kim? Is it not Saturday today? Was not Kimberly supposed to make my breakfast?" I demanded.

"Sure, it is Saturday. It is always Saturday to you. It will always be Saturday to you. If you had listened to me, maybe it would have become Sunday, Monday or maybe Friday. Ha ha ha. Have you thought about that Hmm? Have you even thought about that, George? Oh, oh, oh no siiir, Right? It is Sir, isn't it, George?"

"You've gone mad Chinelo! What the hell is wrong with you? Where is everybody?"

"Oh, I've gone mad? I cannot believe you! Now, it is me who has gone mad. Tell me Sir, who is in prison Hmm? Who is locked up and whining, craving for breakfast? When I told you to hurry back to save your family, did you listen to me Hmm? No, you did not listen. When I told you that Stella was ruining the family, your family, did you listen? No, you did not. So, what was I supposed to do? Tell me, was I supposed to just sit there and watch her? Was I supposed to throw my life away? What choices did she leave me Hmm? Now, everybody is in hell! You're in hell. Stella is in hell. Your children are in hell. And me, where do you think I am Hmm? Do you think this is what I wanted Hmm? Do you think I am happy Hmm? I had to do what I had to do . . .!

I felt my temperature rise sharply. What in the hell was going on? With fake hair on her head and fake tears in her cheeks Chinelo taunted me? Changing form right before my eyes! "Good heavens," I yelled, "what the hell is going on . . .?" I screamed.

I woke up suddenly to the ear shattering sound of a bunch of keys banging on the side of my bunk bed. My cell mate was already up, sitting on the bunk above me and explaining something to the female correction officer who had ceased banging on my bunk.

"He appeared very exhausted last night. He has spoken very little since he returned from court," he was saying to the correction officer. "He seems to be having a nightmare now."

"I'm sorry, but he has to get up now, the Marshals are coming for him," she said to my cellmate. And then turning to me, she continued, "Did you hear me, Mr. Udeozor? Get up. If you need a shower, go and get a quick one and be ready in fifteen minutes. The Marshals are coming for you." Before I could gather my thoughts, she was gone.

I swung my legs out from underneath the pile of beddings and blanket. The cell felt as though it was spinning and silence rang around me. No one spoke, but I could feel my cellmate's eyes resting on me from above. My head buzzed. The events of the previous day and my nightmare filled my mind as if a large bucket had dumped them in there. I was now fully awake and could hear nothing but the sounds of my breathing. I could not shake a terrible premonition that a lot more ill omen than the visiting Marshals awaited me. Images from the nightmare still hung suspended in my thoughts. What did it all mean? I remember wondering about Chinelo's parents and how they could, in good conscience, watch as my family was being ripped in shreds only because I tried to make their lives more livable! "What leeches they are!" I thought, very distraught. "What sort of parents are they, to have spawned such hellish monstrosity as a daughter?" The picture of her sneering face at my cell door refused to fade away as I slowly raised my exhausted frame up from the bunk. I had no inkling that I had had my last rest on that bunk as I scurried away to the bathroom for a three minute hot shower.

When I returned to the cell, my Bunkie, Ola was waiting. "Why are the Marshals coming for you?" he asked.

I sat down heavily on the bunk. "I have no idea." I replied.

"You did not know they're coming? You mean you do not have; like a doctor's appointment or another court visit?"

"None that I know of, I'm really confused." I said weakly.

In a minute, I was dressed in my green jumpsuit, ready for the Marshals and just in time for the correction officer who waved as she approached my cell for me to hurry up. Ola and I walked up to her together. While Ola began handing out breakfast trays—a chore we had tackled together as Pod Representatives for the past three months, I was ushered to a table with a breakfast tray already sitting on it. The correction officer advised me to "step on it with that food, as it might be a while before you see any more decent meals." As I silently wolfed the scrambled eggs, two strips of bacon and some fruit down, it became crystal clear to me that this was the last I would see the interior chambers of the Montgomery County Detention Center. The much dreaded journey to the Federal Prison to serve my time was under way already.

As I ate, I began scribbling on a paper napkin. I wrote my sister's telephone number and my identity number down. I said a quick prayer and motioned to Ola to join me. I handed him a paper napkin with the solemn request to find a way to make contact with my sister and inform her about the new developments. Her planned family visit for the next morning had been involuntarily and forcibly terminated by the visit of the United States Marshals. Despite knowing that prison life is transitory by design and that bonded relationships may be terminated at any instant without fanfare, prison inmates appear even more inclined than any other segment in humanity to form bonds of friendship. Ola and me who, in the free world probably would have ended up as mere acquaintances, had grown so close and protective of each other that even though we knew this day was coming, we could do nothing to prepare for it. Now that it became reality, we found the process of parting devastating. Words were not necessary to express the anxiety we felt for ourselves knowing that now we would be forced to contend with our individual predicaments without the support and sympathy of each other. In very few words, we wished each other good luck just as the correction officer beckoned from her workstation for me to get moving.

The long walk from Pod C to the prison intake lounge was a familiar one to me. I had traversed it numerous times over the past eight months. But on the eighth of October 2008, that walk appeared a momentous pilgrimage to me. Although I had frequently felt humiliated at the hands of prison officials, I understood that their actions were usually dictated by prison policies with which they were required to comply. Nevertheless, MDDC had been home for me for eight months of my life which would still have been significant had MDDC been hell itself. I willed my senses of sight, smell and hearing to record every possible detail of the scene for posterity; The Pod, the passageway through which I wheeled many a food cart, the barber shop—scene of numerous prison dramas, the visitation area—scene of many impersonal and unfulfilling, yet crucially important family visits, the Leisure and Law Libraries, the Classrooms and Chapel which all did wonders for my sanity. It had not been a pleasure ride; my life in this institution, but now that I was leaving it for good, to another unknown destination, MDDC began to look to me, like a paradise lost.

Unlike the other visits from the Marshals, when I got to the intake area, they were already there, waiting. I had little time to look around for the last time. They had already apparently completed the paperwork. The correction officers on duty took away every last item which I had brought along on the off chance that they might allow me to travel with them—my prescription eye drops, spare prescription glasses, medicated shampoo and hygiene kit. I was then stripped down to my nature in the raw, and given the usual squat and cough treatment.

The first of many shocking acts of humiliation which I had to endure followed immediately thereafter; Right after the strip-squat-and-cough treatment, I hurriedly put my boxer and tee shirt back on. As I pulled up my jumpsuit, one of the Marshals stopped me short. He grinned and handed me a blue jumpsuit made of a light, porous paper material through which my entire nakedness could be seen, save what was concealed by my boxer. It was in this garment alone, in the sub-zero temperature outside that I was handcuffed, shackled and ushered into the Marshal's waiting van and away to a destination which, as usual, remained undisclosed until arrival.

Sixty Six

It seemed as though my every step had been dogged by an invisible stalker determined to always undermine my liberty. I had been abducted from my home during Christmas celebrations, detained, in violation of my due process rights and a court order to release me. I had, for three years, been incarcerated in horrid, inhuman conditions while I fought unknown forces whose identities were concealed until the last minute. My already battered family life had taken its death hit when I was extradited from Nigeria back to the United States and forced at the age of fifty two to negotiate away my dignity and honor. At least, I thought, I could spend the next few weeks before I was whisked away, trying to apply the salve of a father's love on the bleeding hearts of my children. But that wish had now, unfortunately, been denied me. Now, in the very heart of the modern world's bastion of freedom, liberty and happiness, I sit seminude, in shackles, in the inner chamber of a paddy wagon, a box-like wagon which feels like a meat freezer in the obscenely cold weather, circumnavigating, it seemed, the entire streets, highways, and alleyways of the state of Maryland.

I lifted my head and looked around at the faces of the men sitting around me. They were mostly tense, and judging from their looks, they were men mostly chiseled out of villainous clay. We must have been on the road for over two hours since the U.S. Marshals handed me off to the operators of the paddy wagon at the courthouse at Greenbelt and it seemed we were as yet, not close to our destination. From where I sat, I could see street signs as we whisked past them, but none long enough to read what they said. All I could think was, "Lord, what's going on? You're still with me, are you not?"

Minutes later, as if an affirmative answer to my question, I saw, a short distance from the road we were on, the outline of a barbed wire fence. The journey which began at 3:00am in the morning was apparently finally coming to an end. Sure enough, the signal light switch started clicking and we were shortly admitted into Charles County Jail. Due to the circuitous journey which brought us to the jail, I could not estimate how far we were from Montgomery County Maryland, but I was sure it could not be terribly far—nowhere within the state of Maryland is terribly far, it is not one of the very large states, but it felt to me as though we were in limbo....

With every inimical experience I had in the prison system, I learned to inoculate myself against the punishment intended by those who designed the system. It seemed astonishing to me however, that there was no dearth of ideas in the system for the humiliation of inmates, designed to keep them compliant. At Charles County Jail, I was promptly given a taste of their own design of inmate hospitality.

Before inmates are admitted into their facility, they are required to pass some form of healthcare check; among the mandatory checks is the tuberculosis test. During my intake processing, I informed the nurse screening me that I had received a TB shot less than six months earlier after which I had severe skin reaction which had not healed. I showed her the partially healed scar and informed her that the doctor at MDDC ordered an x-ray which showed that I was negative to tuberculosis but was positive-reactive to the TB virus. The doctor had advised me to not submit to further testing or x-rays until after one year. After my explanation, the nurse ignored me, pulled out her needle and TB vial and ordered me to make a fist for her. When I refused her order, demanding to know why she wouldn't listen to me, she looked at my face for the very first time. I must have looked like Frankenstein because she trembled and called the Sheriff's Deputy who stood right outside the Plexiglas door that separated her little cubicle from the hallway. The Sheriff's Deputy appeared between both of us like Jack in the box.

"He's gonna need to be taken into quarantine!" She cried, pointing at me and backing away from where I sat.

The deputy was calm and appeared not fazed by the nurse's drama. He turned to me and with a heavy baritone asked, "What seems to be the problem?"

As calmly as I could, I explained the situation to him. I noted as he listened to me that the nurse was livid. She had her nose turned up and apparently upset that the deputy saw fit to give me audience.

"Please get the doctor. The doctor here would understand. I do not need to be quarantined. I have no disease whatsoever. Better yet, look up my record on your computer or call the Montgomery County Detention Center. They will confirm what I've just told the nurse," I implored them.

"I'm not going to have this!" the nurse declared belligerently, "if he would not take the shot, then have him taken to isolation!"

The deputy although sympathetic with my plight, surrendered to the "professional" authority of the nurse. He advised me to reconsider my position. He said, "Sir, you do not want to be taken to isolation now. The doctor has closed and gone home and since it is Friday night, she will not return to work until Monday. Believe me, it will be difficult for you in isolation. The TB shot may hurt, but for sure, it cannot hurt as much as isolation."

"This is clearly wrong," I complained, "I feel I'm being bullied but I have no escape or choice, do I? Go ahead and give me the shot. But I guarantee you, you will wish you hadn't."

And she indeed did. It was the most painful shot I'd ever been given. I would not wish a cobra the fortune I wished for her that night.

Minutes later, while cooped in a cell nursing my pain from the TB shot, a correction officer came for me. I followed him to a storage area where he handed me a tub that contained two orange jumpsuits, a towel, blanket, sheets and a hygiene kit. When I picked up the tub and made to exit, he quipped, "not so fast." He then asked me to strip down to my toes. "Nothing new," I thought as I complied, expecting him to give me the usual squat-and-cough treatment. But no, he ordered me into the shower which had been obscured by curtains. "Get in there for decontamination." Confused, I turned to face him wondering what he meant. But he wasted no time in showing me into the shower. He then grabbed what looked like a sprinkler and began spraying me with a liquid that reeked of a hospital ward. I did not scream and run out of that tight corner only because I knew that there was nowhere to run, but that was my first impulse. I could not tell whether that correction officer took notice, but I came close to dropping on my rumps. My thoughts had made a mortal journey to Nazi Germany. I thought he was about to gas me! Meanwhile, his role played, the officer said to me as he exited; "now go ahead, take a shower and be out in two minutes." That was the conclusion of my second welcome ritual.

I was once again cooped up in a new waiting cell. Finally, someone remembered we might need food like other humans. We were served a meal. Because of the hunger I felt, I could not tell what the food tasted like or what it was. My tray was empty before those thoughts even occurred to me. It was not until well past midnight that a correction officer came in with a cell assignment for me and the other inmates. But the relief I felt at the prospect of a restful sleep promptly vanished when I got to my assigned cell. The jail was overcrowded at that moment due to unexpected extra intake. We were to share the cells, four inmates in each cell—two new intakes plus the two originally assigned to the cell that were already fast asleep on their bunks. Needless to say that these original two were not happy to receive us—they were downright hostile, but considering that we were bigger, bulkier guys than they were, they only huffed and puffed. It was the first time since my unspeakable experience in Nigeria's dungeons that I was forced to sleep on a hard concrete floor, and although I had a blanket, beddings and a pillow, my sleep was just as restless.

As one must expect after a restless sleep, a fitful sleep, or no sleep at all, upon waking up, one is drained of all energy. I remember hearing loud noises around me but lacking the requisite energy, I could not even prop myself up, let alone rise to my feet. After gradual mental and physical manipulation, my brain and limbs picked up some activity. While I worked on waking up, all elements of my body constitution were yet to respond when a correction officer threw our cell door open. I was startled and immediately jarred into full consciousness. Only then did I notice that the other cell occupants were already finishing the eating of their breakfast. The correction officer called out two names. The second name called was mine. He held the door open for us to pick our belongings up and follow him. It took me under sixty seconds to roll up my blanket, towel and beddings, straighten out myself and stump out of the cell. We were ordered to line up behind six other inmates, all eight of us balancing our full tubs between our outstretched arms and our posterior parts. Like worker ants, we were marched in a single file by the right side of narrow, endlessly long hallways, each inmate pulled out of the file at his designated pod along the hallway. I was the third inmate pulled out. Once I walked through the entrance to my designated pod, the door was shut behind me. Unlike the arrangement at Montgomery County, there was no correction officer posted within the pod. The supervising officer had a small duty post across from the pod out of which he remotely monitors activities within the unit. Shortly after arriving at my cell, I learned that our housing unit was designated for federal inmates only. We were subject to Federal Bureau of Prisons rules which differed considerably from the rules applicable to all other inmates who were the permanent resident inmates. They were under the county jail rules. Because I had no idea what that meant, I asked for clarification. My new cellmate, a scrawny, eagle-eyed criminal—by his own proud admission, said; "We are federal gangsters and they are local gangsters." When I continued to gaze at him puzzled, he sneered at me and continued in a petulant tone, "Where the hell are you from nigger? We are charged with federal crimes and they are not. They are charged with state or county crimes. We are serving federal time, they're serving state time. You feel me?" I knew right away that I would not get along with this middle aged guy and I began immediately saying my prayer that I would not have to spend much time in the same space with him.

In all, I spent six days at Charles County Jail. Most of those six days were indistinguishable from each other. Breakfast was brought in by a correction officer at about 6:00 in the morning, after which, inmates were locked down until count time at 10:00 AM. Shortly thereafter, inmates are let out for recreation, television and games. Lunch was served between 11:00 AM and noon. Again, inmates are locked down at 2:30 PM for the 4:00 PM count. Dinner was served shortly after the count, usually at about 5:00 PM. Rotational provisions were made for library visits where a limited number of books may be checked out. The routine at Charles County Jail turned out to be much less restricting and less stressful than the routine which I left behind, perhaps a compensation for the obvious superiority of the facility and practices of the newer, better run Montgomery County Detention Center.

My otherwise uneventful stay at Charles County Jail was briefly punctuated by a single occurrence that shed a bright light on the thinking that may have earned me the ire of my judge. On the evening of my fifth day at the jail, a nerdy, fiendish looking Caucasian man apparently noticing that I usually kept a lone company with myself, walked over to where I sat watching television. He took a seat next to me and said hi. I was a bit uneasy owing to his weird personality, but I returned his greeting. After a few minutes, he slowly and mechanically turned his head toward me. Without moving my head, I withdrew my line of vision from the television to keep the fellow covered in case he made any untoward move in my direction. I was unsure whether he noticed my alertness, but he began talking. I assumed he was talking to me since it was just the two of us at that table and the four chairs around it.

"I have court tomorrow morning." he said.

"Oh, really? Good luck." I replied.

"Yes, I'm going before Judge Messitte for sentencing."

I was jolted as if I stepped on a high tension wire. That name struck me dumb for more than a fleeting moment. I did not know how to react. Was this a set up—an attempt to elicit a reaction from me? But to what end? Of what value would my reaction be to Judge Messitte? He had already given me the most prison time he could. Strange as it was, it had to be a coincidence. But I had to find a response with carefully chosen words all the same.

"That judge's name sounds familiar. In fact, I believe he was my judge as well." I offered in reaction, paying close attention to his body language when he responded.

"Really?" he exclaimed with genuine surprise.

I nodded in response, still keeping watch for signs of a snare.

"Oh, then you can tell me, was he fair to you?" He continued, "Do you consider him a good judge?"

"I cannot tell much about him. I believe he did not deliberate on my matter at all. I think his mind was made up already before he even came into court for my sentencing and he did not permit anything said in court to influence him. Otherwise, I cannot say anything about him because I do not know him."

"I guess I'm gonna have to find out in the morning," he concluded.

By the next morning, I had all but forgotten about that conversation when the nerdy fellow poked his face into my cell door, his thick glasses moving ahead of him. He asked me to wish him luck, and I quickly indulged him, wishing him the best but secretly nursing a foreboding feeling for him, knowing as I did that Judge Messitte would most likely dash his high sense of expectation.

But later that evening it was me who was in for the shock of my life. Nerdy approached me after dinner at my usual table as I watched the evening news on CNN. He had a surprising broad grin on his face and he began speaking even before he took a seat.

"I thought you said Judge Messitte was tough," he said.

"Yes," I replied. "To me, he was. Emm, he was very mean to me."

"Well, I cannot say why, but he seemed very nice to me. He listened very attentively to me and afterwards he asked me a few questions and man, I was so relieved when he gave me thirty six months!"

"Judge Messitte listened to you?" I asked, incredulous.

"Yes, he was like a father to me. He knows I have a problem. I basically pleaded with him that I cannot help myself. That I'm a low down dirty bastard. That I was abused as a child and ever since, I became sort of like a misfit. You know, I get to spend less than one year with the feds. Most of my time is already served. I'm going home in six months!" He declared jubilantly.

It was with great difficulty that I survived the pressure of resentment which welled up as nerdy concluded his observations about our judge. He blamed me for not doing as he had. He said, "One inmate told me this was all I needed to do. Just put yourself at the mercy of the judge. He likes that. He will recommend treatment for you and he will give you a light sentence and a chance at rehabilitation."

Sixty Seven

From my second row seat, I could not see much of the road ahead of us, but I could see some of the oncoming traffic. The only thing I could tell for sure was that we were heading north. The slaphappy wipers kept sweeping away rivers of rain water from the windshield as we inched onward toward yet another unknown destination. It was impossible to tell whether the tires of our 18 passenger van were on the proper lane as most of the road was covered with a mixture of rain water and frost-like droplets. As our van kept nudging forward I kept wondering why our escorts would not pull over to the side of the road like all other vehicles were doing. Although we were prisoners, we had not expressed the will to spill our blood on this treacherous highway and that seemed likely with every turn of the steering wheel. Amazingly, the journey proceeded without incident. After about one hour of holding my breath, I quit expecting the worst. If we crashed, then we crashed. It would not change a thing how much I worried.

Right then my thoughts migrated back to the subject that had occupied my mind since the previous night—Judge Messitte and his ruling in the case of the nerd. I had tossed and turned as I chewed over nerd's words in my mind. Sure, he had been right. The judge had been impatient with the two who had nothing but kind words to say about me, about my character and about my charitable activities. Then, when he had given me the opportunity to address the court, he had been impatient, and downright repulsed by the notion that the man described in the hideous testimonies of the "victim" and the PSI Report of the probation officer, could stand before him and suggest that he is not the lowlife he believed him to be.

Less than ten minutes into my testimony, the judge, failing to conceal his irritation, had ordered me to stop my speech, a speech which he had requested in the first place, and he had asked how long I wished to speak. When I informed him that I needed only fifteen more minutes, he had called for a recess—apparently, fifteen minutes had sounded like an eternity to him—an eternity listening to my self-righteous rants. The fact that I had based my entire plea for mercy on the plight of my children meant nothing to him!

When he returned from recess, I had tossed my prepared speech and quickly concluded my address of the court. I was no fool. The judge's biased inclination was seeping like nuclear waste right out of his robe. As I had expected all along, he was relieved that he did not have to listen to my tortuous speech any longer. He wasted no time in imposing the highest end of the sentencing guideline recommendation on me. My attorney at that point turned toward me and said, "I don't know what to say George, but the judge just screwed you." As I sat wondering how, that same judge could be described as a father figure; I decided that my attorney could not have chosen a more succinct phrase to describe what the Judge did to me on October 7, 2008. He screwed me!

Through the windshield of the van I began to make out the kind of road signs, the structures and the oversized billboards that give a clear indication that you are either at an airport or approaching one. Visibility had been poor from the very start of our journey. It had been one of those endlessly gloomy days. We had as usual been woken up at about 3:00 AM. About ten of us had been processed, cuffed, shackled, and led into a waiting van. We had been herded to a courthouse in Baltimore, Maryland where more of the paperwork and prisoner horse-trading was done. At the end, I was the only one among the bunch from Charles County Jail in the group of inmates that ended up traveling north in the 18 passenger prison van. Now, about five or six hours after we departed Baltimore, we were approaching an airport. Where in the world were we and what were we doing at an airport in this god-awful weather? I was about to find out.

The van slowed to the posted speed. Through the haze I could see the signs of Fed Ex, DHL and other cargo companies all lit up by flood lamps mounted on tall steel poles. Finally, I was able to glimpse a billboard that informed that we were at Harrisburg Pennsylvania, at the cargo terminal of Harrisburg Airport.

I swallowed in horror because the word Conair jumped into my mind. Who on earth had not seen the movie Conair? I admit it was a strange, unwieldy thought, but I could not shake it off. Such fate could not apply to me, I thought uneasy. Could we possibly be headed anywhere onboard a Conair flight? Images from the movie—of inmates on restraints, mass murderers, bandits and rapists flashed through my mind. It was difficult to keep from coming unglued, but I knew that that would only cause my family more anguish. I had assured them I would survive this ordeal and come out whole. I therefore did the only thing I could under the circumstances; I prayed for strength and waited.

I have little knowledge of how the systems which order and control the lives of Americans were created. I have even less knowledge of how they evolved into what they are today. But what I do know is that I have felt the full impact of the American Justice System in the last six years. My account has so far chronicled my experiences within the system that decides guilt or innocence and freedom or punishment. Now that the system had finally decided that I was guilty and had handed down my punishment, the system was about to uncover an open secret—a sort of Pandora's Box to me, about the inner workings which operate it. It was at the Harrisburg Airport that the box was first opened and the memory of that scene remains today in my mind, the watershed event of my entire prison experience.

When the rain, after first falling in bucket loads, gives way to other factors which complicate the weather—darkness, fog or just plain October cold nastiness, all you yearn for is a warm bed and layers of comfortable bed covering. But instead of that good fortune, October 14th, 2008 presented me with scenes out of the dark ages of human horse trading.

I leaned against the steel cable mesh which was meant to protect against escape of prisoners, searching for the profile of the dreaded Conair aircraft. Visibility must have been less than 100 feet. I could only make out a large area with people milling around in no particular order as we approached slowly. Instead of the aircraft which I feared, our van pulled alongside a few other vans similar to ours. Across from us, about 50 feet away, rows upon rows of large travel buses stretched as far as eyes could see. As our driver switched off the ignition, I was able to cover a larger area of vision, being that we were no longer in motion. It was then that the scene gradually unfolded, revealing the blood curdling activities reminiscent of a world gone by—a world which I never had personal knowledge of, but which apparently, amazingly reappeared out of the dark ages. On that chilly, messy, dark October afternoon, I saw what my ancestors must have seen and experienced what they must have experienced those many years ago—lost and helpless in Sheol.

I knew very well what was in the offing. Harrisburg Airport is a modern airport and nothing untoward goes on there. But how could I help feeling the way I did when the scene before me reminded me of no other human engagement but the scene at a slave auction?

Some of them were dressed in jumpsuits, some in tee shirts and trousers, others in garbs of various description and hue. They were mostly men and mostly disheveled. Some of them appeared outright infernal. They filed out, grouped in small numbers as they wobbled and staggered to the command of the United States Marshals. They were inmates in transit but due to my rather callow experience with the world underground, they appeared to me, like nothing but merchandise at an auction. They might as well have been cattle at a farm market getting inspected by their purchasers!

I watched in stupefied horror as inmates were ordered in near freezing weather and slush-covered ground with their handcuffs, shackles and chains in place, to squat down and cough, to open their mouths, lift and wiggle their tongues, to remove their shoes and socks and raise their feet for the inspection of their soles. My heart hammered away against my ribcage as I watched our escort crisscross the very well organized and ordered makeshift work areas negotiating the fate of her human cargo of which I was one. I knew it would not be long and therefore I shut my eyes and waited patiently for the inevitable.

I did not have to wait too long, for shortly after I shut my eyes, the escort returned. She first led the women, who numbered only four, to the side of our van. Before I could readjust my sitting position, she ordered the rest of us out of the van. The men were then split into about four groups. There were only three of us in my group. While the driver kept watch over us, the escort led the women away. While we waited, I spotted several Marshals who were heavily clad standing at spacious intervals around the perimeter of the open area. They each had their fingers trained on the triggers of either pump action or automatic weapons which they cradled in their arms. I looked over to the gentleman keeping watch over us and wondered whether he seriously believed that had he not been there, any of us might consider making an escape attempt. Somehow I knew that we all knew the answer to that thought.

My innards began rolling. The air around us which was already chilled grew heavy, almost solid. It was as if I breathed rocks. When I lifted my head as we plodded along with our escort, I saw only two kinds of people: men and women who stood erect and tall, even the short ones among them appeared tall, and a second group—men and a few women who were bound, shackled and stooping, even the tall among us, appeared cut down low. Those who stood tall gave the orders and those who stooped followed those orders. If this scene varied from the slave auction scenes of those hundreds of years ago, I felt it could not have been in too many ways. But then, I had endured too much, come too far. I could have been rendered delusional by agony. One thing I know, even today in one of my soberest of days, the 14th of October, 2008 remains to me, the day I saw and felt the way my ancestors felt hundreds of years ago.

Just like the lamb meekly submits to the lamb owner's will, we submitted to the orders of those who had charge over us—those who stood erect and tall.

After their business with us was completed, those of us still on our feet were herded into our master's waiting vehicles. Those who had wilted from exhaustion were assisted into their designated transportation vehicles. There were of course those prisoners who needed physical persuasion to comply with orders. It appeared the escorts were well equipped with the tools for that job. Eventually all prisoners were seated in one of the endless rows of prisoner transport vehicles spread out in the open area. Because of poor visibility, I was unable to observe whether any of the aircrafts parked outside of our immediate handling area was a Conair aircraft and whether any inmates got the dubious pleasure of riding in one of them. I was personally thankful to have been spared that treat. Not to suggest that my seat in the large travel bus equipped with its vast array of security bars and hard wood seats was about to offer me a pleasure ride to wherever on earth our destination was.

And so, I rode in solitude, surrounded by strange men who, just like myself, were shackled and chained, most of us showing signs of exhaustion and anxiety. Unlike me however, many of the other passengers seemed to know one or two others in our bus. They moved around and paired up or sat within earshot of themselves. I sat near the window as if in a dream, looking at faces which I had never seen before and probably will never see again after our ride. I listened as they discussed matters which were indifferent to me as though I was not there—matters to do with crime and law and society. They spoke in a language I could hardly understand, except that they were words whose meanings I could decipher when the words were separated.

They made statements such as; "that cat's a disciple, but you ask me, he aint shit . . . He is non but a rat . . . moafukka gave me 120 months . . . shit, that crazy cop violated me . . . they careered me and gave me life . . . I've been designated, I mo be here a minute, then I'm off to Coleman."

I strained to grasp even one sentence but failed. Even though in the months to follow I was to easily understand such language and even hold discussions using similar terminologies, during our bus ride outbound from Harrisburg Airport they might as well have been speaking in tongues. None of what they said resonated with me.

And then, once again I began perceiving how really alone I was in the world and how, in spite of the security and reassurances provided by family and friends, the journeys which shape us are ultimately travelled alone. It was during those lonely moments in isolation with my thoughts that I was able to think broadly, clearly and profoundly about my mission here on earth. I could suddenly see the whole of life outside the vision of eternal hope, outside of deception and false expectations of fairness from a world which is everything but fair—a world which lures us toward indulgence in dreams never to be realized and delivers the opposites of its promises.

From the signs posted along the crowded interstate highway I could see that we were travelling westward. As we penetrated the countryside of the State of Pennsylvania, I began daydreaming that I was on a solo adventure ride through the most luxuriant natural vegetation I ever saw. As the air got lighter and visibility improved, I was awestruck at the beauty of nature brought on by the transition from spring to fall. The continuous stretches of billions of oak trees and their hundreds of color shades interspaced between vast farmlands which sprawl through the accent over unknown rocky mountain ranges and through tunnels unlike any I have ever traversed. What a waste of adventure! I lamented.

Still my innards roiled, my joints ached and my thoughts silently rattled within my chest like bagged popcorn popping in a microwave oven. Where were we headed and what lay in wait for me there?

Sixty Eight

Finally the lit up sign appeared; Correctional Corporation of America (CCA), Youngstown Ohio. Based only on its location and the drive up to the unassuming entrance, CCA would ordinarily not have caught my attention. But shortly after our bus exited the freeway which had carried us for nearly six hours, I returned my attention to the many signs pointing in several different directions. I quickly deduced that we were at the northeastern tip of Ohio State, one of those locations where one state intersects with another and a simple hop could change the operating jurisdiction and laws—State line, if I am correct. As our bus looped, braked and turned, I was never sure which state we were in—Ohio or Pennsylvania. But once I saw the CCA sign, I knew we had arrived at our destination. I did not need to be told. The fence told everything.

The snowflakes which had disappeared on contact with earth as we journeyed to CCA had begun taking hold by the time our bus pulled to a stop at the facility entrance gate. At least one inch of the white vapor had accumulated like an endless blanket over everything in sight. There was no way of telling what time it was. To find out, we had to wait until we got into the facility. While waiting, I watched as both of the armed guards who had accompanied us for the long ride from Harrisburg Airport assumed their monitoring positions while we were slowly accounted for, one inmate at a time. As usual, owing to the position of the letter "U" in the order of alphabets, my last name Udeozor made me one of the last inmates to be processed and admitted into the intake hall. Finally, I was able to get rid of the transparent jumpsuit which had me shivering while we traveled across three state lines half naked in near freezing temperatures. For the first time during my entire ordeal, I went through the invasive body search and groping without complaint in my eagerness to again feel the warm comfort of plain cotton material on my skin. To my surprise, instead of exchanging one jumpsuit for another, I was presented with three sets of uniforms, boxers, tee shirts, soft shoes, and shower shoes. When I picked up one of the uniforms, it broke into two. It was only then I realized that the uniform was two pieces of clothing—one pair of trousers and one shirt. My days dragging around inside oversized jumpsuits seemed to be over. It remained to be seen.

It is candidly a mystery to me why it takes a virtual eternity to process an inmate for admission into a detention facility but that is the way it is. It does not seem to make a difference which facility it is, although the county facilities appear the worst culprits. It took us all of seven hours to be processed, going by the time piece at the intake hall. After arriving at CCA about 9:00 PM, it was not until long past 4:00 AM that we were finally shepherded, our property containers in tow, through the most interminably long hallways I've ever walked within one building. From the look of the hallways after every turn, I began to wonder if we weren't walking in circles. Every long corridor looked just like the one before it or the one coming up next. Eventually, we were brought to the pod identified as ours. Only four of us from our group of about sixteen were let into the pod. The remaining twelve or more continued the pod-chase further up or around the next turn.

By the time I got to my designated cell, I could hardly put one foot ahead of the other. As luck would have it, I was assigned an empty cell—no cellmate. I dropped my property container on the floor, pulled out the sheets and blankets and wrapped my body with them like and Egyptian mummy. I shut my eyes and slept like a corpse.

~

C-h-e-o-w…! C-h-e-o-w . . .! C-h-e-o-w…! The sonorous baritone yelled from somewhere nearby. My eyes popped open and the world around me was gone! Vanished!

Where was my cellmate? How did I end up on the bottom bunk, tied up? What was happening? My mind raced as my heart doubled its pumping. Slowly, all began to come together as I lay puzzled, peeping through the beddings and attempting to untangle myself from the bed sheet bondage I felt I was trapped in.

Finally free, I dashed to the door, squinted through the narrow glass panel. A mass of human bodies were gathered, spread out in the shape of the letter V, all of them squeezing through the only door out of the pod as though through a funnel. The last time I witnessed a chaotic rush similar to this was at MDDC, as inmates scrambled to the food line for their food trays. This time however, the exodus was headed toward the exit door. There was thankfully no sign of stampede, so I took the time to brush my teeth and rid myself of the ugly wrinkled look before joining the crowd which had thinned down to just a handful of inmates. At the door, a rotund, balding, retirement age officer held the door open for the crowd. I asked him what the rush was about. "Ah!" He beamed, "Its c-h-e-o-w time, run along. Go get it. Scrambled eggs, cakes, cookies, sugar, sugar, sugar. Go on; get it before it's all gone! Ha ha ha . . ."

He clearly did not notice my shoulder drop and my expression swing from one of extreme anxiety to that of disbelief. He was in no mood for chatter, and so shooed away the few of us remaining in the pod out into the hallway.

The hallway, just like a highway, was divided in the middle by two solid yellow lines. The inmates; there seemed one million of them... us, were restricted to the right lane. Officers dressed in black trousers and white shirts policed the unruly crowd like a procession of a large herd of cattle. It was no mystery that correctional officers were positioned along the hallway despite the metal detectors because metal detectors cannot stop a fight. Indeed, shortly after we merged into the breakfast procession line, a bloody fight broke out right after the metal detector door. At least five inmates were involved and what a bloody rumpus it was! I saw very little of the actual blows but the trail of blood looked gory. It seemed that each one of the fighters was in a hurry to inflict maximum hurt, for each of them knew quite well that they had but a few seconds before the officers bore down on them. In what seemed less than one second, correction officers of every description; male, female, young, old, agile, sluggish, came bounding toward us, their keys jangling as they shouted orders at inmates. We were quickly spirited back to our pod where we remained locked down in our cells for the next one hour.

When I finally made it to the dining hall, I found it a truly spectacular scene. Nowhere else had I been in my entire fifty two years of existence where so many people could be fed complete meals in a matter of two or three minutes! It was then that I understood why the aged officer beckoned and shooed us along like we were a herd of cattle, for indeed the meal procession was orchestrated in the fashion of cattle grazing. It was not therefore surprising that the great hall was appropriately renamed The Chow Hall. The term dining hall clearly did not fit the many rituals and schemes which take place within minutes, the least of which was the eating of the meal. It was only a small fraction of us to whom eating was the primary reason for regular attendance at the chow hall feeding rituals.

From feeding to recreation, to reading, I had to entirely reprogram my way of life for the fifth time in less than one year. If the popular aphorism "We are what we eat," were indeed factual, then while in prison I have had no choice but to become a new man, for my digestive system had never experienced a larger selection of meals and snacks which seemed to flip from cold to hot to heavily preserved. From one institution to another, breakfast ranged from hot breakfast meals to cold, sugar drenched pastries. My system usually reacted to these changes with changes of its own. At Youngstown Ohio, I recall experiencing hyperactive mood swings for the first time in my life. I made no connection between my activity level and the meals I ate until during my routine institutional physical. The doctor on duty who conducted my physical remarked casually that I could reduce my risk of future ill-health and my current activity level by carefully monitoring my diet. I pressed him for further insight into what I should do and how. My questions led to the doctor giving me a slew of medical information about my health and advise which has been tremendously useful to me, including the regulation of my activity level through dieting.

I spent my first two days at CCA Youngstown in virtual seclusion while I tried to understand the system while staying away from the constant commotion which appeared ever present among the highly restive inmate population. During those two days I kept mostly to myself, only responding to greetings from some inmates who were either out of curiosity or plain natural friendliness adept at making the first gesture toward strangers. I had learned very little by the third day when during dinner at the chow hall a group of young inmates converged on an eight-sitter table where I had just taken the first seat. One of them walked up behind me and said, "Hey ol G, sit on that table over there, if you don't mind." I followed his hand signal to the table next to mine which had about two vacant seats. Still looking straight into my eyes, he concluded his request; "me and my homeboys wanna talk." His homeboys were already taking up the seats around me so that I had to oblige. Until I returned to my cell, all I kept turning in my head was the expression "ol G." What did it mean?

I did not wait for long because shortly after I entered into my cell, I got my first visitor. His name was Craig. Craig had observed my exchange with the rude young men at the chow hall, and being an elderly man of wisdom, had noticed how uncomfortable the experience made me. He felt the need to explain and reassure me that I had nothing to worry about these unruly kids.

"I hope you're not upset by those kids' rude behavior." He said. "They just don't know any better. They can't even tell that they did anything wrong, running a man like you, old enough to be their daddy, off from this table! Why? I've cautioned them, and they're sorry."

"Thank you sir, that was very kind of you." I said, genuinely thankful and pleased.

"Sure George," he said, "that is your name, isn't it?"

"Yes, sure, I'm sorry, I didn't introduce myself." I replied embarrassed.

"Nothing missing," he said, "it's alright, won't you come downstairs and watch the news with me? It comes on at 7:00 PM."

"Sure."

And that was how Craig and I became buddies, and also how I learned everything I got to know about CCA Ohio and much, much more. I cannot forget the very first of his lessons to me. On our way downstairs to watch the news, I had asked Craig what ol G stood for. After laughing heartily he turned to me and said, "Boy oh boy George, now I know you really do not belong here. Ol' G stands for Old Gangster. Is this the first time you've heard the expression?"

"Yes," I answered truthfully. But within me, my heart had begun doing a double take. I needed desperately to look in the mirror. It was the first time I felt truly depressed about Judge Messitte's ruling. "Me? Old Gangster?"

As we watched the news, the pictures appeared and went like flash cards before my face. I got nothing from the news but I thanked Craig for a wonderful evening before I retired to bed. As there was no mirror, I had decided that I would visit the barber shop the next morning as Craig had advised. "The mirror there is large and revealing," he had joked.

Having not seen a mirror since the day of my sentencing two weeks earlier, I gazed at myself astonished at the image of my father staring back at me from somewhere behind the life-sized imager. It stunned me into speechlessness. Not only was age beginning to gain its inevitable triumph over me, it was also reminding me of who I ought to be—one who never quits. That was the man in that mirror. Or maybe a disheveled form of him. But certainly not the one who had been kicked about by the ghosts of his past and vilified by a justice system that had been deceived and defrauded by a perfidious young woman.

I stood there as if frozen in time, while memories of my father's encounter with his boss fifty two years earlier violently and inexplicably flooded into my head and chest. It felt as though the memories were from events which had occurred in my own life. Perhaps a time traveler can explain how this could have happened, but for these few moments I became my father. He was an inspector of police in the defunct British Colonial Administration of Nigeria under Her Royal Majesty the Queen of England. In those days, only Britons and a handful of Nigerian born policemen made it to my father's rank, which meant that my father was a bright and dependable officer—an honorable man. When therefore, a British Officer his own rank insulted my father, perhaps only as a prank, the British Officer did not, could not, account for what hit him. Only that Mr. Udeozor attempted to yank his head from his body. I could hear and I could see the British Officer as he trembled before their boss, licking the blood off his busted lip while he gave his account of what happened. I could sense the bile well up in their boss's guts when he sent for "that ape officer" who assaulted a "Royal Police Officer." I could also see my father stand his ground and refuse to be dishonored or intimidated. Then, when in a bid to teach the "disrespectful African Officer" a lesson of discipline by slapping him with summary demotion without due process, I could see my father yank out his badge and slap it on his boss's desk, showing him his back before slamming the door shut. I could see it all, just as if I had been there. I could see it, just as if it was happening there and then—really only because that was my father standing in the mirror before me.

The two barbers and another inmate had been waiting for me to move aside as there was only one mirror in the tiny room. They had evidently kept me under their observation for a short while and must have concluded that I was perhaps an incomplete entity. The barber to whom I was assigned for a shave and haircut held up his clipper and said, "Ol G, m-a-n, are you here? Yo, you with me? Am I not getting through? What's up?" I looked at him without responding and handed him my ID card. He turned to the other two who exchanged glances with him and moved over to the mirror. He showed me to his chair and proceeded to prepare me for the business at hand.

When I spoke, they were all startled. "He speaks, hallelujah," he yelled. I told him to give me a good haircut. "I'll give you a great haircut," he promised, "the greatest you ever had." We all laughed and chatted till he finished. Back at the mirror, a new image smiled back at me—the image of the warrior. The warrior I thought I had lost to life's relentless assaults. "Thank you dad," I whispered silently in my heart, "for breathing the fight back into the warrior."

Sixty Nine

With my restored fighting spirit and a gut full of fire, thanks to the spirit of my father, I felt poised to take my fight for justice to the United States Court of Appeals. With communication between me and my attorney frozen while I was in transit to my unknown new home, the clock was still ticking and the thirty day time clock for the submission of my appeal was in danger of running out. I had to do something quickly.

My new life at CCA Youngstown was meanwhile gradually falling into a routine as it usually did in prison. While getting acclimatized to my new environment and the new routine, the main fight of my life—a desperate quest for justice could not wait. With the assistance of my new friends; Craig and my barber shop pals, I went hastily into action. If Judge Messitte thought he had seen the last of me, then, he figured it all wrong. I was heading for the Appeals Court.

With the very limited resource materials available for legal research at CCA's make-shift law library, it was difficult to read up on the grounds and procedure for appeal in my case. Also, because I was not allowed to bring any of my legal paperwork and paperwork from the court proceedings, I had to rely solely on the sketchy details stored in my memory. Nevertheless, with those sketchy records, I was able to put a Notice of Appeal together and filed it on time. Although I had requested that my attorney, Michael Citara Manis, immediately appeal my sentence, I did not wish to leave anything to chance. Just in case he had failed to file a notice, my notice would ensure that I did not lose my right.

After ensuring that my notice was received on time, I began spending every possible library time I had, reading and recording all the information I could uncover on the subject of Involuntary Servitude. Interestingly, it was not the law books that provided me with the insight I needed to educate me on this debased global phenomenon. It was rather the many very penetrating articles I read in such news magazines as Foreign Policy and The Economist that provided me with the most insightful information of all. Also, International newspapers such as USA Today and Wall Street Journal which we received on an irregular basis were equally helpful.

From what I was able to glean out of these and other media sources, I realized that the ferocity with which I was pursued was as a result of timing. It turned out that when the United States President George W. Bush came under great pressure from the United States Congress, diplomats, human rights groups and other concerned entities to join the fight against human trafficking, he sympathized with their cause. Unfortunately for me, when the president approved the use of the full might of U.S. law enforcement in the battle against servitude sometime about the year of our Lord 2002, my erstwhile ward, my mother's goddaughter, had discovered some tricks that saw her take advantage of the fired up mood of U.S. law enforcement to achieve her goal. With her sights focused narrowly on securing a green card and also securing a better life for her family, an objective she judged my family too slow at bringing to fruition, she decided to do whatever it would take to achieve those objectives.

The more I researched, the clearer it became to me that in those early days following the president's approval of the fight, law enforcement had very limited cases to support the claims of those who heaped pressure on the president to-declare this war against slavery. Now, the president's signature had of course opened the floodgate on cash, a gate which had to be kept open. The pressure from Congress, diplomats, human rights advocates, et cetera, now shifted on to law enforcement and media agencies, more out of the necessity to justify the free flow of cash than out of the age honored ideal of social justice.

Feeling the pressure, law enforcement, working in tandem with the media and in the modern American inclination to varnish every threat against society, small or large, real or imagined, in order to justify budgets and other related expectations, went out scouting for "slaves." While on their search, I suspect that they found some slaves because there really are slaves out there. And wherever there are slaves, there are bound to be slave masters. So, when Chinelo Anyadiegwu ran out into the hands of slave hunters whose hunting was experiencing a disturbing dry spell, identifying herself as a slave, the hunters brought out their biggest guns. Now, nothing I said or did could persuade the hunters to pull their drawn guns back without firing. Instead of the guardian that I had always been to her and the big sister which she was to my children, Chinelo declared herself a servant to us claiming that she was an exploited and mistreated servant at that.

To the ears of the law enforcement agencies concerned and to the media, Chinelo's claim was nothing short of the Sound of Music. To the human rights advocates who assisted her and those others who helped pile pressure on the president to declare war on slavery and by so doing, open the door to the bottomless cash vault, that music represented the sound of success. To the justice system which helped railroad me into prison, that sound of success represented proof to the electorate that they remain as tough on crime as ever. To the electorate, that proof represented further proof and justification that taxpayers' money was being well spent and therefore reason to support the government and maintain status quo.

However, to all those who suffer deprivation, poverty and disease for no other earthly reason but for the location of their birth and domicile, I wonder if they were asked to be the judge in my case, would they find me guilty of involuntary servitude? How and why is it even deemed justifiable by civilized society in the twenty-first century to expend the mind numbing amounts they do, waging war against human trafficking while at the same time doing next to nothing to combat the poverty which inspires and feeds that trade? From my findings as I researched, it became clear to me that a vast number of individuals and agencies do a lot of good work as humanitarians toward alleviating poverty. But their efforts, laudable as they are, come up short, inadequate to have the level of impact which could put human traffickers out of business. In a very inexplicable twist, the governments of the rich nations whose citizens "invest" in trafficked humans (slaves) form "equal" partnerships with the governments of the poor nations whose citizens "profit" from human trafficking ostensibly to combat the illegal trade. Sadly, I failed to see any attempts to form equal partnerships to combat other illegal trading between the same governments which further impoverish the poor nations thereby promoting the evil trade which they both profess to abhor. To my mind, the result is inevitable; *a vicious cycle in which the rich nation is in effect perpetuating and sustaining the conditions which give rise to the illicit trade in the first place!*

I truly believe these partnerships rank among the worst deceptions ever perpetrated against human kind. There is nothing equal about them! They are fraudulent. They are unequal. They are unjust. They amount to the enslavement of poor nations by rich nations!

It was at Youngstown Ohio Correctional Corporation of America that I quit beating myself up for the mistakes that I made in enabling my accuser to violate the immigration laws of the United States. If the United States, against whom she committed wrong, would forgive her and even reward her for her assistance in making the case for a half-hearted war against slavery, then why should I not forgive myself for deceiving the United States in order to save her life?

From this juncture, I had determined that brooding over the severity of the punishment meted out to me could work in one of two ways; for good or for bad. I chose the first. In order for good to result from my situation, I reasoned, I had to sustain my renewed fighting spirit, and sustain the fight against my conviction regardless of the rulings on my appeal, or how long it took. The fight against poverty is a fight worth dying for. I would be prepared to wait forever, but I certainly hope it does not take that long to win the war.

All in all, I spent a total of three months at CCA Youngstown, Ohio. For much of that time I did not know why I was there or whether my entire period of incarceration would be spent there. Nobody routinely offered that information. What I was told was that I was to await my designation to a Bureau of Prisons (BOP) facility where I would serve my time. When I asked how long that process would take, I was given a vague answer. "It usually takes between two weeks to two months" they would say, "but many inmates have spent a few years here, sometimes they serve out their time and go home from here."

And so, the first month came and went. By the end of my second month at CCA, I had seen enough inmates come and go that I had begun wondering whether I would end up spending my entire prison term at Youngstown. I had also seen enough skirmishes between various inmates within and outside the pod to begin wondering when I would be drawn into one. From what I could see, any situation could spark conflict among all manners of inmates.

The pod was usually a scene of thorough going revelry. For three hours in the morning, and up to six hours from the late afternoon, all the way into the night, inmates gorged themselves with food purchased weekly from the commissary, and wine secretly brewed out of fruit and sugar stolen from the kitchen. At the end they gazed at each other with malignant glances. I could never understand why these young men took the chances they did. All I know is that these scenes were usually followed by scuffles and in many cases, all out fights. During such fights, I usually withdrew into my cell, giving up television viewing simply to avoid witnessing any of the absurd stupidity. Surprisingly, most of the time, they finished their fights undetected. The wounded always ensured that their scars were well concealed, for it was in the best interest of both brawlers that not a peep was heard of the fight by the authorities. The consequences were usually quite dire for both, and sometimes even for any eye witnesses. The foolishness of these thrill seekers is somewhat of major comic relief. The trouble makers were usually known to inmates, sometimes even to the officers. Many of them were usually revolving door offenders. You could see them sway from table to table where their targets played cards, checkers or chess. You could see them smelling out their choices for confrontation and then stumbling onto their game, provoking a verbal exchange. Without question, you knew this was a result of idleness. It was usually at this point that I withdrew into my cell. At the end of it all, Craig generally gave me a detailed update of how it all went down.

~

When at the end of December 2008, I was still one of the very few inmates remaining out of the groups that arrived in October, I became quite distraught. I had been unable to reach my attorney, Michael Citara Manis. My family members, with whom I was in constant communication, had no news about any progress on my appeal. From within the CCA, there was equally no news about the process of my designation to the Bureau of Prisons facility chosen for me. I had no one to turn to for update on these crucially important issues. I was in effect, sitting in limbo at CCA, Youngstown.

Then, two weeks later, on the morning of January 10, 2009, at about 2:30 AM, the long awaited knock on my cell door suddenly interrupted my sleep, catching me entirely off guard. I had to forfeit a substantial amount of my valuables including a radio and several batteries which I had loaned for use to another inmate. That's just the way things are in prison. When the jailer calls, ready or not, the prisoner must answer.

I had lived for three long months without getting handcuffed and shackled even once. That was the longest break from the harrowing prisoner transfer ritual to which I simply could not acclimatize myself. And so, when once again we were cooped up at the intake area and the clanging, jangling sound of chains, handcuffs, and shackles filled the air around us, that ominous feeling associated with the unknown, with uncertainties, returned. I made sure to be the last in line to be disrobed, groped handcuffed and shackled. The little extra time helped me say my prayers and switch off the thin layer of protection with which I guarded my battered ego, even though it actually only existed in my head. In actuality, I had no ego to protect before my jailers.

The ride in the prisoner transport bus was unexpectedly short. Through the windows and through a continuous flurry of snowflakes which came down in sheets, I watched anxiously as we wound our way through the highways to the steps of an airplane. In my state of mind, I found nothing objectionable anymore. It was all very surreal. Three months earlier, I had been terrified at the prospect of getting ushered into a Conair flight. Now, I welcomed it, almost with some eagerness. My only anxiety came as a result of the thickness of the layers of snow on the ground—at least twenty four inches. But what choice did I have? I could not decide to opt out of the flight, could I?

Just then, as if to prove me a coward, a young Caucasian man balked. He would not move. To the United States Marshals, he said, "You cannot force me into that airplane. I refuse to board. If you dare touch me, I will sue your asses individually and collectively. I will own your asses!" The Marshals kept calm and informed him that he was getting on that flight, the easy way or the hard way. Meanwhile, as they argued, other Marshals guided us, stooping and wobbling up the steps and into Conair Flight No. USM.

The best description of seat arrangement aboard Conair is simply that it was not designed with passenger comfort in mind. It was however, not exactly as fiendishly laid out as the Conair in the movies. But it flew same as all other passenger birds of the sky.

Shortly before we departed, we were presented a scene which set off a round of roaring laughter down the aisle. The young Caucasian male who would not be forced on board or he would sue and own the asses of the United States Marshals, could be seen carried overhead by three U.S. Marshals. He was wrapped inside a strait jacket and gagged in the mouth. His eyes, rounder than two silver dollars were terrified and shining—a mixed color of blue and red. As he wiggled and moaned until he was strapped lengthwise on a row of three seats. He remained in that position for the duration of the entire flight.

It was during takeoff that I realized, per the announcement of the pilot that we were at Pittsburg Airport. We were however not given any information as to our destination. But when we arrived, we could all see from the posted signs that we were taxiing into a terminal building at Oklahoma City Airport.

Anyone who says, or even insinuates that the American Bureau of Prisons does not have something to show for the tax payer's money their system receives, would certainly be guilty of malice. It blew my mind that this entire terminal wing with all the facilities attached; from gangway to the main five story structure was a transit prison. Arriving inmates never walk under the open sky for the duration of their incarceration there, yet they have access to all the amenities of any regular correctional institution. Going by what I witnessed on the 14th of January 2009, I am convinced that if organization and structure were all that were required to mend and reform the broken souls admitted into the system, then employers would never find a better agency from which to recruit prospective candidates for their labor needs. But unfortunately, organization and structure alone cannot mend troubled souls.

The gangway through which we entered the terminal building was long and winding. As we travelled the carpeted structure, I could not tell that we were already within the building proper, until the Marshals began ushering us to sitting positions on the long single benches fastened along both sides of the wide hallway. As we took our seats, inmates who required assistance due to some handicap or other special needs were brought to the front of the line, rattling and jangling their restraints, wheelchairs and crutches as they went by. Then, from the end of the inmate line-up which was obscured from view by the arched hallway, loud howling, hooting and jeering broke out. In my pensive mood, I quickly judged the crowd as harsh. Who in their right minds would deride the handicapped in such vile, insensitive manner? I was still silently disparaging the insensitive attitude of the hooters when I too, saw the object of their jeering. Behold! It was no less than an inverted man—the one and same who would sue the Marshals and afterwards own their asses. Yes. He was this time, strapped upside down on an inverted implement on wheels. This time, not a peep escaped his wide open mouth as he rolled along the intake corridor. Oh, how sorry he looked!

As the events of January 14, 2009 continued to unfold while the Marshals methodically freed our cuffed wrists and unshackled our knackered bodies, I was in deep thought, and ponderous with amazement.

Could the signs I was reading be correct? Had we made it to our destination or were we being transferred elsewhere? By the way, where were the other passengers—the regular air travelers through this airport?

I kept gazing at the proceedings incredulous, as reality slowly and surely unfolded. The entire airport edifice, aircraft, terminal building and all were one and the same; Bureau of Prisons property. I was in the process of admission, not transfer to a connecting flight, but rather, into another prison facility! Well, I'll be dammed, I thought, an airport prison!

With impressive administration, we were unshackled and processed. We however, did not escape the long, long hours it took for the usual assignment of identity tags, hygiene needs, healthcare needs, et cetera, before finally being assigned to our housing units. My housing unit was on the fourth floor of the sprawling facility which is better known as The Transfer Center.

From the moment I arrived inside my assigned cell, I was immediately drawn to the view from the cell window. It was the most delightful view I had seen since the beginning of my checkered travel through what I now perceived as the most ubiquitous penal system in the world. It seemed that January was the time to see the beauty of Oklahoma Airport's landscape. Viewed from my window, acres of tarmac lay buried under the cover of snow which glowed luxuriantly under the glare of one hundred flood lamps. The lamps, sparsely arranged in line with the hedges, appeared to mark the boundary between the prison terminal and the main general aviation terminal. Daily, I sat by that window, a book in hand, lost in my mind's four major occupations; first, how was my appeal of Judge Messite's ruling going? Had it been filed? How are my children coping in their lives and would they understand what happened at that courtroom? Second, where is the institution to which I have been designated? I had been given the institution information—SCP-MNA, which I was informed, stood for Satellite Camp, Marianna. What was it like? I spent hours wondering, visualizing, anticipating. I knew that once there, I could finally activate my plans. Third, I would alternate my attention between the first two activities, the book in my hand and finally rest my mind on the fourth and final activity; my thoughts would travel through the airport terminal across the tarmac, seized with an irresistible desire to see the rest of Oklahoma and to jet away from there to a fantasy land and walk through the gardens of sweet smelling flowers—groves of roses. My mind would relax and ingest the music of nature at an imaginary waterfall anywhere in the world. I would revisit every beautiful location I had ever set my feet on, silently in my mind; Bermuda, Hong Kong, Shanghai, Berlin, Hamburg, Cologne, even Rostok, my favorites; London and Paris too.

Every other activity which occurred for the three months that I spent at the Oklahoma Transfer Center was painfully monotonous. Outside of my four usual occupations, every new day was an exact replay of the day before it and the day that followed. Surprisingly when the D-day finally came, I was thrown into a state of panic. I had become so used to my new routine that the thought of starting over, losing that window view, adapting to new authority and prison personnel, living among new groups of strangers, and adapting to new meals and dining schedules, tormented me. Although I had no alternative options such as staying back or choosing a different location, I had to convince and motivate myself to suppress the feeling of foreboding which had seized my thinking faculties.

The one recent occurrence which helped convince me that the transfer to Marianna was for good was the letter which I received only a few days earlier. After months of dodging the pressure from me and my family, my attorney finally decided to respond to my inquiries. His response was however bad tidings to me. He had artfully crafted a persuasive letter to me, urging me to withdraw my appeal. As he put it, I had no meritorious grounds for appeal owing to the terms of my plea deal. I realized then that I was on my own and decided that at Marianna, I would make my appeal a completely personal affair.

Seventy

It has been twenty months since that rambling two-day journey from Oklahoma City to Marianna, Florida, yet it remains stubbornly iffy to my mind how we made it all the way here without incident. That is of course, without any incident of the usual kind, since in reality, it is unlikely that a group of felons could be transported from point A to point B without any fisticuffs at all.

Although I usually stayed out of the way, there was hardly a dull moment within the inmate population. From the detention centers in Maryland to Chuck County Jail, from CCA Youngstown Ohio to The Transfer Center in Oklahoma City, the story was usually the same. Always the same wrangling over television remote control, squabbling over imaginary "saved spots" from which to get clear view of the television, clashes between rival gangs over control of loots from the kitchen or continuation of other turf related wars within or outside the prison, clashes over allegations of snitching to authorities, described as "talking to the POLIS."

All those aggravating situations were now hopefully behind me, I hoped as I tried without success to read the signs posted at the entrance of the Marianna prison complex. All I could tell for sure was that at last, we had made it to my designated prison. The final terminus . . . Maybe. Hopefully.

On the morning of March 9th 2009, at about 8:30 AM, one full plane load of inmates, including myself, were swept away from our airport terminal prison—The Transfer Center. In such blistering winter weather, only the rubber hearted may travel in shackled restraints, bumping ceaselessly through the clouds of the sky without getting the shakes. Through it all, until we landed, my heart was in my mouth. I sat bowed down, saying a silent prayer until we were safely on the ground. We had arrived at a special security wing of the Atlanta Hartsfield Airport. From there, we were whisked off in a prisoner transfer bus and a long ride through the middle of Atlanta ultimately found us at a holdover facility at which there was a total lack of love or joy as implied in the name of the city—Love Joy!

In the twenty four hours we spent at Lovejoy, I mourned every single hour as it slowly ticked by. Perhaps because we had just arrived from a prison where the keepers seemed warm and friendly, and the food left you satisfied, the officers at Lovejoy appeared unfriendly, aloof and determined to starve us into oblivion. Like forgotten animals in a laboratory cage, we roamed about in our housing area, bumping into one another, each of us looking desperately in the direction of the entrance for the sign of a food cart or to sniff the sweet aroma of anything edible as a sign of reassurance that they had not forgotten our stomachs. When at 1:00 AM on March 11th 2009, barely 24 hours after we were processed into the facility, an officer arrived with a list and began calling some names out, it was with the greatest feeling of enthusiasm that I welcomed the funny sound of the name he uttered. I knew of course, that he meant to say my name, so I responded with a mixture of relief and eagerness. The rest of that morning's drama is forgotten history marked by hunger, interminable administrative processing, the usual strip search-squat-cough, handcuff/chain treatment, and a bus ride which took twice the normal time required for the journey, leaving us all jaded.

As I stepped gingerly down and out of the van, trying hard to avoid being tripped by the leg chain around my ankles, I felt the cool morning zephyrs blowing refreshingly over our heads as though a welcome gesture from nature. Only five of us, the men alone remained of the total number of eight who traveled in our van, the three women having earlier been dropped off at the female camp facility only minutes earlier.

Today, after twenty months of nondescript living as a non-person, a mere number without which I would be invisible to the system, I can now see and appreciate the depth of Robert Kennedy's words when he said:

> ***"Some people look at things* as *they are and say, 'why?' I look at things as they can be and say, 'why not?'"***

The Robert Kennedy philosophy of "why not" indeed sums up the story of my life. I must confess that this fact never registered in my mind until I arrived at the Federal Correctional Institution at Marianna tagged with a prison registration number.

At all Bureau of Prisons facilities, inmates are required to secure a job. At the FCI facilities there are three main job providers; UNICOR, acronym for Unique Corporation which belongs to Federal Prison Industries. UNICORP mainly features jobs in textiles, furniture and electronics refurbishing and recycling fields. The second job provider is the commissary which deals on various canteen items—hygiene products, healthcare products, packaged foods and clothing/footwear. The third job provider is the Bureau of Prisons through various institution departments—Education, Kitchen, Laundry, Religious Services, Health Services, and Land Maintenance.

When, through a combination of luck and tenacity, I secured the only opening at the law library at the time, I thanked my stars and went to work. My job as a law clerk was a dream realized. From knowing next to nothing about the world's most convoluted justice system, I quickly went to about average understanding of why my original thoughts and assessment of the system were badly flawed. Most of the issues I originally viewed as straightforward, it turned out, were usually anything but straightforward.

Upon assuming my position, I realized that in their effort to remain true to the guaranteed rights protected to the free people of the United States dating back over three hundred years, successive law makers, the courts which interpret the laws and those empowered to enforce them had, for reasons I have neither the knowledge nor the credentials to intelligently review, critique or criticize, continuously expanded their roles until the system of justice delivery attained its current unmanageable gigantic size. The system, I quickly observed, sustained its stupendous growth until it is currently hard pressed to continue to deliver the rights and freedoms guaranteed in the nation's constitution by the nation's founding fathers.

I arrived at FCI Marianna determined to seek judicial remedy in my case. Since my attorney had effectively retreated from representing me by persuading me to sign a prepared notice withdrawing my appeal, I decided to represent myself. My job as a law clerk at the law library provided me the opportunity I needed to quick-study the legal and judicial systems. The quick-study gave me a glimpse into the aw-inspiring maze known as the American Juris Prudence. By all accounts, the law library at FCI Marianna which some may consider adequate for legal research offers only a peripheral view of the ubiquitous system, yet it sheds enough light on the system for me to understand that no justice system, not even in our jet-set computer age can deliver all the access, equity and fairness it promises. There are bound to be casualties due to neglect, oversight, abuse of discretion, abuse of process, discrimination, recrimination—a plethora of grievances which the overwhelmed system simply may never be able to address. I could easily sense the possibility of my grievances falling through the cracks.

This glimpse into the system under great pressure was informative enough for me to realize that I had to streamline my own demands on it down to requests for which I had a good chance of receiving some consideration. I therefore focused on achieving two goals while serving the remainder of my time at Marianna:

1) To engage the system that imprisoned me by using the channels available to me through the Law Library in persuading any appellate level arbiter to take judicial notice of the whole truth about my case and decide whether to offer me some reprieve.
2) To tell my story in its entirety in the hopes that those people whom I love, my children in particular, who became victims due entirely to no fault of their own would at least know the truths which conversation and explanations cannot fully clarify to them.

On November 25th, 2009 I filed a motion with the United States District Court for the District of Maryland requesting the court to 'Vacate, Set Aside or Correct the Sentence which was imposed against me.

This motion filed under the Statute 28 USC § 2255 is one of the many post-conviction remedies available, designed to challenge a conviction or a sentence, other than direct appeal. Because all post-conviction remedies are subject to rules and time controls, and given that Attorney Cirara Manis who represented me during the negotiation of my plea agreement had persuaded me to withdraw my appeal of the sentence which even he judged as unusually harsh, I chose this motion as a first step to begin seeking judicial remedy. I recognized that my choice of motion could be inimical to Mr. Citara Manis's professional standing, so I sought to contact him before proceeding with the action in case he would offer an alternative vehicle but my efforts failed, whereupon, I filed the motion citing the following in support:

GROUND ONE: Udeozor was denied effective assistance of counsel as guaranteed by the Sixth Amendment to the United States Constitution.

Supporting Facts:

A.) Counsel was ineffective for failing to perform minimum investigation research and litigate Udeozor's case in general.

B.) Counsel was ineffective for failing to properly advise Udeozor of matters related to plea negotiations and the guilty plea process.
C.) Counsel was ineffective for failing to adequately explain to Udeozor the elements and nature of the offense under 18 USC § 1584, and applicable sentence exposure, pursuant to USSG (U.S. Sentencing Guideline) § 1B1-1 application, Note 1(L) and USSG § 2F14.4(b)(1)(B).

GROUND TWO: Udeozor's plea was not made voluntarily and intelligently as required by the Due Process of Law Clause, Sixth Amendment.

Supporting Facts:

A.) Udeozor's plea was involuntarily induced by false promises from counsel.
B.) Counsel was ineffective for failing to call witnesses on petitioner's behalf.
C.) Counsel failed to provide petitioner with an opportunity to review the discovery materials.
D.) Counsel failed to have any meaningful discussions with the petitioner about the facts of the government's case against him or to listen to his explanations of those facts.
E.) Counsel failed to advise the petitioner that the restitution ordered to pay was only an issue if damage caused was a direct result of criminal conduct charged.

GROUND THREE: Udeozor was deprived of effective assistance of counsel as guaranteed by the Fifth and Sixth Amendments.

Supporting Facts:

A.) Counsel was ineffective for not filing a motion to suppress.
B.) Counsel was ineffective for inducing petitioner to withdraw his direct appeal.
C.) Counsel was ineffective for failing to move to withdraw Udeozor's guilty plea.

During the negotiation of my plea deal, I never once met with either the prosecutor or the probation officer who prepared the Pre-sentence Investigation Report for my case for the court. Being completely non-versed in law and poorly informed on the legal ramifications of plea agreements I relied entirely on Attorney Citara Manis's good judgment at the meetings held between himself and the government. As it turned out, the entire strength of the government's case against me which informed my attorney's acceptance of the plea deal offered by the government, and the pre-sentence investigation report of the probation officer lay in the prejudiced, perjured and highly inflammatory allegations which were made at my wife's trial. Both parties at that trial played the same game. They both capitalized on my absence to dump allegation upon allegation on me in the hopes of winning the court's sympathy. As any rational thinking person who understands the American giving spirit should expect the "victim" must be protected, and I believe this is rightly so. Except in this case, Chinelo Anyadiegwu was not the type of victim she pretended to be.

When I pointed these sticking points out to my attorney, registering my objections to Chinelo's manipulation of the system, he basically reminded me that what mattered most was my freedom. I had indeed related to him that being with my children was paramount in my mind. I would gladly take any fall so long as I gained early release in order to begin the difficult task of reconciling with them and hopefully healing the wounds of our broken past. That prospect was the carrot dangled before me, and with my eyes fixed on that carrot, that prize, I signed my name on the plea agreement document accepting some of the vilest, most egregious allegations even as loaded with falsities as they were, as true! Much as I believe in Attorney Citara Manis's sincerity during the process of plea bargaining, I still insist that he was ineffective for persuading me to give up my right to pursue the appeal process.

It is fair to say that my epiphany two years earlier, in front of the barber's mirror at C.C.A. Youngstown Ohio, did much more than renew my fighting spirit. For while I was drawing up my battle plan for a fight against the injustice done to me by way of the aforesaid motion, my entire attitude to life was undergoing cataclysmic changes. It was in the writings of John C. Maxwell that I read some time ago that a difficult crisis can be more readily endured if we retain the conviction that our existence holds a purpose—a cause to pursue, a person to love, a goal to achieve.

It was this renewed fighting spirit and the fact that all worthy causes must be pursued to a logical end that drove me to file the 28 USC § 2255 Motion although I realized that the process could outlast my prison term and that I may be released prior to the conclusion of the process. I am determined to apply this principle to every assignment I take up in the future because I know now that if I don't design my own life plan, chances are that I will fall into someone else's plan. And guess what they have planned for me? Hardly anything good.

Until fate railroaded me into prison, I had identified such a plethora of purposes for my life that I would have needed many lifetimes to achieve even a fraction of them, which is my way of admitting that during the course of my life until I became imprisoned, I had an overactive imagination or even a lack of focus. The only thing that had really kept me going was that providence always managed to hand me "success" in most of my endeavors. Otherwise my name would easily have made anybody's list of God's most unserious creatures.

Finally now, at the most inauspicious period in my life, in the midst of strange, mostly unwholesome men, betrayed and banished by two for whom I risked everything, I found a cause (or two) to pursue, people to love, and a goal (or two) to achieve. Now, I know that it is nothing against me to fall down flat. It is to lie there and fail to get up that is disgraceful. Today, the harder I'm thrown, the higher I bounce.

As I begin the final countdown toward my release from prison, I marvel every day at how the Heavenly Father has taken evil and turned it into good, has used a creature like Chinelo to reveal the hidden purpose of my life—quite the opposite of the intended hurt. It is remarkable, even miraculous that I have been preserved and shepherded through a system better equipped than any other to test a man's resolve to do right—a system where mere survival is a matter of seasoning, not reasoning.

My survival through it all has signaled to me without a scintilla of doubt what I must do—what I've already begun doing and must continue to do to the best of my God-given ability for the remainder of my days.

It is now one year since I filed my motion to vacate, set aside or correct my sentence. I am yet to receive the decision of the court one way or another—granting the requested relief or denying it. In the period which has elapsed since then however, a lot has happened. As they say, a lot of water has passed under the bridge.

The government, after twice requesting an expansion of time in which to respond to my motion, finally on the 26th of May, 2010, responded. As expected, they opposed my request for relief and held that I entered into the deal intelligently and competently. It was now up to the court to decide based on my grounds and argument, and the government's opposition to them whether to grant my prayer.

Meanwhile, I discovered that twenty months as a law clerk can expose any diligent person to a respectable amount of information, as it has done me. I have also in that period met all descriptions of the human species. The result is that I can honestly say that my prison experience, although not an experience worth embracing, could be made to yield many victories. For nowhere else in society is one forced to share every aspect of his living on a daily basis with total strangers who also happen to be adept crime practitioners. By living within such close proximity of these rejects of society, it is astonishing what one is able to learn about those who are deemed wholesome and are embraced by society. As a direct result of my own experiences, many vistas of my being have become illuminated, which were previously dormant and untapped. Today, I wholly subscribe to Walt Emerson's assertion that; "What lies behind us and what lies before us are tiny matters compared to what lies within us."

During a recent visit from my nephew Ralph Dikas, I made a statement which confounded him for a while before finally, he slowly began nodding his head in agreement with me. I said to him and I continue to hold fast that at the end of my time in prison, those who imprisoned me might end up wondering if they hadn't done me a favor by jailing me!

As to the expectations from my motion outstanding in court requesting for relief; I have lowered those expectations. The reason is simple. In the ensuing period since the filing of that motion, my path has intersected with a gentleman, much my elder who is a seasoned man of law. He has given me a deeper insight into the process of selecting the appropriate motions with which to seek selected reliefs. Regrettably, I had chosen the wrong vehicle for the relief I was seeking. I am however, not discouraged. My choice of vehicle has not been a nullity. It is the sum of all the silly mistakes which I have made in my life, not the things I got right that will guarantee that I shall never walk this road again.

I have a little over seven months until the day I walk through the gate which I have seen only once in the last twenty months. A gate which swallowed me, body and soul, but will not throw me out despite being daily, just a few yards from where I remain waiting patiently.

Although I am still here, in the limbo of prison, I look forward with nostalgia to my freedom. After years and years of receiving visitors, my senses are abuzz with curious sensation about how it would feel to walk free again, free at last, to again become myself, a visitor of others—those who visited me, those who remembered me when I was in prison . . . and those who gave up on me and forgot me.

And so, until the slow hands of the clock announces, ever so slowly, that the time has come for me to move on; to the next phase of my fieldtrip through earth, I leave you my friends, with these words from another unknown traveler like me, his own journey through life:

LITTLE BY LITTLE

Little by little the time goes by-
Short, if you sing through it, long, if you sigh.
Little by little an hour a day,
Gone with the years that have vanished away.
Little by little the race is run;
Trouble and waiting and toil are done!

Little by little the skies grow clear;
Little by little the sun comes near;
Little by little the days smile out,
Gladder and brighter on the pain and doubt;
Little by little the seeds we sow
Into a beautiful yield will grow.

Little by little the world grows strong,
Fighting the battle of right and wrong;
Little by little the wrong gives way
Little by little the right has sway.
Little by little all longing souls
Struggle up nearer the shining goals.

Little by little the good in men
Blossoms to beauty, for human ken;
Little by little the angels see
Prophecies better of good to be;
Little by little the God of all
Lifts the world nearer the pleading call.

Epilogue

***"Experience has shown,
that even under the best of government,
those entrusted with power
have, in time, and by slow operation,
perverted it into tyranny . . ."***

***"A society that will trade a little liberty for a little order
will deserve neither and loose both"***
~ Thomas Jefferson, 3rd U.S. President.

***"There is no one so enslaved
as the one who believes they're free"***
~ Goethe

I was all alone in the world.

The cold concrete bench upon which I sat was located inside the visitor's waiting patio in front of Federal Correctional Facility (FCI), Marianna, Florida. It was about 2:00 p.m. in the afternoon of July 19th, 2011. I had just been granted parole to a halfway house in the nation's Capital Washington D.C. to serve the remaining 175 days of my 2,910 days prison term in partial freedom. As I sat alone in absolute stillness, the only sound I could hear was coming from snack and soda machines humming to the rhythm of electricity. I was in the middle of acres upon acres of parking lot full of silenced vehicles, day dreaming about life in a halfway house—a form of pre-freedom Purgatory with no cells, no guards and no prison uniforms!

I listened to time as it silently whistled by and vegetation as it fluttered at the edges of the parking lot in response to invisible forces of nature. It was all incredible and surreal.

Could it be true, I wondered, that my nightmare was at its end? I waited as instructed, knowing that soon, a vehicle will appear and I would be whisked away by a prison official and I would thereafter never reside within prison walls ever again.

Suddenly, the silence was broken by the piercing screech of car tires causing me to jump onto my feet. Behind the wheels of a white Chrysler P.T. Cruiser was the Unit Team Manager of the dormitory which had until that fateful day been my home. For the past thirty months while I resided in the dormitory known as Mohawk B Unit, the lady behind the wheels of the white Chrysler served as the Unit Manager of Mohawk B. That meant that for thirty months she was my Unit Manager, and sometimes my Case Manager as well. But on this day, destiny had transformed me from a case (a mere number) in her long list of cases, to a passenger in the front seat of her car.

For the first ten minutes, as she drove me to the Greyhound Bus Station in Dothan Alabama, we sat surrounded by nothing but the cloud of silence in which I decided to bury my thoughts. Then as if she remembered a forgotten assignment, she turned her radio on, breaking the silence and then followed its sound up with a question;

"How're you today?"

"Fine."

"How does it feel to be free?"

"Good."

"Are you hungry?"

"Yes."

"Do you want to get something to eat?"

"Yes, sure"

"O. K. I know just the place. It's a new Publix Super Store, just opened in the area. Their Deli section is fantastic. You'll like it."

"O. K. then."

Meanwhile, I noted the long pauses between each of my answers and the next question. The pauses suggested that our one directional prison code of communication no longer applied. In other words, I was now free to initiate conversation or change the topic if I wished. But I could think of nothing to say until she opened the door with her next question.

"Now that you're free, what are you going to do?" She asked.

"Ha. Am I really and truly free?"

"Well, yea. You're free, technically. Unless you decide to screw it up. You can choose what to eat, what to wear, even where to go . . . mmm, I mean, it would be better if you went straight to your designated halfway house and not deviate elsewhere. That would be the quickest way back to prison."

"So, I am not really free then, am I?"

"Well, not entirely. But if you follow the rules, you'd be surprised how quickly time would pass and you'd be entirely free. It will surprise you, how many inmates violate the rules and are back in prison shortly after their release."

"No, it would not surprise me. In my short time at F. C. I., I cannot count the number of inmates I witnessed as they departed, only to return... in some cases, up to two times in just six months following their release."

"There you go. It is easy to violate. By the way, do you plan to go back to your family and start over?"

"Sure. I want to re-establish my relationship with my family. That is the main reason I elected to return and face the charges against me. Now that I have paid my debt to society, I must return to my longsuffering children, hoping that we would be able to put our nightmarish past behind us. We have a lot of thorny issues to resolve and lay to rest. God help me."

"Indeed, you're going to need God's help. I hope you believe in prayer. How about your wife by the way? Are you in touch with her?"

"Not really. I've reached out to her numerous times but she has never replied or reciprocated my gestures. I guess I have my work cut out for me."

"Indeed, you do . . . Hell hath no fury like a woman scorned. I'm sure you've heard that expression before . . ."

I offered no response to her comment although I agreed with her.

After a long pause she resumed;

"Here we are." she announced as we pulled into the Publix parking lot. "Let's go get something to eat."

"Sure, I'm famished."

She walked into the store and I followed behind her, her figure a series of uninspiring straight lines, quite distinct from the series of dangerous curves exuded by most other women within view. It dawned on me then that beauty looks and feels better to the senses of an unrestrained spirit, for while inside the prison, my mind had learned to neither recognize nor appreciate good looks in all female staff members as a general rule. And so, my presently unrestrained eyes danced all over the store, feeding themselves on the beauty of nature, people and their wares. I kept track of my escort by her scent which followed her as she walked across the store floor. From the faces of those I fed my eyes on, it was evident that they had witnessed a pair like us before—a late model bulldyke leading a frightened man of color. Not exactly a threat to the dominant forces of our path of travel.

For the first time in about 40 months, I stood before a checkout clerk in a store and paid for my purchases with my own cash. It felt good. It felt like freedom.

Unfortunately for me, this much cherished, most uplifting, incredibly tasty feeling of euphoria only lasted a bit over two days. It grieves my heart to recall how painfully close I came to being returned to prison under one week after I was paroled from Marianna Florida to Washington D.C. The seed which threatened this cruel turn around journey was apparently sewn one day prior to my release but I did not know it then.

The Mohawk B Unit Secretary had on that day, summoned me to "sign your release papers" as she put it. The "papers" were quite a stack stapled together in one thick bundle. When she indicated where I was to sign, she appeared in a desperate hurry—very detached and unfriendly. I asked for a moment to read the document before signing. She exploded;

"Can't you see the queue behind you? You think I'm here for you alone? What do you think I want you to sign, your death warrant? They're just release documents! That is . . . if you want to leave tomorrow. Look, I don't have time Mr. Udeozor, if you want to leave tomorrow, sign here. I can't wait for you to read every page. This is not a death warrant here, just an agreement that you will follow the rules of your parole and not escape once you are released."

"Is that all this is about?" I asked.

"Yes. What else d'ya thank?" She slurred, pontifically reassuring me, even showing me the first two pages of the document. Those pages were indeed on point, detailing my bio data and my travel itinerary along with a Greyhound bus ticket.

I leaned over her desk and signed the documents without reading the rest of the pages—a bad move which came back to haunt me in the days, weeks and months immediately following my release. In fact, as it later turned out, the agreement I signed may as well have been my death warrant.

It is important to add here that I also failed to properly interpret the devious flash in the eyes of my escort when, during our drive to the Greyhound Bus Station she commented that I would need divine assistance to overcome the obstacles awaiting me on the outside. She obviously knew about the landmines and other intrigues lying in wait for me in my 175 days at the halfway house. She helped to package them.

Looking back today, I find it very unsettling that despite the lessons I had supposedly learned after first signing away my honor in the Pre-Sentence Investigation Report (PSR) and then my right to appeal the negotiated plea deal, I would still offer my neck like a lamb to his shepherd for slaughter—without strategic and thoughtful deliberation. Somehow, despite the hand I had been deviously dealt repeatedly, I still subconsciously clung onto the childlike belief and trust that the System would serve and protect me and my rights—regardless of what reality had taught me.

On the other hand, I wondered, "Was it wrong that I should believe in, and trust the system to protect me? Was not this belief and trust in the system what set the United States of America apart from every other nation on earth? Despite my travails and frustrations with the system, was there any other nation under the sun which has embraced all assortments of alien cultures, religious doctrines, ethnicities, races and genders, constitutionally and judicially guaranteeing all and sundry their individual and collective rights? Was not that the reason myself and millions of others from around the world are here in the first place?" As if in answer, I recalled the sage words of the third president of the United States;

> **"Experience has shown, that even under the best government, those entrusted with power have, in time and by slow operation, perverted it into tyranny . . ."**

There it was! I whispered. The explanation that had long eluded me! As I mentally began racing through the odyssey of my recent past, I started feeling the pleasure of being alive again. I was greatly relieved by the knowledge that my belief and trust in the system were not misplaced after all. It was not the system that I needed to direct my fight against. That fight would be futile—waged against the wrong adversary. More importantly, the system which I would be fighting had been protecting me all along. It was the individuals who had, in the discharge of their duties chosen to ignore or downgrade the truth either because doing so was convenient or I was not, in their calculations, worth the energy required to search for the truth when I was easily expendable. And regrettably, they owned the power to do as they pleased—the system entrusted them with it in the hope that they would use it dutifully!

"If you want a black man destroyed, you assign that task to his own kind. No person of another race, nobody else, no other creature can achieve a more thorough, more complete, more pleasing performance of that assignment. Your mission would be successfully accomplished—beyond your dreams, and you'll have plausible deniability to boot. You had nothing to do with it! Thank you very much...." When this statement was made by another inmate while I was in prison, I challenged the statement as both outrageous and unfounded. However, the events which began unfolding only days after I walked out of the prison gates left me wondering whether my challenge was not a result of naiveté on my part. The inmate with whom I argued who was black as well insisted that under the spell of greed and jealousy, many blacks will turn against their own kind but not necessarily against people of other races. To buttress his argument he cited instances in history such as Lumumba, Nkrumah, Malcolm X, and a host of victims similarly betrayed by none other than their own kind.

One must admit that disturbing thoughts such as these are usually swept into the secret chambers of the mind because the subject is much too offensive and emotional. But when an incident of a related nature such as an act of betrayal occurs, one is forced to dredge up the thoughts for re-examination—perhaps there are valuable lessons to learn from the experiences of past victims.

Life in prison had seemed like the worst of times in my life. What I did not know was that the coming fire would burn with the degree of severity I suffered at the hell of E.F.E.C. Halfway House. This halfway house is run entirely by my own kind.

E.F.E.C., acronym for Efforts From Ex-Convicts is located in the heart of the District of Columbia. When this halfway house was named as the location where I had to serve the remaining 175 days of my prison term as part of the Bureau of Prison's pre-release program designed to gradually return ex-offenders into mainstream society, I felt nauseous—the kind of nausea that results from knowing you're being set up for an unknown tragedy, but at the same time, a sensation close to joy for knowing that you will overcome. With one part of my mind I kept hoping that the intuitive feeling that I was being set up would turn out to be wrong. But the incident which set off my sense of skepticism bore all the hallmarks of treachery.

Shortly after I submitted a request for the approval of my pre-release program, a member of my family was able to confirm that my request had been approved. She was given details of the approval which included the location of the halfway house, my travel date and my program start date. However, only a few weeks prior to my parole date, a probation officer visited my family with the troubling news that the location of my program had been changed. A different halfway house, E.F.E.C. in Washington D.C. now superseded the original halfway house which was located in Rockville, Maryland. Even more troubling was the hint that the conditions of my probation sounded unexpectedly draconian. Although this news was very troubling, I refused to let it dampen my yearning and resolve to breathe the air of freedom once again. I had come this far without capitulating to the machinations of Satan. Why yield to his authority now?

My resolve however, did not ease the queasiness in my stomach at this agency's unusual name. I had been informed by inmates from Washington D.C. that E.F.E.C. halfway house catered to a weird class of inmates and was run entirely by ex-convicts. What manner of return to society could be heralded by an agency administered entirely by ex-convicts? I wondered. Surely, ex-convicts cannot be expected to provide the dignified or subtle re-entry into the free world which ex-offenders desperately need. I was being released from a medium security prison which was set up by the Department of Justice and administered by seasoned administrators and professional law enforcement officers, to a halfway house run entirely by ex-convicts?

I had imagined that society would prefer that the re-entry of ex-offenders into their communities be supervised by the very best professionals in that field. It was rumored among the inmates that the system approved this idea based on important political considerations among which were: First, to offer some "reformed" ex-convicts who would run the halfway house another chance in life. Second, to give recently released inmates the benefit of being welcomed by a "reformed" ex-offender staff because it was believed that they would better understand and meet the needs of other convicts at their point of pre-release, having successfully gone through the same process themselves. However, given the daily mayhem I had witnessed in prison despite the quantum of human and material resources invested, it seemed to me as though I was being cast from my frying pan into fire. As indeed I was.

When I entered into a plea agreement with the government, my understanding of the criminal justice system was scant and juvenile. As a result, like Forrest Gump, I wadded through the system in an otherworldly state of mind, rising to the position of Law and Resource Clerk at the Education Department of the Federal Correctional Institute, in the midst of some of the world's most dangerous criminal elements. I refused to be cowed by the perilous nature of prison life or to believe that what I did not know could and would hurt me in that environment. And, although I continue even today to learn through experience and education that the system sees the truth as meaningless if it cannot be proved, I have, perhaps due to the laws of pre-destination continued to evade the gun sights of many with malicious designs toward me.

One such an individual was a gentleman who was the coordinator of the halfway house when I arrived there for my re-entry program. He and the entire members of his staff were black, as was I. He was my own kind, with the possible exception that he would be a perfect instrument for the immolation of his fellow black men. I do not judge this gentleman by any other yardstick but his own actions. Although he outwardly endeavored to arrange himself with the poise of gentility, he relished his acts of sadism, and in my case was clearly and particularly enthused by the melancholy effects those actions had on me.

Faced by each other, the coordinator and I were petrol and fire. That was our chemistry—spontaneous combustion. Our only moment of civility with each other was during the formality of introduction. That was all. After he introduced himself as the Coordinator of the halfway house and also as my Case Manager, he paused as if to accord me enough time to decipher the fact that I stood before a man of authority—an important "big" man in government. In only a few words, he let it be known to me that as far as the halfway house was concerned, it was he who laid down the law. He it was, who assigned all residents to their various Case Managers. All Case Managers also had to report to him. In addition to his duties as coordinator, he assigned some cases—some special cases to himself. In other words, he was Case Manager Supreme—not subordinated to any higher authority. He omitted to mention that there were others who functioned at a level higher than himself. By the time he finished speaking, it had become clear to me that I was dealing with a grossly outsized ego. The room was full of him even though he was the smallest man in it. I held my breath and waited.

After these introductory formalities, the coordinator, in an altered tone, and with the practiced eloquence of a serpent, delivered three of the most scorching directives I'd ever heard in my life to me. Peering into a thick folder he began; "I have assigned your case to myself. I am your Case Manager . . . my, my, what do we have here?"

Still holding my breath I managed to keep my anxiety from surging to the surface. He continued; "I have to prepare three passes for you. You are going to have a very busy week. First, you must report to CHIPS to register for the drug abuse counseling program. Next, you have to report to CSOSA on Indiana Avenue to be registered as a sex offender. And finally, you will register and participate in a sex offender treatment program at Clinical and Forensic Clinic at Silver Spring.

The range of emotions which passed through my body and senses came and went in rapid spurts—from nausea to disbelief to resolve. I immediately understood which way this coordinator and I were headed—we were headed down a nasty, slippery slope. There was no room for pretentions or dilly dallies. His manner of speaking had demonstrated to me that he expected nothing short of obedience and compliance from me—no objections, no explanations.

I knew then that my moment to fight had finally arrived. I was not going to become marked a pervert for life with the brand between the itchy fingers of this man, an ex-convict who clearly delighted at inflicting pain on any inmate unfortunate enough to end up in his roster. Marking me with the pervert brand was no doubt, the coordinator's intention. Sure, I was alarmed and highly curious about the origin of his pernicious disposition toward me, but there was precious little time to spend brooding over it. In the days and weeks that followed, I learned from the active rumor mill at the halfway house that the coordinator's sadism stemmed from the deep seated resentment he harbors against humanity for the mark seared all over him some years earlier with the pervert brand. Now that the same brand had been placed between his fingers he had become empowered to burn even deeper marks on all who followed behind him, regardless of the circumstances of their arrival at his halfway house and on his odious list.

From the beginning of my ordeal, the various official handlers of my case had sought to fit me into one of the many boxes into which offenders are usually consigned. These boxes, designed to keep offenders in check in order that society is protected would, to my mind, serve society well, if those who end up inside the boxes are those for whom the boxes were designed. The sex offender registration box is the pervert box which in present day United States, nobody decent should be lumped into by mistake or without careful evaluation. Sadly, as devastating as the lifetime effects of becoming labeled a sex offender can be, the one-way road into that box openly admits both the guilty and the innocent without discrimination. Sadly also, the sex offender box has no exit doors. All admissions are for life; because mere accusation of sexual deviancy, whether true or false usually leaves something of an indelible stain, let alone getting dumped into the exit-less offender box of grime.

"Sir," I replied the coordinator, "there must be a mistake somewhere in that folder. It is not possible that anybody could have recommended that I participate in any of the aforementioned programs. To begin with, I have never used illicit drugs in my entire life. I do not consume alcohol except occasionally at social events and I have never ever molested anybody sexually. Moreover, most significantly, I was not convicted of any drug or sex related offence."

With those words, I incurred the E. F. E. C. coordinator's unqualified wrath. He thundered; "What did you just say, huh? Who the hell do you think you are nigger? I'm asking you, convict! You listen to me, and you listen good. You are nobody! Nothing . . . Nothing but a number! Do you hear me? You are nothing but a friggin number! You're gonna register alright. Yes, yes, yes sir . . . you're gonna register for the two programs and you gonna be in the sex offender register. Now, you go on, get out of here. And tomorrow, you get your butt on outa here. You will start tomorrow with C. H. I. P. S. You will go there and we will get paid . . . And let me warn you right now, when you get there, you better play along with everybody else because if I hear of any problem from you, I will personally get the U. S. Marshals to come and take your ass back to the prison you came from. You will be back there in a snap. You hear me? Now, go on, get out! Step out of my office!" I held my ground, refusing to leave. "Sir," I intoned loudly, "you cannot make me do this. You can't make me declare myself a drug abuser and a sexual deviant! I have done nothing to deserve this, and I do not think you can make such a unilateral call on your own sir. I have never used drugs and I most certainly have never molested anybody sexually, young or old."

"Oh yeah?" the coordinator barked in a virulent voice. He flipped the pages of the folder through three different pages showing me three signatures and asking in that icy voice; "whose signatures are these, huh? Mm . . . Let me guess, perhaps you didn't sign these either, huh? You come in here . . . talking about . . . oh, I didn't do it. Whining to me as if I made you do what you did! You know what? I don't really care if you did it or not. You're a convict. And sure, all convicts are innocent . . . huh fellas?" he concluded, turning to face the other case managers who all had sheepish grins plastered all over their faces, their white teeth flashing in between fits of laughter. "Everybody here is innocent," he resumed. "Guys, isn't that the truth, huh?" The mockery in their laughter was meant to shame, ridicule and disgrace, but instead I became even more resolved to fight the looming injustice with every ounce of my ability.

But those signatures were mine! Just three days earlier, the secretary of my former unit at F.C.I. Marianna, Florida had extracted those signatures from me. When I demanded to read the entire document before signing, she had initially flared up, and then in a calm voice, berated me for being suspicious of her motives; " . . .this is not a death warrant here. Just an agreement that you will follow the rules of your parole and not escape once you are released . . ."

As I recalled my exchange with the secretary in the face of the coordinator's present assault on my rights, I became highly incensed. Either the secretary had lied to set me up for my current troubles or this man was lying boldfaced, implying that my fate had already been sealed when I signed those "release documents." Either way, it did not really matter to me any longer. I was going to fight. I was not a drug user or sexual deviant and nobody was going to make me one by fiat. I stormed out of the coordinator's office feeling like a boxer at the end of a brutal first round. Was that the beginning of a meltdown? I certainly hoped not, because the fight had merely just begun.

It is said that the face mirrors a man's soul, and that we can read there what is written in his heart. I began my mornings for the next 170 days following my arrival at the halfway house by reading the face of the coordinator. It was clear; not to me alone, that sadism had long resided in his heart. His entire existence began and ended on a daily basis, at the halfway house. He apparently had no other life outside that enterprise. He usually arrived just before 6:00a.m., and departed only after all other staff members under his supervision had long gone home. Oftentimes, even after he left the halfway house, his aura still hung in the air, always managing to keep peace away from the house, like the smell of burning sulfur keeps mosquitoes from entry.

It is fair to say that I was not always his only target. Other inmates usually complained about his overbearing, wannabe strongman attitude toward any resident who thought of himself as anything but a number. For as long as I was at the halfway house, I constantly violated the coordinator's directive to never think of myself as anything but a number. He judged me a snub for having the audacity to try and delist my name from the list of nameless souls who he described as government property worthy only to be represented by numbers. My name is George Chidebe Udeozor. I am not a number, I said.

Because I had by this time, learned one of the most valuable lessons about survival in the arena of American Jurisprudence, or in any arena of American life for that matter, it appears that with me, the coordinator finally met his waterloo. That lesson is that there is a rich history behind every aspect of American life, and understanding that history is the key to survival in America. I am no master of American history but my ordeal unwittingly thrust me at the core of the nation's life. All I had to do was follow the cultural compass which that experience placed in my hand.

I fought and defeated the coordinator by choosing wisely when to fight and when to lie low. Armed with the knowledge of the source and true limits of his powers, I departed the halfway house on the morning after our first encounter to a location in Washington D.C. North East ostensibly to enroll in the drug abuse recovery program. Halfway house rules mandate inmates to strictly follow the directions written on their passes or destination sheets and to report back to the halfway house within the time period specified in the pass. Veering off the natural route to or from the specified destination, or failing to return within the specified time period was a punishable violation of the rules. However, to be in violation, concrete proof of the violation is required. With these rules in mind, I proceeded to do what needed to be done, within the rules, to prove that I was not required to participate in the drug treatment program. From way above the coordinator's presumed infinite powers; a directive was issued dropping me out of the program. My first win thus went into record.

Because in America almost all contentious issues are viewed from the vantage point of winners and losers, and being that historically Americans generally gravitate heavily toward winners or perceived winners, it has become near impossible in this land, for those considered losers to survive, even when the truth is transparently in their favor. It was only in the context of my win that a good number of the staff and all of the other inmates began to express their support and offer their advice on how I should duel with the coordinator. They knew I was on the right side of justice in my fight, yet they had to deal with me discretely because they would not dare draw the coordinator's fury to themselves.

The coordinator reacted very badly to my successful move to protect myself from unjust treatment. Because he interpreted the outcome of my fight for justice as a win for me and a loss for himself, the vicious win-or-lose cat-and-mouse game between us intensified. The danger of this game for me was its potential to permanently emasculate me from restoration as a worthy father to my children and a contributing member of society.

It was remarkable yet again, how God took my woebegone situation, an unjust affliction, and made it right just at the nick of time. For I do not credit my triumph over the coordinator and his chicanery to any overt act of genius or bravery on my part; I was terrified of the man the entire time. Every new dawn seemed to bear with it, tidings of my last morning in purgatory, and if the coordinator got his way, I'd be headed in reverse, straight back to the hellhole I had just come from. I watched time after time as one inmate after another was manacled and removed by United States Marshals. What kept me going was the fact that I knew I was not fighting to save myself—the damage to me had already been inflicted. I was fighting to save my children's memory of their father. Failing to fight now would inscribe the wrong record of the true facts in their memories.

The coordinator became clearly feral when I informed him the next morning that I was not required to participate in the drug treatment program. His face became the picture of panic as sweat began trickling down his forehead. It terrified him to consider a loss to me.

"Who the hell said that to you?" he asked struggling to get his eyes into focus.

"The doctor who runs the program." I replied.

"Bullshit! He did not say that to you! And . . . even if he did, I don't care. You are gonna be in that program! We're going to get paid, period. Not even the doctor can change that order! Only the BOP can do that."

I felt pity for him seeing how my bit of good news distressed him. With my best effort I faked a contrite look when I broke the news to him; "the order did come from BOP."

That made him mad. "Hey Mister, didn't I warn you to co-operate . . . to play along at the CHIPS program? Do you know what I can do to you?" he asked, standing there like a defeated politician whose own sense of celebrity had just been trampled by an insignificant.

"Sorry Sir," I stammered, "what did I do wrong?"

That made him even madder. He stomped away, unable to utter another word and from that moment on, all other prejudiced hostilities he secretly held against me erupted from within, spreading like shingles all over his person any time we came in contact with each other.

Owing to the coordinator's badly soured disposition toward me and his avowed promise to deal harshly with me, even those sympathetic with my fight could not shield me from harm as they would under normal circumstances. Ordinarily, while an inmate resides in a halfway house, his assigned case manager had his back or he had his ass. This unspoken relationship of loyalty or perfidy combined with the inmate's conduct determined whether he made it to the actual date of his final release or whether he got sent back to prison on a violation of parole.

In my case, after the rumble over the drug treatment program, my case manager and coordinator let it be known to all that he had my ass and that he had decided what to do with it—return it to prison. He took several steps to ensure that he acted within the law or appeared to be acting within it when he carried out his dastardly act. First, he structured my day movements outside the halfway house to allow me very limited amounts of time to accomplish the object of each outing. This way, he kept me constantly hyped-up and vulnerable to any number of his plans of attack. His ultimate goal was to set me up to violate my parole and be returned to prison.

The first test of his reinforced resolve came on August 24th 2011. On that date, he sent me to the Sex Offender Registration Center (CSOSA) on Indiana Avenue to get registered. Prior to this day, he had blocked every attempt I made to obtain legal assistance for help on that matter. He did so by scheduling me for job search programs any time I put in a request to seek legal assistance. My greatest undoing at this time was my clearly unmasked fear of any talk of a return journey to prison. My case manager seized on every chance he got to remind me that he was the one man with the authority to visit that nightmare on me. He wielded that threat to his maximum amusement during these times.

When I arrived at the CSOSA office, I knew that I was walking the fine line between darkness and light. Refusing to be registered, I had been informed, constituted a violation of one of my pre-release conditions and therefore a sure ground for immediate return to prison. Although I knew that for me, registration as a sex offender was not ordered by any court and therefore would be unlawful, I was mortally afraid of risking the humiliation of spending even a moment in confinement—a fear which the coordinator was aware of, and capitalized on. I was not and never have been a sex offender. I was not charged with a sex offense. I was not convicted of a sex offense. The court did not order a sex offense treatment for me. My quagmire therefore was; *"where was this order really originating from, and who wanted so badly to have my reputation and image destroyed?"*

Whoever that contemptible fellow was, he came within a heartbeat of ruining the most important thing of value to me—my children's memory of their father. And for what? I hope someday to be able to answer this question and to unmask the evil genius behind it. Suffice it to say that after the most nerve-racking cat-and-mouse game in which my entire being rested on a very precarious balance, I triumphed over and over again against the coordinator. And if I might indulge in a measure of immodesty, it seems to me that good triumphed repeatedly over evil. In the end, the coordinator failed to keep any of his unjust promises—it was ruled that I was not to be registered as a sex offender, and I was neither forced into any unnecessary programs nor was I returned to prison.

From the moment the verdict was entered in my case I made a deliberate effort to stay out of the coordinator's way until the day of my final release. On January 10, 2012, it was a shamed and defeated coordinator who held the door open for me to walk through the halfway house door—a free man! "Do not come back," he said to me, his eyes fixed on an imaginary, distant object which only he could see.

Washington D.C. is the face of freedom to the world. As I walked away from one among the extensive web of snares designed to entrap the enemies of peace and keep the face of freedom safe and pretty, I decided to spend a few hours flirting with the beauty and magnificence of our world's bastion of freedom.

I walked down Seventh Street through Chinatown to the Judiciary Square. In my thirty four years of living in the United States, sixteen of those years as a citizen, I must have traversed the great monuments sprawled out before me dozens of times without giving any of them a second look. I hardly even wondered what activities occurred within their bowels. To me, such engagements were meant for tourists, not for area residents such as myself. In the past four months however, I had been inside scores of these buildings, engaged in more activities than I thought possible in my entire lifetime in my effort to rebuild myself and re-enter society once again.

These experiences which kept me living on edge as I awaited the outcome of decisions being made in my case also left me in awe of the United States of America.

As I have noted earlier, ***there is a rich history behind every aspect of American life.*** At the core of American life is the average citizen's near obsession with freedom and liberty. Now standing on the same grounds they stood on, and looking at the monuments which immortalize the men and women who had most sacrificed of themselves for the protection of these God-given rights and attributes, I began to wonder where I fit into all these. How and why did I even end up in this place?

I found a concrete bench and sat on it. I was immediately struck by the quantum of police presence visible from where I sat. It was striking that while I felt completely safe, I could not help wondering whether or not I was truly free yet. At that moment, the words of renowned philosopher Goethe jumped into my head and I paraphrase; ***"There is no one so enslaved as the one who believes they're free."*** I have long forgotten the context in which I first read these words, but they resonated with me just as if the author was speaking to my view of life in the world today.

In my reverie, I began introspectively reviewing the import of this philosopher's belief vis-à-vis my release from prison. It seemed to me that from the moment of my parole on July 19th 2011, officials of the various agencies charged with supervising my re-entry into society were instead keener at spending the resources meant for that purpose in preparing me for a return trip to prison. For while I was contending with the matter of a pesky halfway house coordinator, the U.S. Probation Office in Washington DC was at the same time, in a bewildering move, attempting to have the conditions of my probation modified. This attempt, had it succeeded, would have made my life in freedom a living hell. The still unanswered questions which agitated my mind then were; "Who wanted so badly to have my image and reputation destroyed beyond what my conviction had already done to it, and to what end? Also, who stood to benefit from such egregious injustice to me?"

The more I rotated these questions in my mind, ruminating on them, the more unsettled I became about all the possible directions to which their possible answers led. The most disturbing of these possibilities however was the one which seemed to flow directly out of my debates with other inmates while I was incarcerated. They had contended that the amorphous American Prison Industrial Complex was the main culprit. They had argued that this ubiquitous body applied a vice-like stranglehold on anyone who became unfortunate enough to be snagged by their network of snares. They claimed that this network wraps its shenanigans around you which forces you, lures you or seduces you into one of its snares. In the end they argued, you become their property, to be toyed with in a condition of legalized involuntary servitude, and recycled until you were used up or dead. I, on the other hand had argued that prison was like a sabbatical from life gone awry. I even ventured to suggest that the experience should be turned into an opportunity and made to yield results as though it was positively motivated in the first place—not the punishment that it was intended to be. I had often wondered why we saw the same issues so differently. Now, I could not only see their point of view, I could also see why we were unable to see eye-to-eye on them.

Although I have refused to be snagged by one of those ever spinning wheels of the snares which are undoubtedly out there and which are as real as the real world itself, I can honestly say that it has taken much more than wisdom and gallantry on my part to keep from getting recycled. It has taken Divine Intervention.

Based on the apparently valid claims of my opponents in those spirited debates, I now concede to their expressed opinion that my position on the system is an exception to the established rule. For it is hard to imagine how a young person who hails from a broken home, a home devoid of love and one in which any form of abuse happened, even if randomly, would not capitulate to the level of pressure which the officials and agents of the dreaded ubiquitous complex brought to bear on me. Indeed, these officials and/or agents were usually tone deaf to my loud proclamations that I was not abused in my youth or at any other time in my life except perhaps the abuse I was now suffering in their hands. It made little difference to them when I told them that I have always enjoyed the love and support of my family and friends and that I have never and will never abuse anybody. They preferred instead and applied pressure on me, to explain away the imaginary crimes which they suggested I might have unconsciously committed or partaken in. Whether this strategy helps to lower or prevent crime is a debate for which I am not qualified or one in which I wish to engage. I simply know that it did not take acts of wisdom or heroism for me to live through the horrors of incarceration within and outside prison walls and yet survive unscathed. It took the love and support of my family and friends. Most of all, it took the love of God.

Having vented all my frustrations with the clogs endemic in the system which I had to overcome to regain my freedom, the time is rife to celebrate being an American. I am sure that until now my readers are most likely unaware how beholden to this great nation I truly am. My complaints and whining are actually lamentations of a utopian from Amawbia—Amawbia being in my opinion, one of the obscurest spots on earth from which to launch a successful quest for the American Dream. The fact that it was even possible for me to venture out on my own impetus and succeed to the extent that I did at achieving the dream is nothing short of confounding. To then receive a second chance after violating some laws of the land in my ill-contrived effort to extend those same dreams to another is a miracle which is only possible in America. I believe that the time I served in prison is truly a small price to pay for the chance I have again received. And although some within the system do overstep their mandates in their personal hustle for gain, as they did in my case, I challenge anybody anywhere on planet earth to present their proof of a more accommodating, more forgiving and more just society. I guarantee that none can be found.

I reiterate that I lament my ordeal, only as an American who enjoys the God-given, constitutionally protected rights of life, liberty and the pursuit of happiness. As a citizen of two nations, I wear two skins—An American skin and a Nigerian skin. At this stage of my life, asking me to shed either of my two skins would be tantamount to asking me to wash half the color away from it.

If Americans and the rest of the world all accept that life, liberty and the pursuit of happiness are God-given rights; is it not by inference prudent to expect those rights to be universally protected? As one who struggled to become an American citizen for exactly those reasons, I feel I am representative of millions whose rights are sometimes compromised or even trampled when conflict arises due to clashes between our culture of birth and our adopted American culture. When such conflicts lead to complications during a legal battle, I believe that the exercise of caution in applying the laws is critical. To my mind, this is the only way to avoid unjustly creating numberless collateral victims unnecessarily over issues which have simple culture-based resolutions. Criminalizing alien cultural practices does not serve the cause of justice. Important lessons are lost while contentious issues remain unresolved. When viewed from a distance an unexamined freckle on the skin might appear like a blemish to the eyes. In the same vein, failure to perform a proper review of the cultural dynamics at play when trying an immigrant in court would tend toward misdiagnosis and exaggeration of an offense, and ultimately the miscarriage of justice. In my own case, I believe that the freckles on my Nigerian skin appeared like a blemish on my American skin only because it was not examined closely.

In my American skin, even as an immigrant and a first generation American, I may not always be free to do as I like, but I have the ability always to demand my rights and know that they will be respected. Although there are some who might consider me undeserving of my God-given rights, as though God granted them to me in error, I honor the constitution of the United States which guarantees them to me and the system which strives to protect the rights of all.

When I wear my Nigerian skin however, I become a Nigerian. In this skin, I prepare myself for the Nigerian brand of freedom—embroidered freedom. For in Nigeria, freedom is limitless; it can be found everywhere, but rights are found only on printed paper! You claim your rights at your life's peril. While at home in this magnificent land, I often wander about, wondering what to do with my oodles of freedom when none of my rights is respected or protected. As I wander about, free like a bird, I do so holding onto my dear life because I dare not invoke my nation's negligence and constant violation of my rights when God calls me to give an account of what I did with my life. I believe that the third president of the United States of America best captures the dangers of high handedness in government when he asserted that;

"A society that will trade a little liberty for a little order will deserve neither and loose both."

My future engagements in the two nations that I love will draw their mantras from the sage words of President Thomas Jefferson and those of other noble human individuals who believe in the unified destinies of all human beings. Admitted, I possess neither the eloquence nor the sagacity of gifted world leaders. I have neither the deep pockets nor the influence of the wealthy. But there is none alive with whom I would trade places. "Out of many, one"—the high and mighty often prefers to think of himself as THE ONE. But I think him foolish. With our world getting smaller by the day and earth's population fusing together despite our clear and obvious differences and the bigoted activities of ignoramuses, I believe that the only way forward for humanity is to begin tolerating and loving one another so as to be on the right side of the ultimate story of the world when it is finally told.

Because in my life, I have always preferred to view the cup as half full rather than half empty, it has been possible for me to navigate life's obstacle courses with a smile on my face. I pray the Almighty grants me the tenacity to keep the smile in place as I embark on my life's future adventures. The one thing of which I can be sure is that while life will never excite me if I backed away from ever taking a chance, choosing wisely has taken on a new meaning to me . . .

Acknowledgements

Six months after my illegal arrest and detention, it had become clear to me that the treaty of extradition between Nigeria and the United States was in the process of being unconstitutionally applied in my case. From that point on, through my ordeal in prison, and the process of researching and penning down the contents of this book, certain people played pivotal roles which greatly eased my many burdens.

I am grateful to:

- My sisters Chinwe and Christine who stood stoically and protectively by me, setting the record straight about the plethora of false and defamatory information being spread about me.
- My brothers Gilbert, Paul and Bernard upon whose shoulders it fell to sustain me when I could no longer bear the cross by myself.
- My barrister, Festus Keyamo, for the brilliant legal battle he fought on my behalf and the reassuring warmth of his friendship.
- My court appointed attorney, Michael Citara Manis, whose appreciation of my plight and effort to reunite me with my children helped reassure me that despite its many flaws, the American Justice System remains the fairest on our strife-ridden planet.
- My friend Angela Laws for her tireless effort in the typing and conversion of hundreds of pages of the original manuscript into its final form.
- My friends Arize and Sharon Ogudo, young Chelsea Gatewood and her parents for their contributions in the typing of portions of this work.

From the bottom of my heart, I thank you all and pray the almighty treats your needs with the same love and kindness with which you've treated mine.